KYOTO CSEAS SERIES ON ASIAN STUDIES 1
Center for Southeast Asian Studies, Kyoto University

THE ECONOMIC TRANSITION IN MYANMAR AFTER 1988

Market Economy versus State Control

T0351934

Edited by

Koichi Fujita, Fumiharu Mieno and Ikuko Okamoto

NUS PRESS

Singapore

in association with

KYOTO UNIVERSITY PRESS

Japan

The publication of this volume was partially funded by the Kyoto University Foundation.

© 2009 NUS Press

NUS Press
National University of Singapore
AS3-01-02, 3 Arts Link
Singapore 117569
www.nus.edu.sg/nuspress

ISBN 978-9971-69-461-6 (Paper)

Kyoto University Press
Kyodai-Kaikan (Kyoto University Hall)
15-9 Yoshida-Kawaramachi, Sakyo-ku
Kyoto-city 606-8305
Japan
www.kyoto-up.or.jp

ISBN 978-4-87698-468-8

National Library Board Singapore Cataloguing in Publication Data

The economic transition in Myanmar after 1988: market economy versus state control / edited by Koichi Fujita, Fumiharu Mieno and Ikuko Okamoto. – Singapore: NUS Press in association with Kyoto University Press, c2009.
p. cm.
Includes bibliographical references and index.
ISBN-13: 978-9971-69-461-6 (pbk.)

1. Burma – Economic policy – 1988–. 2. Burma – Economic conditions – 1948–. I. Fujita, Koichi. II. Mieno, Fumiharu.
III. Okamoto, Ikuko, 1967–.

HC422
338.9591 – dc22   OCN297144911

Typeset by: Scientifik Graphics
Printed by: Mainland Press Pte Ltd

KYOTO CSEAS SERIES ON ASIAN STUDIES 1

Center for Southeast Asian Studies, Kyoto University

THE ECONOMIC TRANSITION IN MYANMAR AFTER 1988

Market Economy versus State Control

CONTENTS

PART TWO: The Economy of Agriculture and Labour

LIST OF TABLES

Chapter 2

Chapter 3

Chapter 6

Chapter 7

Chapter 8

LIST OF FIGURES

Chapter 4

Chapter 5

Chapter 6

Chapter 7

ACKNOWLEDGMENTS

The authors very much appreciate the Kyoto University Foundation and the Global COE Programme "In Search of Sustainable Humanosphere in Asia and Africa" of Kyoto University for their generous financial assistance for the publication of this book. The authors also thank Professor Takatoshi Ito, Professor Masao Kumamoto, Professor Nobuyoshi Nishizawa and Professor Sandra Wang for their contributions with background papers.

INTRODUCTION

Myanmar's Economic Transformation after 1988

Koichi Fujita, Fumiharu Mieno and Ikuko Okamoto

Under British colonial rule, Myanmar became the largest rice exporter in Asia. With a typical primary commodity exporting economy, depending almost solely on rice and teak wood, the country achieved some degree of economic prosperity. However, in the development process, basic industries such as rice milling, transport, finance, and insurance were occupied by the British people, while in rural areas land was increasingly concentrated in the hands of a particular group of Indians ("Chettiars"). The bitter experience of "exploitation" by foreigners was, without doubt, one of the most important factors behind the adoption of an inward-looking economic system in Myanmar after independence, a system that was consolidated after 1962, under the name of the "Burmese Way to Socialism".[1]

The inward-looking import substitution policy of industrialization pursued in Myanmar largely was a failure, resulting in many inefficient state economic enterprises (SEEs) and widespread poverty. The economic contradictions became intolerable by the mid-1980s and finally resulted in a large-scale political unrest in 1988 (Takahashi, 2001; Myat Thein, 2004; Tin Maung Maung Than, 2007). Subsequently, a newly installed military government, led by the State Law and Order Restoration Council (SLORC),[2] made a series of bold decisions to open and liberalize the economy. This move toward a market economy in Myanmar was in line with a world-wide trend, paralleling shifts elsewhere in Southeast Asia, such as in Vietnam, Laos and Cambodia. However, in Myanmar's case, the instability of the political regime forced it to adopt a somewhat different course, since the country could not expect much assistance from the international community to push forward reforms.[3]

The economic problems the new government faced in 1988 were two-fold; one was how to reform the inefficient socialistic economic system in conformity with a market economy and the other was how to develop the agricultural and underdeveloped industrial and service economy, thus alleviating mass poverty. What policies did the government adopt, and to what extent did Myanmar succeed in solving the two basic problems? Under what kind of international economic and political opportunities and limitations did Myanmar have to undertake the economic transition? And finally, what kind of problems is Myanmar now facing, and where is the country heading?

By carefully analyzing economic policies and performance in various sectors, this book presents an overall picture of economic transformation in Myanmar from 1988 into the early 2000s. Several research publications analyse Myanmar's economic transformation after 1988 (Mya Thein, 2004; Tin Maung Maung Than, 2007).[4] These works provide a comprehensive outline of the historical change of the economy and of the economic policy making. The present book applies solid economic analysis to the changing structure of the economy by delving deeper into important economic segments, using both micro and macro data. Official statistics in Myanmar are rather unreliable and need to be treated with caution,[5] but by synthesizing both macro and micro pictures, the authors reveal aspects of the economy not well captured in previous research, and present the economy in transition as closely as possible.

The book consists of two parts. One concerns "Macro Economy and Industrial Structure", the other, "The Economy of Agriculture and Labour". In each part, however, instead of simply presenting an outline of the economy and changes over time, we offer interpretations of the changing "structure" of the economy.

Myanmar's Economy in Transition

At the primary stage of economic development, the contribution of the agricultural sector is very large in terms of production, employment and export. Development in this context means transforming such an agrarian economy into an industrialized one, and the critical issue for the government is how to construct a balanced relationship between agricultural and non-agricultural sectors in each stage of development, aiming at a long term benefits.

In the socialist period Myanmar tried to squeeze resources from the agricultural sector, especially from the rice sub-sector, and to use those resources to promote industrialization based on import substitution through construction of SEEs. These efforts mostly failed. As a result, Myanmar's economy in

Table 1 Changes in Sectoral GDP Shares (%)

	1990	1995	2000	2004
Manufacturing				
Myanmar	7.8	6.9	7.2	9.2
Vietnam	12.3	15.0	18.6	20.3
Laos	10.0	14.1	17.0	19.2
Cambodia	5.2	9.5	17.0	20.2
Agriculture				
Myanmar	57.3	60.0	57.2	54.6
Vietnam	38.7	27.2	24.5	21.8
Laos	61.2	55.2	52.5	48.6
Cambodia	55.6	50.4	39.5	36.0

Source: ADB, *Key Indicators*, various issues.

the late 1980s was still agrarian, with inefficient SEEs and "fatigue" in the agricultural sector. The major issue for the government was to build a new relationship between agricultural and non-agricultural sectors for promoting long term development.

The situation faced by Myanmar in 1988 was fairly common among the former socialist economies at the beginning of a transition to a market economy. In this context, it is useful to compare the experience of Myanmar with the experiences of the other former socialist Asian countries, in particular China starting in the late 1970s and Vietnam a decade later.

Failure of Industrialization-led Growth in Myanmar

The economic transformation of Myanmar after 1988 was characterized by an extreme delay in industrialization, especially in the export-oriented manufacturing sector. This becomes clear when we compare Myanmar with other transitional economies in Southeast Asia, including Vietnam, Laos and Cambodia (Table 1). The share of manufacturing in GDP rapidly increased in all of these countries except Myanmar, reaching more or less 20 per cent in 2004. In Myanmar, manufacturing was stagnant during the period, staying at about 7–9 per cent and the share of agricultural sector remained very large, accounting more than 55 per cent of GDP.

These figures do not mean that Myanmar's economy was totally stagnant whereas the other countries achieved rapid economic growth. On the contrary, the economic growth rate in Myanmar during the period was as high as, or even higher than, in other countries. In other words, the contribution of the non-manufacturing sectors, especially that of the agricultural sector, was remarkable in Myanmar.

The key question here is why Myanmar developed as it did, in sharp contrast with other Asian transitional economies.

Major Policy Reforms in Myanmar after 1988

The new military regime that came to power in September 1988 immediately announced and implemented several bold market liberalization policies including (a) liberalization and/or authorization of private enterprise activities, including internal trade activities, (b) liberalization and/or authorization of international trade (including border trade), and liberalization of foreign direct investment (FDI), (c) financial sector reforms, including allowing of private banking (Table 2). The first reform implemented in 1987 was liberalization of the agricultural marketing system, including changes in the procurement and rationing of rice (see Chapter 6). Regarding this important reform, two points should be noted; first, in general, agricultural commodity prices started to rise rapidly after the reform, faster than the other commodities; and second, the state procurement system was soon re-introduced for some important crops, including rice, cotton, sugarcane, rubber, and jute, although generally the quota was reduced. The significant point is that the government continued to procure these crops from farmers at less than open market prices. Rice was procured mainly for rationing to the "target group", including military and civil servants while other cash crops were procured for state-owned agro-processing industries. The second important point is that rice export remained a monopoly of a government agency (Myanma Agricultural Produce Trading), which was responsible for the procurement of rice from farmers. After sufficient amounts had been procured for internal rationing, rice was exported.

Reforms and/or liberalization lagged behind in the following two critical areas; reforms in the foreign exchange market, reforms in the SEEs. As discussed elsewhere in this book in greater detail, the failure of reforms in these two areas continued to a serious and a fundamental constraint for long term economic development in Myanmar, and for the development of the export-oriented manufacturing sector in particular.

Rapid Agricultural Growth

Although Myanmar did not succeed in the industrialization-led growth and postponed fundamental reforms in core sectors, such as foreign exchange

Table 2 Major Economic Reforms in Myanmar, 1987–96

1987	* Removal of government monopoly on the domestic marketing of paddy and some important crops
1988	* Introduction of Union of Myanmar Foreign Investment Law * Removal of restrictions on private foreign trade * Regularization (Opening-up) of border trade
1989	* Introduction of State-Owned Economic Enterprises Law * Revocation of the 1965 law of establishment of socialist economic system * Establishment of Joint Ventures with SEEs and private sector * Re-establishment of Myanmar Chamber of Commerce and Industry
1990	* Introduction of Myanmar Tourism Law * Allowing 100 per cent retention of export earnings * Introduction of Private Industrial Enterprises Law * Introduction of the Central Bank of Myanmar Law * Introduction of Financial Institutions of Myanmar Law * Introduction of Myanmar Agricultural and Rural Development Law * Introduction of Commecial Tax Law
1991	* Introduction of Promotion of Cottage Industries Law
1992	* Announcement of lease inefficient state-owned factories * Approval of the establishment of four private banks for the first time * Introduction of Tariff Law * Approval of Foreign Exchange Remittance through Myanmar Foreign Trade Bank
1993	* Introduction of Foreign Exchange Certificates (EFCs) * Introduction of Myanmar Hotel and Tourism Law * Introduction of Myanmar Insurance Law
1994	* Introduction of Myanmar Citizens Investment Law * Approval of representatives offices of 11 foreign banks * Introduction of Science and Technology Development Law
1995	* Announcement of the formation of Privatization Committee * Opening of the licensed foreign exchange center of FECs in Yangon * Establishment of Myanmar Industrial Development Committee
1996	* Permission granted to local banks to conduct foreign banking business and to pay interest on foreign currency deposit * Establishment of Myanmar Securities Exchange Center * Introduction of Computer Science Development Law * Establishment of Myanmar Industrial Development Bank and Myanmar Livestock and Fisheries Development Bank * Official rate of exchange for levying custom duties changed to 100 kyat per US$ (raised to 450 kyat in 2004) accompanied by reduction of tariffs

Source: Prepared by the authors.

and the SEEs, the economy did not experience a complete collapse and continued to demonstrate some "strength" throughout the period. Rapid agricultural growth was an important factor supporting this unexpected economic strength. Table 3 indicates the growth rate of Myanmar's economy after 1988 and the contribution of each sector, and it is clear that the agricultural sector played a major role, especially up to the mid-1990s.

One of the reasons Myanmar was able to pursue such an agriculture-led economic growth was the rapid "normalization" of the relative price structure between agricultural and industrial commodities (Chapter 5) that grew out of reforms in the agricultural marketing system in 1987. Agricultural commodity prices, which had been kept extremely low during the socialist period, started to rise sharply, and farmers responded quickly to these policy-induced price changes. Especially notable was the tremendous growth of new export crops such as pulses and beans. This growth was in line with the so-called "vent-for-surplus" theory (Hla Myint, 1971), in that it made use of hitherto unutilized land and labour in the dry season.

Limitation of Myanmar's Agriculture-led Growth

Though this steady growth of the agriculture sector, supported by price normalization, helped to maintain the strength of the economy in transition, its growth and contributions to the national economy was less than it might have been. Some critical limitations to Myanmar's agricultural growth will be elaborated here, by referring to the experience of the other Asian transitional economies, namely China and Vietnam.

First, the positive impact of price normalization on production was short-lived in Myanmar. This was also the case in China, where agricultural reforms started in 1978 brought dramatic increases in agricultural production in response to the stimulus of policy-led higher agricultural prices, supported by organizational reform, especially the resurgence of the farm household as a production unit. However, the agricultural growth rate of China fell after 1984, just 5–6 years into the reforms. In Myanmar, the agricultural growth started to slow down from 1996/97, mainly because of the stagnation of rice production. This means that price normalization had lost its initial impact by this time. We believe that the sluggish growth of the agricultural sector in the same period is the main cause for the slowdown of Myanmar's overall economic growth after the mid-1990s. The critical issue here is the difference in the path after the first-stage development potential was exhausted. China could continue and accelerate growth through mainly the development of rural industries, while Myanmar could not. Why did a distinct difference occur?

Table 3 Myanmar's GDP Growth and Contributions of Each Sector

	1989/90	1990/91	1991/92	1992/93	1993/94	1994/95	1995/96	1996/97	1997/98	1998/99	1999/00
Growth rates											
GDP	3.71	2.81	-0.66	9.69	6.02	7.48	6.94	6.44	5.74	5.77	10.95
Agriculture	5.24	2.00	-3.92	12.40	4.66	6.70	5.46	3.77	3.05	3.54	10.50
Livestock & Fishery	-3.97	-0.56	5.73	4.55	4.81	6.04	2.98	11.85	7.11	9.35	16.79
Forestry	28.43	8.25	-1.68	-3.28	0.99	-14.27	-4.53	2.12	2.82	3.20	4.59
Mining & Energy	30.58	-1.16	10.94	20.03	10.96	14.87	16.67	9.87	25.39	12.89	36.31
Manufacturing	11.25	0.12	-4.03	10.82	9.40	8.50	7.55	4.60	5.00	6.20	14.54
Power	14.12	5.04	6.74	31.14	24.42	4.78	6.55	12.84	17.75	-5.41	14.19
Construction	32.72	35.78	17.14	11.18	11.75	15.65	27.17	24.60	9.80	6.34	4.41
Trade	5.30	2.40	-2.46	8.85	4.65	7.05	5.66	4.95	4.96	6.32	9.54
Transport	9.72	3.51	5.85	9.06	9.20	11.21	6.36	6.00	6.53	5.65	11.96
Communications	11.64	3.95	16.55	26.02	8.49	20.42	24.60	21.69	28.09	11.64	10.99
Finance	-85.70	16.70	17.86	15.06	38.43	47.30	34.80	21.90	14.40	17.00	12.57
Social & Administrative Service	17.94	4.24	4.32	2.92	7.22	6.78	6.16	5.60	6.29	6.50	7.01
Rental & Other Services	1.51	3.46	2.55	3.60	3.50	3.99	6.28	5.94	6.05	6.58	5.76
Contributions											
GDP	100.0	100.0	-100.0	100.0	100.0	100.0	100.0	100.0	100.0	100.0	100.0
Agriculture	54.4	27.8	-229.5	47.9	29.7	33.9	29.6	21.7	19.2	21.6	33.1
Livestock & Fishery	-8.6	-1.5	62.3	3.6	5.8	5.8	3.1	12.6	8.9	11.8	11.5
Forestry	11.0	5.2	-4.8	-0.6	0.3	-3.0	-0.8	0.4	0.5	0.6	0.4
Mining & Energy	6.0	-0.4	14.6	2.0	2.0	2.2	2.9	2.0	6.0	3.6	5.7
Manufacturing	26.4	0.4	-55.4	9.8	13.8	10.4	10.0	6.6	7.9	9.7	12.1
Power	2.3	1.2	6.9	2.3	3.5	0.7	0.9	2.0	3.2	-1.1	1.4
Construction	12.9	23.8	64.0	3.4	5.7	6.5	13.1	15.2	7.9	5.3	2.0
Trade	32.0	19.4	-84.5	20.3	17.0	20.5	17.7	16.5	18.3	22.9	18.4
Transport	9.3	4.7	33.5	3.8	6.1	6.2	3.9	4.0	4.8	4.2	4.7
Communications	2.1	1.0	18.0	2.3	1.4	2.7	3.9	4.4	7.2	3.6	1.9
Finance	-78.7	2.8	14.4	1.0	4.2	5.5	5.9	5.1	4.3	5.5	2.4
Social & Administrative Service	28.6	10.2	44.5	2.2	8.0	6.2	6.0	5.8	7.3	7.5	4.3
Rental & Other Services	1.9	5.6	17.7	1.8	2.6	2.3	3.8	3.9	4.4	4.8	2.2

Source: Central Statistical Organization (CSO), *Statistical Yearbook* (1998, 2002).

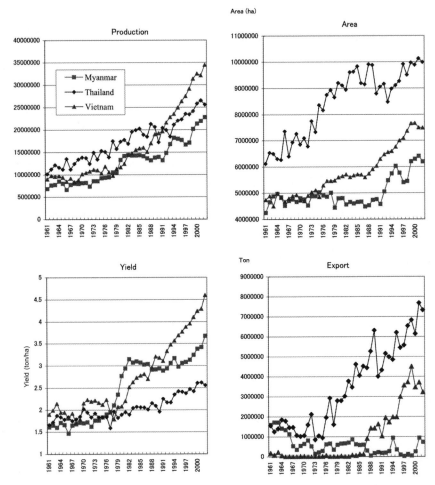

Figure 1   Performance of Rice Sector in Myanmar, in Comparison with Vietnam and Thailand

Source: FAO, *FAOSTAT.*

A second point is that Myanmar could not fully utilize its potential in the development of rice sector. Comparison with the case of Vietnam makes this point clearer. Vietnam attained a remarkable increase in rice production and export starting in the late 1980s (Figure 1). The divergence between the two countries is largely caused by rice export policies. Vietnam promoted rice exports, albeit carefully, by introducing an export quota system,[6] while Myanmar continued to ban private exports, a policy that also inhibited development of rice milling, the country's largest manufacturing activity. Thus the impact of rice export liberalization extended far beyond the rice sector itself. Why did the two countries adopt such different rice export policies?

To understand the issues outlined here, and the reason Myanmar was different from China and Vietnam, we believe that full attention should be paid to the differences in the historically formulated agrarian structures in these countries.

Myanmar has an unequal agrarian structure compared to China or Vietnam. Myanmar's land reform programme in the 1950s was highly imperfect (Takahashi, 1992), and a large pool of landless agricultural labourers (30–40 per cent of rural households on average) continued to remain in rural areas throughout the socialist period. However, China implemented a thorough land reform in the early 1950s that was followed by agricultural collectivization through the formation of communes. In the case of Vietnam, when country started economic reform and liberalization in 1986, the number of landless labourers in rural areas was small, even in the Mekong delta where socialist policy influence was minimal.

Our hypothesis here is that the agriculture-led growth in Myanmar was constrained by its inequitable agrarian structure.

First, regarding rice export policy, it is evident that if exports are allowed, the domestic market price will increase, all other things being equal. Because rice is a staple food, the government has to be very sensitive to the problem of higher rice price, especially at the early stage of economic development.[7] Even a slight increase in the rice price can easily endanger the livelihoods of many urban people. However, the problem becomes much more serious in Myanmar, where in addition to the urban population there are numerous net rice purchasers in rural areas, in the form of poor landless agricultural labourers. This explains, at least partly, why Myanmar government did not dare to liberalize rice export even gradually, in contrast with Vietnam.

The Myanmar government might have been hesitant for another reason. The landless agricultural labourers were entitled to rice rations in the socialist period, but after 1987 when the agricultural marketing system was reformed, they were deprived of this entitlement and suddenly thrown into the volatile rice market (Chapter 6). It is easy to understand why the Myanmar government was concerned about the price of a staple food, especially after experiencing serious social unrest in 1988.

Second, whereas the benefit of the rapid agricultural growth accrued to almost all rural residents in China under an egalitarian agrarian structure, in the case of Myanmar, the benefit was largely limited to the farmers, by-passing large numbers of landless people (Chapter 7). In addition, agricultural growth in Myanmar mainly relied on the expansion of cropped land area with no outstanding productivity growth (Chapter 5), whereas in China, agricultural growth was largely based on an impressive improvement in productivity. As a result, economic disparity in rural areas widened and the poverty of landless people remained a serious problem in Myanmar.

The difference in the nature of agricultural growth also explains why rural industrialization was possible in China, while it was not the case for Myanmar. Because agricultural growth was accompanied by productivity improvement in China, surplus labour was available for other sectors. A typical Lewis-type industrialization with an unlimited supply of labour took place. Second, equitable and productivity-enhancing agricultural growth largely solved problems of rural poverty and food supply in China, which created a vast market for non-food consumer goods in rural areas. Rural industries in China produced a wide variety of consumer goods for the rural population.

In sum, the rapid agricultural growth in Myanmar apparently slowed down from 1996/97, basically due to the exhaustion of the first-stage development potential induced by the price normalization, as also happened in China. However, in the case of Myanmar, an inequitable agrarian structure with a large number of landless agricultural labourers hampered further development, in the sense that it did not allow rice export liberalization, and it failed to create the conditions necessary for further growth based on non-agricultural development.

Growth of Liberalized/Authorized International Trade and FDI

While the rapid recovery and development of Myanmar's economy after 1988 was primarily a product of the agricultural growth, the high economic growth was also reflected by the trade and service sectors. The contribution of trade to GDP growth was the second largest after the agricultural sector in the early 1990s, and FDI rapidly expanded until 1996, stimulating non-manufacturing sectors such as construction, tourism and the hotel industry. Furthermore, in the mid 1990s, increased FDI is found in the manufacturing sector.

In contrast to agriculture, which experienced an obvious slowdown in growth during the mid-1990s, the trade and service sectors continued to show substantial growth even after the Asian economic crisis. As a result, Myanmar's economy recorded a fairly high and sustained growth.

Dampening of Economic Growth in the Mid-1990s

The apparent slowdown of the Myanmar's economy that became apparent around 1996/97, in our view, was primarily caused by the limitation imposed on agricultural growth in the first half of the 1990s. The constraint was, as stated earlier, deeply rooted in the historically formulated inequitable agrarian structure in Myanmar.

Myanmar's economy was also affected by changes in external economic relations during the Asian economic crisis in 1997/98. The decelerated export and FDI inflow caused the growth rate to decline. However, the direct and immediate influence of the Asian economic crisis was in fact not very large; Southeast Asian countries such as Thailand, Malaysia, and Singapore experienced falls in FDI and exports, but these declines were not dramatic.

Subsequently, however, Myanmar government began to change its attitude to economic liberalization; some initiatives were suspended and others even reversed. The changes were a defensive response to a severe shortage of foreign reserves, and they aggravated the deterioration in economic condition, which generated a vicious circle.

Flaws in the Macro-economy after the Mid-1990s

Over-valued exchange rate and macroeconomic instability

After the mid-1990s, the price distortion arising from the artificial and fixed exchange rate that over-valued the kyat became serious. As is discussed in Chapter 1, the distortion appeared in the form of "import bias" and created conditions unfavourable to exports, which virtually closed off development of the export-oriented manufacturing sector. The distortion grew worse in a cyclical process of fiscal deficit, inflation and further falls of market exchange rate against the over-valued official rate.

The stagnation of state economic enterprises

That the stagnation of the state economic enterprises (SEEs) underlies the worsening fiscal deficit gradually became obvious in the late 1990s. After the slowdown of economic growth starting in the mid-1990s, the failure of the reform of SEEs became apparent. This large but inefficient sector consumed a vast government subsidy.

The revised State-owned Economic Enterprise Law in March 1989 confirmed SEE monopolies in 12 prescribed fields, and allowed private enterprises to operate in many other areas. Nevertheless, the SEEs continued to occupy a significant position in the economy. In 1998, more than fifty SEEs were operating. They employed 0.3 million people; about 1.5 per cent of the total working population, but contributed 20 per cent of GDP (Nishizawa, 2001). The share of GDP was not significantly lower than in 1987/88 (23.5 per cent) or in 1996/97 (22.8 per cent).

The SEEs dominate communication (100 per cent), electricity (99.9 per cent), social and administrative services (89.4 per cent), construction (69.3 per cent), banking (62.2 per cent), mining (51.7 per cent), forestry (44.1 per cent) and transportation (34.0 per cent). The share is relatively low in processing and manufacturing (28.7 per cent), commerce (22.1 per cent), and agriculture (including livestock and fishery) (0.3 per cent), according to figures for 1996/97. Although reliable information on SEEs after the end of the 1990s is very rare, indirect and scattered evidence suggests that the SEE sector has expanded. As the construction of sugar factories described in Chapter 5 indicates, this trend is related to assistance from China. Mizuno (2004) provides further evidence that new factories producing cement, ceramics and many other goods have been built with support from China.

On the other hand, although the SEE sector was large, it did not experience significant growth after 1988. As discussed in Chapter 4, under the regulation of their fund-raising and the State Fund Account System, serious soft budget constraints have regularly occurred and gotten worse. Clearly, the management efficiency did not improve in this process, and the stagnation and large deficit associated with this sector made national budgetary conditions worse.

"Import bias" and underdevelopment of the export manufacturing sector

Private manufacturing can be regarded as the sector most seriously affected by the influence of "import bias" arising from the highly distorted foreign exchange market. The most typical case, medium and large rice millers, is analyzed in Chapter 6. In addition to "import bias", the prohibition of private rice exports denied these medium and large rice millers any opportunity to renovate their facilities, and they failed to escape from stagnation and decline.

One of the characteristics of Myanmar's manufacturing sector is that the SEE sector is biased towards large-scale heavy industries, while the private sector mainly consists of small-scale enterprises engaged in light industry, such as food, textiles and timber. There was a dramatic increase in the number of private manufacturing enterprises after 1988, but growth was moderate in terms of GDP share and other macroeconomic indicators

(Kudo ed., 2001; U Tin Htut Oo and Kudo eds., 2003 for agro-based industries). As noted above, Myanmar's private manufacturing sector is apparently stagnant when compared with neighbouring countries.

Government policy towards the private manufacturing sector was not completely laissez-faire. Measures such as establishing industrial zones with certain infrastructure can be seen as a form of promotion of private manufacturing. However, these measures were negated by the revival or strengthening of various restrictions, and by the absence of infrastructure investment in electricity and telecommunications (Chapter 2). Most of the revival, maintenance and strengthening of restrictions is directly or indirectly related to measures for acquisition of foreign exchange earnings by the government. In this sense, the victims of unfavourable export conditions arising from "import bias" were private manufactures.

Unexpected Strength of Myanmar's Economy

Myanmar's economy, continued to register moderate growth until recently, and has not faced any risk of complete collapse, as is sometimes suggested. In other words, it showed strength much more than we expected. The main reason, in our view, is that certain positive factors continued to affect the economy, such as a relatively high growth rate in the agricultural sector, the rapid development of the financial sector, the emergence and the development of the garment industry in the late 1990s, inflow of FDI from China and Chinese people that is not officially recorded, and the rich resource base in Myanmar, exemplified in the development of natural gas exports in very recent years. It is entirely possible that Myanmar will follow a "staple" development path by depending on agriculture, precious stones and natural gas for some time to come, a situation that is compatible with the country's resource endowment.

Prospects for Myanmar's Economy

Development based on the country's rich natural resources will eventually lead to the depletion of these resources. As the long-term declining trend of the labour wage rate indicates, the economy has been gradually impoverished in its fundamentals (Chapter 7). In fact, the wage rate for unskilled labourers in Myanmar is extremely low ranging from 40 to 50 cents per day when converted at free market exchange rates. Even in the poorest neighbouring countries such as Laos and Bangladesh, the wage rate is around 1–1.5 US dollars per day. Export-oriented industrialization is indispensable and, without any movement in this direction, there are few prospects for full-scale economic development and poverty reduction. It should be emphasized that the very low money wage rate in Myanmar is a great advantage for promoting labour intensive industrialization, although as noted earlier, agricultural productivity growth is an important pre-requisite. The major hindrance to export-oriented industrialization is the unfavourable condition associated with the macroeconomic structure, essentially caused by the fiscal deficit and parallel exchange rate system. Reforms are most urgent in the foreign exchange market and the SEE sector.

Outline of the Book

Macro Economy and Industrial Structure

As noted earlier, this book is divided into two parts. Chapters 1 to 4 analyze the macro economy and industrial structure in relation with their external economic relationships.

The relatively high growth of the Myanmar economy in the early 1990s accompanied a substantial change in industrial structures. The new regime adopted various market liberalization policies, including the liberalization/authorization of private trade, authorization of private investment including FDI and reform of financial institutions. Thanks to these policies, the economy broke away from the deadlock of the latter half of the 1980s and achieved rapid expansion. However, Myanmar started to experience an economic malaise after the mid-1990s, the result of instability in the economic structure, an unfavourable external economic environment, serious fiscal deficits, inefficient SEEs, and the failure of the exchange rate system. Chapter 1 which analyzes the causes, the processes and the impacts of each of these issues and highlighting the development of private enterprise and its pattern of capital accumulation, is the key element in the first part of the book. This chapter explains capital accumulation in these private enterprises while analyzing the systems of foreign exchange control, finance, banking and industrial structure, in the context of changes in the whole national economy.

The chapter emphasizes the impact of a dual exchange rate system, with multiple official and semi-official exchange rates and various parallel market rates, on Myanmar's economic transformation process. Obviously Myanmar has failed to reform the foreign exchange market, which is a critical element for opening the economy. The disparity between the official rate and parallel rate has been increasing year after year. Until recently, the official rate was kept at about 6 kyat per US dollar, while market rate reached about 1,300 kyat per dollar (April 2006), more than 200 times the official rate.

Facing circumstance where it earned almost no foreign exchange revenue, the government took measures to absorb foreign exchange earnings from the private sector by implementing compulsory exchange at a disadvantageous rate, taxing exports and imposing government monopolies over trade in particular commodities. This arrangement created an "import bias" that was a strong disincentive to private sector participation in export-oriented activities.

The "import bias" generated by the distortion in the foreign exchange market discouraged investment in export manufacturing. The capital accumulated from exports of agricultural, fishery and mining exports under trade liberalization was directed into non-manufacturing sectors, such as the construction, financial and real estate sectors, rather than investment in manufacturing. This chapter strongly argues that this situation is the fundamental factor that inhibited industrialization.

Chapter 1 also provides a new perspective on the recession after the mid 1990s. While Myanmar started to suffer from economic malaise after the mid-1990s, it escaped serious negative consequences from the Asian economic crisis and sustained moderate economic growth until after 2000. Although rates of growth exceeding 10 per cent after 1999–2000 in government statistics cannot be taken at face value, it is most likely that the country achieved moderate growth of around 5–6 per cent per annum even in the late 1990s. The chapter points out various contributing factors such as a rise in Cutting, Making and Packaging (CMP) processing in the garment industry, an invisible increase in the capital flow mainly from China and Chinese investors, and the expansion of exports of natural gas.

Chapter 2, "Industrial Policies and the Development of Myanmar's Industrial Sector in the Transition to a Market Economy", focuses on the development process of the manufacturing sector and its structural problems. Although it did not play a central role in economic development, the manufacturing sector achieved some growth in the early 1990s. The liberalization of the manufacturing sector and "pent-up" demand for daily commodities stimulated private manufacturing in the early 1990s. However, persistent and worsening trade deficits led the government to reverse its policy and shift back to SEE oriented production, strengthening the SEE monopoly, particularly over heavy industry, and imposing heavy taxes on the private export industries. Chapter 2 raises two particular issues relating to the situation after the mid-1990s: the failure of SEEs to deal with infrastructure defects and the success of garment manufacturing. It shows that Myanmar suffers from infrastructure shortage caused by inefficient and insufficient investment in infrastructure, mainly due to the monopoly of SEEs. Despite such adverse circumstances, private manufacturing survived and even grew as a garment

CMP sector, making a kind of "enclave" where producers could minimize the unfavourable policy environment. The chapter concludes, however, that the failure of the government has gotten very serious, and the effort of the private manufacturing sector has almost reached its limit.

Chapter 3, "Trade, Foreign Investment and Myanmar's Economic Development in the Transition to an Open Economy", analyzes Myanmar's foreign economic relations in terms of trade and foreign direct investment. The chapter examines changes in the pattern of exports and imports after changes in trade policy. In particular, it shows that while the country experienced trade deficits in the 1990s, export products and trade partnerships both evolved, and conditions improved faster in 2000. The chapter also describes foreign direct investment in the 1990s and 2000s. While increased foreign investment was mainly directed to the domestic and energy sectors in the 1990s, shifts in focus occurred after that. The overall evaluation of the contribution of the external sectors to growth is also pointed out.

Chapter 4, "The Financial Sector during the Transition to a Market Economy in Myanmar", discusses financial reforms after the enactment of three financial laws in July 1990. The chapter describes the transformation of the financial system in Myanmar that followed, and explores the development of private banks. It also describes the bank run of February 2003 and the government response to it, and evaluates the characteristics of the Myanmar's financial sector in comparison with those of Cambodia, Laos, and Vietnam.

Many private banks were established in the early 1990s by entrepreneurs as a way of re-investing the capital they accumulated through trade and other activities. Despite negative real interest, deposits in these banks expanded until they accounted for more than 70 per cent of total bank holdings in 2001. The chapter examines the cause and the results of the bank run, and shows that Myanmar's banking system had reached a stage at which it could no longer sustain stable relations with other sectors of the economy. The chapter also examines the fund mobilization of SEEs, and the different roles of state owned and private banks in comparison with the other Indochina countries.

The Agriculture and Labour Economy

The second part of the book contains four chapters that focus on the transformation of the agricultural sector after 1988 (Chapter 5), the rice marketing system (Chapter 6), rural labour (Chapter 7) and the urban informal sector (Chapter 8).

Chapter 5, "Overview of Agricultural Policies and Development in Myanmar", reviews government policies and the resulting performance of the agricultural sector after the transition to an open economy in 1988. The chapter first clarifies how rapid agricultural growth after 1988, and especially up to the mid-1990s, was induced by a surge in agricultural prices. Dramatic increases in production and export were achieved for some export crops, such as pulses and beans; even rice, for which export liberalization was not allowed, registered a high growth in production due mainly to price increases.

This chapter then highlights contrasts in the government policies applied to different sub-sectors within agriculture. While the government intervened heavily in some important crops such as rice, oilseed crops, and several cash crops (such as sugarcane and cotton) on behalf of agro-based SEE factories, it largely neglected the remaining sub-sectors, including pulses and beans, and prawns, which have rapidly become important sources of exports.

There has been ongoing pressure to increase the production of crops such as rice and oilseeds, because they are indispensable for the diet of Myanmar people. The major objective is to stabilize the prices of such important food crops at low levels to avoid social unrest. The same aggressive policy to achieve increased production implemented for industrial crops supplied as raw materials to the SEEs. Such a policy had a negative influence on the farmers, especially when it was not profitable for them to increase production. For example, increased production of rice was promoted aggressively through the crop planning system and the summer paddy programme, even after the mid-1990s when rice farmers faced deteriorating terms of trade for rice production. Another example is that the government strongly encouraged the introduction of new oilseed crops such as sunflower, although farmers were reluctant because of the lower profitability.

In sum, agricultural policy is basically unaltered from the way of thinking in the socialist era. Increased production, with little consideration of the quality of the product or profitability for farmers, continued to be the sole objective in the case of products indispensable for sustaining the regime.

On the other hand, with respect to the crops/products that are less important for the people's diet, such as pulses and prawns, the government's position was neutral and practically speaking they operated under laissez-faire conditions. These crops/products achieved a remarkable growth in production and export, supported by the expanding international demand. As noted earlier, this self-sustaining growth of pulses and prawns led by the private sector was one of the important factors that supported the "unexpected" strength of Myanmar's economy.

Chapter 6, "Transformation of the Rice Marketing System after Market Liberalization in Myanmar", analyzes rice marketing policies and the transformation of the rice marketing system after 1988, one of the areas where government attention was always concentrated. The "first liberalization" in the late 1980s (when the procurement system was abolished but then partly revived, while rice export remained prohibited) and its impact on the rice marketing system, are examined in detail. The chapter also offers analysis of the "second liberalization" in April 2003 (when the procurement system was totally abolished, and private rice export briefly allowed but then banned again).

The processing and marketing of rice are a critical non-agricultural activity in Myanmar. Many (marginal) entrepreneurs entered the business after the first "liberalization", and it showed steady growth thereafter. However, owing to the vital importance of rice, millers and traders continued to face restrictions and interventions. Overall policy was never directed toward upgrading the rice marketing sector or improving its efficiency, but rather imposed constraints on the sector's development. Chapter 6 explains Myanmar's transition to a market economy after 1988 by focusing on the difficulties faced by rice millers and traders during the economic transition.

As mentioned above, a very large number of individuals survive solely by selling their labour in Myanmar. Some are found in the urban informal sector, but most are in rural areas working as agricultural labourers. Chapter 7, "Agricultural Labourers in Myanmar during the Economic Transition: Views from the Study of Selected Villages", provides an in-depth analysis of households of agricultural labourers in rural Myanmar. This chapter demonstrates unique features of Myanmar's rural economy that create initial conditions for economic development and differ from those in other transitional economies. First, the scale of agricultural labour households is estimated as follows: 30–50 per cent of the total rural population consists of non-farm households, with 20–40 per cent households of agricultural labourers. Second, surveys in rural area, show that the real wage rate (in rice equivalent) of labourers decreased by about 40–50 per cent between 1970s and the early 2000s. The chapter also finds that reductions of real wages occurred in the course of a shift of the payment from wages in-kind to wages in cash. Further, in this chapter the "poverty" of households of agricultural labourers is examined by looking at the deterioration of income distribution, serious debt, poor asset holding and educational backwardness.

Chapter 8, "Urban Informal Sector Labourers in Yangon", provides valuable information on a topic that has received little attention in the past. Based on interviews, the chapter describes the characteristics of these labourers, the profitability of different categories of work, and household economy. It analyzes seven categories of workers: shop owners, shop employees, restaurant waiters, vendors, taxi drivers, trishaw (*hsai car*) drivers, skilled labourers, unskilled labourers, waste collectors, refuse collectors and slipper/umbrella repairers.

Notes

Chapters 1, 4, 5, 7 and 8 of this volume are revised versions of Chapters 1, 3, 5, 7 and 8 in Fujita, Koichi ed. 2005. *Myanmar Iko Keizai no Henyo* [*Myanmar's Economy in Transition*], Chiba: Institute of Developing Economies (in Japanese). Chapter 6 was originally published in Japanese in the Fujita's volume and is an expanded version of Chapter 7 "Transforming Myanmar's rice marketing", in Monique Skidmore and Trevor Wilson eds., *Myanmar: the State, Community and the Environment*, Canberra: Asia Pacific Press. Chapters 2 and 3 are revised versions of the following discussion papers published by the Institute of Developing Economies: "Stunted and Distorted Industrialization in Myanmar", *IDE Discussion Paper Series* No. 38, October 2005, and "Trade, Foreign Investment and Myanmar's Economic Development during the Transition to an Open Economy", *IDE Discussion Paper Series* No. 116, August 2007.

[1] For a discussion of economic management under the "Burmese Way to Socialism" and its consequences, the following are useful: Steinberg (1981); Hill and Jayasuriya (1986); Mya Maung (1970, 1991); Myat Thein (2004) and Tin Maung Maung Than (2007).

[2] SLORC was re-organized and renamed the State Peace and Development Council (SPDC) in 1997.

[3] Explanations of the difference in the pace as well as the performance of the reform in the initial stage of the transition between these neighbouring countries, see Myat Thein and Mya Than (1995: 249–54).

[4] Other examples are Kyin Maung Kyi *et al.* (2000) and Mya Than and Myat Thein (2000). The former covers economic conditions up to the mid-1990s and focuses on policy recommendations. The latter is a collection of papers on Myanmar's domestic finance mobilization, pointing out limitation as well as future directions.

[5] For example, Turnell (2006: 78–80), discusses official statistics.

[6] See Nicholas and Goletti (2000) for the Vietnamese case.

[7] Even in Thailand, the domestic rice price was kept at a low level for a long time by a so-called "rice premium" system. The gap between the domestic and the international price remained as large as 40 per cent, and was reduced to 10 per cent only after the mid-1980s when full-scale industrialization started (Choeun *et al.*, 2004).

PART ONE

Macro Economy and Industrial Structure

CHAPTER 1

Characteristics of Capital Accumulation in Myanmar, 1988–2003

Fumiharu Mieno

Introduction

This chapter examines the characteristics and mutual linkages between Myanmar's macroeconomy, industrial structure and financial system. These linkages emerged during the capital accumulation process following the liberalization of external economic relations in the late 1980s. It also considers the recent difficulty experienced by the Myanmar economy. There are three basic questions to be answered. First, what kinds of industries and firms have played a central role in economic growth and capital accumulation since the economic reforms of 1988? Second, how did the financial system, which is expected to provide the essential function of efficient resource allocation in the capital accumulation process, emerge and take shape? Third, what effect has the nature of the capital accumulation process had on recent macroeconomic instability? We examine each aspect of the economy: the macroeconomy, industrial structure, emergence of private firms and banks, and their method of financing expenditure. We then examine the relationship between the structure of the economy and macroeconomic conditions in the twenty-first century.

Based on economic performance, we divide the 15 years since the economic reform into three different phases: 1989–96, the start of the post-reform period, when there was strong growth; 1997–2000, when the economy suffered partially from the Asian financial crisis but continued to achieve growth; and, after 2000, when the macroeconomic conditions became unstable. After taking power in September 1988, the State Law and Order Restoration Council adopted new economic policies that moved Myanmar away from its traditional closed economy. The external economic activities, namely foreign trade, border trade and foreign currency holdings, were liberalized or authorized. Laws for private and foreign investment were established. The financial system was reorganized from a socialist mono-bank system into a two-tier system, and was opened up for entry by private firms. Under this series of policy reforms, Myanmar experienced high growth during the early 1990s. An increasing volume of foreign investment was attracted into the construction, tourism and mining sectors. The trade activities also expanded, while the increasing amount of importation of capital goods maintained a trade account deficit.

During the second phase, 1997–2000, the economy continued to grow despite a significant downturn in the external economic conditions due to the Asian financial crisis. The financial crisis caused a fall in exports for the major trading partners, such as Singapore, and a sudden fall in foreign investment, whereas the trade deficit continued to expand owing to the persistent increases in the importation of capital goods. The government responded to these circumstances by strengthening its control over remittances and foreign currency holdings. On the other hand, the domestic economy continued to expand, driven by the construction and financial sectors.

In the third phase, after 2000, the macroeconomy became unstable. After 2001, inflation surged and the real exchange rate depreciated. The local asset markets appeared prosperous until 2002, but fell subject to panic during the banking crisis of February 2003. In 2004, the economy appeared to contract, although this is difficult to confirm because of the lack of reliable data.

We argue in this chapter that the economic structures that were developed in the 15 years after 1988 in Myanmar produced the recent macroeconomic instability for the following reasons. Although Myanmar achieved substantial growth led by the private sector for this 15-year period, distortions persisted and even become more serious. Fiscal reforms relating to the privatization of state-owned economic enterprises (SEEs) were limited, and no drastic reforms of the exchange rate system were implemented, resulting in an unstable macroeconomy and other problems, such as fiscal deficits, inefficient production and the underdevelopment of the financial system. However, this 15-year period also brought substantial economic growth and capital accumulation driven by the expanding trade and capital inflows. Economic growth was led by trade surpluses during the first stage following the authorization of trade, and during the second stage, until 2002, by the non-manufacturing sector, including construction, finance and real estate, as reflected by the distortion of prices. The export manufacturing sector also developed under unfavourable conditions in the late 1990s in the form of the garment industry, which operated on a process on commission basis and gave the economy an atmosphere of being in the early stages of industrialization. After 2003, the economy appeared to contract, but it was supported in 2004 by increased capital inflows, mainly from China, and by Chinese business networks and increasing natural gas exports to Thailand.

With the government avoiding drastic reforms, the Myanmar economy became seriously distorted and unstable despite the high growth experienced during these periods. A move towards industrialization, generally regarded as a necessary condition for sustainable economic growth, has not been evident. However, the difficulties facing the Myanmar economy have been minimized, supported intermittently and partially by the plentiful natural resources and rich external economic networks, in both a formal and informal fashion. The common view that Myanmar's economy is facing catastrophe appears incorrect, but the current structure of the economy seems inappropriate for nurturing sustainable growth.

Studies or even general information about the Myanmar economy are scarce. Nishizawa (2000), Takahashi (2001) and Myat Thein (2004) are among the few comprehensive works that cover the economic policy and conditions of this period. Mya Than and Myat Thein (2000) examine the Myanmar financial system in the 1990s. Following these previous studies, our objective is to uncover the mechanism of the growth and capital accumulation processes. The other major data sources used in this chapter are official government statistics, notes from interviews conducted in 2004 and 2005, and the results of some questionnaire-based company surveys that we conducted. Reflecting the weak evidence above, our view may be little more than a hypothesis. Meanwhile, considering the scarcity of the available information and research on the Myanmar economy, we believe that our approach is valuable, at the very least, as a discussion platform.

The structure of the chapter is as follows. Section 1 explains our view of the relationship between the capital accumulation process and the macroeconomy. Section 2 discusses individual aspects of the economy, such as growth rates, industrial structure, foreign investment, trade, fiscal conditions and the macroeconomy along with the regulations on external economic relations. Section 3 focuses on the microeconomic relationship between private firms and banks, examining the characteristics of both the private sector and the financial system that have emerged under the macroeconomic distortions. The final section concludes the discussion and provides a possible interpretation of the recent economic conditions.

Basic Economic Structure

Characteristics of the Liberalization of External Economic Relations

In the 1990s the government implemented various economic reforms centered on external economic relations, which are typical of the types of reform implemented in transition economies. First, the banking sector was reorganized and separated from the fiscal process. Through the Central Bank Law, Financial Institution Law and other laws enacted in 1990, the financial sector was redeveloped into a two-tier system consisting of a central bank, banks specializing in agricultural or foreign currency, and the ordinary state-owned banks. Furthermore, the government authorized private sector entry into the banking industry, and between 1992 and 1997 many private businesses acted on this approval.

Second, the government liberalized external economic relationships. External trade had been largely prohibited in the closed economy, but from 1989 restrictions were gradually loosened. Imports were admitted under a license system. Border trade, long viewed as smuggling, was also gradually authorized in the mid-1990s.[1] Foreign investment was encouraged within a new legal framework — the Union of Myanmar Foreign Investment Law in 1988 and the Myanmar Citizens Investment Law[2] in 1994 — and a Myanmar Industrial Development Committee is established in 1995. As a result, large amounts of foreign direct investment (FDI) were attracted to the construction, tourism and mining sectors.

Meanwhile, the transitional reforms in particular areas were seriously delayed or ineffectively implemented. In the fiscal sector, the reform of the SEEs was virtually not-existent. Furthermore, when the accounting systems of the SEEs were unified into a single account, the State Foundation Account in 1990, and placed under the budgetary process, the discretionary capacity of individual SEEs was restricted, in contrast to the general reformist trend. Although a stated objective of the government, privatization of the SEEs was never fully implemented, and took place only in small enterprises, such as cinemas or factories, producing commodities for daily use (Nishizawa 2000, Chapter 6).

Another aspect of the delay is found in the exchange rate system. While reforms were necessary for the activation and expansion of international trade, drastic changes to the exchange rate regime were avoided, and the confusing exchange rate policies that were implemented seriously distorted the domestic economy. Despite the vast inflow of foreign currency through trade and foreign investment, the government rigidly restricted foreign currency holdings, allowing them only in accounts with the Myanmar Investment and

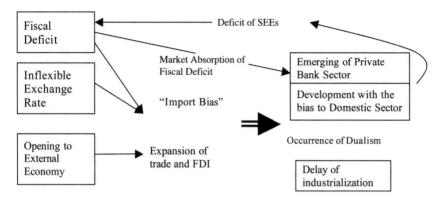

Figure 1   A Principle View

Commercial Bank (MICB) or the Myanmar Foreign Trade Bank (MFTB). Myanmar nationals were only allowed to hold foreign cash in the form of Foreign Exchange Certificates (FECs), which were introduced in 1993. The exchange rate was pegged to the SDR at around an unrealistic six kyat per US dollar in the formal statements, and the government required nationals to use the FEC rate as the formal rate in their transactions, usually known as the "centre rate" (meaning "the rate at the authorized exchange centres"), in their transactions.[3] The centre rate significantly overvalued the kyat because of the fall in the market exchange rate, discussed later, and there were illicit markets for FECs and the US dollar. The disparity between the formal and market rates under the parallel rate regimes, and accompanying macroeconomic distortions, became progressively more severe.

The Basic Viewpoint: Linkages between the Policy Factors

In this subsection, we present an overview of our observations. Figure 1 summarizes how the policies implemented in the 15 years after 1988 affected economic growth and capital accumulation, and how these factors influenced each other.

First, the large fiscal deficits caused chronic inflation, resulting in a decline in the real exchange rate. The worsening fiscal deficit was caused not only by excessive expenditure by the central government but also by deficits run up by the less competitive SEEs following the reforms.[4] While the inflation rate was volatile depending on the period, the average inflation rate from 1994 to 2002 was 30.5 per cent, mainly due to the monetization of the fiscal deficit. Alongside the surge in prices, the market exchange rate declined by around 60 per cent annually.

Second, with an unrealistic official rate and a growing disparity between the centre rate and the market exchange rate after 1997, liberalization of trade and increased FDI led to strong growth in the domestic non-manufacturing sectors, which mainly utilized imported capital goods as inputs. The appreciation of the kyat for domestic firms forced them to adopt the fixed centre rate and created circumstances favourable to the importers of capital goods and inputs but disadvantaged the exporters of the final products. The mixture of trade liberalization and an inflexible exchange rate system created price distortions that were favourable to non-tradable goods, or non-manufacturing sectors, such as the construction and hotel industries, which largely depended on imported capital goods. This scenario was unfavourable for the export manufacturing.[5]

Third, until the mid-1990s rising FDI was directed towards such sectors as the construction, tourism and hotel industries. The domestic firms have rapidly grown within these sectors. Excess demand for foreign currency under the exchange rate disparity after the mid-1990s required the rationing of foreign currency, either at the official rate or centre rate, where it was allocated primarily to the SEEs, and to private firms as part of their import licenses. Several private firms that obtained licenses grew rapidly and diversified their business within the non-manufacturing sector. Major private banks have emerged from these types of business firm.

Fourth, the emergence of private firms in the domestic sector resulted in a decline in the competitiveness of the SEEs in the local market, which, in turn produced a worsening fiscal deficit. The allocation of import licenses also brought a new distinction in the market between the non-manufacturing sector and the export-manufacturing sector, or between firms with access to import licenses and those without.

Finally, the financial sector significantly expanded from the mid-1990s through the new entry of the emerging, non-manufacturing conglomerates. However, because of the constraining factors of the interest rate ceiling, business regulation, negative real interest rates and a lack of information, the emerging financial system failed to act as a financial intermediary. Funds mobilized through the financial system were solely directed to firms close to the banks and operating in the domestic, non-manufacturing sector. Businesses in the export-manufacturing sector suffered from a scarcity of accessible funds, but the expanding the banks helped finance the deficit when the government dispatched a compulsory allocation of treasury bonds (TBs) in late 1999. This move reduced inflationary pressure during 1999–2000, despite the expanding deficit. However, the relationship also raised the possibility that the operations of the financial sector would directly influence the inflation rate.

Developments in the Myanmar economy after 2000, such as the rapid depreciation in the market exchange rate, the boom and bust of the asset markets, and the economic contraction in 2003, grew out of the economic restructuring of the 1990s.

The Macroeconomy, Industrial Structure and Regulations

Economic Growth

First, let us briefly examine the economic growth rate, although this most basic economic indicator must be interpreted with caution. According to Table 1, which shows Myanmar's GDP figures according to the official statistics, Myanmar recorded substantial growth after the mid-1990s. The average rate of GDP growth from 1994–96 was 6.9 per cent, and growth in excess of 5.0 per cent was achieved in 1997 and 1998, when the Asian economic crisis hit the region. The difficulty in evaluating the GDP data is that there is skepticism about the reliability of the official statistics after 1999, for example, between 2001 and 2003 when government statistics show more than 10 per cent annual growth. Furthermore, the release of GDP data after 2002 was substantially delayed.

Some external economic intelligence sources have stopped quoting government statistics, and release their own estimates. Table 2 shows the estimated growth rate from various secondary sources. *Country Reports* by the Economic Intelligence Unit (EIU) estimates the real growth rates for 2001 and 2002 to have been 4.6 per cent and 5.3 per cent, respectively. *Regional Outlook* 2005, published by the Institute of Southeast Asian Studies in Singapore, places the growth rate for the same periods at 5 per cent. Both sources anticipated a decline in 2003–4 and a slight recovery in 2005,[6] but they differed on the magnitude of the recession in 2004, with the former estimating negative growth, the latter around 3 per cent positive growth.

Myanmar achieved persistent, significant growth until the mid-1990s, and managed to maintain strong growth even after the Asian financial crisis of 1997. It was not until 2003 that the economy went into recession.

The Fiscal Conditions, Money and Prices

Next, we focus on the relationship between fiscal conditions and inflation. While the worsening fiscal conditions induced chronic inflation through the monetarization of the fiscal deficit, the mechanism was temporarily

Table 1 GDP Growth Rate

	1993/94	1994/95	1995/96	1996/97	1997/98	1998/99	1999/00	2000/01	2001/02
Nominal GDP, Million Kyat	360,321	472,774	604,729	791,980	1,119,509	1,609,776	2,190,320	2,552,733	3,523,515
Nominal GDP, Growth Rate		31.2%	27.9%	31.0%	41.4%	43.8%	36.1%	16.5%	38.0%
Real GDP, Million Kyat	58,064	62,406	66,742	71,042	75,123	79,460	88,157	100,275	992,394*
Real GDP, Growth Rate		7.5%	6.9%	6.4%	5.7%	5.8%	10.9%	13.7%	10.5%

Note: *the base year for 2001/02 of real GDP is 1995/96, and that of the others is 1985/86.

Sources: Asian Development Bank, *Key Indicators*, 2003 (internet version); Central Statistical Organization, *Statistical Yearbook*, 2002.

Table 2 Estimations of Real GDP Growth

	1999/00	2000/01	2001/02	2002/03	2003/04	2004/05	2005/06
EIU 2002/Nov.	10.9	13.6	5.4	4.6			
EIU 2003/Nov.	10.9	13.6	5.3	5.3	2.5		
EIU 2004/Sept.				5.3	−1.0	−1.1	1.1
Regional Outlook		5.5	5.0	4.5	3.2	3.0	3.7

Note: The figures in italics are estimates.

Sources: Economic Intelligent Unit (EIU); ISEAS, *Regional Outlook: Southeast Asia 2005–2006* (2005: 114).

moderated in the late 1990s, when the emerging private banking sector started to absorb the TBs.

Table 3 summarizes the budgetary conditions and the means of financing the deficit according to the official statistics. Information on the budgetary conditions is available only for the period from 1999–2000. The size of the SEEs' account is two to three times that of the central government. The deficit of the central government declined after 1997, while, in contrast, that of the SEEs appeared to increase.

The government statistics provide no information on the financing of the deficit. Most of the deficit appears to have been absorbed by monetarization via the Central Bank. The quantity of TBs on issue was small prior to 1997, but expanded rapidly after 1998. Comparing the quantity of TBs on issue with the balance sheets of the banks, the absorption increased annually and, by 2000, around 30 per cent of the total deficit had been absorbed by the market through bank deposits.

It is believed that the market absorption through the private banks helped to moderate inflation. Figure 2 represents the trend consumer price index (CPI) growth rate. Although the average rate from 1999–2003 was a high 36.5 per cent the inflation rate was moderate from 1998–2000 when the market absorption started.[7] This fortunate set of conditions occurred because the private banking sector was emerging. Table 4 shows that the money supply from 1993–2001 in the form of bank deposits (demand deposits and time deposits) rapidly expanded. It was during this period that the potential demand for deposits was realized by the emerging financial sector, and a method of financing the fiscal deficit by the market was constructed. Despite this development, the mechanism was very temporary in nature. After 2001, the growth of deposits weakened and, in turn, the currency expanded, resulting in the reemergence of inflation.

Table 3 Fiscal Balance and its Financing

Table 3-1 Fiscal Balance

Central Government	1980/81	1985/86	1990/91	1994/95	1995/96	1996/97	1997/98	1998/99	1999/00
Revenue	6,498.4	7,716.2	14,203.1	32,340.3	40,077.2	55,012.1	88,181.3	117,293.5	107,312.1
(to GDP)				6.8%	6.6%	6.9%	7.9%	7.3%	4.9%
Tax and Tariff	3,710.6	4,621.9	9,416.7	20,101.2	22,643.7	31,357.0	49,429.2	56,653.0	49,919.8
Income from SEEs	1,712.3	1,936.2	3,433.8	8,194.8	10,508.6	16,642.4	26,864.2	43,689.2	44,417.6
Others	515.8	742.6	1,239.2	3,611.1	6,145.6	6,580.5	10,238.7	15,551.6	12,493.1
Investment*	278.3	84.8	1.7	3.8	34.5	10.9	38.1	875.7	4.1
Grand and Aid	281.4	330.7	111.7	429.4	744.8	421.3	1,611.1	524.0	477.5
Expenditure	5,830.9	8,014.3	21,708.2	48,493.2	65,527.5	80,439.6	98,462.0	124,751.9	145,403.3
(to GDP)				10.3%	10.8%	10.2%	8.8%	7.7%	6.6%
Current Expenditure	3,999.7	5,547.3	15,381.6	27,654.0	32,875.3	37,009.9	47,836.7	62,953.2	84,523.4
Capital Expenditure	1,218.7	2,051.9	6,050.1	20,145.4	31,820.9	42,919.6	50,365.0	60,918.7	60,396.1
Redemption for Debt	524.5	354.4	180.3	615.3	818.5	510.1	260.3	878.7	383.8
Others	88.0	60.7	96.2	78.5	12.8	0.0	0.0	1.3	100.0
Fiscal Balance	667.5	-298.1	-7,505.1	-16,152.9	-25,450.3	-25,427.5	-10,280.7	-7,458.4	-38,091.2
(to GDP)				-3.4%	-4.2%	-3.2%	-0.9%	-0.5%	-1.7%
Fiscal Balance**	-1,044.8	-2,234.3	-10,938.9	-24,347.7	-35,958.9	-42,069.9	-37,144.9	-51,147.6	-82,508.8
(to GDP)				-5.1%	-5.9%	-5.3%	-3.3%	-3.2%	-3.8%

Table 3–1 continued

State-owned Economic Enterprises	1980/81	1985/86	1990/91	1994/95	1995/96	1996/97	1997/98	1998/99	1999/00
Revenue	18,323.2	22,719.2	31,414.9	72,719.0	87,221.3	108,608.2	185,004.6	242,244.3	315,553.7
(to GDP)				15.4%	14.4%	13.7%	16.5%	15.0%	14.4%
Expenditure	22,674.1	28,044.1	36,361.4	87,373.3	101,853.6	135,578.9	233,248.8	328,948.3	388,163.2
(to GDP)				18.5%	16.8%	17.1%	20.8%	20.4%	17.7%
Redemption for Debt	1,712.3	1,936.2	3,433.8	8,194.8	10,508.6	16,642.4	26,864.2	43,689.2	44,417.6
Balance of SEE Account	-4,350.9	-5,324.9	-4,946.5	-14,654.3	-14,632.3	-26,970.7	-48,244.2	-86,704.0	-72,609.5
(to GDP)				-3.1%	-2.4%	-3.4%	-4.3%	-5.4%	-3.3%
Balance of SEE Account**	-2,639	-3,389	-1,513	-6,460	-4,124	-10,328	-21,380	-43,015	-28,192
(to GDP)				-1.4%	-0.7%	-1.3%	-1.9%	-2.7%	-1.3%
General Government									
Revenue	23,109.3	28,499.2	42,184.2	96,864.5	116,789.9	146,977.9	246,321.7	315,848.6	378,448.2
(to GDP)				20.5%	19.3%	18.6%	22.0%	19.6%	17.3%
Expenditure	26,792.7	34,122.2	54,635.8	127,671.7	156,872.5	199,376.1	304,846.6	410,011.0	489,148.9
(to GDP)				27.0%	25.9%	25.2%	27.2%	25.5%	22.3%
Fiscal Balance	-3,683.4	-5,623.0	-12,451.6	-30,807.2	-40,082.6	-52,398.2	-58,524.9	-94,162.4	-110,700.7
(to GDP)				-6.5%	-6.6%	-6.6%	-5.2%	-5.8%	-5.1%

Unit: Million Kyat, Percentage to GDP.

Notes: The accounts of the Development Committees are excluded because of the trivial amount. Therefore, here, the general government is defined as the consolidated account of the Central Government and the SEEs.
 * Expressed as "Investment" in the original text.
 ** The calculation under the treatment that "Income from SEEs" in the central government revenue table is counted to the SEE account side.

Table 3-2 Financing the Fiscal Deficit

	1980/81	1985/86	1990/91	1994/95	1995/96	1996/97	1997/98	1998/99	1999/00	2000/01	2001/02
(1) Borrowing appeared in the budgetary statistics		1,745.1	2,645.6	1,260.7	1,151.2	1,235.3	656.8	1,290.5	2,295.9	981.6	n.a
Domestic Debt		56.1	344.5	505.0	556.8	560.8	306.0	224.5	294.4	174.9	n.a.
External Debt		1,689.0	2,301.1	755.7	594.4	674.5	350.8	1,066.0	2,001.5	806.7	n.a.
(2) Fiscal Deficit – (1)		–1,938.3	–2,977.4	–11,190.9	–29,656.0	–38,847.3	–51,741.4	–57,234.4	–91,866.5	–109,719.1	n.a.
(3) Amount of TB issued					54.7	872.4	2,390.5	4,213.5	25,653.1	42,195.5	60,295.7
(4) (2) – (3)		–1,938.3	–2,977.4	–11,190.9	–29,601.3	–37,974.9	–49,350.9	–53,020.9	–66,213.5	–67,523.6	n.a.
Rate to GDP											
(1) Borrowing appeared in the budgetary statistics	47.4%	47.0%	10.1%	3.7%	3.1%	1.3%	2.2%	2.4%	0.9%		
Domestic Debt	1.5%	6.1%	4.1%	1.8%	1.4%	0.6%	0.4%	0.3%	0.2%		
External Debt	45.9%	40.9%	6.1%	1.9%	1.7%	0.7%	1.8%	2.1%	0.7%		
(2) Fiscal Deficit – (1)	52.6%	53.0%	89.9%	96.3%	96.9%	98.7%	97.8%	97.6%	99.1%		
(3) Amount of TB issued	0.0%	0.0%	0.0%	0.2%	2.2%	4.6%	7.2%	27.2%	38.1%		
(4) (2) – (3)	52.6%	53.0%	89.9%	96.1%	94.7%	94.2%	90.6%	70.3%	61.0%		

Source: Central Statistical Organization, *Statistical Yearbook* (2002: 318, 321, 326–7).

Table 3-3 TB Balance Classified by Holders

	1980/81	1985/86	1990/91	1994/95	1995/96	1996/97	1997/98	1998/99	1999/00	2000/01	2001/02
TB balance				97.5	969.9	3,324.4	7,490.6	32,313.1	72,602.8	130,424.5	131,918.5
Classification A											
Public				89.7%	10.6%	5.3%	3.4%	1.2%	0.6%	0.4%	0.4%
Private Business				10.3%	89.4%	94.7%	96.6%	98.8%	99.4%	99.6%	99.6%
Classification B											
Private Banks				41.0%	51.0%	34.2%	59.5%	28.6%	81.4%	77.5%	81.1%
Others				59.0%	49.0%	65.8%	40.5%	71.4%	18.6%	22.5%	18.9%

Note: "Classification A" is based on the Table of "Issues of Treasury Bond", "Classification B" is calculated from the "TB balance" minus "TB held by private banks" in the consolidated balance sheet table.

Source: Central Statistical Organization, *Statistical Yearbook* (2002: 318, 321, 326–7).

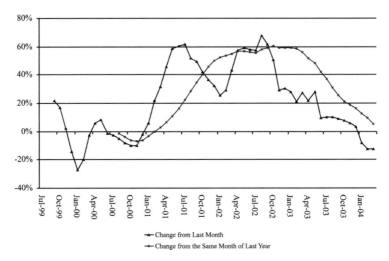

Figure 2 Growth in the Consumer Price Index (Sept. 1997 to Mar. 2004)

Source: Central Statistical Organization.

Distortion in Exchange Rates

Inflation caused by the monetarization of the fiscal deficits was directly related to a continuous fall in the market exchange rate, which increased the overvaluation of the inflexible authorized rate (the centre rate). It contributed to an import bias and conditions that were favourable to non-tradable goods by distorting the domestic price system.

As mentioned previously, while the exchange rate system in Myanmar is pegged to the SDR in the formal statements, the reality is a complicated mixture of multiple authorized rates and the curbside (market) rate. After the introduction of FEC in 1993, the centre rate was used as the applicable rate at the public exchange service centre and for import/export transactions. The FEC market rate was set by the curbside market and, in most cases, the disparity between the market rate for FEC and for the US dollar was extremely high.

Figure 3 traces the trends in these rates between January 1997 and May 2004. The official rate (which is rarely applied to private transactions) remained at around six kyat per US dollar. The free market rate for the US dollar was around 180 kyat until 1997; the figure fell to 300 kyat and remaining at this level until mid-2000, but subsequently declined steadily, reaching 1,100 kyat by the end of 2002. After February 2003, the rate recovered to 900 kyat, possibly reflecting the demand for kyat during the banking crisis.[8]

Table 4 Money Supply

Table 4-1 Money Supply (Government Statistics)

	1993	1994	1995	1996	1997	1998	1999	2000	2001
Currency	68,663	90,659	119,207	159,786	n.a.	n.a.	n.a.	n.a.	n.a.
Demand Deposit	6,319	7,664	12,593	17,079	n.a.	n.a.	n.a.	n.a.	n.a.
State-owned Bank	5,560	6,358	8,907	11,374	n.a.	n.a.	n.a.	n.a.	n.a.
Private Banks	759	1,306	3,686	5,705	n.a.	n.a.	n.a.	n.a.	n.a.
Quasi Money	n.a.	n.a.	105,568	161,649	197,710	288,537	420,098	648,606	449,815
Saving Deposit	n.a.	n.a.	53,730	82,617	100,858	151,158	216,956	335,653	412,936
Time Deposit	n.a.	n.a.	51,838	79,032	96,852	137,379	203,142	312,953	36,879
M1	74,982	98,323	131,800	176,865	205,577	272,672	325,637	409,654	n.a.
M2	n.a.	n.a.	237,368	338,514	403,287	561,209	745,735	1,058,260	n.a.
M1*	n.a.	n.a.	185,530	259,482	306,435	423,830	542,593	745,307	n.a.

Average Annual Growth

	1993	1994	1995	1996	1997	1998	1999	2000	2001
Currency		32.0%	31.5%	34.0%					
Demand Deposit		21.3%	64.3%	35.6%					
Quasi Money				53.1%	22.3%	45.9%	45.6%	54.4%	-30.6%
Saving Deposit				53.8%	22.1%	49.9%	43.5%	54.7%	23.0%
Time Deposit				52.5%	22.5%	41.8%	47.9%	54.1%	-88.2%
M1			31.1%	34.2%	16.2%	32.6%	19.4%	25.8%	
M2				42.6%	19.1%	39.2%	32.9%	41.9%	
M1*				39.9%	18.1%	38.3%	28.0%	37.4%	

Table 4-1 continued

	1993	1994	1995	1996	1997	1998	1999	2000	2001
Rate to GDP									
Currency	1.5%	1.3%	1.5%	1.4%					
Demand Deposit	0.2%	0.3%	0.6%	0.7%					
Quasi Money			17.5%	20.4%	17.7%	17.9%	19.2%	25.4%	12.8%
Saving Deposit			8.9%	10.4%	9.0%	9.4%	9.9%	13.1%	11.7%
Time Deposit			8.6%	10.0%	8.7%	8.5%	9.3%	12.3%	1.0%
M1	20.8%	20.8%	21.8%	22.3%	18.4%	16.9%	14.9%	16.0%	
M2			39.3%	42.7%	36.0%	34.9%	34.0%	41.5%	
M1*			30.7%	32.8%	27.4%	26.3%	24.8%	29.2%	

Unit: Million Kyat, Percentage to GDP.

Notes: M1 is defined by the sum of the currency and demand deposit in the original source. However, the amount of demand deposit is unnaturally small compared with the deposit. Thus, we also calculate alternative M1* defined by M1 plus saving deposit.

Sources: For Quasi Money in 1993–96: Central Statistical Organization, *Statistical Yearbook* (2002: 317). For other items in 1993–96: Central Statistical Organization, *Statistical Yearbook* (2001: 317): For M1 in 1997–2000: various source from the Government of Myanmar.

	1995	1998	1999	2000	2001	2002	2003
Currency	119,207	256,605	296,471	378,000	551,343	793,275	1,163,953
Demand Deposit	12,593	45,672	74,007	121,663	208,792	292,806	83,545
Quasi Money	53,730	151,158	216,956	335,653	449,815	538,082	380,012
Saving Deposit	46,419	127,759	191,811	300,704	399,534	456,556	354,434
Time Deposit	7,311	23,399	25,145	34,949	50,281	81,526	25,578
Total Deposit	66,323	196,830	290,963	457,316	658,607	830,888	463,557
M1	131,800	302,277	370,478	499,663	760,135	1,086,081	1,247,498
M2	185,530	453,435	587,434	835,316	1,209,950	1,624,163	1,627,510
Annual Growth Rate							
Currency			15.5%	27.5%	45.9%	43.9%	46.7%
Demand Deposit			62.0%	64.4%	71.6%	40.2%	-71.5%
Quasi Money			43.5%	54.7%	34.0%	19.6%	-29.4%
Saving Deposit			50.1%	56.8%	32.9%	14.3%	-22.4%
Time Deposit			7.5%	39.0%	43.9%	62.1%	-68.6%
Total Deposit			47.8%	57.2%	44.0%	26.2%	-44.2%
M1			22.6%	34.9%	52.1%	42.9%	14.9%
M2			29.6%	42.2%	44.8%	34.2%	0.2%
CPI			17.6%	-6.3%	50.9%	57.2%	17.4%
Rate to GDP							
Currency	19.7%	15.9%	13.5%	14.8%	15.6%	20.5%	27.3%
Demand Deposit	2.1%	2.8%	3.4%	4.8%	5.9%	7.6%	2.0%
Quasi Money	8.9%	9.4%	9.9%	13.1%	12.8%	13.9%	8.9%
Saving Deposit	7.7%	7.9%	8.8%	11.8%	11.3%	11.8%	8.3%
Time Deposit	1.2%	1.5%	1.1%	1.4%	1.4%	2.1%	0.6%
Total Deposit	11.0%	12.2%	13.3%	17.9%	18.7%	21.4%	10.9%
M1	21.8%	18.8%	16.9%	19.6%	21.6%	28.0%	29.3%
M2	30.7%	28.2%	26.8%	32.7%	34.3%	41.9%	38.2%

Note: The percentage to GDP in 2002–03 is calculated under the assumption of 10% GDP growth.

Source: Asia Development Bank, *Key Indicators (internet version)*, 2004. The rate to GDP in 2002–03 is calculated under GDP growth rate is assumed as 10%.

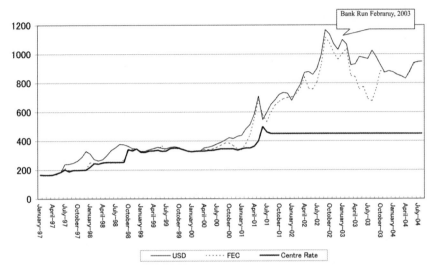

Figure 3 Trend in the Exchange Rate (Market Rate, Centre Rate)

Note: Yearly average (average of January to August 2004).

Source: Various Sources.

In the market for FEC, the centre rate was set at 200 kyat per US dollar in mid-1997, but reduced to 300 in mid-1998, where it remained until July 2001, when it was adjusted to 450 kyat. No further adjustment was attempted despite a continuous fall in the market rate, and the spread became more than double the market rate.

It is likely that serious, complicated distortions arose due to the fact that there were at least four exchange rates in effect: the formal rate, the centre rate, the market rate of the dollar cash and the rate for FEC. Exporters were obligated to settle their foreign currency transactions in the MICB or MFTB, where the centre rate was applied. The effective rate for exporters was made even higher by a 10 per cent export tax (8 per cent for the garment industry). On the other hand, importers raised foreign currency by exploiting an import license or from the curbside market. The import bias caused by the inflexible exchange rate has been strengthened by the sharp fall in the market rate.

The Industrial Structure

Let us now review the industrial structure formed during this 15-year period under the strong import bias and the resulting favourable conditions for the non-manufacturing sectors. Table 5 shows that there was a gradual decline in agriculture's share of GDP during the 1990s, and the rise of construction,

Table 5 The Composition of GDP

	1993/94	1994/95	1995/96	1996/97	1997/98	1998/99	1999/00	2000/01	2001/02
(1) Real GDP									
Agriculture	63.0%	63.0%	60.0%	60.1%	58.9%	59.1%	59.9%	57.2%	57.2%
Mining and Energy	0.7%	0.8%	0.8%	0.9%	0.7%	0.6%	0.6%	0.7%	0.5%
Manufacturing	6.8%	6.2%	6.9%	7.1%	7.1%	7.0%	6.5%	7.2%	7.8%
Construction	1.4%	1.6%	2.2%	2.4%	2.4%	2.3%	1.8%	1.8%	2.2%
Trade	21.5%	21.5%	23.2%	22.6%	23.0%	23.5%	24.0%	24.0%	24.3%
Other Service	6.5%	6.9%	6.9%	6.8%	7.9%	7.6%	7.1%	9.0%	8.1%
(2) Nominal GDE									
Total Consumption	88.6%	88.3%	86.6%	88.5%	88.2%	88.2%	87.0%	87.7%	88.7%
Total Investment	12.4%	12.4%	14.2%	14.7%	12.5%	12.4%	13.2%	11.8%	11.7%
Trade Account	-1.0%	-0.6%	-0.9%	-0.8%	-0.7%	-0.6%	-0.3%	-0.3%	-0.2%
Export	1.2%	1.1%	0.8%	0.7%	0.6%	0.5%	0.4%	0.5%	0.5%
Import	2.2%	1.8%	1.7%	1.5%	1.3%	1.1%	0.7%	0.6%	0.5%

Source: Central Statistical Organization, *Statistical Yearbook* (2002), for (1) pp. 307 and 309, and for (2), p. 308.

trades and other services supported by the construction boom in hotels and buildings, financed by FDI, and the expansion of agricultural exports after the liberalization of trade. Meanwhile, the share of the manufacturing sector remained at very low levels of around 6 to 7 per cent.[9] It is worth noting that, during the period of economic growth and reform in the 1990s, the degree of industrialization, a requirement for sustained growth, was limited.

The picture is similar for the expenditure side (gross domestic expenditure or GDE). According to the components of the nominal GDE, the share of investment has remained constant at between 11 or 12 per cent, although a slight increase to 14 per cent occurred in 1995 and 1996 when the FDI inflow was strong. This low rate suggests that Myanmar never reached the stage where the economy enters a phase of high growth following a change in industrial structure and active investment.[10]

Trade, FDI and the Industrial Structure

The greatest change after 1988 occurred in the area of trade and FDI. Once again, there was a biased environment that was favourable to domestic non-manufacturing industries.[11] As discussed in Chapter 3, approved FDI increased staring in 1993 and peaked in 1996, but then declined sharply in connection with the Asian financial crisis in 1997, which returned FDI to the levels of the early 1990s. FDI was mainly directed towards the hotel, tourism, construction and oil/natural gas sectors during the 1990s. In the manufacturing sector FDI only increased in 1996. Before the crisis, the major investing countries were Myanmar's neighbours, such as Singapore and Thailand, and Western nations.[12] Following the crisis, investment fell significantly because of the recession in most Asian countries, and due to political reasons in the Western countries.

It is difficult to understand the nature of the capital inflows after 1997. It is true that approvals of FDI fell sharply, as will be discussed in Chapter 3, but that does not necessarily mean that there was a corresponding fall in capital inflows. Figure 4-2 shows that the capital inflows in the balance of payments decreased marginally after 1998 and remained at their new level until 2001. The difference between the capital inflows for the two set of statistics may arise from differences in the definition of FDI in the statistical sources, or differences in the treatment of capital goods imports for garment production, which grew rapidly in the late 1990s.[13] In any case, capital inflows remained at higher levels than is generally evident from the approval basis statistics, at least prior to 2001.

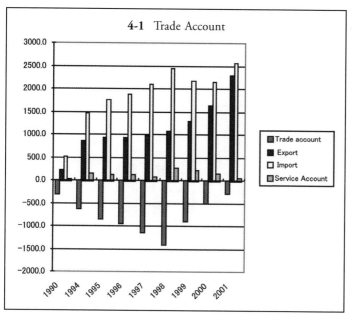

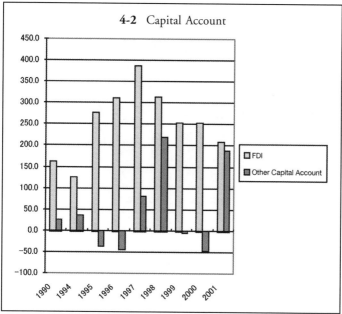

Figure 4 Trade Account, Capital Account in Balance of Payment
Unit: Million US$.

Source: IMF, *International Financial Statistcs.*

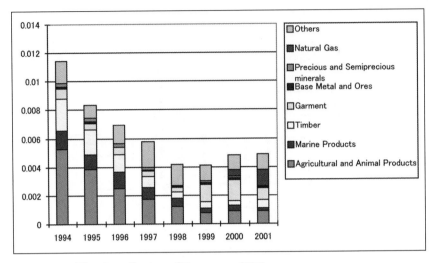

Figure 5-1 The Contribution of Exports to GDP

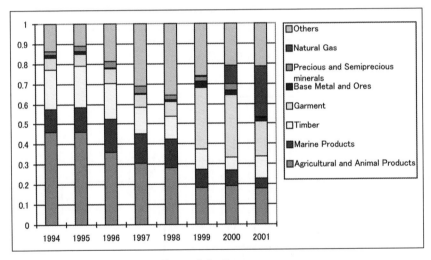

Figure 5-2 The Component Share of the Export

Note: Calculated from nominal values.

Source: Central Statistical Organization, *Statistical Yearbook* (2002: 193).

Both imports and exports continued to expand following the reform. As shown in Table 4-1, import growth increased more quickly than that of exports, resulting in an increasing trade deficit, particularly prior to 1999. Figure 5-1 shows that the share of exports in GDP (in other words, the share of foreign demand in the total demand) continually declined after

1994, implying that the expansion of domestic demand was always greater than that of export demand during the growth process of the 1990s.[14] This conclusion is consistent with the view that the growth in the 1990s was led mainly by the domestic non-manufacturing sector.

A structural change in trade occurred around 2000. After that date, the control of import licenses was tightened and direct import restrictions have even been employed in order to reduce the trade deficit. Exports increased sharply at this time, resulting in a decrease in the trade deficit. Figure 5-2 shows that, while the major export items in the 1990s were agricultural, livestock, marine products, and timber, these primary products were replaced by garments in 1999 and 2000, and by natural gas in 2001.[15] Intermittent factors, such as the temporary expansion of garment exports and the commencement of exports of newly developed natural gas supplies contributed to the favourable turnaround of the trade account.[16]

The Stagnation of the State-owned Economic Enterprises

Finally, let us examine the stagnation of the state-owned economic enterprises (SEEs). According to Nishizawa (2000: 123–24), 58 SEEs employed about 280,000 labourers in Myanmar in 1998. The heavy industry and import substitution sectors were central to this. When privatization was attempted in 1995, only a small number of firms, involved in cinemas, garment production and daily commodities, were listed (Nishizawa, 2000: 143) and most of the heavy industry remained state-owned.

Table 6 shows the trend in the share of value added by ownership. The share of state ownership was 38.4 per cent even by the middle of 1980, which was relatively low compared to the 56.8 per cent that was privately owned.[17] This contrasts with Myanmar's neighbouring transition economies, Vietnam and China, where the SEEs created a large value-added component in production. The share of state ownership declined to 22.5 per cent in 1995 and 1996, when the growth of the private sector accelerated. While the share of the SEEs largely declined in the commerce, trade and finance sectors, where the growth of the private sector was remarkable, a decline also occurred in the manufacturing sector, where SEEs originally held the largest share, particularly in heavy industry. The implication is that the SEEs have been unable to compete with the domestic private firms and with imported goods.

The business structure in Myanmar has remarkable characteristics compared with other transition economies. On the one hand, the privatization of the SEEs or the expansion of the independent control within them was

Table 6 The Share of Added Value by Ownership (%)

	1984/85			1992/93			1995/96		
	State	*Cooperative*	*Private*	*State*	*Cooperative*	*Private*	*State*	*Cooperative*	*Private*
Agriculture	0.3	4.5	95.2	0.2	1.9	97.9	0.2	1.6	98.2
Stockbreeding, Fisheries	1.8	1.4	96.8	0.8	1.3	97.9	0.4	1.3	98.3
Forestry	31.0	4.6	64.4	44.9	0.6	54.5	40.7	0.9	58.4
Mining	88.5	2.5	9.0	56.9	1.0	42.1	59.0	0.8	40.2
Manufacturing	55.2	2.8	42.0	28.4	2.4	69.2	27.4	0.8	71.8
Electricity	99.9	0.1	0.0	99.9	0.1	0.0	99.9	0.1	0.0
Construction	80.7	1.2	18.2	83.8	0.1	15.2	85.7	0.2	14.1
Transportation	36.6	5.3	58.1	41.4	1.8	56.8	36.2	0.0	62.4
Communication	100.0	0.0	0.0	100.0	0.0	0.0	100.0	0.0	0.0
Finance	98.8	1.2	0.0	88.3	9.6	2.1	72.8	11.8	15.4
Social and Administrative Service	98.8	1.2	0.0	91.3	0.9	7.9	90.2	0.4	9.5
Rental Service	13.3	5.5	81.2	6.6	2.2	91.2	5.7	1.9	92.4
Commerce and Trade	46.5	10.4	43.1	23.3	6.0	70.8	23.0	2.4	74.5
Total	38.4	4.8	56.8	22.1	2.7	75.2	22.5	1.6	75.9

Sources: Nishizawa (2000), p. 121, Takahashi (1999), p. 310: original source is Government of Myanmar, *Review of The Financial, Economic and Social Conditions*, each year.

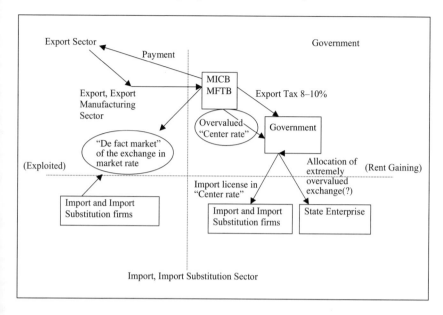

Figure 6 Distortion of the Exchange Rate and Firms

rarely realized and these enterprises have become isolated from the market. However, the private sector has recently become more important and SEEs seem to be losing their significance, becoming isolated from the expanding competitive markets. Furthermore, the firm structure exacerbates the fiscal deficit.

The Private Sector and the Financial System

The Overvaluation of the Kyat and the Formation of Private Firms

Let us now examine the microstructures of the business activity, upon which the macroeconomic and industrial structural characteristics outlined above are based. The primary characteristics of the firms' structures are: the existence of a dualism caused by the import bias created by the exchange rate system, with a limited number of large firms diversifying into the domestic non-manufacturing sectors; and the many small firms producing export products or domestic final goods.

Figure 6 summarizes how the series of regulations is related to foreign currency holdings and how the overvalued kyat influences the firms and the SEEs. Under the current regulations, the exporters, the exporting manufacturing sector and the domestic final producers are subject to heavy taxation.

The taxation system consists of two components: the overvalued exchange rate and a direct export tax. Both of these are implemented by strict government control in specialized government banks for foreign currency holdings. The rents obtained from these mechanisms are thought to be allocated primarily to the SEEs, and secondly to importers and the import-substituting industries that hold import licenses and have access to foreign currencies through an overvalued kyat.

Exporters are allowed to utilize their foreign currency earnings to fund their own imports. In practice, however, the right to use foreign currency is itself subject to market transactions between the exporters and importers. This implies that importers without import licenses are also subject to taxation through price transfers in the foreign currency.[18,19] Under such mechanisms, import bias and the resulting situation causes a disparity between the two groups of firms: one through taxation and one through obtaining rents.

In such a situation, the growth rates of the two groups should differ, and rent-seeking activities after obtaining a license and other means of obtaining foreign currency will be vigorously pursued. The process of capital accumulation under these circumstances caused dual structures in private business to be formed: a small number of large firms operated in the domestic non-manufacturing sector with successful access to the rents, and many small-scale exporters or export manufacturers, who were adversely affected by the heavy taxation system, on the other side.

Large Firm Conglomerates and Private Banks

An important feature of the private banking sector is that most of the major banks were created from the major business groups that were engaging in the export of primary sector products and in the non-manufacturing sector activities such as construction and real estate. Let us consider the cases of Yoma Bank and Asia Wealth Bank as examples based on the information obtained interviews in September 2003, and from Wang (2004).

Table 7 lists the private banks that were in existence in the late 1990s. Since the Financial Institution Law was enacted in 1990, between two and five new banks were established every year, until 1997.[20] The Asia Wealth Bank, which was the largest bank in 1999, was established in 1994 under the initiative of the Olympic Group, one of the largest construction conglomerates.[21] Following the economic reform of 1989, the founding family started their business by trading in agricultural products in South and Southeast Asia, subsequently becoming involved in cross-border trade in marine products. In 1992, the family established the Olympic Corporation and

Table 7 Private Banks in Myanmar

	Total Asset	Deposit	Share of Deposit	Year Established	No. of Branches
1 Asia Wealth Bank Ltd.	52,051	12,698	27.32%	1995	39
2 Myanmar May Flower Bank Ltd.	14,937	8,261	17.78%	1994	24
3 Myanmar Oriental Bank Ltd.	11,180	3,559	7.66%	1993	14
4 Myawaddy Bank Ltd.	14,671	3,257	7.01%	1993	6
5 First Private Bank Ltd.	6,112	1,750	3.77%	1992	15
6 Myanmar Citizens Bank Ltd.	2,899	1,509	3.25%	1992	1
7 Myanmar Industrial Development Bank Ltd.	3,545	990	2.13%	1996	2
8 Co-operative Bank Ltd.	1,543	656	1.41%	1992	8
9 Yangon City Bank Ltd.	n.a.	4,302	9.26%	1993	1
10 Yoma Bank Ltd.	n.a.	4,551	9.79%	1993	42
11 Myanmar Livestock and Fisheries Bank Ltd.	n.a.	1,793	3.86%	1996	7
12 Innwa Bank Ltd.	n.a.	817	1.76%	1997	8
13 The Myanmar Universal Bank Ltd.	n.a.	815	1.75%	1995	25
14 Tun Foundation Bank Ltd.	n.a.	813	1.75%	1994	5
15 Sibin Tharyar Yay Bank Ltd.	n.a.	244	0.52%	1996	1
16 Asian Yangon International Bank Ltd.	n.a.	144	0.31%	1994	n.a.
17 Kanbawza Bank Ltd.	n.a.	136	0.29%	1994	22
18 Co-operative Promoters Bank Ltd.	n.a.	122	0.26%	1996	n.a.
19 Yadanabon Bank Ltd. (Mandalay)	n.a.	33	0.07%	1992	n.a.
20 Co-operative Farmers Bank Ltd.	n.a.	20	0.04%	1996	2
Total	n.a.	46,471			
Base Period	March, 1999	March, 1998		March, 2000	March, 2000

Notes: The total asset of First Private Bank Ltd. (5) is at the end of 2000. Banks Three Co-operative banks (8, 18, and 20) were merged into new Co-operative Bank Ltd. in 2004. The units for total asset and deposit are million of Kyat.

Sources: Total Asset: balance sheet of each bank, Deposit: Myat Thein and Mya Than (2000: 89), Table A4.1, A4.2, Established Year and No. of Branches: Wang (2003), (the number branch of Co-operative Bank Ltd. (8) is at March in 1998).

entered the construction and real estate business. The Asia Wealth Bank was founded under a holding company established by the Olympic Corporation with about 90 joint contributors, the majority of whom were involved in the jewelry business. According to the hearing in September 2004, the purpose of the entry into the banking sector was to finance their construction and trade business. By 1995, the bank had exceeded its breakeven point. Four of the bank's eight board members at the bank are also on the board of the Olympic Corporation. The group operates 15 firms that are engaged in construction relations (7 firms), exports (2) and agriculture (2).[22] Of these, only two firms are engaged in manufacturing (fertilizer production and processing).

The Yoma Bank (established in 1993) is a 100 per cent subsidiary of the two holding companies that are part of the same family business: First Myanmar Investment (FMI), one of the largest holding companies in Myanmar, with the status of a public company; and Serge Pun and Associates (SPA), with the status of a foreign corporation. The Myanmar Chinese founder of the FMI and SPA groups started his Myanmar business ventures after enjoying success in Hong Kong and Thailand. Starting with the importation of cosmetics, the group grew to include over 40 subsidiaries and affiliations[23] owned by the FMI, the directors of the FMI and SPA, and by cross holdings.[24] Judging by the 51 firms listed in Wang (2004), their core businesses are finance, real estate, services (hotels, golf courses, and hospitals) and trade. The manufacturing side of the business appears negligible. Among the group's firms, Yoma Bank is owned 100 per cent by FMI. Their major clients were the trade sector in the early years and are currently real estate development businesses.

Both of these cases illustrate the growth achieved by the private sector through first accumulating capital from export businesses following the liberalization of trade in the early 1990s, and then reinvesting it in order to expand their business to the non-manufacturing domestic sectors in fields such as construction, real estate and finance. The domestic investment decisions were rational under the condition of import bias. The banking sector, the largest entity in the financial system, was formed in association with the capital accumulation process of the domestic sectors.

The Development of the Banking Sector[25]

Table 8, showing the consolidated balance sheet of the private banks, illustrates the growth process and operational features of the banking sector. As described above, the private banks grew rapidly. The average annual growth

Table 8 The Balance Sheet of Private Banks

Assets	1992	1993	1994	1995	1996	1997	1998	1999	2000	2001
Total Assets	522	2,400	6,676	20,231	48,966	85,062	139,849	230,588	384,101	597,174
Current Assets	273	881	2,188	6,884	13,810	17,655	33,190	36,246	52,725	82,290
Cash in Hand	114	322	581	3,339	4,599	8,913	15,838	19,691	31,358	54,101
Reserves in Central Bank	154	547	1,584	2,397	8,093	6,258	11,027	8,233	10,616	16,297
Earning Assets	194	1,347	3,591	10,434	29,156	56,862	89,960	157,150	262,351	418,700
Loans	180	1,294	3,516	9,719	26,223	50,488	60,866	97,066	159,807	309,561
Securities	14	14	35	220	1,799	1,920	19,864	973	1,466	2,089
Treasury Bonds (TBs)	0	39	40	495	1,135	4,454	9,230	59,110	101,078	107,051
Fixed Assets	4	34	72	236	1,086	1,886	2,408	4,120	6,760	9,781
Others	51	139	825	2,678	4,914	8,660	14,291	33,072	62,266	86,403
Distribution of Assets										
Current Assets	52.3%	36.7%	32.8%	34.0%	28.2%	20.8%	23.7%	15.7%	13.7%	13.8%
Cash in Hand	21.8%	13.4%	8.7%	16.5%	9.4%	10.5%	11.3%	8.5%	8.2%	9.1%
Reserves in Central Bank	29.5%	22.8%	23.7%	11.8%	16.5%	7.4%	7.9%	3.6%	2.8%	2.7%
Earning Assets	37.1%	56.1%	53.8%	51.6%	59.5%	66.8%	64.3%	68.2%	68.3%	70.1%
Loans	34.4%	53.9%	52.7%	48.0%	53.6%	59.4%	43.5%	42.1%	41.6%	51.8%
Securities	2.7%	0.6%	0.5%	1.1%	3.7%	2.3%	14.2%	0.4%	0.4%	0.3%
Treasury Bonds (TBs)	0.0%	1.6%	0.6%	2.4%	2.3%	5.2%	6.6%	25.6%	26.3%	17.9%
Fixed Assets	0.8%	1.4%	1.1%	1.2%	2.2%	2.2%	1.7%	1.8%	1.8%	1.6%
Others	9.8%	5.8%	12.4%	13.2%	10.0%	10.2%	10.2%	14.3%	16.2%	14.5%

Table 8 continued

Liabilities and Capital Account	1992	1993	1994	1995	1996	1997	1998	1999	2000	2001
Borrowings from Central Bank	0.0	63.9	0.0	0.0	275.0	4,713.5	564.2	715.4	922.9	9,108.0
Notes payable	134.0	118.0	200.2	174.7	278.0	564.9	848.7	624.1	922.9	1,342.9
Deposits	230.0	1,577.5	4,839.6	15,705.1	37,013.6	58,156.4	110,783.8	186,168.5	324,580.2	487,100.8
Demand Deposits	93.8	758.8	1,305.8	3,722.3	5,698.3	14,279.3	32,382.4	58,409.1	102,477.1	187,699.6
Time Deposits	136.2	818.7	3,533.8	11,982.8	31,315.3	43,877.1	78,401.4	127,759.4	222,103.1	299,401.2
Liabilities from banks	0.0	1.0	31.0	176.3	346.8	825.6	1,271.0	1,105.6	2,239.6	8,096.4
Other Liabilities	6.5	224.3	763.9	2,628.3	6,321.6	13,438.1	17,468.8	28,611.7	36,303.0	64,222.3
Capital Account	151.5	415.3	841.7	1,546.2	4,731.2	7,363.1	8,912.6	13,362.8	19,102.4	27,303.3
Paid up Capital	152.0	411.2	811.9	1,495.7	4,527.7	6,648.6	7,170.3	10,677.7	14,295.9	19,503.5
Retained Earrings	−0.5	2.8	7.1	0.6	18.6	92.5	257.2	259.7	273.2	384.5
Capital Surplus	0.0	1.3	22.7	49.9	184.9	622.0	1,485.1	2,387.6	4,484.2	7,349.5
Stock Premium	0.0	0.0	0.0	0.0	0.0	0.0	0.0	37.8	49.1	65.8
Liabilities and Capital Account										
Borrowings from Central Bank	0.0%	2.7%	0.0%	0.0%	0.6%	5.5%	0.4%	0.3%	0.2%	1.5%
Notes payable	25.7%	4.9%	3.0%	0.9%	0.6%	0.7%	0.6%	0.3%	0.2%	0.2%
Deposits	44.1%	65.7%	72.5%	77.6%	75.6%	68.4%	79.2%	80.7%	84.5%	81.6%
Demand Deposits	18.0%	31.6%	19.6%	18.4%	11.6%	16.8%	23.2%	25.3%	26.7%	31.4%
Time Deposits	26.1%	34.1%	52.9%	59.2%	64.0%	51.6%	56.1%	55.4%	57.8%	50.1%
Liabilities from banks	0.0%	0.0%	0.5%	0.9%	0.7%	1.0%	0.9%	0.5%	0.6%	1.4%
Other Liabilities	1.2%	9.3%	11.4%	13.0%	12.9%	15.8%	12.5%	12.4%	9.5%	10.8%

Table 8 continued

	1992	1993	1994	1995	1996	1997	1998	1999	2000	2001
Capital Account	29.0%	17.3%	12.6%	7.6%	9.7%	8.7%	6.4%	5.8%	5.0%	4.6%
Paid up Capital	29.1%	17.1%	12.2%	7.4%	9.2%	7.8%	5.1%	4.6%	3.7%	3.3%
Retained Earnings	−0.1%	0.1%	0.1%	0.0%	0.0%	0.1%	0.2%	0.1%	0.1%	0.1%
Capital Surplus	0.0%	0.1%	0.3%	0.2%	0.4%	0.7%	1.1%	1.0%	1.2%	1.2%
Stock Premium	0.0%	0.0%	0.0%	0.0%	0.0%	0.0%	0.0%	0.0%	0.0%	0.0%

	1992	1993	1994	1995	1996	1997	1998	1999	2000	2001
Growth of Total Asset		359.8%	178.2%	203.0%	142.0%	73.7%	64.4%	64.9%	66.6%	55.5%
Growth of the Deposit		585.9%	206.8%	224.5%	135.7%	57.1%	90.5%	68.0%	74.3%	50.1%
Growth of the Loan		620.1%	171.7%	176.4%	169.8%	92.5%	20.6%	59.5%	64.6%	93.7%
Growth of TB holding			2.6%	1137.5%	129.4%	292.3%	107.2%	540.4%	71.0%	5.9%
Growth of deposit minus CIP growth rate						54.5%	60.4%	52.4%	76.1%	15.6%

Unit: Million Kyat, Percentage or Growth Rate.

Source: Central Statistical Organization, *Statistical Yearbook* (2002: 315).

rates of total assets and deposits were 155.1 and 195.5 per cent, respectively, for the period 1993–99. Although this explosive expansion can be explained by the fact that this period included the establishment of these banks (that is, with the founders' cash swelling the deposits), the fact that deposit growth continued until 1999 suggests that the potential demand for deposits was huge in the household and business sector.

Loans on the asset side also grew but at a much slower rate than that for deposits. Primarily, this was caused by the high rate of liquid assets on hand, reflected in two figures: first, the high inflation rate (24.1 per cent on average from 1994–99) and interest rate ceilings, which made the real interest rates negative and therefore the lending business less profitable, and probably discouraged the private banks from expanding their lending activity. Second, the difficulty experienced by the newly emerging banks in finding new and appropriate customers for loans as quickly as they accepted deposits, as it took a substantial amount of time to acquire information regarding lending transactions.

The slow expansion of lending is also related to the issue of TBs and expansion in the growth rate of bonds on issue after 1999. The ratio of TB holdings relative to total assets was 6.6 per cent in 1997, which increased to between 18 and 26 per cent after 1999. This suggests that between 27 and 38 per cent of the fiscal deficits was financed through the absorption by TBs during this period, temporarily lowering inflation in 1999 to 2000.

Turning to the operational structure of the banks, the negative profits continued in real terms because of the negative real interest rate. The interest rate ceiling was set at 10 per cent for deposits and 15 per cent[26] for lending in the 1997–99 period, while the inflation rate averaged 26.2 per cent. The banks survived only because their total assets grew rapidly with the expansion of deposits, so that the profits in nominal terms exceeded the inflation rate.[27] This implies that a high rate of deposit growth is a necessary condition for the banks' positive earnings.

The holding of TBs increased after 1999. TBs are not an asset in high demand since they yield only a 9 per cent in return in 2000, which is less than the deposit rate, and they are not tradable in a secondary market. TBs were allocated to banks by the government and utilized as the criteria for the upper limit of Central Bank lending on which banks without access to the money market largely depend.[28] In other words, the financing mechanism of the fiscal deficits was developed through compulsory bond holdings by the banks as a part of the reserve rate regulation.

In summary, the continuous expansion of deposits prior to 2000 was crucial both for the banks' profits and the financing of the fiscal deficit, and was linked to the expansion of the bond issue. When the rate of growth in deposits declined after 2000, the inflation rate increased and the difficulties surrounding banking operations led to problems in the banking sector in 2003.

The Characteristics of Fund-raising in the Manufacturing Sector

The dualism in the private firms and the emergence of the banking sector suggests that while banks maintained close links with the non-manufacturing sector and large firm conglomerates, most firms in the manufacturing sector, particularly those producing products for export, were relatively independent of the banking sector. We conducted a questionnaire-based survey of sample firms in Yangon regarding their production and fund-raising behaviour in 2003. Based on the results, the characteristics of fund-raising and the relationship between these firms and the financial sector, we examine how capital accumulation in the manufacturing sector has occurred, and whether it has been realized through financial intermediation by the banking sector.

The scope of the survey

The survey focused on privately-owned firms. The data include firm profiles, balance sheets, various financial details and the characteristics of the owners. The data cover 167 medium- and small-sized firms in the manufacturing, trade, and service sectors.

The survey was conducted between October and December 2003 as a joint project with a private information company in Yangon. The surveyed industries were classified into the export, manufacturing and service sectors, with 10 subsectors. We selected a large number of potential sample firms from each subsector, and contacted them in advance to invite them to participate in the survey. Next, enumerators visited the firms' head offices and interviewed the managers using the prepared questionnaires.

Only 89 of the 167 firms had data available about their balance sheets, financing for investments, and sources of working capital. Some of the larger firms that own private banks and belong to major business groups were not included, due primarily to the survey design and sample selection.

Establishment and previous career

Table 9 indicates the previous careers of the firm owners. Most of the sample firms were established after 1989, implying that the reforms led to the creation of new private businesses. Comparing the three periods, the largest number of firms prior to the reform were created through self-employment followed

Table 9   Parent Body of Newly Established Firms

	Before 1988		1989–96		After 1997	
Staff of Government or SEEs	1	6.3%	10	22.7%	2	6.9%
Trader	4	25.0%	16	36.4%	6	20.7%
Self Employment	8	50.0%	11	25.0%	18	62.1%
Person abroad	0	0.0%	2	4.5%	3	10.3%
Others and unclear	3	18.8%	5	11.4%	0	0.0%
Total	16		44		29	

by trading, whereas most of the firms were created from trading in the period from 1989–96 and subsequently from self-employment, after 1997. This allows the following interpretation. During the early 1990s, entrepreneurs gained profit mainly from external trading businesses but after the Asian economic crisis and the ensuing downturn in the external economic conditions, they developed their business to the second-stage. This trend is common among business groups related to the Asia Wealth Bank and Yoma Bank, which accumulated capital through trading businesses following the liberalization of trade in the early 1990s, and later from their domestic businesses.

Capital structure in the balance sheets

Table 10 shows the capital structure of all of the sampled firms, classified by sector and size. The balance sheet data covers the years 1999–2001, classified by the three major sectors and their subsectors. The values in the table indicate the averages for the three years.

For all firms combined, the debt ratio is 15.9 per cent, comprised mainly of bank borrowing (6.0 per cent), accounts payable (4.1 per cent) and other liabilities (3.0 per cent). The debt ratio is surprisingly low, which implies that the firms in the sample were primarily self-financing. Only 33 of the 89 sampled firms (37%) utilized bank loans as a tool for fund-raising.

Debt financing is higher in the export sector (with a debt ratio of 21.5 per cent and bank borrowing of 11.1 per cent), and lower in manufacturing (13.7 per cent and 4.7 per cent, respectively). At the subsector level, debt financing seems most common in agriculture (with 24.6 per cent of firms exporting agricultural products, 26.0 per cent for livestock and 20 per cent for the manufacturing of agricultural products). The ratio for construction was relatively low at 2.5 per cent.

There does not appear to be a direct relationship between firm size and debt financing. Based on their assets, the firms were classified into three

Table 10. Capital Structure of Sample Firms

	All Sample	Size			Export			
		Large	Medium	Small		Textile	Agric. Product	Livestock
No. of Sample	89	11	48	30	12	5	5	2
Debt Ratio	15.9	10.3	18.6	13.8	21.5	16.7	24.6	26.0
L1 Deferred Payment, Note Payable	4.1	1.8	4.0	5.2	3.9	4.9	1.4	7.6
L2 Bank Borrowing	6.0	5.6	8.1	2.7	11.1	5.1	17.0	11.5
No. of Firms Borrowing	33	4	11	4	8	2	4	2
Rate of Firms Borrowing	37.1	36.4	22.9	13.3	66.7	40.0	80.0	100.0
L3 Borrowing from Affiliates	0.8	1.0	0.6	1.0	1.8	2.7	0.0	4.3
L4 Borrowing from Owners and Managers	0.9	0.0	1.2	0.6	2.3	1.3	4.3	0.0
L5 Borrowing from Others	1.2	0.2	1.2	1.5	0.3	0.0	0.3	1.1
L6 Other Liabilities	3.0	1.7	3.4	2.8	2.1	2.7	1.7	1.5
Capital Account	83.1	87.5	80.1	86.2	78.5	83.3	75.4	74.0
C1 Paid up Capital	37.2	46.7	35.5	36.5	42.2	52.1	32.3	42.5
C2 Retained Earrings	27.8	31.3	24.3	32.0	25.6	20.6	28.1	31.5
C3 Capital Surplus and Others	18.1	9.4	20.3	17.7	10.7	10.6	15.0	0.0

Table 10. continued

	Manufacturing				Service			
		Agric. Product	Industries	Consumers Product		Service General	Construction	Consumer service	Retail, Distributor
No. of Sample	47	3	33	11	30	6	7	8	9
Debt Ratio	13.7	20.0	10.9	14.1	17.2	7.4	13.8	13.7	29.6
L1 Deferred Payment, Note Payable	3.2	0.0	4.0	3.2	5.7	4.3	5.0	1.6	10.9
L2 Bank Borrowing	4.7	16.7	3.0	4.2	6.0	0.0	2.5	8.6	10.4
No. of Firms Borrowing	16	1	13	2	9	0	3	3	3
Rate of Firms Borrowing	34.0	33.3	39.4	18.2	30.0	0.0	42.9	37.5	33.3
L3 Borrowing from Affiliates	0.6	0.0	0.0	0.8	0.7	0.0	0.8	1.2	0.7
L4 Borrowing from Owners and Managers	0.5	0.0	0.8	0.4	0.8	0.0	2.7	0.8	0.0
L5 Borrowing from Others	1.5	3.3	1.6	1.3	1.0	0.4	0.7	0.8	1.9
L6 Other Liabilities	3.3	0.0	1.5	4.2	2.9	2.7	2.1	0.8	5.7
Capital Account	85.8	79.9	86.8	86.0	80.7	92.6	86.2	86.3	63.4
C1 Paid up Capital	41.4	30.6	46.3	40.7	28.8	23.1	45.2	31.2	17.6
C2 Retained Earrings	26.4	19.3	25.7	27.3	30.8	49.1	22.5	25.0	30.3
C3 Capital Surplus and Others	18.0	30.1	14.8	18.0	21.1	20.4	18.6	30.1	15.5

Unit: Percentage to Total Assets.

Note: The total of items does not necessarily match one hundred per cent due to the inconsistency of original data.

Characteristics of Capital Accumulation in Myanmar   59

Table 11 Method of Fund-raising for Equipment Investment and Working Capital

Table 11-1 Equipment Investment

	All 28	Export 4	Manufacturing 18	Service 6
Self Financing: Investment from Affiliates	8.9	0.0	13.9	0.0
Self Financing: Investment from Owner	60.2	52.8	62.5	58.3
Bank Borrowing	22.8	33.3	14.2	41.7
Family, Relative and Friends	0.0	0.0	0.0	0.0
Others	8.1	13.9	9.4	0.0

Note: Calculated from the 28 firms which implemented equipment investment in the late five years. Bank borrowing is positive in 9 firms.

Table 11-2 Working Capital

	All 89	Export 12	Manufacturing 47	Service 30
Self Financing	78.1	63.6	82.8	76.7
Bank Borrowing	13.5	29.2	12.3	9.2
Family, Relative and Friend	4.2	2.5	2.8	7.2
Foreign Counterparts	0.0	0.0	0.0	0.0
Others	3.7	4.8	2.1	5.7

Note: Bank borrowing is positive in 32 firms.

groups: large-size (over 10 million kyat), medium-size (1–10 million kyat) and small-size (under 1 million kyat). A comparison shows that the medium-sized firms are most dependent on debt financing, while the large- and small-sized firms appear moderately dependent on debt. The larger firms appear to be estranged from the bank loan market.

Fund mobilization for investment and working capital

Table 11 illustrates the methods for fund-raising for investment in equipment and working capital. For the last five years, 28 of the 89 firms have invested in equipment, but bank loans have been used in only nine cases. In all of these cases, loans were obtained from a single bank rather than from a syndicate. According to the table, the share of bank loans relative to the total firm debt is high, at 22.8 per cent. Debt in the form of shares appears to be moderately higher in the export and service sectors, while it is lower in the manufacturing sector. This trend is questionable, however, because of the small sample size. For working capital, only 32 of the 89 firms borrowed from banks, and the share of bank loans used for fund-raising is, on average, 13.5 per cent of the total.[29] Similar to the investment in equipment, shares appear to be more common in the export sector.

The financial intermediation by the banks seems to function well for supplying working capital to the trade (export) sector. This is a traditional form of banking activity, and partially supports investment in equipment. Bank loan transactions are prevalent in the export and service sectors, but less so in the manufacturing sector.

Implications

Firms operating within the export manufacturing and final goods sector that are subject to taxation finance their business solely through self-financing, with bank borrowings extremely rare. The total assets of the private banks increased from the mid-1990s, in part because of an increase in loans. There-fore, our observations in this subsection imply that bank loans are not out of reach for these firms, but borrow and lending will primarily occur within groups of firms.[30] From the perspective of social function, the banks do not play a role in efficient fund allocation, probably because their ability to act as financial intermediaries is slight and in an early stage of development. It can be said that financial intermediation is divided between the two groups of sectors and firms.

The export manufacturing sector and final goods sector face un-favourable conditions because of their isolation from a developed financial system. In the process of growth and capital accumulation since 1989, the newly developed business structures in Myanmar have been in conflict with industrialization.

Concluding Remarks: The Myanmar Economy in the Twenty-first Century

We have examined the structure of capital accumulation. As summarized in the first section, and examined in detail in the second and third sections, the growth in the Myanmar economy from 1989–2003 was high, but the structures formed were unstable. These were linked to fiscal deficits, a distorted exchange rate system, the development of the domestic private sector, and the stagnation of the SEEs, and the bias in the financial system.

This chapter concludes by providing a possible explanation of the change in the economy after 2000.

Until 2002, the Myanmar economy was in an unusual macroeconomic situation. The country faced hyperinflation and worsening fiscal deficit, but its trading sectors were performing well and its asset markets were booming.[31] In 2003, with the start of the banking crisis, the asset values fell sharply and the economy went into recession. The contraction of the economy continued in 2004, but entered a recovery phase in 2005.

The boom in the asset markets until 2003 reflected the structural characteristics of a financial system that had been formed in the 1990s. While bank deposits expanded, following the formation of the banking system, from the mid-1990s to 2000, the growth rate in deposits slowed after 2001. In the same period, deposits with informal financial companies, called General Service Companies (GSCs),[32] increasingly replaced bank deposits, and the price of real estate in Yangon surged. This situation reflects the fact that the demand for bank deposits, stimulated by the emergence of the financial infrastructure, became further diversified into riskier and more profitable assets in 2001 and 2002. Furthermore, there is a possibility that the asset-holding decision of households and the business sector were affected by the recurrence of inflation after 2001.

Because the profit structure of the banks depends on the continuous growth of their asset base through deposits, the slowdown in the number of new deposits became a major issue for banks. In 1999, a new method of financing fiscal deficits was created, and 30 per cent of fiscal deficits were dependent on the issue of TBs to banks. Under these conditions, the slowing of deposit growth caused the market absorption channel to malfunction and caused a recurrence of inflation. In other words, the new financial channel linking the fiscal and financial sector brought with it the possibility that the condition of the financial sector might affect inflation.[33] Whether or not the rumours about the trigger of the banking crisis in early 2003 are correct, we can see the factors that principally contributed to the crisis: the relationship between the slowdown in deposit growth, the erosion of bank profits, and the weakened capacity to absorb the fiscal deficit.

It appears that, following the banking crisis, inflation and the depreciation of the market exchange rate were moderate, and the economy contracted.[34] The external economic sector, particularly trade, remained stable even after 2000, despite the turmoil in the domestic economy. Looking at exports, many garment factories grew rapidly from 1999–2001 and started to contribute to an improved trade account, replacing agricultural products as the major export commodity. After 2002, the country began to export

natural gas, and these exports became more important than the export of
garments, which faced a ban from the US for political reasons. During this
period, exports increased substantially and this development together with
the import restriction policy brought improvements in the trade account.[35]
Furthermore, the capital inflow from China expanded from 2003–4. In
summary, while the financial sector and non-manufacturing sector faced
a depression, triggered by the banking crisis in 2003, the economy experienced macroeconomic stability, and trade performance and capital inflow
improved.[36]

On the other hand, and importantly, in contrast to the changes in the
private sector the government failed to improve its operations. The reoccur-
rence of hyperinflation and the cessation of the release of official statistics on
budgetary accounts can be seen as indirect evidence of the worsening of the
fiscal conditions. Furthermore, the disparity between the centre exchange rate
of 450 kyat to the dollar and the market rate of 800–1,000 kyat increased
in the early twenty-first century.

In 2004, the economic conditions improved, despite a worsening fiscal
situation. However, without a drastic resolution of the SEE and exchange
rate system issues, the economy remained exposed to the risk of serious
macroeconomic instability and bottlenecks in the move towards greater
industrialization.

Notes

[1]   Numerical information on border trade, however, remains unavailable to the
        public and hence is unclear.

[2]   It is often suggested that some Myanmar Chinese citizens have extensive business
        networks in other countries, which enables them to contribute to the formal and
        informal capital inflow of Myanmar (interviews in September 2004). Mizuno
        (2004) examines in detail the characteristics of trade and capital flow with China.

[3]   There is no information on how and where the formal rate is applied. While it
        functions as a subsidy to the imports of SEEs, it has been abolished in practice
        and is used only in the official statistics. Nevertheless, it is highly possible that
        ad hoc application of the rate is utilized as a type of subsidy.

[4]   Also, the sanctioning of the donor countries and multi-national institutions for
        development assistance is thought to be another potential factor involved in
        worsening the fiscal conditions.

[5]   Such circumstances are considered to be favourable for most SEEs operating in
        the import-substitution sectors.

[6]   The prospect of the expansion of investment from China and an improvement
        in Chinese relations, combined with the growth in natural gas exports, were

suggested as reasons for forecasting a recovery in 2005 in interviews conducted during September 2004.

[7] Some point to the decline in the rice price as another factor reflecting the temporary cessation of the price rise. Rice is overwhelmingly the largest component of the CPI basket in Myanmar.

[8] The market exchange rate became very volatile after 2000.

[9] This becomes clear when Myanmar is compared with its Indochinese neighbours. Cambodia increased its secondary industry's share of GDP from 15.1 per cent in 1994 to 24.1 per cent in 2000, with the garment industry increasing its share from 2.0 to 9.5 per cent.

[10] However, the investment rate, measured by the fixed 1985 prices, monotonically increased from 16.4 per cent in 1990 to 32.0 per cent in 2000. While this increase may have been affected by deflator bias, it also suggests the possibility that the value of the nominal investment is undervalued because of the application of unrealistic official exchange rates to the components of investment spending, and the fact that the investment rate was marginally higher than our observation. Likewise, the proportions of imports and exports in nominal GDP appear unrealistically small in Table 5.

[11] Foreign direct investment and external trade are discussed in detail in Chapter 3.

[12] Their investments are mainly directed to the mining sector (oil and natural gas).

[13] The possibility that investment from abroad by Chinese Myanmar citizens is treated as domestic investment in the statistics implies that the level of capital inflows in the balance of payments may have been underestimated.

[14] Although we consider the nominal values here in order to examine the trend in individual export goods, we should note that the rate of imports and exports in nominal GDE seems unrealistically small, as seen in note 10. However, the export rate measured by the real value using 1985 fixed prices also declined from 1993–96.

[15] Garment exports stagnated after the ban on US exports was introduced in 2003.

[16] It is worth noting that the growth trend is not driven by the development of certain leading sectors, and so may be regarded as unsustainable.

[17] Note that agriculture and other primary sector producers are included under private holdings in Table 6.

[18] As a case in point, in order to avoid perceived unreasonable taxation, firms tend to curb the settlement in an informal way, such as utilizing foreign cash raised in the curb market, using a non-monetary method with their foreign partners, or locating the settlement base outside Myanmar.

[19] According to the hearing at firms and banks in Yangon conducted in September 2004.

[20] In the banking sector, apart from the private banks, there are five state-owned banks, with substantial assets. However, their number of transactions with private businesses is very limited. A few private banks merged after the banking crisis of 2003.

21 This bank caused the banking crisis of 2003, and most operations were frozen by the authorities until mid-2004.

22 These are classified according to the company names listed in Wang (2004). The remaining four unclassified firms are processing (1), hospital (1), unclear (2).

23 There were 38 firms in the group in total, according to the hearing in September 2003, 51 in Wang (2004) and 37 in the pamphlet of the SPA issued in 2001.

24 For example, the share of both Yangon Land, a real estate developer in the group, held by FMI, and Yoma Bank is 37 per cent, respectively. The remaining share is allocated to several directors of the SPA, according to the hearing in September 2003. As a foreign corporation, the SPA is not entitled to hold shares.

25 The objective of this subsection is to outline the characteristics of the growth of the banking sector, and our focus is limited to information on consolidated balance sheet data up to 1999. Chapter 4 discusses the details about the development related to the banking crisis of early 2003. For more details, see related articles in *Burma Economic Watch*, various volumes from 2003–4 and Turnell (2003).

26 Up to September 2004.

27 According to the hearing in September 2003.

28 See note in Chapter 4.

29 Questionnaires regarding fund-raising for working capital (flow level) were limited to questions related to bank borrowing, borrowing within one's family, and/or self-financing. In fact, trade credits in the form of expanding deferred payments functions as working capital. Care should be taken in interpreting the results shown in Tables 10 (which shows the share of methods at the stock level) and 11.

30 It is obvious that the SEEs do not receive funds, because they are not allowed to transact with private and state-owned banks.

31 As a proxy for the price of real estate, Wang (2004) provides information on the trend in apartment rents, comparing apartments of similar location and condition, and collecting the data from *Living Color*, a local economic magazine. As the table below indicates, the rental price was almost constant from 1997–2002, and increased suddenly from late 2002 to early 2003.

Rental Price of Apartment (625sq ft)   Kyat Million

	1997	2000	2002/6	2003/2	2003/8
Sanchaung	5	4	0.8	25	15
Kyaukmyaung	4.5	3.5	5	20	10

Source: Wang (2004).
   Original source is *Living Color*, September 2003.

32 GSCs suddenly grew in the early twenty-first century, paying an interest rate in excess of 5 per cent per month on deposits. The bankruptcy of some GSCs was one direct trigger of the banking crisis of 2003. Wang (2004) identifies at least 14 major GSCs. See also Chapter 4.

33   It is also highly likely that the compulsory allocation of TBs eroded the profit base of the banking system.

34   The amount of deposits recovered in 2003 and 2004, however, with many deposits shifting to several medium-sized banks that were unaffected by the banking crisis (see Chapter 4).

35   In this period, imports were restricted by direct controls and strict import licenses.

36   However, it is difficult to see how these sectors can become new leading sectors, replacing the stagnating domestic sectors.

CHAPTER 2

Industrial Policies and the Development of Myanmar's Industrial Sector in the Transition to a Market Economy

Toshihiro Kudo

Objectives

Since the Industrial Revolution in Britain, economic development and the process of industrialization have often been treated as synonymous. Independent Myanmar, like other countries, hoped for the transformation of its agrarian economy into a modern industrial one. For many years it pursued industrialization within the framework of a socialist planned economy, using state-owned economic enterprises (SEEs) established through either nationalization programmes or new public investment. The results after half a century were disappointing, and Myanmar was reduced to Least Developed Country status in 1987.[1]

In 1988, the State Law and Order Restoration Council (SLORC), reconstituted in 1997 as the State Peace and Development Council (SPDC), took power and abandoned the socialist economic system, setting its sights on a so-called market economy instead. More than 20 years have passed since Myanmar introduced this new policy, and industrial development in Myanmar has not progressed smoothly. Table 1 clearly shows that the country has stagnated compared to Cambodia, Laos and Vietnam (CLV), which embarked on a transition towards a market economy at about the same time as Myanmar. The CLV countries successfully increased their share of the industrial sector throughout the 1990s and at the beginning of the new century.

Myanmar's industrial sector also underwent considerable changes during this period. Its private industrialists responded well and swiftly to the new economic opportunities provided by the liberalization measures and the

Table 1 GDP by Industry (%)

	Primary Industry			Secondary Industry		
	1980	*1990*	*2003**	*1980*	*1990*	*2003*
Myanmar	47	57	55	13	11	13
Cambodia	–	56	36	–	11	28
Laos	–	61	49	–	15	26
Vietnam	50	39	23	23	23	40

Note: Myanmar for 2003* is based on figures of 2002.

Source: ADB, *Key Indicators*, various numbers.

"open-door" policy. Private sector industrial development was observed in the first half of the 1990s. However, the government ultimately maintained their predecessor's SEE strategy for industrial development. There was no serious reform of SEEs and they even expanded to take part in the new projects.

This chapter describes industrial development from the 1990s to 2005, and the mechanisms behind the growth or stagnation of Myanmar's industrial sector. Which factors promoted or impeded the national industrial development? How did the government's industrial and trade policies influence its performance? What is the relationship between the private enterprises and the SEEs? Addressing these research questions here will contribute to a better understanding of the underlying causes that promoted or hindered economic and industrial development in Myanmar.

To facilitate examination of the factors that promoted or hindered development, the author has categorized the industries studied into three groups: (a) domestic market-oriented industries, including import-substitution ones and construction businesses; (b) export-oriented industries, such as garment manufacture; and (c) infrastructure services, including electricity, transportation and communications. The three categories exhibit quite different development paths, reflecting their marketplaces (domestic and overseas), contrasts between the players in private enterprises and SEEs, the differentiated impact of the open-door policy, and government policy objectives for each category.

In the second section, the contribution of the industrial sector to the national economy is briefly examined. The third section explores the development of import-substitution industries and the construction business under the open-door policy. The research period is divided into three parts: namely, preliminary development, with the release of pent-up demand in the first half of the 1990s; the slow-down, during which the foreign currency problems surfaced after 1997; and the revival of the SEEs after 2000. Firm-level survey data obtained by our study team will be used to support the argument.[2]

The fourth section describes the rapid growth of the export-oriented garment industry in the late 1990s, which continued until 2003. This industry is a private sector-driven success story, an industry outside the remit of the interventionist government. The fifth section deals with the infrastructure, in which the SEEs dominate the supply and markets. The primary mandate of the SEEs within the infrastructure sector was to provide services at low prices, which they unquestionably did, but the pricing policy eventually eroded their financial capability.

By way of conclusion, the nature of Myanmar's industrial policies and the industrial development that can be attributed to these policies will be briefly summarized.

The Performance of the Industrial Sector in the National Economy

Myanmar's secondary sector (energy, mining, processing and manufacturing, electricity generation and construction; see Table 2) grew relatively more rapidly than the economy as a whole throughout the 1990s and at the start of the new century, although the pace of industrialization was not comparable to neighbouring countries, as mentioned before (Table 1). This growth was led by not only the manufacturing sub-sector, which lay at the core of the secondary sector, but also by other sub-sectors, such as construction, mining and electricity generation (Table 2). The private sector was the engine for their growth, and the involvement of the private sector increased remarkably in mining, construction and manufacturing, although public sector activity persisted to some degree. Myanmar's industrialists quickly entered the industries that were newly opened to them, but did not become involved in energy and electricity generation because the government continued to impose an entry ban under the State-owned Economic Enterprises Law, enacted in 1989.[3]

The number of registered private industries is shown in Table 3.[4] The first half of the 1990s saw a rapid increase, reflecting local industrialists' quick response to the new economic opportunities. There was a slowdown after 1997, when the Asian economic crisis occurred, but growth picked up in the early twenty-first century, continuing up to May 2005, when the number of registered private industries declined for the first time. These private factories were accommodated in industrial zones that were mostly

Table 2 GDP Growth, Contribution and Ownership by Sector

	GDP Average Annual Growth Rate				Share in GDP		Share of Private Sector	
	FY1986–89	FY1990–93	FY1994–97	FY1998–2000	FY1986	FY2000	FY1986	FY1998
Primary Industry	-3.3%	3.5%	4.8%	9.4%	49.0%	42.7%	92.9%	97.0%
Agriculture	-3.8%	3.6%	4.7%	8.3%	40.3%	33.6%	93.4%	97.9%
Secondary	-3.9%	7.6%	10.6%	12.5%	12.4%	17.8%	42.6%	62.4%
Energy	–	–	0.5%	49.3%	–	0.5%	–	0.0%
Mining	-4.3%	3.0%	20.3%	21.0%	0.9%	1.9%	8.0%	88.2%
Processing & Manufacturing	-4.9%	3.9%	6.4%	14.4%	9.2%	10.1%	54.2%	70.8%
Electric Power	3.8%	16.3%	10.4%	7.6%	0.5%	1.1%	0.0%	0.0%
Construction	-0.8%	18.6%	19.1%	4.9%	1.7%	4.2%	10.8%	54.0%
Tertiary (Service Trade)	-3.2%	4.4%	7.2%	9.9%	38.7%	39.5%	46.3%	60.3%
Gross Dom. Product	-3.3%	4.4%	6.7%	10.1%	100.0%	100.0%	68.6%	76.3%

Note: Real GDP based on 1985/86 constant prices. FY stands for Fiscal Year (April–March).

Source: Central Statistical Organization (CSO), *Statistical Yearbook* (2003).

Toshihiro Kudo

Table 3 Number of Registered Private Industrial Enterprises

	Number	Growth (%)
FY 1990	27	–
FY 1991	23,848	883 times
FY 1992	25,081	5.2%
FY 1993	28,528	13.7%
FY 1994	31,540	10.6%
FY 1995	33,278	5.5%
FY 1996	35,348	6.2%
FY 1997	35,786	1.2%
FY 1998	35,915	0.4%
FY 1999	36,152	0.7%
FY 2000	37,649	4.1%
FY 2001	38,254	1.6%
FY 2002	39,604	3.5%
FY 2003	42,429	7.1%
FY 2004	43,435	2.4%
FY 2005*	41,875	–3.6%

Note: * as of May, 2005.

Source: Ministry of Industry (1).

designated and constructed by the government. The Shwe Pyi Tha Industrial Zone was constructed in the suburbs of Yangon in 1990, and since then the government has constructed more than 18 industrial zones nationwide.

The open-door policy produced a remarkable increase in external trade throughout the 1990s and up to 2003, although exports and imports did not grow in parallel (Table 4).[5] Myanmar was unsuccessful in exporting "Made-in-Myanmar" industrial products, with the sole exception of garments (Table 5). Until the mid-1990s exports were mainly primary commodities such

Table 4 Trade Growth (%, times)

	1986–89	1990–93	1994–97	1998–2001	2002–2003	1988→1997	1997→2003
Export	0.0%	23.6%	4.9%	25.7%	–1.8%	2.7 times	2.4 times
Import	2.4%	23.9%	22.1%	–5.4%	9.8%	5.2 times	1.0 times

Source: UN Comtrade.

Table 5 Export/Import Composition by Commodities

	Rank	Items	FY1986–89	FY1990–93	FY1994–97	FY1998–2001	FY2002–03
Export	1	Gas, natural and manufactured (34)	0.0%	0.0%	0.0%	13.9%	28.4%
	2	Articles of apparel and clothing accessories (84)	1.7%	4.3%	12.3%	31.5%	25.5%
	3	Cork and wood (24)	43.7%	40.7%	30.3%	18.4%	15.5%
	4	Vegetables and fruit (05)	7.3%	14.6%	15.9%	9.9%	11.3%
	5	Fish, crustaceans, molluscs, preparations (03)	8.2%	9.6%	15.1%	8.8%	6.0%
	6	Cereals and cereal preparations (04)	4.6%	3.9%	5.0%	1.4%	2.8%
	7	Footwear (85)	0.0%	0.1%	0.3%	0.8%	1.0%
	8	Non-metallic mineral manufactures, n.e.s. (66)	8.5%	8.2%	5.5%	1.9%	0.9%
	9	Non-ferrous metals (68)	1.8%	0.4%	0.3%	2.0%	0.9%
	10	Cork and wood manufactures (excl. furniture) (63)	0.5%	0.5%	0.8%	1.1%	0.8%
Import	1	Petroleum and petroleum products (33)	2.3%	6.3%	5.7%	12.8%	13.0%
	2	Textile yarn, fabrics and made-upart (65)	9.5%	10.7%	7.7%	10.4%	11.1%
	3	Machinery specialized for particular industry (72)	6.1%	4.1%	5.5%	7.1%	6.3%
	4	Road vehicles (incl. air cushion vehicles) (78)	7.0%	8.6%	6.0%	3.5%	5.5%
	5	Power generating machinery and equipment (71)	6.0%	3.8%	3.3%	3.4%	5.0%
	6	Iron and steel (67)	7.2%	6.8%	7.1%	5.5%	4.7%
	7	Electrical machinery, apparatus & appliance (77)	7.4%	3.8%	4.0%	4.0%	3.8%
	8	General industrial machinery & equipment (74)	5.9%	3.7%	4.0%	4.3%	3.8%
	9	Manufactures of metal, n.e.s. (69)	4.1%	2.6%	2.9%	3.4%	3.3%
	10	Fixed vegetable oils and fats (42)	0.7%	5.3%	5.6%	3.5%	3.1%
	20	Tobacco and tobacco manufactures (12)	1.5%	5.2%	5.4%	1.8%	1.5%

Note: Based on SITC 2 digits. Figures in apparenteses indicate the SITC codes.

Source: UN Comtrade.

as teak, gem stones, rice, beans and pulses, and fish and prawns. Garment exports increased in the mid-1990s and gained momentum between 1998 and 2001, accounting for 32 per cent of total exports during this period. At the start of the twenty-first century, natural gas from the Andaman Sea started to be exported to Thailand, becoming the biggest export commodity in 2002 and 2003.

The Import-Substitution Industry and Construction Businesses

The open-door policy unleashed people's pent-up demand for consumer goods, providing economic opportunities for local firms. It was natural for burgeoning private industries to target domestic rather than export markets, and to concentrate on consumer goods rather than capital goods. The private sector did not have the production facilities, technology, or marketing channels for exporting their products and no hope of developing an export trade.[6] They began import-substitution industries at the outset.

Preliminary Import-Substitution: Exploiting Pent-up Demand

Shortly after the SLORC took power in 1988, the government allowed private businesses to engage in external trade and started to legitimize and formalize the border trade with neighbouring countries, hitherto an activity deemed illegal. Opening up external trade to private enterprises vastly increased the number of exporters and importers.

Imported goods poured into the emerging consumer goods markets. The people had been cut off from purchasing daily commodities and durables during the socialist period, and most of the demand for such products was supplied by a black market that was reliant on an extremely inefficient, illegal border trade. Once people had ready access to such products, demand skyrocketed. According to Myanmar government statistics, while consumer goods occupied 6 and 12 per cent of total imports in FY 1980 and FY 1985 respectively, the corresponding figures for FY 1990 and FY 1995 were 35 and 42 per cent (CSO, 2003: 210).[7]

Myanmar's businesses faced competition from imports; nevertheless, there was room for the domestic industries to embark on straightforward assembling, mixing and processing activities. For example, the so-called "3 in 1" Coffee Mix, a packet mix powder consisting of coffee, cream and sugar combined, became popular following the introduction of the open door policy. Traders imported the three ingredients (sugar, cream and coffee powder) and then carried out the very simple process of mixing and packing using imported machinery. They imported sugar because the quality of domestic sugar was poor, but gradually began to purchase domestic sugar that met the quality standards for instant products. The manufacturers also set up printing businesses so that they did not need to import ready-printed plastic packages from abroad. In this way, the local content of the "3 in 1" Coffee Mix increased, even though the coffee and powdered cream were still imported.

This product would never have materialized without the release of people's pent-up demand and without the possibility of importing raw materials and machinery. Although imported goods competed with domestic products, they made the growth of import-substitution industries in the private sector both possible and feasible. Private industry expanded quite rapidly in the early 1990s.

Manufacturers of consumer goods accounted for about 70 per cent of the 23,675 private industries registered with the Ministry of Industry (1) in 1992.[8] The majority were rice mills and edible oil mills. Among the newly established businesses, the manufacturers of consumer goods appeared at an earlier stage than other types of industry. According to our firm-level survey, among 27 survivors from the socialist era, 18 were manufacturers of consumer goods, such as foods, slippers and traditional medicine (Table 6). Myanmar industrialists established new factories in this sector throughout the 1990s.

Private construction firms also emerged immediately after the introduction of the open-door policy. The demand for new and rehabilitated houses, hotels and office buildings had been suppressed during the socialist period, and construction firms enjoyed the same kind of sudden market improvement as the producers of consumer goods. The private sector's construction activities in Yangon created a "boom" situation in the first half of the 1990s (Table 7). The rapid growth in the construction sub-sector was made possible by the improved access to imported building materials under the open-door policy. For example, cement imports increased from 2,000 tons in FY 1990 to 285 thousand tons in FY1995, 590 thousand tons the next year, and 1.05 million tons in FY 1997 (CSO, 2003: 209).

However, the construction boom was relatively short-lived; it petered out in 1997, when the property and real estate bubble burst in the main cities of Myanmar. In retrospect, however, this construction boom was important for the burgeoning private industries since it gave them a chance to accumulate capital to some extent in the early stage of their development. Many of today's business groups that engage in a variety of business lines originated in the construction industry.

Table 6 Year of Establishment of Private Firms

	Manufacturing					Construction	Services		Total
	Garments	Agri & Marine	Industrial Goods	Consumer Goods	Sub-total		For Business	For Consumer	
Up to 1988	1	2	3	18	24	0	0	3	27
1989–1992	0	7	7	13	27	8	4	2	41
1993–1996	2	5	6	12	25	5	5	4	39
1997–2000	8	4	7	18	37	2	6	7	52
2001–2003	2	2	1	1	6	0	0	2	8
Total	13	20	24	62	119	15	15	18	167

Source: Author's survey, 2003.

Table 7   Private Building Activities in Yangon

	FY1985	*FY1990*	*FY1995*	*FY2000*	*FY2002*
Application Submitted	1203	2012	6841	1344	2209
Application Approved	1111	1821	5201	1490	2143
Completed Construction	–	407	1112	918	708

Note: New buildings only.

Source: CSO, *Statistical Yearbook* (2003).

Frustrated Development: The Foreign Currency Shortage

The high economic growth experienced shortly after the open-door policy, however, turned out to be short-lived. In retrospect, the business climate had begun to change even before the Asian economic crisis of mid-1997. A trigger for policy changes was an apparent expansion of the trade deficits in the mid-1990s. Once the government liberalized trade, imports grew far faster than exports, the performance of which had slowed by the mid-1990s (Table 4).

The relatively poor export performance in the mid-1990s was probably due to delays in reforms in the agricultural sector, where the major export commodities were still under government control, with the exception of beans and pulses. Two new export commodities, garments and natural gas, emerged in the late 1990s and early 2000s. The emerging domestic import-substitution industries did little to alleviate the overall demand for imports, since they depended heavily on imported machinery and imported raw materials. According to our firm-level survey, more than 90 per cent of firms used foreign-made machinery and equipment to varying degrees. Of these, about half utilized more than 50 per cent of foreign-made machinery and equipment for their production.

Foreign exchange reserves became extremely limited in 1997, when capital flows slowed as a result of the Asian economic crisis. ODA had been long suspended, for political reasons. During 1997, the gross reserve coverage had slipped below 1.5 months of imports and the coverage of net reserves fell to about a month of imports (IMF, 1999b: 26). As foreign exchange reserves dwindled, the government imposed a series of restrictions on the exchange and trade system. The establishment of the Trade Policy Council (TPC) seems to have marked a turning point. The TPC, an extra-ministerial committee, was formed in July 1997, with the vice chair of the SPDC as chair and the Minister for National Planning and Economic Development as secretary. The TPC laid down important policies not only on external trade but also on other economic matters. These policies include an export-first policy with the following provisions:

*   imports are allowed only against export earnings
*   limits are imposed on non-essential imports
*   there is a 10% export tax
*   the advanced purchase of certain industrial crops is allowed
*   there is market-price-based taxation on imported vehicles
*   import restrictions are imposed on motor vehicles
*   there is a monthly grant for palm oil import
*   a lowered FEC limit is placed on overseas bank transfers
*   there is strengthened revenue collection from Myanmar Investment Commission (MIC)-approved projects
*   under-priced import vehicles are subject to inspection.

A number of these provisions appear to have been made to capture foreign exchange earnings for the government budget (Kudo ed., 2001: 40–42).

The imposition of new restrictions on the exchange and trade system deprived private firms of free access to imported goods, causing a slowdown in their economic activity. However, the period from 1998 to 2001 brought a sudden and unexpected boom in Yangon's garment industry led by the domestic private firms, and phenomenon that will be examined in detail later in this chapter. Companies that lost access to imported raw materials flooded into the export-oriented garment industry, which successfully avoided import-related problems by adopting CMP (Cutting, Making and Packing) consignment arrangements.

The Survival and Revival of the SEEs

The number of SEEs did not decrease throughout the transitional period towards a market economy. On the contrary, their number increased from 597 establishments in FY 1985 to 1,132 in FY 2002 (Table 8). There were only 19 new public industrial enterprises created between FY 1985 and FY 1990, but the number grew by 92 between FY 1990 and FY 1995, and by around 20 to 30 per year during the next five years. Thereafter, growth was spectacular, with 53 public industrial enterprises established in FY 2001 and 231 in FY 2002. The numbers suggest that a substantial government programme to develop state-owned factories was launched around this time.[9]

Table 8   Public Industrial Enterprises

	Total Number	Growth (number)
FY 1985	597	–
FY 1990	616	19
FY 1995	708	92
FY 1996	753	45
FY 1997	771	18
FY 1998	802	31
FY 1999	824	22
FY 2000	848	24
FY 2001	901	53
FY 2002	1,132	231

Source: CSO, *Statistical Yearbook* (2003).

What are the government's objectives with regard to these programmes? From September 2001 to January 2002, the *New Light of Myanmar*, a state-run English newspaper, featured a series entitled "Industrial Development" that explained the government's thinking.[10] Most of the articles described the government's efforts to rehabilitate old state factories and establish new ones. Very little reference was made to private industry, and the investment and business climate was not mentioned at all. What the authors of the articles appreciated above all was the quantity of goods produced rather than the value of the production. The factories' performances were assessed by the volume of production, which was measured by tonnage, miles and pieces. For example, an article on the textile and garment industry included the following statement:

> Thus, the requirement for the entire nation is 187,574 million pounds of cotton yarn and 801.6 million yards of cloth. At present, the industries can fulfill 13 percent of the yarn requirement and nine percent of the cloth requirement of the nation. Thus, it is clear that the textile and clothing factories are much needed for the nation.[11]

The Ministry of Industry (1) gave top priority to three slogans: "leap-frog the era through industrial might", "double production" and "patronize locally-made products".[12] Thus, the main objective of the government's industrial policy was to increase the volume of production to achieve a domestic self-sufficiency in terms of quantity without, however, paying much attention to customers' preferences. A direct corollary is the rather anachronistic proliferation of SEEs in the early twenty-first century.

Industrial Policy and Import-Substitution Industries

The strong demand for goods and improved access to imported raw materials made it possible for the local entrepreneurs to enter the manufacturing and construction sub-sectors. From FY 1986 to FY 1998, the share of the private sector increased from 54.2 to 70.8 per cent in manufacturing and from 10.8 to 54.0 per cent in construction, while the role of SEEs declined accordingly (Table 2).

Why did the government allow the private sector to grow faster and occupy a bigger portion of the economic activities in these sectors? This question would be irrelevant in a genuine market economy, where the private sector can engage in economic activities as freely as they wish, but it remains relevant in Myanmar, since many private economic players, including industrialists and farmers, are not allowed to conduct business as freely as they might wish.

One answer, the author believes, is that the government allowed the private businesses to grow as long as they remained in their own sphere, and did not seriously encroach on the SEEs' activities. The government resorted to restrictions and regulations whenever the private firms had interests that clashed with the major SEEs. As far as the import-substitution industries were concerned the emerging private firms and SEEs did not compete for customers in the product markets. The consumer goods markets were huge and growing, and the supply was insufficient to meet demand. Private firms could not afford to produce capital goods and consumer durables, leaving the SEEs as the only local producers in this field. Under such a market environment, the growing private sector did not seriously affect the businesses of the SEEs.[13]

The two sides did not seriously compete for raw materials, although the tightened import controls after 1997 gradually promoted competition between them for imported raw materials. A notable exception was the agro-based industry. Agro-processing private firms did compete with the SEEs for domestic raw materials, such as cotton and sugarcane.[14] The government restricted private-sector procurement of those raw materials in order to secure sufficient raw materials for the agro-processing SEEs. The lack of raw materials seriously impeded the development of private firms. The case of agro-based industry clearly shows government willingness to place restrictions on the private sector to support the SEEs.

With the economic slowdown, the tightened import controls and the proliferation of SEEs, the private sector was gradually crowded out from both the products and raw materials markets. Their scope was eroded by the public sector companies and by government intervention. They needed new business opportunities, and found them in export-oriented production.

The Export-Oriented Garment Industry

The exceptionally brisk development of the garment industry had become apparent by the late 1990s, but the US sanctions imposed in July 2003 caused considerable damage. This section investigates how the garment industry grew despite Myanmar's overall economic and industrial stagnation.

Growth under the MFA regime

The manufacture of garments for export is a recent development in Myanmar.[15] First, state-owned and military-related textile and garment factories started production for overseas buyers and customers in the early 1990s, when foreign firms, especially companies from Korea and Hong Kong, established joint ventures with these factories. Others established wholly-owned factories funded entirely by foreign capital. Domestic firms started to enter the garment industry in the mid-1990s, but "boom" conditions in the garment industry developed only in the late 1990s, led by the local private firms.

Exports serve as the most reliable performance index for the garment industry. Most of the garment industries in Myanmar, like those in other developing economies, operate on a Cutting, Making, and Packing (CMP) basis. Overseas buyers do everything but the production; they find customers, design the clothes to detailed specifications, and procure and supply raw materials to plants in Myanmar. These plants do the cutting, sewing, and packing, and then re-export all of their products.

Figure 1 shows the export performance in Myanmar's garment industry, based on the UN Comtrade and import data relating to 22 major countries.[16] According to the UN Comtrade, the export of Myanmar-made clothes increased steadily through the 1990s up to 1998, when it reached about US$270 million. The following two years, 1999 and 2000, brought remarkable growth and produced a garment industry "boom" in Yangon. At this time, garments occupied about 40 per cent of the total exports of the country that were the top export item. The surge peaked in 2001, when the value of exports reached US$868 million.

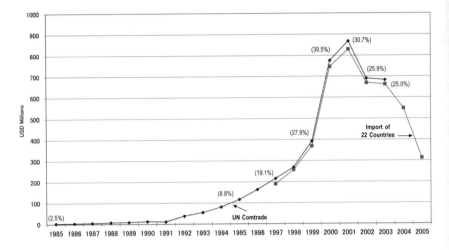

Figure 1   Myanmar's Garments Export

Note: Figures in parentheses show garments share in total exports.

Sources: UN Comtrade and World Trade Atlas.

The export-oriented garment industry in Myanmar grew based on market demand from the US and the EU. Throughout the 1990s, about 90 per cent of the demand for Myanmar-made clothes was provided by the US and EU markets. According to Table 9, 45 per cent of Myanmar-made clothes went to the US market in 1997 and 50 per cent to the EU. Subsequently, the US market share steadily increased, reaching 54 per cent by 2000.

Table 9   Major Importers of Myanmar Garments (US$ Millions)

	1997	1998	1999	2000	2001	2002	2003	2004	2005
EU (15 Countries)	94.1	118.0	155.1	276.1	348.8	307.2	339.9	457.4	236.9
Japan	1.1	2.3	2.1	4.6	7.5	15.0	32.2	44.8	52.7
Singapore	n.a.	n.a.	10.8	26.5	28.4	22.2	29.2	23.6	7.5
Korea	0.1	0.0	0.2	0.7	3.3	1.7	5.0	6.3	7.4
Canada	7.8	6.3	11.6	31.6	29.5	22.0	19.9	12.3	5.0
Malaysia	0.0	0.0	0.0	0.0	0.5	1.6	2.8	3.2	2.7
Australia	1.5	2.7	3.6	2.5	3.0	0.3	0.2	0.3	0.2
USA	85.3	127.8	185.7	403.5	408.0	298.6	232.7	0.0	0.0
Total (22 Countries)	189.8	257.2	369.1	745.5	829.0	668.5	661.8	547.9	312.4

Note: The figures include HS61 (Knit Apparel) and HS62 (Woven Apparel).

Source: World Trade Atlas.

Why did the garment industry in Myanmar receive orders from the US and EU? An important reason was that, under the Multi Fiber Agreement (MFA), Myanmar enjoyed an unrestricted quota position (either no quotas, or non-binding ones). The MFA, which came into force in 1974, applied quantitative restrictions (quotas) to imports from developing countries. It was followed by the Agreement on Textiles and Clothing (ATC), which came into force with the establishment of the World Trade Organization (WTO) in 1995. The US and EU applied quotas under the MFA/ATC regime (Norås, 2004: 13–15),[17] and the MFA ended on 1 January 2005.

In the absence of quotas for the EU market; Myanmar could export freely as long as orders continued to come in. The US imposed quotas but on just six woven items, including men's shirts and trousers. Knitwear had no quotas. Buyers came to Yangon searching for either no quota or unfilled quota items. The export of no quota items contributed to the rapid growth of the garment industry in Myanmar. As an example, the export of knitwear to the US, on which no quotas had been imposed, accounted for nearly 70 per cent of the total exports to that country during the rapid growth period of 1997–2002.

At the same time, the export volume of six quota items also increased remarkably in 1999 and 2000, facilitated by the improved use of quotas. It is said that the quotas had long been monopolized by the Myanmar Textile Industry (MTI), a SEE under the Ministry of Industry (1), the Union of Myanmar Economic Holdings Limited (UMEHL), a military-related enterprise, and their joint ventures with foreign firms. Even though there were no announced reforms in the allocation of quotas, there certainly were changes, so that the private firms, including those that were 100 per cent foreign, could have access to them. As a result, the export volume of items with quotas constituted about 20 per cent of the total export volume to the US in 1999 and 2000. The garment industry in Myanmar clearly benefitted from the MFA regime for its support of rapid growth.

The CMP-based "Enclave"

There are, of course, factors other than the MFA quota, such as the availability of abundant, cheap labour and the "China+1" diversification strategy of the buyers. These factors contributed substantially to the growth of the garment industry in Myanmar, but they also posed challenges to the garment industry, and determined its destiny in line with the market demand, international competitiveness, capital formation, human resources, technology transfer, and so on.

Here, however, we focus on the *system* that made possible the development of this industry in the midst of Myanmar's overall industrial stagnation. How did the garment industry overcome the tightened import controls and worsened access to imported raw materials during this period? It did so by utilizing the CMP system. Garment manufacture is a labour-intensive, export-oriented industry that has swiftly shifted its production bases from one county to another, in search of ever cheaper labour costs and ever more attractive quotas. The industry utilizes conventional technology and the initial investment, mainly the purchase of sewing machines, was relatively small. The raw materials are not excessively heavy or bulky, and can also be transported at reasonable costs. The nature of the product makes the CMP arrangement possible in the garment industry. In other words, the CMP system can create "enclaves" in which all raw materials are provided from abroad and the products are processed by domestic workers, then exported again to the overseas markets, avoiding messy domestic and international transactions and settlements.

The most important advantage of the CMP system was that Myanmar industrialists did not need to pay for imported raw materials, such as fabrics and buttons. Instead, almost all of raw materials, except for small items such as carton boxes and plastic bags, which could be procured domestically, were provided by overseas buyers through their own financing and at their own risk. The actual payment is merely the remittance of processing fees to the Myanmar Foreign Trade Bank (MFTB) and/or the Myanmar Investment and Commercial Bank (MICB), two state-owned foreign exchange banks, by overseas buyers after the receipt of the products. Myanmar industrialists did not need to concern themselves with the controls surrounding imports and exports, or by tedious procedures, as in other sectors. In particular, they could have access to imported raw materials without "export earnings" under the CMP arrangement.

By contrast with CMP, the so-called "FOB" production modality, in which suppliers receive the full price of a garment exported rather than just payment for assembling it, involves the more active participation of local industrialists in matters such as the procurement of raw materials, the design of clothes and marketing.[18] The "FOB" production modality requires the economy and its industrialists to have better-developed upstream industries, stronger industrial linkages, better access to financial facilities, improved business coordination and more risk-taking attitudes, most of which are not currently found in Myanmar. As far as can be ascertained, there is no "FOB" modality of production in Myanmar, whereas 10–15 per cent of garment factories in Vietnam engage in "FOB"-type production and export.

Although Goto (2002) asserts that a shift from CMT (CMP)[19] to FOB does not necessarily guarantee increased value-added and international competitiveness, the viability and feasibility of "FOB" operations are closely related to better investment and to a more favourable business climate, in which local industrialists can take more risks. The *de facto* impossibility of "FOB"-type production and export in Myanmar implies a poor investment and business environment, including import controls.

The CMP arrangement is, of course, applicable to other industrial sub-sectors and is already present in industries such as shoes, electronics, and medical and optical appliances. However, the arrangement is used rarely and with limited success in Myanmar, probably because it demands a larger initial investment, more highly trained workers, and a more reliable infrastructure. Given the present investment climate and industrial fundamentals in Myanmar, the CMP arrangement could create "enclaves" only in relatively straightforward lines of production, such as garment manufacture.

Industrial policy and the export-oriented garment industry

The rapid growth of the garment industry was led by the private sector. Table 10 shows that the private sector, particularly local companies, increased its export share during the boom period from the late 1990s up to 2002. As was the case with the import-substitution industry up to 1997, the government simply allowed private sector firms to grow by themselves, provided that this did not affect the businesses of the SEEs.

At the outset, the MTI, the only SEE in the field of textile and garment manufacturing in the early 1990s, established several joint ventures with foreign companies (Kudo, 2005b: 18–20).[20] However, the MTI devoted increasing attention to upstream industries, such as spinning and weaving, and apparently lost interest in the downstream garment industry, leaving it in the hands of private businesses, both local and foreign.

The garment industry grew by following an export-led development strategy. In a sense, it developed along the same lines as beans and pulses in the 1990s, the cultivation of which expanded rapidly by utilizing untapped domestic resources, including arable land and labour during the dry season (Chapter 5). The sudden emergence of the Indian export market provided farmers and merchants with the opportunity to use these idle resources more fully and effectively. As for the garment industry, large export markets were provided by the US and the EU under the MFA, and unemployed and/or underemployed labour was mobilized from both urban and rural areas for this extremely labour-intensive industry. The garment industry's usage of conventional technology and low requirements for initial investments made

Table 10 Myanmar Garments Export by Type of Firms (%)

	Type of Firm	FY 1993	FY 1994	FY 1995	FY 1996	FY 1997	FY 1998	FY 1999	FY 2000	FY 2001	FY 2002	FY 2003	FY 2004
Public Sector	SEEs	0.9%	0.6%	0.5%	0.4%	0.2%	1.4%	0.0%	0.2%	0.0%	0.0%	0.0%	0.0%
	Foreign JV with SEEs	62.3%	75.4%	61.6%	57.6%	42.9%	34.9%	3.9%	9.7%	7.8%	7.2%	4.6%	1.6%
Private Sector	Private Local	4.3%	2.1%	2.8%	4.7%	12.1%	31.4%	73.9%	62.3%	67.5%	65.9%	61.4%	59.8%
	100% Foreign	0.0%	0.0%	2.6%	2.6%	6.5%	9.7%	12.2%	17.6%	13.8%	16.8%	23.6%	26.2%
	Foreign JV with Private Firms	0.0%	0.7%	1.2%	2.1%	0.7%	0.7%	0.9%	3.8%	4.0%	2.7%	3.0%	3.5%
	Foreign JV with UMEHL	32.5%	21.2%	31.2%	32.7%	37.6%	19.9%	2.6%	6.4%	6.9%	7.4%	7.4%	8.9%
	Miscellaneous Exporter	0.0%	0.0%	0.0%	0.0%	0.0%	2.1%	6.3%	0.0%	0.0%	0.0%	0.0%	0.0%
Total		100.0%	100.0%	100.0%	100.0%	100.0%	100.0%	100.0%	100.0%	100.0%	100.0%	100.0%	100.0%

Note: UMEHL is a military–affiliated company.

Source: Export Data reconstructed by the author.

Table 11 Infrastructure Access and Stocks (%)

	Water Supply access	Sanitation access	Electricity access	Telephone access	Internet access
Myanmar	72	64	5	1	0.1
Cambodia	44	22	17	4	0.2
Lao PDR	58	30	41	3	0.3
Vietnam	49	25	81	9	4.3
Thailand	93	98	84	50	11.1
China	76	39	99	42	6.3

Source: ADB, *Connecting East Asia* (2005: 9).

it possible for local entrepreneurs who had neither high-level technology nor large amounts of capital, to enter the industry, employing low-wage workers.

Moreover, private garment manufacturers successfully avoided competition with the public sector for scarce foreign currency and imported raw materials by means of the CMP arrangement. They exported all of their products to the overseas markets, which lay beyond the reach of the SEEs. The rapid growth of the garment industry led by the private sector had no affect on the SEEs, so the Myanmar government simply let matters unfold. Indeed, the success of this sector was neither intended nor promoted by the government.[21] On the contrary, it was a self-sustaining growth led by the private sector through export market incentives.

Infrastructure Development: A Failure of the SEEs

While the private-sector-led growth flourished in the manufacturing and construction sub-sectors under the open-door policy, the infrastructure sub-sector, long monopolized by the SEEs, recorded serious failures in providing much-needed services. Insufficient coverage and the poor delivery of public services have seriously hindered the industrial development of the country.

Inadequate access

All over the world, firms with access to modern telecommunications services, a reliable electricity supply, and efficient transport links stand out from those without these facilities (World Bank, 2005: 124). Private firms in Myanmar lack almost everything, even compared to poor countries, such as Cambodia and the Lao PDR (Table 11). Myanmar's private firms themselves recognize the negative impact of poor infrastructure on their economic activities. Our

Table 12 Rating of Problems by Private Firms

	Big problem	Problem	No Problem
Domestic/local banking	47	53	67
Inadequate infrastructure	21	49	97
Frequent changes of systems and insufficient information disclosure	20	58	89
Regulations/procedures for import	16	30	121
Foreign currency related problems	11	36	120
Non-disclosure of customs-related information	11	34	122
Levies for domestic transportation	8	35	124
Export Tax	6	13	148
Regulations on foreign currency remittance	5	28	134
Regulations/procedures for export	4	20	143
International banking	4	10	153
Monopoly of SEEs	3	17	147
Others	2	1	164

Source: Author's survey, 2003.

survey indicated that the need to improve an inadequate infrastructure is one of the most urgent priorities of Myanmar businessmen (Table 12).

The failure of the socialist regime to invest sufficiently in infrastructure has severely handicapped the country in its drive towards a market economy. The present government has made a serious effort to build up the infrastructure, but indices and survey results suggest that little, if any, progress has been made.

Insufficient investment

The allocation of public investment underwent a drastic change in the 1990s, and became more balanced and appropriate for a market economy (Table 13).[22] An increased share of public investment has been devoted to infrastructure development, including public works (construction), transport and communications, with a smaller share of expenditure allocated for the production and services sectors, such as industry and trade. The share of the industrial sector (manufacturing) fell considerably, from 36 per cent in FY 1980 to 18 per cent in FY 1985 and 6 per cent in FY 1999. As far as the

Table 13 Public Investment by Sector, Composition (%)

	FY1980	FY1985	FY1990	FY1995	FY1996	FY1997	FY1998	FY1999
Agriculture	11.5	11.9	5.4	16.7	11.0	13.2	20.5	14.2
Livestock and Fisheries	6.9	2.8	1.0	0.2	0.3	0.2	0.2	0.1
Forestry	3.5	4.1	2.9	1.0	1.6	1.4	1.1	1.5
Mines	7.4	1.5	1.2	0.4	0.2	0.1	0.1	0.0
Industry	36.1	17.7	4.8	0.9	1.7	2.3	2.3	5.7
Energy	5.3	22.0	8.0	3.4	4.8	6.7	4.8	6.6
Construction	3.6	6.0	9.5	12.1	11.9	20.5	15.7	20.3
Transport and Communications	12.6	12.7	12.3	15.4	17.4	16.6	15.4	15.0
Social Services	2.3	9.1	20.3	10.9	16.0	11.4	6.4	8.0
Finance	0.5	0.5	3.2	1.5	0.8	1.0	0.6	1.1
Trade	2.2	3.6	2.5	2.0	1.4	1.1	0.7	0.8
Defence	4.8	5.6	15.6	31.9	30.5	22.6	29.7	22.9
Administration	2.0	1.7	5.9	3.5	2.4	2.7	2.6	3.8
Development Committees	1.3	0.7	7.5	0.0	0.0	0.0	0.0	0.0
TOTAL	100.0	100.0	100.0	100.0	100.0	100.0	100.0	100.0

Source: CSO, *Statistical Yearbook* (2003).

production sector was concerned, spending on agricultural development was given priority. Agriculture absorbed 14 per cent of total public investment in FY 1999. Although the detailed budget allocation within the agricultural sector is unknown, the emphasis seems to have been on infrastructure development, including the construction of dams, reservoirs and irrigation systems. This is a significant departure from the past public policy of investing heavily in publicly-owned industry.[23] The figures in this table do not reveal the real significance of the capital investment in the infrastructure sector. Here, the author calculated the capital investment of the SEEs per thousand of the nominal GDP, a method that makes it possible to capture the real economic value of investment.[24]

It is rather surprising to see that the figures shown in Table 14 declined in the 1990s. Although the government proudly claimed that it had spent heavily on infrastructure development since seizing power, spending in actual terms declined. The government invested far less in infrastructure development in the 1990s than in FY 1985. No single infrastructure sector received more capital investment in the 1990s than in FY 1985 or FY 1990. The figures do not support the generally held impression that the SLORC/SPDC government emphasized infrastructure development far more than the previous socialist regime. The government has constructed many roads, bridges, dams, power plants, airports and so forth (Ministry of Information, 2003), but it had failed to mobilize sufficient resources for constructing infrastructure that is in line with overall economic growth.[25]

Due to poor investment policies in the 1990s, infrastructure facilities and services have not shown any improvement. Table 15 shows that infrastructure capacity and/or services even declined in some sectors during the 1990s; for example, the air freight total for FY 2002 was only 60 per cent of that for FY 1990, while the number of passengers travelling by road in FY 2002 was only 40 per cent of the figure for FY 1990.[26] In most respects, the provision of the infrastructure failed to keep pace with the growth in GDP. The figures indicate a worsening, or at best stagnation, of the infrastructure supply capacity.

Financial loss due to policy-directed low product prices

The shortage of public investment capital was not the only reason for lacklustre infrastructure development in the 1990s. The inefficient management of the SEEs within the infrastructure sector also hampered growth. Most of the SEEs simply failed to carry out daily business activity.

Apart from capital investment, the SEEs in the infrastructure sector lost money on their day-to-day operations. As shown in Table 16, most of

Table 14 SEEs' Capital Investment in Main Infrastructure Sectors, as of GDP (%)

	FY1985	FY1990	FY1995	FY1996	FY1997	FY1998	FY1999
Energy	25.1	5.4	2.3	3.5	4.1	2.4	2.5
Myanma Oil and Gas Enterprise	1.1	0.5	0.0	0.3	0.2	0.3	0.5
Myanma Electric Power Enterprise	11.8	4.7	2.2	3.0	3.7	1.9	1.9
Public Works	0.2	0.2	0.7	0.4	0.1	0.1	0.1
Transport (Water, Air)	8.1	1.7	0.8	1.9	1.4	0.6	0.5
Rail Transport	3.6	3.1	5.8	7.6	5.8	3.0	2.7
Myanma Railways	2.6	2.9	5.7	7.5	5.6	2.9	2.6
Road Transport	1.0	0.2	0.1	0.2	0.1	0.1	0.2
Telecommunications, Post & Telegraph	1.7	2.6	1.3	1.3	1.1	0.8	0.6
Industry	19.6	3.0	0.6	0.6	0.8	0.7	1.4
Industry (1)	15.8	3.0	0.4	0.6	0.7	0.4	1.0
Industry (2)	3.7	0.1	0.1	0.0	0.1	0.2	0.4

Source: CSO, *Statistical Yearbook* (2003).

Table 15 Performance Indexes for Infrastructure Development

	FY 1985	FY 1990	FY 1995	FY 2000	FY 2002	Increase from FY 1985 to FY 2002	Increase from FY 1990 to FY 2002
Electricity							
Electric Power, Installed Capacity (MW)	684	804	982	1,171	1,190	1.7	1.5
Electric Power, Generation (Million KW)	2,119	2,643	3,762	5,118	5,864	2.8	2.2
Electric Power, Consumption (Million KW)	1,460	1,675	2,262	3,268	4,691	3.2	2.8
Transport							
Railways: Passengers (in thousands)	55,012	53,180	53,928	60,486	61,763	1.1	1.2
Railways: Freight (in ton miles)	271,848	306,861	551,594	750,040	723,098	2.7	2.4
Airways: Passengers (in thousands)	466	416	637	448	500	1.1	1.2
Airways: Freight (in ton miles)	1,209	688	482	705	435	0.4	0.6
Inland Waters: Passengers (in thousands)	20,313	27,481	24,979	23,270	24,199	1.2	0.9
Inland Waters: Freight (in ton miles)	307,535	325,643	322,601	344,381	370,872	1.2	1.1
Road: Passengers in Yangon (in thousands)	82,994	97,391	116,703	37,061	37,879	0.5	0.4
Road: Freight (in ton miles)	157,638	76,842	147,393	189,893	208,847	1.3	2.7
Arterial Highways (miles)	14,417	14,951	17,299	17,874	18,112	1.3	1.2
Registered Motor Vehicles (number)	141,015	178,500	302,833	442,264	466,708	3.3	2.6
Communications							
Telephones (number)	59,343	86,333	169,530	282,853	351,763	5.9	4.1
Mobile Phones (number)	–	–	5,234	26,960	94,736	–	–
e-mail subscribers (number)	–	–	289 (FY 1998)	3,273	12,706	–	–
Internet users (number)	–	–	–	40	7,240	–	–
Real GDP (Million Kyat, 1985 Prices)	55,989.3	50,259.5	66,741.6	100,274.8	135,972.6	2.4	2.7

them could not even cover operational costs from their revenues. Moreover, the deficits increased considerably in FY 1997 and FY 1998; for example, Myanmar Electric Power Enterprise (MEPE), which had recorded a surplus ever since FY 1980, suddenly plunged into the red in FY 1998 and FY 1999. Enterprises running various modes of transport followed the same pattern. The five SEEs engaged in waterways and airways went into the red in FY 1997 and FY 1999; Myanmar Railways was in deficit in FY 1998 and FY 1999 after generating a comfortable surplus for many years; and Road Transport suffered losses in FY 1996 and FY 1997. The telecommunications, posts and telegraph sector was an exception and enjoyed a relatively substantial surplus up to FY 1999.

What accounts for the deterioration of the SEEs? The main problem was unreasonably low-prices for services. Most of the tariff rates charged by the public utilities owned by the SEEs were suppressed grossly below the parallel market prices. Three salient examples (electricity, post and telecommunications and petroleum) will be discussed below. In addition to setting low prices, the SEEs favoured particular groups, such as other SEEs, military units and related enterprises, and governmental officials, offering these clients cheaper tariff rates. Moreover, revisions of rates often lagged behind the rapid devaluation of the kyat, but most inputs for producing services depended on imports, including fuel and imported spare parts, creating significant foreign exchange costs. This seems to have contributed to the serious deterioration of the financial situation of the SEEs.

The SEEs are strictly controlled by various ministries, in other words, by the government. In 1989, the budget for all SEEs was consolidated into the State Fund Account (SFA), a practice that deprived them of their financial independence. When the SEEs lose money, they receive subsidies in compensation. When they make a profit, they pass it on to the SFA; thus, they have no financial incentive to increase revenues or reduce costs. The management of the SEEs is also highly centralized and they lack managerial independence. The government tell the SEEs how much they should invest each year, how much they should produce in terms of products and services, at what prices they should sell their products and services, and so forth. In reality, the SEEs are part of the government.

SEEs in the fields of electricity, communications and petroleum distribution

We will examine three key SEEs in the fields of electricity, communications and petroleum distribution to highlight the nature and difficulty of the management of the SEEs within the infrastructure sector.

Table 16 SEEs' Current Cash Budget (Kyat Million)

Industry ((1) & (2))	FY 1980	FY 1985	FY 1990	FY 1995	FY 1996	FY 1997	FY 1998	FY 1999
Receipts	4,435	5,491.4	6,377.2	10,691.4	13,388	17,660	24,558.8	32,387.7
Expenditures	4,448.6	5,129.4	5,744	10,907.8	12,452.6	17,522.6	27,596.2	33,269.6
Surplus/Deficit	–13.6	362	633.2	–216.4	935.4	137.4	–3,037.4	–881.9
% of Receipts	–0.3%	6.6%	9.9%	–2.0%	7.0%	0.8%	–12.4%	–2.7%
MEPE	*FY 1980*	*FY 1985*	*FY 1990*	*FY 1995*	*FY 1996*	*FY 1997*	*FY 1998*	*FY 1999*
Receipts	209.2	430.6	795.6	2,771.1	3,227.5	3,450.8	3,599.6	19,680.8
Expenditures	201.9	412.3	658.5	2,599.8	2,721.6	3,120.7	4,976.9	20,614.1
Surplus/Deficit	7.3	18.3	137.1	171.3	505.9	330.1	–1,377.3	–933.3
% of Receipts	3.5%	4.2%	17.2%	6.2%	15.7%	9.6%	–38.3%	–4.7%
Telecommunications, Post and Telegraph	*FY 1980*	*FY 1985*	*FY 1990*	*FY 1995*	*FY 1996*	*FY 1997*	*FY 1998*	*FY 1999*
Receipts	96.6	255.9	445.1	1,834.5	2,256.2	3,401.7	4,248	5,168
Expenditures	65.7	130.9	316.9	1,527.8	2,066.6	2,403.2	3,558.9	4,491.2
Surplus/Deficit	30.9	125	128.2	306.7	189.6	998.5	689.1	676.8
% of Receipts	32.0%	48.8%	28.8%	16.7%	8.4%	29.4%	16.2%	13.1%
MPPE	*FY 1980*	*FY 1985*	*FY 1990*	*FY 1995*	*FY 1996*	*FY 1997*	*FY 1998*	*FY 1999*
Receipts	393.9	795.6	1,958.6	5,070.2	4,907.2	30,142.6	48,686.1	61,705.6
Expenditures	519.1	808.8	2,020.6	5,139.3	5,323.4	32,988.5	55,467.8	61,289.5
Surplus/Deficit	–125.2	–13.2	–62	–69.1	–416.2	–2,845.9	–6,781.7	416.1
% of Receipts	–31.8%	–1.7%	–3.2%	–1.4%	–8.5%	–9.4%	–13.9%	0.7%

Table 16 continued

Transport (5 SEEs: Water & Air)	FY 1980	FY 1985	FY 1990	FY 1995	FY 1996	FY 1997	FY 1998	FY 1999
Receipts	630.9	827.7	1,111.8	2,362.6	3,202.1	3,445.9	5,455.3	5,029.7
Expenditures	637.4	759.8	899.1	2,006.9	2,519.8	3,759.6	5,297.7	5,482.3
Surplus/Deficit	-6.5	67.9	212.7	355.7	682.3	-313.7	157.6	-452.6
% of Receipts	-1.0%	8.2%	19.1%	15.1%	21.3%	-9.1%	2.9%	-9.0%

Myanmar Railways	FY 1980	FY 1985	FY 1990	FY 1995	FY 1996	FY 1997	FY 1998	FY 1999
Receipts	291.4	349.3	835.1	2,065.4	2,570.5	4,237.7	5,190.9	5,250
Expenditures	283.8	304.3	672.3	1,902.8	2,066	3,162.2	5,414.7	5,457.9
Surplus/Deficit	7.6	45	162.8	162.6	504.5	1,075.5	-223.8	-207.9
% of Receipts	2.6%	12.9%	19.5%	7.9%	19.6%	25.4%	-4.3%	-4.0%

Road Transport	FY 1980	FY 1985	FY 1990	FY 1995	FY 1996	FY 1997	FY 1998	FY 1999
Receipts	173	214.9	349.1	711.7	663.5	1,086.6	1,265.2	1,158
Expenditures	159.8	171.6	299.8	677.7	731.1	1,197.6	1,176.4	1,148.6
Surplus/Deficit	13.2	43.3	49.3	34	-67.6	-111	88.8	9.4
% of Receipts	7.6%	20.1%	14.1%	4.8%	-10.2%	-10.2%	7.0%	0.8%

Grand Total	FY 1980	FY 1985	FY 1990	FY 1995	FY 1996	FY 1997	FY 1998	FY 1999
Receipts	17,946.2	22,335	31,327.4	87,185.1	108,555	184,921.2	242,155.5	315,141.7
Expenditures	18,121.6	22,503.3	32,219.1	91,624.6	119,936.5	214,639.7	309,587.1	365,695.2
Surplus/Deficit	-175.4	-168.3	-891.7	-4,439.5	-11,381.5	-29,718.5	-67,431.6	-50,553.5
% of Receipts	-1.0%	-0.8%	-2.8%	-5.1%	-10.5%	-16.1%	-27.8%	-16.0%

Source: CSO, *Statistical Yearbook* (2003).

MEPE

The supply of electricity in Myanmar is monopolized by the Myanmar Electric Power Enterprise (MEPE), an SEE that falls under the jurisdiction of the Ministry of Electricity. The State-owned Economic Enterprises Law of 1989 stipulated that electricity generation should be performed exclusively by public enterprises. MEPE is the sole provider of electricity generation and transmission nationwide.

The total installed capacity of electricity was 1335 MW in May 2005 (CSO, 2005: 28). The per capita consumption of electricity was 108 KW, which is amongst the lowest in the world. Only 5 per cent of Myanmar's population has access to electricity, a far lower percentage than in Cambodia (17 per cent) and the Lao PDR (41 per cent; Table 11). Demand for electricity tends to increase more rapidly than GDP in any economy during the early stages of economic development and this was true of Myanmar. To make matters worse, in FY 2001 around 15 per cent of electricity was lost during generation, transmission and distribution, further widening the demand/supply gap. The Economic Intelligence Unit (EIU) has estimated a 220 MW shortfall in electricity supply in Myanmar around 2004 (EIU, 2004: 20).

Because the supply of electricity is unreliable and insufficient, industrial firms depend on generators that run on diesel fuel. The market price of diesel is high, while the technical efficiency of electricity generation by small-scale generators is low. Independently generated electricity is expensive compared to power supplied through the grid. Moreover, the tariff rates are multi-tiered, and foreigners, both residents and organizations, must pay in US dollars or FEC, which makes the real charge for electricity for this group far higher than for others. A foreign garment factory located on Mingalardone Industrial Estate, one of the best industrial parks in Myanmar, experienced frequent, lengthy power failure and had no alternative but to use its own generator. In 2004, the firm's energy costs, including electricity from the grid and diesel oil, amounted to 1.4 times its labour costs.[27] Even in the highly labour-intensive garment industry, energy costs more than labour. Thus, the cheap labour costs in Myanmar have been offset by the expensive infrastructure services.

MPTE

The Myanmar Post and Telecommunication Enterprise (MPTE), a corporation that falls under the jurisdiction of the Ministry of Communications, Posts and Telegraphs, has long enjoyed a monopoly over the provision of telephone services. Their services are notorious for suffering from frequent disconnections, lengthy waiting times for connections, and high prices in the parallel market. As a result of the inadequate coverage and unreliable services, the market rates for telephone lines vary considerably from one telephone number to another. International phone calls are extortionately expensive; for example, it costs 4.5 US dollars per minute to phone Japan from Myanmar.

Mobile phones are scarce and for privileged customers only, such as military cadres, high ranking government officials and the so-called crony businesspeople. Some mobile phones are resold to actual customers who have a pressing need for telephone services and can afford to pay the extravagant market prices.

As for internet providers, the government has allowed one private company to enter this market, a move that appears to have improved the Myanmar's internet environment. Nonetheless, internet accessibility lags far behind neighbouring countries, where liberalization has progressed far further. The internet café is a recent phenomenon, found only in Yangon, Mandalay and other big cities. Internet access through personal computers at home is far beyond the wildest dreams of the majority of the population, and even the issuance of email accounts is relatively limited.

MPPE

The Myanmar Petroleum Products Enterprise (MPPE) is the sole enterprise responsible for the distribution and sale of petroleum products in Myanmar. MPPE has 4 main fuel terminals, 26 sub-fuel terminals, 11 aviation depots and 256 filling stations nationwide.[28] MPPE presents a typical case of an enterprise that has fallen prey to rent-seeking activities. In June 2005, their filling stations were selling petrol and diesel at the official rates of 180 and 160 kyat/gallon respectively, whereas the free market rates for these two fuels were approximately 2,000 and 2,300 kyat/gallon respectively.[29] Such pricing naturally creates gross shortages at the official prices, but the MPPE has arbitrary power over allocation. In principle, car owners in Yangon are entitled to two gallons per car per day, although some privileged groups, such as government officials, other SEEs, and military units, are allowed extra allocations. All of these surplus allocations are resold on the parallel market, providing windfalls for the sellers. The fuel is then distributed to actual consumers by "black" merchants who, although operating beyond the law, are openly present, buying and selling fuel immediately next to the filling stations that have supplied them.

These pricing policies made the MPPE one of the biggest loss-making SEEs in Myanmar, accounting for about 10 per cent of the total losses by SEEs in FY 1997 and FY 1998 in current cash budget terms. Imports of refined mineral oil grew as demand expanded, and increased approximately nine-fold between FY 1990 and FY 2003. The share of total imports of refined mineral oil also increased, from less than 5 per cent in the mid-1990s to 13 per cent in FY 2003. This import trend suggests that MPPE's present deficit is growing, and, moreover, its supply of subsidized fuel deters other SEEs and privileged groups from introducing managerial and structural reforms, resulting in more distorted resource allocations.

Industrial Policy and Infrastructure Development

It is probable that the present government genuinely intended to build a sufficient infrastructure for national economic development, as they often claim, although budgetary difficulties and increased defence expenditure constrained the capital investment in the infrastructure and the low-priced services failed to recover even daily operational costs, which eventually harmed the financial capability of the SEEs.

Why did the government fail to invite private sector participation in infrastructure development? And why, having abused their monopoly of the market, did they not charge the customers more expensive tariff rates? The answers to these questions are probably related to the government's objectives regarding the provision of infrastructure services. The government intended to provide infrastructure services as cheaply as possible. Such services are indispensable to people's daily lives and to industrial development. In a sense, infrastructure services are political goods and the government must be solely responsible for them.

Whatever the government's true objectives, however, it would be difficult for the SEEs to finance huge infrastructure constructions and simultaneously operate their businesses in a proper manner, as long as the government sticks to its goal of providing infrastructure services at low prices. The SEEs in the field of infrastructure development will fail to survive independently, resulting in stunted infrastructure in Myanmar.

Conclusion

Myanmar's open-door policy drastically changed the business environment for the private sector. Public demand for consumer goods and the improved access to imported raw materials facilitated the entry of local entrepreneurs into import-substitution and the construction business in the first half of the 1990s, although by the mid-1990s, as the trade deficit expanded and the foreign reserves dwindled, the government gradually tightened import controls and restricted private business activities. The bursting of the property and real estate bubble and the Asian economic crisis of 1997 seriously affected Myanmar's economy and gave birth to the Trade Policy Council (TPC), which laid down new, and rather ad hoc, regulations and restrictions on trade and exchange systems. In addition, the government revived state-owned economic enterprise programmes and accelerated the construction of state-run factories in the import-substitution industries from around 2000, and public enterprises pushed aside burgeoning private sector in the import-substitution industries by gaining privileged access to raw materials and to markets.

However, the open-door policy provided opportunities for private sector companies to grow by serving export markets. A new economic sphere that opened up for private firms after the Asian economic crisis was the garment industry, which expanded rapidly thanks to large orders from the US and EU markets under the MFA regime. The major players were local industrialists who had engaged in import-substitution or construction in the previous period, and they successfully avoided import-related problems by utilizing the CMP arrangement. The MTI, the only SEE in this field, prioritized the upstream industries, such as spinning and weaving, but left the downstream garment industry for export in the hands of the private sector.

The infrastructure sector had long been monopolized by the SEE, and had failed to keep pace with the overall economic growth. The government's objective in this area is to provide services that are indispensable to both people's daily lives and industrial development at low prices to the population, the privileged sector in particular. The government probably intended to stabilize commodity prices by providing a low-priced infrastructure and utility services.

How can we characterize the industrial policies in Myanmar after 1988? The government allowed the private sector to develop as long as it did not harm the public sector or did not compete with SEEs. The garment industry provides a good example of this arrangement. The government did nothing to promote it, but also did nothing to impede it.[30] By contrast, the government continues to allow public enterprises to monopolize infrastructure services.

There are some commonalities between agriculture and industry. One is a similarity between rice in agriculture and infrastructure services in industry; another between beans and pulses in agriculture and garments in industry. The former set of commodities is far more important according to the government's evaluation and, as a result, falls under government control. The latter set of commodities is less important according to their criteria, and falls outside the remit of government interests.[31] The policy consequences are also similar. The former recorded prolonged stagnation, whereas the latter registered brisk growth.

If industrial policies remain unchanged, the only option for industrial development in Myanmar is private-sector-driven, self-sustaining growth in fields that fall outside government intervention and public sector enterprises. However, the sphere of freedom for private sector activities has been shrinking as the government strengthens its control over the private sector and the international community closes export markets to Myanmar goods. Without fundamental policy changes and serious reform programmes, including those related to the SEEs, broad-based industrial development is not possible in Myanmar.

Appendix: A Survey of the Private Firms in Myanmar

Objectives

A study team from the Institute of Developing Economies (IDE) conducted a survey of private firms in Myanmar in 2003 with the aim of gaining an overview of the current situation regarding the private sector and the business environment in Myanmar. The questionnaire was prepared and tested by the study team and the data collection was entrusted to a marketing and research company working under the supervision of the IDE study team.

The Samples

A total of 167 private firms were selected from Yangon and Mandalay. With regard to the former, the sampling was based on the sector classification provided by the *Yangon Directory 2003*. For Mandalay, we chose samples mainly from the manufacturing sector, since this area is famous as a production centre in Myanmar.

The sample firms were originally classified into ten categories: namely, exporters of garments, exporters of agricultural produce, exporters of marine products, manufacturers of agricultural produce, manufacturers of industrial products, manufacturers of consumer products, construction, services for businesses, services for consumers, and the retail trade.

For convenience of description and analysis in this paper, the author streamlined these ten categories into three broad sectors containing seven categories. The three sectors are manufacturing, construction and services. The manufacturing sector is further divided into four categories (namely, garments, agricultural and marine products, industrial goods and consumer goods), while services are divided into the two groups of services for businesses: software, advertising, and consultancy, and services for consumers, such as restaurants and hotels. The figures for each category are shown below.

Sector Classification of Samples

		Yangon	*Mandalay*	*Total*
	Garments	12	1	13
Manufacturing	Agriculture and Marine	18	2	20
	Industrial Goods	18	6	24
	Consumer Goods	41	22	63
Construction		13	1	14
Services	For Businesses	15	0	15
	For Consumers	17	1	18
Total		134	33	167

Field Surveys

The field surveys were conducted by trained enumerators. The author of this paper participated in the field surveys on several occasions in order to obtain first-hand knowledge from the interviews with the founders, owners and managers of the private enterprises as well as to ensure that the surveys were of reasonable quality. The field surveys were conducted between October and December 2003.

Notes

1   For details, see Myat Thein (2004).

2   For an outline of the survey, see the *Appendix: A Survey on Private Firms in Myanmar*, provided at the end of this chapter.

3   This law stipulates the 12 economic activities that the public sector should monopolize, including petroleum and natural gas exploration and exploitation, electricity generation, teak extraction, postal and telecommunications services, and broadcasting and television services.

4   According to the Private Industrial Enterprise Law, enacted in November 1990, any private industrial enterprise using energy of three horsepower and above and/or employing ten or more wage-earning workers is required to register with the Ministry of Industry (1). The procedures relating to the Private Industrial

Enterprise Law were prescribed on 1 February 1991, in which the relevant authorities requested that the existing private industrial enterprises should apply for registration within 120 days, during which time they would be allowed to continue their production activities before receiving a directive from the Directorate.

5   See Chapter 3 for details.

6   There were exceptions for the straightforward processing of pulses and beans, and fish and prawns, which are agricultural and marine products rather than manufactured ones.

7   FY stands for the Fiscal Year, starting from April and ending in March.

8   Including food and beverages, clothing, household goods, and printing and publishing.

9   The timing of such a policy change coincided with the start of natural gas exports to Thailand, which obviously alleviated the shortage of foreign currency in Myanmar. Immediately following the gas exports, Myanmar's foreign reserves increased from 238.9 million US$, equivalent to 1.2 months of imports, in July 2001, to 400.2 million US$, equivalent to 2.2 months imports, in August 2001 (IMF). At the same time, the Chinese economic cooperation programmes seem to be supporting the construction of state-owned factories in Myanmar, although accurate information is unavailable in this regard; see Kudo (2006) for more details.

10 The series consisted of 17 articles, starting on 17 September 2001 and ending on 25 January 2002.

11 New Light of Myanmar, *Industrial Development-2*, 21 Sept. 2001.

12 These slogans are displayed in every state-run factory.

13 Some products produced by SEEs competed more with imported goods than with items produced by local private firms. For example, as the import volume of textiles increased during the first half of the 1990s, the SEE's production of fabric declined from 38.1 million yards in FY 1990 to 10.9 million yards in FY 1997. The government imposed import restrictions, and SEE production recovered to 25.6 million yards in FY 2000. See Kudo (2008) for details.

14 See Chapter 5 for a more detailed discussion of agro-based industry, and U Tin Htut Oo and Kudo (2003) for a crop-wise overview.

15 This section is drawn mainly from Kudo (2005b).

16 Twenty-two countries that are major importers of Myanmar-made clothes were selected, based on the author's field survey in Yangon in 2005.

17 For convenience, "MFA" rather than "ATC" is used in this chapter.

18 Based on his survey of Vietnamese firms, Goto classified the so-called "FOB" contractual arrangements into three types. The first type is where Vietnamese firms purchase input materials for processing from suppliers that are designated by foreign buyers (FOB Type I). The second type is where Vietnamese firms receive garment samples from foreign buyers (FOB Type II). The third type is where the Vietnamese firms initiate the production of garments based on their own design, with no prior commitment of any kind from foreign buyers (FOB

Type III) (Goto, 2002). The term "FOB" here has no relationship with "Free on Board", "FOB" as defined under Incoterms.

[19] CMT (Cutting, Making and Trimming) is the term generally used in Vietnam for what is known as CMP in Myanmar.

[20] There seem to be several reasons why foreign companies chose state-owned and military-related enterprises as their counterparts in the early 1990s. First, state-owned and military-related enterprises appeared to be reliable and secure, since they were in power. Foreign companies shunned political risk after the military government opened its door to foreign capital in 1988. Second, private entrepreneurs and enterprises had not yet developed at that time. There were no capable private enterprises, in terms of both managerial and technological skills or financial capability. Third, these companies expected to enjoy the quota allocation of the US market by forming joint ventures with public and semi-public entities. Fourth, and most importantly, 100 per cent foreign investment in the garment industry was probably not yet permitted by the government, even though it was legally permissible under the Foreign Investment Law of 1988 (Kudo, 2005b: 19).

[21] The only favourable practice implemented by the government was a rather flexible allocation of quotas to private firms from 1998, until then they were monopolized by the MTI and some military-related companies, although the quota utilization ratio remained extremely low. However, there was no explicit announcement of the change, and it was probably implemented step-by-step at the operational rather than at the policy level.

[22] The fiscal data of the Myanmar government, including that relating to the SEEs, is available only up to FY 1999, even in the latest issue of the *Statistical Yearbook, 2005*.

[23] Myat Thein also commented on the more-balanced public allocation by the SLORC/SPDC government, stating that, "The new emphasis given to infrastructure development, and especially transport, also seems to be in accord with the market-oriented policy. The large proportion of public investment in the social sector, however, was taken up largely by defence" (Myat Thein, 2004: 133). As Myat Thein pointed out, "defence" increased its share from 6 per cent in FY 1985 to 32 per cent in FY 1995; such an allocation cannot be regarded as *balanced*.

[24] Note that the ratio between the capital investments of the SEEs to the nominal GDP is also problematic because a significant portion of the capital investments involved foreign imports valued at the much over-valued exchange rate which, in turn, depressed the ratio significantly.

[25] In retrospect, the author doubts whether the more *balanced* allocation of public investment in the 1990s resulted solely from the sudden suspension of ODA, which had previously been poured into SEEs in the industrial sector (Kudo, 1998). He believes that the apparently renewed allocation policy was not created through a resolute change in public investment policy that was in accord with a drive towards a market economy.

26 Note that the figures may not include private services; for example, some private airline services and many private bus services started their operations in the 1990s.

27 Personal communication from the factory manager in June 2005.

28 The energy sector of the Myanmar's government homepage is available at <http://www.energy.gov.mm/>.

29 Personal interviews with taxi drivers in Yangon in June 2005. The government increased the official prices of petrol and diesel increased to 1500 kyat/gallon on 20 October 2006.

30 Regarding the government's regulation and taxation of the garment industry, see Kudo (2005a: 33–35).

31 See Chapter 5 in this volume for a detailed discussion.

CHAPTER 3

Trade, Foreign Investment and Myanmar's Economic Development in the Transition to an Open Economy

Toshihiro Kudo and Fumiharu Mieno

Introduction

Myanmar's transition into a market economy began with a series of open-door policies. Soon after the military took power in 1988, the State Law and Order Restoration Council (SLORC), later re-constituted as the State Peace and Development Council (SPDC), allowed private sector businesses to engage in external trade and retain their export earnings, and started to legitimize and formalize the border trade with neighbouring countries, an activity hitherto deemed illegal. Following this, in November 1988, foreign investment was permitted under a new a Foreign Investment Law. These changes released Myanmar's economy from the isolationist foreign policy of the quarter-century long Socialist era and launched an effort to re-integrate the country with regional and world markets.

Myanmar opened its doors to the rest of the world during a period of globalization and regionalization, and, consequently, the open-door policy drastically changed Myanmar's external economy. Foreign trade rapidly increased during the 1990s and up to 2005, and foreign direct investment flowed into the country, albeit with some fluctuations. As the volume of trade increased, Myanmar expanded its trade relations with its neighbouring countries, becoming integrated into regional markets. The commodities that made up exports and imports also changed during the transitional period.

With advances in globalization and regionalization, an export-oriented and foreign investment-driven development strategy has become an orthodox and promising policy for developing economies. Myanmar, which experienced a hostile international economic environment, did not follow such a development strategy and apparently failed to achieve rapid economic growth. Nevertheless, even in Myanmar the open-door policy and the attendant growth in trade were the most powerful forces affecting the process of economic development and industrial change.

This chapter examines the development of, and changes in, Myanmar's external sector during the transition to an open economy, and the relationship between overseas trade and economic performance. Progress towards an open, market-based economy is also evaluated. The first section reviews the open-door policy itself and trade performance, and evaluates the extent to which the economy of Myanmar depends on foreign trade. The second section discusses changes in the trading partners, and indicates the regionalization of trade that has resulted from the enhanced importance of cross-border trading transactions. The third section examines inflows of foreign investment, and evaluates their impact on Myanmar's overall economic growth. In the conclusion, the authors summarize the discussion and outline some policy implications.

The Open-Door Policy and Trade Performance

Opening the Door

During the socialist period, the Myanmar government, for many years, pursued self-reliance in both political and economic terms. The idea of self-reliance was, in practice, translated into a closed-door or inward-looking policy, which actually suited the control-oriented socialist economic system. As far as its economy was concerned, Myanmar cut itself off from the rest of the world. In the absence of inflows of foreign capital, agriculture was the most important, and indeed almost the only, reliable resource available to the government for financing their industrial projects. As a result, agriculture was heavily exploited and lost its growth potential. From the 1970s onwards, the agricultural sector no longer earned a significant amount of foreign currency (Myat Thein, 2004: 73–81).

Against this background, the socialist government started to accept foreign aid. Coincidentally, some western allies, Japan and West Germany in particular, were happy to provide considerable amounts of official economic assistance to this non-aligned nation, which the United States basically regarded as a countervailing power against Communist China. As for the Myanmar socialist government, Official Development Assistance (ODA) seems to have come in the form of politically low-cost foreign capital rather than private foreign investment (Kudo, 1998: 161–62). Between 1978 and

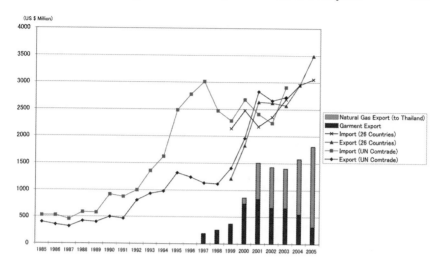

Figure 1   Myanmar's Trade, 1985–2005

Sources: United Nations Commodity Trade Statistics (UN Comtrade); Customs Data of 26 Countries.

1988, ODA provision amounted to US$3,712.3 million, a sum equivalent to 15.1 per cent of Myanmar's total imports for the same period.

Most of the ODA, however, was suspended after the military government came to power. The international donor society adopted a critical stance towards the military regime on account of its poor human rights record, and as a result the newly-born government encountered a serious shortage of foreign currency. To obtain money quickly, the government provided timber and fishing concessions to Thai enterprises; in short, it altered its policy and opted for liberalizing international trade and allowing foreign investments in the territory of Myanmar. Myanmar's transition to a market economy inevitably and primarily meant the adoption of an open-door policy with regard to the international economy.

Growth of Trade and the Economy's Dependence upon Trade

Opening external trade to private enterprises greatly increased the number of exporters and importers in Myanmar. While about 1,000 exporters/importers had registered in FY 1989,[1] the number increased to about 2,700 in the following fiscal year, reaching nearly 9,000 by FY 1997. Accordingly, the trade volume grew. Myanmar's exports grew 6.8-fold between 1985 and 2003 and, during the same period, imports increased by 5.5 times (Figure 1).[2] For the same period, GDP grew by only 1.8 times.

However, despite this increase in the volume of foreign trade, the share of exports and imports of GDP steadily decreased, from 13.2 per cent in FY 1985 to 5.6 per cent in FY 1990 and further to 2.5 per cent in FY 1995, 1.1 per cent in FY 2000, and 0.4 per cent in FY 2003.[3] The external transactions are recorded at the official exchange rate, which has been fixed at approximately 6 kyat per US dollar. As the disparity between the official exchange rate and the parallel market rate has widened, so the volume of external trade recorded at the official exchange rate has become underestimated. The parallel market rate, according to Irrawaddy Online News, was 1,320 kyat per US dollar, as of 20 October 2006. For this reason, among others, it is difficult to measure the openness of the economy simply based on the share of external trade of GDP.

Trade volume per capita can be another indicator for measuring the openness of an economy. Myanmar's trade volume per capita steadily increased from US$25 in 1985 to US$35 in 1990, US$85 in 1995, US$92 in 2000 and US$106 in 2003. Indeed, the increasing importance of imported goods in daily life has been palpable to anyone visiting Yangon since around the mid-1990s. A visit to City Mart, one of the biggest supermarket chains in Myanmar, reveals a very wide range of imported consumer goods, most of which lay well beyond people's reach during the socialist period (Kudo ed., 2001: 24).

Be that as it may, Myanmar's trade volume per capita is still lower than that of the other new ASEAN members, including Cambodia, Laos and Vietnam, all of which launched their drive towards a market economy at almost the same time as Myanmar. Cambodia's trade volume per capita was US$345 in 2003; Laos's was US$140 and Vietnam's was US$561 in the same year (ADB, *Key Indicator* 2005). These figures reflect the underdevelopment of Myanmar's external trade.

Trade Structure and Import Controls in the 1990s

The open-door policy substantially increased Myanmar's external trade throughout the 1990s, up to 2005, although exports and imports did not grow in parallel (Figure 1). Imports grew more rapidly than exports in the 1990s. Imported goods poured into the emerging markets for consumer goods, the demand for which shot up following the many years when daily commodities and durables were in short supply during the socialist period. Moreover, the 1990s witnessed the emergence of the preliminary import-substitution industries, which were heavily dependent on imported machinery and raw materials.[4]

During the 1990s, Myanmar's exports consisted mainly of primary commodities. Among them, cash crops, such as beans and pulses and sesame, and marine products, such as fish and prawns, occupied the lion's share. After the late 1990s, however, the export structure apparently changed. Garment exports surged, followed by an expansion of natural gas exports.

A major cause of the slow growth in exports is thought to lie in the government's maintenance of a monopoly and restrictions on major export items. Teak exports, for example, have been monopolized and strictly controlled by the government. The extraction and exportation of teak lies in the hands of a single state-owned economic enterprise, Myanmar Timber Enterprise (MTE), a company controlled by the Ministry of Forestry under the State-owned Economic Enterprises Law of 1989. Rice exports were monopolized for many years by Myanma Agricultural Produce Trading (MAPT), a government enterprise run by the Ministry of Commerce.[5] Since 1998, the government has also restricted the handling of sesame exports to state-owned and military-related enterprises.[6]

The relatively slower growth in exports, combined with the rapid expansion of imports, generated a huge trade deficit, which, in 1997, reached US$1,879.9 million, 1.7 times greater than that of Myanmar's exports for that year. At the same time, the inflow of foreign direct investment dropped sharply after the Asian economic crisis of 1997. Confronted by a severe shortage of foreign currency, the government reacted by applying a series of restrictions on trade and on the foreign exchange system. In July 1997, a newly-established, extra-ministerial committee, the Trade Policy Council (TPC), was put in charge of strengthening controls on the private sector's economic activities.[7] The TPC imposed many severe restrictions, particularly on external transactions.

The most important policy change was to rescind the "import first" policy and replace it with an "export first" one, under which traders could import only against export earnings. The purpose of these restrictions and controls was to reduce imports, particularly those that the government deemed to be non-essential, including luxury goods. Essential goods are described in list A of the obligatory imports, the share of which should be more than 80 per cent of total imports, according to Ministry of Commerce notice No. 15/98 of October 1998. On the other hand, non-essential articles and/or luxury goods are set out in list B of non-obligatory imports. The share of this category is not permitted to exceed 20 per cent of total imports. The government urged private traders to reduce imports of non-essential and/or luxury goods and to give priority instead of essential goods, that is, goods

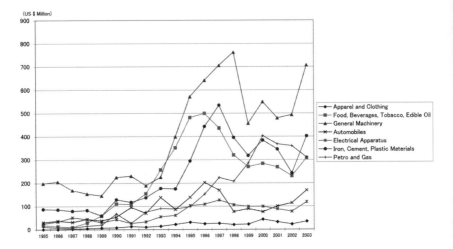

Figure 2 Imports of Major Commodities, 1985–2003
Source: UN Comtrade.

determined by the government to be necessary for economic stability. In
July 1997, the Central Bank set a limit on foreign currency transfers by
private firms (transfers overseas) to US$50,000 per month. The bank there-
after progressively tightened the limit, to US$30,000 per month in January
1999, US$20,000 per month in April 1999 and US$10,000 per month in
August 2000. Private banks were also deprived of foreign transactions, which
subsequently came to be monopolized by three government-owned banks:
the Myanmar Foreign Trade Bank (MFTB), the Myanmar Investment and
Commercial Bank (MICB) and the Myanmar Economic Bank (MEB).

As a result, Myanmar's imports decreased from US$3,010.6 million in
1997 to US$2,469.9 million in 1998 and further to US$2,285.9 million
in 1999. From then until 2002, imports stayed around this level, although
there were fluctuations. Even though the government intended to limit control to the importation of non-essential items and/or luxury goods, Figure 2
shows that the volume of almost all imports decreased substantially. There
were remarkable declines in the import not only of consumer goods, such
as food and beverages and automobiles, but also of machinery and industrial
raw materials, such as iron, cement and plastic resin. The government's new
trade policy deprived the private factories of access to imported machinery
and raw materials, inputs that are indispensable for the preliminary import-
substitution industrial development stage.

Export Growth and Relaxed Import Controls in the Twenty-first Century

Myanmar's external trade sector dramatically improved towards the end of the twentieth century and during the early twenty-first century. According to a variety of sources, the trade account briefly recorded a surplus and from 2001 to 2005 was approximately in balance (Figure 1).[8]

Both exports and imports contributed to this outcome. Strict import controls no doubt helped improve the trade balance, but the most important explanation seems to lie on the export side, and must be sought in the rapid growth of garment and natural gas exports. Garment exports boomed from 1998 to 2001 in response to the strong demand from the US and EU markets, although the expansion of garment exports then lost momentum as a result of the imposition of international trade sanctions. Particularly damaging were the US sanctions of 2003, which banned all imports of Myanmar products,[9] although the decline in garment exports was compensated for by increased earnings from natural gas exports from 2001 onwards, which in fact surpassed the value of garment exports.

Since the early 1990s, two large gas fields, Yadana and Yetagun in the Gulf of Martaban, had been developed by two consortia led by Total/Unocal and Texaco respectively, and from 1998 onwards gas from these fields was exported to Thailand by pipeline. In 2005, gas exports amounted to US$1,497.4 million, more than 40 per cent of total exports. Gas exports greatly improved Myanmar's foreign currency situation. The foreign reserves doubled from US$239 million to US$440 million in August 2001, when the export revenue was apparently paid. By June 2006, they had reached US$939 million. A large portion of the revenue from the gas exports goes to the national treasury, and the inflow of funds improved the foreign currency position of the public sector, including administrative organizations and SEEs. According to government statistics, the public sector recorded a trade surplus of 7,675.1 million kyat, equivalent to US$1,321.1 million for FY 2005 based on conversion at the official exchange rate. This income helped stabilize the local currency, the kyat.

The improved foreign currency position of the public sector may have reduced the government's need to use import restrictions and controls on the private sector to commandeer the foreign exchange earned by the private sector. After a period of stagnation between 1998 and 2001, imports steadily recovered up to 2005, according to data from 26 of Myanmar's trading partners. In short, Myanmar's external trade, both exports and imports, greatly improved in the early twenty-first century.

These facts seem to contradict the widespread impression that the government continues to impose import restrictions and controls. Indeed, many domestic manufacturers have complained that they have found it difficult to obtain imported machinery and raw materials. Moreover, government statistics show that Myanmar's imports declined from 18,377.7 million kyat (equivalent to US$2,734.5 million) in FY 2001 to 11,514.2 million kyat (equivalent to US$1,981.9 million) in FY 2005.

It is difficult to determine which statistics are accurate. It should be noted that the government's rules and regulations, whether on economic or other policies, are seldom modified or withdrawn once they have been announced; for example, an import ban on such things as instant noodles and snacks, announced in 1998, remains effective today, theoretically. Nevertheless, it is possible to buy these "banned" imported items at any supermarket in Yangon, Mandalay or other urban areas. In Myanmar, there is usually a big gap between the announcement of rules and regulations and their actual implementation. Moreover, quantitative controls are often preferred to tariffs and other rule-based policy measures as a means of curbing imports. Import licenses have become a major instrument of trade control and are used arbitrarily. Careful observation is, therefore, necessary in order to identify the real effects of trade-related policies on the trading activities in Myanmar.

The Regionalization of Trade

Myanmar's Enhanced Trade Relations with its Neighbours

The 1988 open-door policy greatly changed the geographical pattern of Myanmar's trade. During the socialist period, advanced countries, such as Japan and West Germany, were Myanmar's major trading partners, mainly because of the trading activities related to the receipt of ODA from these countries. In response to the birth of the military government in 1988, however, Western donors terminated their provision of ODA, and some Western countries imposed economic sanctions on the military government. A hostile international economic and commercial environment encouraged Myanmar to develop trading activities with its neighbours, particularly China and Thailand.

It is perhaps natural that, given the distances involved, Myanmar should trade with its immediate neighbours rather than with far-off, Western countries. Myanmar shares long borders with five neighbouring countries; namely, China (a border of 2,185 km), Thailand (1,800 km), India (1,463 km), Laos (235 km) and Bangladesh (193 km), and is close to China,

Southeast Asia, India and Bangladesh. Among these various countries and regions, there are differences in natural resource endowments and in industrial development, and these various economic and industrial complementarities have contributed to the development of trade throughout the region.

Neighbouring countries welcomed the emergence of an open-door policy in Myanmar towards the end of the 1980s. Just before the end of the Cold War, China departed from its traditional dual-track diplomacy that endorsed party-to-party relations between the China Communist Party (CCP) and the Burma Communist Party (BCP) alongside state-to-state relations. The CCP's covert and overt support of the BCP, which resorted to an armed struggle against the Myanmar government immediately after independence, had long hindered the development of official relations between the two countries.[10] Thailand also abandoned its policy of allowing the ethnic armed groups, notably the Karen National Army (KNA), alongside the border, to create a buffer zone between the two countries. Following these changes, Myanmar abandoned its non-aligned neutralism and began to participate in regional cooperation schemes, such as the Greater Mekong Sub-region Economic Cooperation (GMS-EC) in 1992, the Association of Southeast Asian Nations (ASEAN) and the Bay of Bengal Initiative for Multi-sectoral Technical and Economic Cooperation (BIMSTEC) in 1997 and the Ayeyawady, Chao Phraya, Mekong Economic Cooperation Strategy (ACMECS) in 2003.

These developments contributed to a continuation of the regionalization of trade. The four neighbouring countries (China, Thailand, India and Bangladesh) accounted for 56.5 per cent of Myanmar's exports and 52.7 per cent of its imports in 2003, compared with just 20.4 per cent and 2.7 per cent in 1985 (Table 1). Within this group, China and Thailand are particularly important.

China[11]

Ever since 1988, when Myanmar-China border trade, hitherto an activity deemed illegal, was legitimized and formalized, China has enjoyed an important position in Myanmar's external trade and has consistently ranked high among Myanmar's trading partners. Figure 3 illustrates the trends in the trade between Myanmar and China based on two data sources: UN Comtrade and China Customs, and clearly indicates the unbalanced performance of Myanmar's trade with China. While Myanmar's exports to China increased by only 1.3 times from 1988 to 2003, there was a 7-fold increase in imports from China during the same period, resulting in a huge trade deficit of US

Table 1 Myanmar's Trade with Neighbouring Countries

Export

	1985	1990	1995	2000	2003
Four Neighbours	20.4%	47.7%	42.5%	29.1%	56.5%
China	0.0%	20.9%	11.3%	6.4%	6.2%
Thailand	9.5%	26.5%	16.9%	13.3%	33.0%
India	7.9%	0.0%	12.3%	9.4%	14.9%
Bangladesh	3.0%	0.3%	2.0%	0.0%	2.4%
USA	3.6%	4.8%	6.6%	25.9%	10.9%
Japan	8.8%	8.3%	7.1%	6.1%	5.1%
Germany	2.8%	2.1%	2.0%	4.4%	3.8%
Total (US$ Million)	399	498	1,319	1,958	2,721

Import

	1985	1990	1995	2000	2003
Four Neighbours	2.7%	25.6%	40.6%	41.3%	52.7%
China	0.0%	20.8%	25.0%	19.5%	33.3%
Thailand	2.2%	4.7%	14.2%	19.8%	16.1%
India	0.1%	0.0%	1.2%	2.1%	3.2%
Bangladesh	0.3%	0.1%	0.2%	0.0%	0.1%
Singapore	11.5%	25.0%	25.8%	17.1%	23.8%
Korea	3.1%	4.3%	3.5%	11.4%	6.7%
Malaysia	2.5%	5.8%	9.3%	9.1%	5.1%
Total (US$ Million)	524	913	2,484	2,677	2,904

Source: UN Comtrade.

$797.7 million in 2003, some 4.4 times larger than Myanmar's total trade deficit with other countries for the same year.

Myanmar's exports to China consist predominantly composed of timber, which constituted nearly 70 per cent of exports to China by value between 2000 and 2003. Timber is exported mostly in the form of unprocessed or roughly squared logs, whose preparation requires little labour or technical input. Such a high dependency on timber has caused Myanmar's exports to China to stagnate somewhat, since exports are constrained by the availability of the natural resource in question. Timber extraction and exports in the form of logs seem to have a weak impact on the broad-based economic and industrial development, no doubt because exports of this kind fail to bring about an improved utilization of the existing factors of production, and

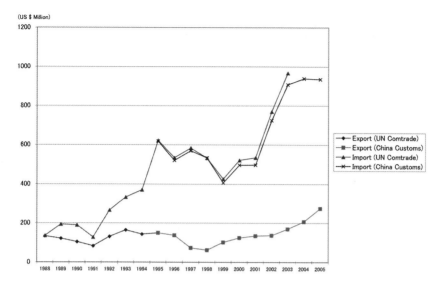

Figure 3   Myanmar's Trade with China

Sources: UN Comtrade; China Customs.

make very little impact so far as expanded factor endowments and linkage effects are concerned.

By contrast, imports from China showed rapid growth on two occasions: one in the first half of the 1990s and the other at the beginning of the twenty-first century. It follows that Myanmar has become increasingly dependent on imports from China. The share of Chinese goods of Myanmar's total imports rose from about a fifth in the latter half of the 1990s to about a third in 2003.

The first phase of rapid growth in Chinese imports to Myanmar was caused by the unleashing of the pent-up demand among the people of Myanmar following the introduction of the open-door policy in 1988. China provided the main supply sources, and Chinese products poured into the emerging consumer goods markets in Myanmar. Shortly after the opening up of border trade with China, Chinese textiles, mostly yarn and fabrics, flooded the Myanmar market. Textiles occupied nearly 40 per cent of total Chinese imports for the period from 1988 to 1991. Subsequently, the share of tobacco increased to 14 per cent for the period from 1992 to 1995.

Myanmar's imports from China had a second phase of rapid growth at the beginning of the twenty-first century. Imports grew at an average annual rate of 22.7 per cent between 2000 and 2003. Textiles, road vehicles,

Table 2 China's Trade with Myanmar via Borders (US$ Million)

	1999	2000	2001	2002	2003	2004	2005
China's Exports via Border	263.3	293.5	261.2	358.3	446.3	500.6	540.6
(Share of Border Trade)	64.8%	59.1%	52.5%	49.4%	49.1%	53.3%	57.8%
China's Imports via Border	55.1	66.9	93.7	105.4	134.5	164.5	223.5
(Share of Border Trade)	54.3%	53.6%	69.8%	77.0%	79.3%	79.5%	81.5%

Note: Border Trade is defined as goods that are cleared and recorded at the Kunming Customs.

Source: China Customs.

power generators, electrical machinery and apparatus, and general industrial machinery increased their share of Myanmar's total imports from China. Such an increase may well reflect the huge inflow of Chinese economic cooperation and the provision of commercial loans from China during the period in question. Chinese economic cooperation expanded towards the end of the 1990s, when successive economic and technical cooperation programs were initiated between the two countries.[12] Most of these programs were tied, whether legally or *de facto*, to Chinese companies, state-owned ones in particular, and consequently led to an increase in imports from China.

Trade between Myanmar and China is heavily dependent on day-to-day, cross-border transactions. According to the district-specific China Customs statistics, border trade represents the bulk of China's trade with Myanmar.[13] In 2005, border trade accounted for 58 per cent of China's exports to Myanmar and 82 per cent of its imports from Myanmar (Table 2). Moreover, in FY 2003, Yunnan Province's share of Myanmar's total border trade was 73 per cent, whereas that of Thailand was 14 per cent (Mya Than, 2005: 39). The border trade is thus important for both Myanmar and Yunnan Province.

The main route for border trade in Myanmar territory is the 460 kilometre-long road connecting Muse on the Chinese border, opposite Ruili in Yunnan Province, with Mandalay, the second largest town in central Myanmar. This road formed part of the old "Burma Road" that was opened in 1936 to supply the Kuomintang (KMT) in Chongqing. It was paved and expanded for truck transportation in 1998 on a Build-Operate-Transfer (BOT) basis by Asia World Company, one of Myanmar's largest private business conglomerates, headed by the son of Lo Hsing-han, a former drugs baron. Before the completion of the new road, it took two days and, during the rainy season, sometimes even a week, to travel from Mandalay to Muse. Now, it takes only twelve to sixteen hours by car.

Border trade between the two countries has been legitimized, regularized and institutionalized since the adoption of the open-door policy by Myanmar's present government. The first border trade agreement was signed in August 1988 by Myanmar Export and Import Services (MEIS) and the Yunnan Machinery Import Export Corporation, allowing bank transactions between the Myanmar Foreign Trade Bank and the Kunming Branch of China Bank. MEIS established border trade offices in Lashio, Muse, Kyukok, Nantkam and Koonlon. According to the Ministry of Commerce (notification No. 7/91), an allegedly new border trade system was administered by MEIS starting in October 1991. The Myanmar and Chinese governments signed a further border trade agreement in August 1994. Under this agreement, a Border Trade Office was established in Muse in August 1995 and a simplified rule of the custom service (one-stop services), were introduced on a trial basis. In August 1996, the office was transformed and upgraded into the fully-fledged Border Trade Department of the Ministry of Commerce. In January 1998, the Muse (105 mile) Office was expanded and started to function as a "one-stop service" border gate.

Both the regularization and the institutionalization of the cross-border transactions and road infrastructure development contributed to boosting border trade between the two countries at the beginning of the twenty-first century. The Myanmar government also promoted all border trade not only with China but also with Thailand, India and Bangladesh to compensate for the economic sanctions imposed by the West, and trade across the border with China became successful to a significant degree so much so, that cross-border trade with China has become a main element of Myanmar's economy.

Thailand

Thailand also occupies an important position in Myanmar's external trade. In 2003, Thailand accounted for 33.0 per cent of Myanmar's total exports and was ranked as the country's single most important export destination. Thailand supplied 16.1 per cent of Myanmar's total imports in that year and was ranked second as a source of Myanmar's imports. As noted in the previous section, natural gas exports via a pipeline greatly augmented Myanmar's exports to Thailand in the early twenty-first century (see Figure 4). Gas exports to Thailand increased from US$114.2 million in 2000 to US$1,497.4 million in 2005, and accounted for more than 80 per cent of Myanmar's exports to Thailand in that year.

The Petroleum Authority of Thailand (PTT), currently the sole purchaser of Myanmar gas, increased imports drawn from the Yadana offshore gas field from 525 million to 565 million cubic feet per day with effect

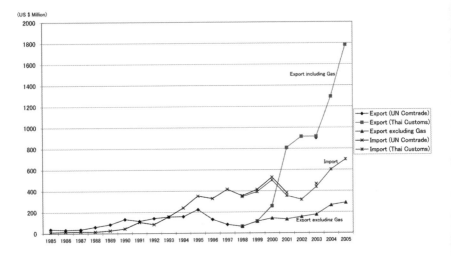

Figure 4   Myanmar's Trade with Thailand
Sources: UN Comtrade; Thai Customs.

from September 2006. High oil prices also caused Myanmar's gas exports to Thailand to increase to US$1,871.2 million in the first 11 months of 2006, a rise of 39 per cent compared with the same period in the previous year. The new large offshore gas fields, known as blocks A1 and A3, are expected to go into production in the foreseeable future, ensuring that Myanmar's gas output and exports will continue to rise in the medium term (EIU, 2006: 29–30). Myanmar's external sector has become increasingly dependent on gas exports and the ensuing revenue.

By contrast, Myanmar's exports to Thailand, apart from natural gas, failed to keep pace with its imports from Thailand. Exports of other primary commodities, such as wood, copper and fish and prawns, have stagnated. Contrary to this trend, between 2002 and 2005, imports from Thailand increased from US$315.1 million to US$696.7 million. Imported goods from Thailand consist mainly of petroleum, plastic resin, food and beverages, electrical machinery, general machinery, and fertilizer. Myanmar exports natural resources, and imports a range of manufactures items, including consumer goods, intermediate materials and capital goods. Such a trade pattern implies that Myanmar has yet to be integrated into the production and distribution networks that have developed in East and Southeast Asia, including Thailand. As was the case with China, trade with Thailand seems to have contributed little to Myanmar's broad-based economic development.

Foreign Direct Investment

The Introduction of Foreign Capital

Shortly after it seized power in September 1988, the military government changed its policy on foreign investment by enacting the Foreign Investment Law (FIL) in November 1988. This law, which permitted 100 per cent ownership by foreign companies, was a novelty for Myanmar. In December 1988, the Foreign Investments Commission (FIC), an administrative body was established to oversee the acceptance of FDI, similar to the Board of Investment (BOI) in Thailand, with the Minister for Planning and Finance as its chair. In April 1992, further organizational reinforcement was achieved and, as a result, two vice premiers assumed the offices of chair and vice-chair respectively, while the Minister for Planning and Finance took the position of Secretary-General. Moreover, fourteen ministers became members of the commission.

In April 1994, SLORC adopted the Myanmar Citizens Investment Law (MCIL) and then established the Myanmar Investment Commission (MIC) to assume the role of the FIC in supervising domestic investment issues, in line with the MCIL. MIC's main function is to evaluate proposed investment plans by examining their financial soundness and technical viability. Under the further organizational changes that were introduced in 2000, the number of committee members was reduced to four and the Minister for Science and Technology was appointed chair of the committee. It is thought that real authority in this field has mainly shifted to the Trade Policy Council (TPC), leaving MIC to function merely as a committee to screen documents submitted in the first stage of the investment proposals.[14]

Myanmar's foreign investment policy is a key component in the restructuring of the whole economy as well as playing an important role in national development. It incorporates three main pillars: the adoption of a market-oriented system for resource allocation, the encouragement of private investment and the promotion of an entrepreneurial spirit, while opening up the economy to foreign trade and investment. In this way, the encouragement of foreign investment can be seen as a development strategy with private initiatives, and one that is dependent on foreign capital. The basic aims underlying the introduction of foreign capital are export promotion, the development of natural resources that require a large sum of investment capital, the introduction of various types of high technology, the promotion of capital-intensive industries, the expansion of job opportunities, the saving of energy consumption, and regional development. Of these aims, it is the introduction of foreign capital that is our main concern, although possibly the most important objective of this policy is export promotion.

As has already been noted, the main exports of present-day Myanmar are primary commodities, such as agricultural, timber, marine and mining products, including natural gas. Because full-scale exploitation has not yet been achieved, the export volume of these products is currently small, except for natural gas.

One of the sectors in which there are high expectations of foreign investment is the development of natural resources, a field that requires considerable capital. As for natural gas, promising gas fields, such as Yadana and Yetagon, have been found, that have made a substantial contribution to export growth. Commercially valuable mines and oil fields have not yet been discovered.

While Myanmar urgently needs to diversify and increase its output of primary products for export, another important issue is the promotion of labour-intensive industries that are capable of producing goods for the export market. In the light of the experience of Malaysia and Thailand, an export shift from primary products to labour-intensive ones, and the promotion of the manufacturing industry will be vital prerequisites for the economic development of Myanmar. Manufacturing labour-intensive products suits the resource endowment of Myanmar and, in this regard, the garment industry seems to be a promising sector. As noted earlier, however, this industry was severely damaged by the imposition of economic sanctions by the US in 2003.

Trends, Source Countries and Receiving Sectors

Trends

Table 3 shows that the average amount of investment on an approved basis before the Asian economic crisis was approximately one billion US dollars, with considerable fluctuations from year to year. In 1996, investment jumped to US$2.8 billion, but it fell sharply between 1998 and 2004 as a result of the economic turmoil caused by the Asian financial crisis and by the Myanmar government's strengthening of its controls over foreign capital.[15] In 2005, the situation improved, following the approval of an extensive hydroelectric project that was to be developed by Thai companies along the Salween River. This boosted the amount of cumulative investment as of March 2006 to US$13.8 billion.

Source countries

In terms of the amount of investment by the countries shown in Table 4,[16] the leading investor is Thailand, followed by the UK, Singapore, Malaysia,

Table 3   Approved FDI Inflows to Myanmar (as of March 31, 2006)

Fiscal Year (April–March)	Enterprises/ Projects	Yearly Amount (US$ Million)	Cumulative Amount (US$ Million)
1989	18	449.49	449.49
1990	22	280.57	730.06
1991	4	5.89	735.95
1992	23	103.79	839.74
1993	27	377.18	1,216.92
1994	36	1,352.30	2,569.22
1995	39	668.17	3,237.39
1996	78	2,814.25	6,051.64
1997	56	1,012.92	7,064.56
1998	10	54.40	7,118.96
1999	14	58.15	7,177.11
2000	28	217.69	7,394.80
2001	7	19.00	7,413.80
2002	9	86.95	7,500.75
2003	8	91.17	7,591.92
2004	15	158.28	7,750.20
2005	5	6,065.68	13,815.88
TOTAL	399	13,815.86	

Note: The figures include those already terminated.

Sources: Myanmar Investment Commission. Some figures are also cited from Myanmar journals and newspapers.

and the US. Each of the three leading countries is responsible for investing over one billion US dollars, and their combined investment accounts for nearly half of the total amount of foreign investment in Myanmar. Western countries, such as the UK, the US, France, and the Netherlands, are among the top ten investors, the others being mainly Asian countries. While these Western countries have criticized the Myanmar government for delaying the introduction of democracy and its abuses of human rights, they have made greater foreign investment in Myanmar than has Japan. The main Asian sources of investment are the Southeast Asian countries located close to Myanmar, including Singapore, Thailand, Malaysia, and Indonesia. Because these countries were severely affected by the Asian financial crisis, they drastically reduced their foreign investment, with negative consequences for Myanmar. In Table 4, Japan, Korea and Hong Kong feature among the Asian sources of foreign investment in Myanmar but the amount of investment from each of these remains relatively small, ranging from 100 to 200 million US dollars.

Table 4   Approved FDI to Myanmar by Country (as of March 2006)

		Amount (US$ Million)	Share (%)	No. of Project
1	Thailand	73.8	55.3%	57.0
2	UK	15.7	11.8%	40.0
3	Singapore	14.3	10.8%	70.0
4	Malaysia	6.6	5.0%	33.0
5	Hong Kong	5.0	3.8%	31.0
6	France	4.7	3.5%	3.0
7	USA	2.4	1.8%	15.0
8	Indonesia	2.4	1.8%	12.0
9	The Netherlands	2.4	1.8%	5.0
10	Japan	2.2	1.6%	23.0
11	P.R. of China	1.9	1.5%	26.0
12	Korea	1.9	1.4%	34.0

Source: Myanmar Investment Commission (MIC).

In terms of the number of companies, Singapore leads, with 70, followed by Thailand. Singapore's investment is concentrated on the hotel construction and tourism industries, as well as on real estate and so on, and accounts for about 70 per cent of the whole. Some Singaporean investment has also gone into light industry, logistics, the wholesale trade, education, ports and industrial estates. Thailand has invested mainly in light industry (rice milling, jewelry, food, timber processing, and agricultural products processing), hotels and tourism, fisheries, and mining. A striking feature of the overall pattern is that the American and European countries have refrained from making new investments as a result of their economic sanctions, while the ASEAN nations, willing to engage constructively with Myanmar, have increased their level of investment. Another notable development is that foreign investment in Myanmar decreased sharply after the Asian financial crisis of 1997.[17]

The receiving sectors

With regard to investment by sector, oil and gas, manufacturing, hotels and tourism, real estate, and construction are the top five categories (Table 5). Since oil had been produced for many years in Myanmar, it was thought that, following independence, promising oil fields might exist. Exploration for new oil fields began in 1971, and a large gas field was found in the Gulf of Moattama in 1982. The Ministry of Energy, which was founded in April 1985, invited foreign oil companies to conduct oil and gas exploration in 1989. Suffering as it did from a shortage of foreign currency, the military

Table 5 Approved FDI to Myanmar by Sector (as of March 2006)

	Sector	Amount (US$ Million)	No. of Project
1	Electricity*	6,054	7
2	Oil and Gas	2,635	71
3	Manufactureing	1,610	152
4	Real Estate Development	1,056	19
5	Hotel & Tourism	1,035	43
6	Mining	535	58
7	Transport Telcommunication	313	16
8	Fishery	312	24
9	Industrial Estate	193	3
10	Construction	38	2
11	Agriculture	34	4
	Total	13,816	399

Note: *expressed as "other service" in MIC classification.

Source: Myanmar Investment Commission (MIC).

government had high expectations for the future development of oil and natural gas, and 71 companies invested approximately US$2.64 billion in this sector, some per cent or more of total investment. The gas field of Yadana has been jointly explored by Total of France, Unocal of the US, PTTEPI (a subsidiary of Petroleum Authority of Thailand) and Myanmar Oil and Gas Enterprise (MOGE) of Myanmar, while the Yetagon field has been opened up by Premier Petroleum Myanmar (PPML), Peptronas Calgary, PTTEPI, Nippon Oil, and MOGE. The amount of capital required for the development of energy and mineral resources is so great that the involvement of foreign capital was probably inevitable.

Next to oil and gas, some US$1,610 million (149 cases) has been invested in manufacturing. Under the Foreign Investment Law, the minimum capital investment permissible in the case of manufacturing is US$500,000, and most manufacturing ventures set up by foreign investors have been started with comparatively small amounts of capital. Garments have been Myanmar's leading export since 2000, which may suggest that the promotion of labour-intensive export-oriented industries should be prioritized in Myanmar's economic development. The reason ASEAN countries sustained their high economic growth over a long period was their successful transition from primary products to manufactured goods as their main exports. In Myanmar, foreign capital could play an important role in such a transition. Myanmar is still basically an agricultural country, producing a substantial quantity of farm-based and forestry-based products. Industries relating to the processing of these products, as well as hotel development and tourism, real estate and construction, are promising fields for future investment.

The present military government decided to promote the tourist industry and hotel development soon after it came to power, and 1996 was designated "Visit Myanmar Year". The roads in Yangon city were considerably improved and many cities were cleaned up in order to create a good impression for foreign visitors. Modern, multi-storey hotels were constructed, and the number of hotel rooms increased rapidly. The Foreign Exchange Certificate (FEC) system was introduced in 1993, partly to avoid the inconvenience to foreign tourists of exchanging their dollars at the official rate. Despite these initiatives, tourist arrivals remained at around 300,000 per annum, on average, although the official figure for tourist arrivals is about 30–40 per cent of the actual total. In expectation of growing demand from foreign business visitors, office accommodation for rent as well as condominiums for lease, mainly to foreigners, have been constructed in the city of Yangon in recent years.

Types of Foreign Business Enterprises investing in Myanmar

As of 31 March 2002, there were 362 foreign enterprises investing in Myanmar, based on the Foreign Investment Law (Table 6), of which 154 were wholly foreign-owned companies, 138 joint ventures and 70 production sharing ventures. The reason so many of these enterprises were wholly foreign-owned is probably related to the problem of exchanging US dollars into kyat at the official rate, which is extremely disadvantageous to foreign investors. Most ventures involve foreign companies exploring for natural resources, such as oil, gas and minerals, on a production sharing basis. The Myanmar partners in foreign capital ventures are generally SEEs (76 instances), followed by 36 instances involving private companies and 19 joint ventures with Myanmar Economic Holdings Ltd. (MEHL). The ministries in charge of the SEEs relating to manufacturing and processing are the Ministry of Industry (1) and the Ministry of Industry (2). The 10 joint ventures under the Ministry of Industry (1) invested nearly kyat 700 million, including US$14.62 million as a foreign portion. There are five joint ventures under the Ministry of Industry (2), as follows:

> Myanmar Fritz Werner Company Limited
> Myanmar Daewoo Company Limited
> Myanmar Suzuki Company Limited
> Myanmar Ekarat Transformer Company Limited
> Myanmar Matsushita Company Limited

Table 6 Form of Organization of FDI (as of March, 2002)   (Billion Kyat)

		No. of Enterprises	Investment	
			Local	Foreign
1	Wholly Foreign-owned	154		157.4
2	Joint Venture	138	72.5	169.8
	(a) State-owned Economic Enterprises	76	30.9	120.3
	(b) Myanmar Economic Holdings Ltd.	19	3.4	20.6
	(c) YCDC	1	.1	.1
	(d) Private Enterprises	36	37.1	27.5
	(e) Co-operatives	4	.4	.4
	(f) JV Corporation	1	.0	.0
	(g) Myanmar Economic Corporation	1	.6	.9
3	Production Sharing	70	.0	122.9
	Total	362	72.5	450.0

Note: YCDC stands for Yangon City Development Committee. The amounts are Kyat-based only.
Source: CSO, *Statistical Yearbook* (2002: 257).

The fact that there are almost twice as many SEEs as private companies among the Myanmar partners of foreign companies possibly indicates a major characteristic of the Myanmar economy. It is more advantageous for foreign investors seeking Myanmar partners to work with SEEs rather than private companies. For example, UMEHL is an institution that was established by incumbent and retired military officers and is frequently chosen as a tie-up partner, probably because, as an influential state enterprise, it receives considerably more preferential treatment than private companies.

Concluding Remarks

This chapter has traced the external economic relationships of Myanmar and the associated policy changes from the early 1990s to the mid-2000s. As for the structure of exports, although some cash crops increased significantly in relative importance as export commodities, the expansion of manufactured exports remained limited. On the other hand, the number of imports rapidly increased, thanks mainly to the rising need for consumer, intermediate and capital goods, causing a serious trade deficit by the mid-1990s. The government dealt with this situation by imposing strict import controls.

The circumstances of the export sector nevertheless underwent a dramatic improvement. The garment industries developed rapidly and, by the late 1990s and early twenty-first century, garments had become Myanmar's main export. Natural gas exploitation and rising gas exports followed after 2002. The current account reverted to positive, reducing the need for import restrictions. Myanmar's trade partners also changed. China emerged as a major trade partner in terms of both exports and imports, mainly due to the flourishing cross-border trade. The economic relationship with China deepened in many sectors, including manufacturing, and Thailand also became a major trading partner, primarily as a result of natural gas exports and an increase in the importation of various necessary goods, including petroleum.

FDI underwent several changes after the early 1990s. Shortly after the open-door policy was adopted, foreign capital rapidly flowed into Myanmar. The major investors came from Western countries, such as the UK and the US, and from their Asian neighbours, including Singapore. Foreign capital was directed mainly towards non-manufacturing sector, such as hotel construction and tourism, and energy development. While the inflow certainly declined during and after the Asian financial crisis, the official statistics are unclear regarding whether this decrease was drastic or slight.

Overall, Myanmar's external economic relationships deepened substantially during the period in question. The contribution of trade to GDP, however, remained very low according to the official statistics, and so far, at any rate, we cannot say that Myanmar's economic structure is closely linked with external trade. The contribution of exports to growth has been intermittent, whether through the garment industry or natural gas development. Likewise, FDI has mostly contributed to the growth of the domestic and energy sectors rather than to export-oriented manufacturing.

In terms of both trade and foreign investment, Myanmar's external sector appears to fluctuate between the open market and the controlled economy but has not yet shown signs of fulfilling its potential contribution to economic growth.

Appendix: Comments on Myanmar's Trade Statistics

In the preparation of this chapter, three different sources of trade data were employed: (1) the United Nations Commodity Trade Statistics (UN Comtrade); (2) customs statistics for 26 countries; and (3) Myanmar government statistics. The characteristics of the three data sets are as follows.

(1)   Statistics Canada has constructed the World Trade Database based on UN Comtrade, and the database retrieval services have been used for

this paper. At the time of writing, the data were available for the period from 1985 to 2003.

(2)   Twenty-six countries were selected as Myanmar's major trading partners, based on the UN Comtrade data. The 26 countries include China, the EU (15 member states), Hong Kong, India, Indonesia, Japan, Korea, Malaysia, Singapore, Thailand and the US. In addition, Canada is included on the export side and Australia on the import side. The 26 countries accounted for 95 per cent of total exports and 99 per cent of total imports of Myanmar for the period from 1985 to 2003, according to the UN Comtrade data. The World Trade Atlas (WTA) database retrieval services are used to determine the 26 countries' trade volume with Myanmar. WTA is based on the customs data for each country. At the time of writing, the data were available for the period from 1999 to 2005.

(3)   For Myanmar government statistics, the *Statistical Yearbook* and *Selected Monthly Economic Indicators* were used. The trade figures contained in these publications are denominated in kyat, Myanmar's domestic currency. Official exchange rates have been used for the conversion. It should be noted that there are large differences between the official exchange rates and the parallel market rates. At the time of writing, the data were available for the period from FY 1985 to FY 2005.

The figures derived from the three data sources are shown in the following table. There are considerable differences between the UN Comtrade/ 26 countries' data on the one hand and the Myanmar government statistics on the other, while the UN Comtrade and the data for the 26 countries are largely consistent. There are many factors responsible for these discrepancies, including whether FOB or CIF trade terms have been used, differences in recording locations for exports and imports, differences in recording periods (calendar years or fiscal years), and the methods employed for rectifying errors and omissions. Among these problems, the most important difficulty is probably differences between the recording locations; that is, whether the trade transactions have been collected at ports or border posts in Myanmar or at locations within the territories of Myanmar's trading partners. The UN Comtrade and the 26 countries' customs data are recorded within the territories of the trading partners, while the Myanmar government statistics are, of course, recorded in Myanmar.

The trade volume of both the exports and imports in the Myanmar government statistics are usually lower than those in the other two data

Comparison of Trade Statistics for Myanmar (US$ Million)

	UN Comtrade		Data from 26 Countries		Myanmar Government		Differences	
	Export (A)	Import (B)	Export (C)	Import (D)	Export (E)	Import (F)	Export: (A) or (C)/(E)	Import: (B) or (D)/(F)
1985	399.1	523.7			316.4	572.5	1.3	0.9
1986	352.1	523.6			333.3	542.5	1.1	1.0
1987	316.8	454.3			251.5	617.7	1.3	0.7
1988	417.8	583.2			342.5	543.7	1.2	1.1
1989	399.1	574.9			426.9	511.3	0.9	1.1
1990	497.5	913.2			472.0	880.1	1.1	1.0
1991	467.4	871.6			470.3	857.8	1.0	1.0
1992	805.0	997.0			594.1	887.9	1.4	1.1
1993	932.8	1,355.3			693.8	1,300.2	1.3	1.0
1994	977.5	1,623.0			909.3	1,401.7	1.1	1.2
1995	1,320.7	2,483.9			899.0	1,836.1	1.5	1.4
1996	1,239.9	2,775.3			936.3	2,009.7	1.3	1.4
1997	1,131.1	3,010.6			1,042.5	2,323.2	1.1	1.3
1998	1,116.3	2,469.9			1,076.8	2,689.2	1.0	0.9
1999	1,406.3	2,285.9	1,214.1	2,139.5	1,437.7	2,613.5	1.0	0.9
2000	1,959.1	2,677.1	1,829.9	2,479.0	1,982.0	2,345.7	1.0	1.1
2001	2,827.3	2,410.3	2,635.1	2,179.8	2,562.9	2,749.5	1.1	0.9
2002	2,659.2	2,242.0	2,617.7	2,352.9	3,035.7	2,268.2	0.9	1.0
2003	2,724.3	2,904.3	2,569.8	2,684.4	2,323.6	2,204.8	1.2	1.3
2004			2,951.6	2,954.1	2,905.9	1,973.3	1.0	1.5
2005			3,489.9	3,054.1	3,583.9	1,998.6	1.0	1.5

Note: Figures from Myanmar Government Statistics are for fiscal-years.

Sources: UN Comtrade; Customs Data of 26 Countries; CSO, SY and SMEI.

series. One reason often suggested for this is the fact that the local traders attempt to evade tax, both export tax and import duties, by under-invoicing and under-reporting their activities. However, strangely enough, the gaps in exports diminished from around 1997 and 1998, even though the introduction of a ten per cent export tax in January 1999 must have meant that traders were more strongly motivated to under-report than previously. By contrast, the gaps in imports widened from 2003 onwards, for which it is difficult to find a single explanation, and the problem may be deeply rooted in the way in which statistics are collected or in the different reporting systems employed by Myanmar and its trading partners.

Notes

1   The Fiscal Year (FY) runs from April and through the following March.

2   Figure 1 is based on two different sources of information, namely the United Nations Comtrade and the customs data from 26 major trading partners; see the appendix of this chapter for a more detailed discussion of Myanmar's trade statistics.

3   Calculated from CSO, *Statistical Yearbook* (2004: 315).

4   See Kudo (2005a).

5   See Chapter 2.

6   The few exceptions are beans and pulses and fish and prawns, all of which categories have enjoyed free trade and rapid growth.

7   See Kudo (2001) for details.

8   According to the UN Comtrade, Myanmar's trade showed a surplus in 2001 and 2002, although it again recorded a deficit in 2003. The data from 26 countries also showed a surplus in 2001 and 2002. Having plunged into a deficit in 2003, Myanmar's trade account remained in balance in 2004, showing a surplus in 2005. By contrast, the Myanmar government statistics recorded continuous surpluses for the period from FY 2002 to FY 2005.

9   On the growth and decline of the garment industry in Myanmar, see Moe Kyaw (2001) and Kudo (2005b).

10   See Lintner (1990, 1994 and 1998) on the historical development of Myanmar-China relations, with special reference to party-to-party relations.

11   This section is drawn from Kudo (2006).

12   See Table 6 (Bilateral Agreements between Myanmar and China since 1996) in Kudo (2006: 23–24).

13   In this paper, the commodities that are cleared and recorded at the Kunming Customs are regarded as "border trade". Since Yunnan Province is land-locked, commodities imported by or exported from Myanmar through Kunming, the capital of the province, are probably transported by land through border gates, such as Muse, Lwejel and Laiza.

14   As mentioned in the previous section, the TPC was established in July 1997, although it apparently exercised a *de facto* authority regarding foreign investment in Myanmar since around 2000.

15   It is noteworthy, however, that the inflow of capital does not decline significantly in the money flow table.

16   The figures in Tables 4 and 5 relate to March 2006.

17   In general, however, we need to consider that the FDI figures in the statistics are based on what has been approved and may differ from the actual inflow, as discussed in Chapter 1. Trends should be treated carefully in considering both the increasing phase before the crisis and the sharp decline thereafter.

CHAPTER 4

The Financial Sector during the Transition to a Market Economy in Myanmar

Koji Kubo, Ryu Fukui and Fumiharu Mieno

Introduction

This chapter explains Myanmar's evolving financial system during the transition period. Economic liberalization was initiated when the military regime relaxed foreign trade regulations in 1989. The process expanded within a few years to encompass an overall reform across the whole economy. After 15 years, some aspects of the reforms, such as the fiscal system and the foreign exchange regime, became deadlocked, but in other areas the reforms encouraged dynamic and autonomous structural changes under private ownership. It has been possible to analyze the financial system as a single case, although this is not a simple process because the reforms resulted in completely new structures replacing the traditional socialist system.

The chapter examines the emergence and evolution of the private banking sector and subsequent changes in it, with a focus on the bank run that occurred in early 2003. Myanmar's financial system is dominated by a banking sector consisting of state banks reconstructed from the monobank system in 1975, which have been in decline, and private banks established in the mid-1990s, which rapidly increased in the number and prominence following the 1990 "Financial Institution Act". The government devised a number of policy schemes designed to enrich and diversify the financial system by supporting the entry of foreign banks, establishing a securities market, and allowing private banks to carry out foreign exchange operations. However, few of the reforms had any effect. After experiencing strong growth, private banks encountered difficulties in 2003 and some banks experienced a run on deposits. After 2003, the private banking sector was in a state of turmoil characterized by bank mergers, the freezing of assets of inefficient banks, and the possibility of further bank runs.

The chapter also compares Myanmar's financial system after the 1990s with those of other transition economies. Problems typical of transition economies are widely observed in Myanmar's fiscal and financial sectors, while the economy retains its unique structure in other areas. For example, the degree of the separation between Myanmar's fiscal and financial sectors is less clear than in other countries in the region, such as Vietnam. This gives the transition process and the development of the banking sector in Myanmar a unique quality.

The Financial System in Myanmar

The Development of the Financial Institutions

This section traces the development of the financial organizations and policies and analyzing the structure of the banking sector that is central to Myanmar's financial system.

Before "Liberalization"

Until 1988, the financial regime under the "Burmese Way to Socialism" was characterized by a monobank system: 24 private banks (14 foreign and 10 domestic) were nationalized in 1963,[1] and further consolidated as the People's Bank of the Union of Burma in 1969. A new banking law was promulgated in 1975 as part of the reform of the financial institutions when the reform of the state-owned economic enterprise (SEEs) was also undertaken. In 1976, the People's Bank of the Union of Burma was reorganized into the Central Bank of Myanmar (CBM) and four specialized financial institutions: the Myanmar Economic Bank (MEB) as a commercial bank, the Myanmar Foreign Trade Bank (MFTB), the Myanmar Agricultural Bank, and the Myanmar Insurance Corporation. Private banks were not allowed to be established at this stage and Myanmar's financial system remained totally under state control. The role of the financial institutions was to provide funds to the public sector, including the SEEs, as part of public finance.

The reform of the financial institutions

In 1988, reforms of the financial institutions were initiated along with a series of economic reforms, seeking to effect a transition to a market-based economy. These reforms were exemplified by the establishment of the Foreign Company Law and the imposition of an embargo on private trade. The first step, taken in 1989, was an increase in interest rates, which had been fixed since 1975. In the same year, the SEEs were prohibited from borrowing from state-owned banks, and the former's books were merged into the State Fund Account (SFA),[2] which was managed solely by the CBM. This measure aimed at reducing the accumulated debt of the SEEs through increasing government control, as the government regarded the self-redressing efforts of these institutions as ineffective (Nishizawa, 2000: 128). In 1990, three new financial laws were promulgated: the Financial Institutions Law, the Central Bank of Myanmar Law, and the Myanma Agriculture and Rural Development Bank Law. From 1992 to 1997, 20 private banks were established under the Financial Institutions Law. Under the Central Bank of Myanmar Law, the role of the CBM was to "maintain the value of Burmese currency within and outside the country", and the CBM was given the authority to carry out monetary policy. The same law changed the governance style of the CBM from direct state control to control by a committee that included officials from the Ministry of Finance and Revenue, thereby guaranteeing the autonomy of the CBM to some degree, if not entirely. These reforms reshaped the financial system in Myanmar — that is, a two-tiered banking system (a central bank and commercial banks) — by separating the financial institutions from public finance.

Further measures were adopted in the mid-1990s. To initiate the development of the capital markets, the Myanma Securities Exchange Center Ltd (MSEC), the first securities company in Myanmar, was established as a joint company by the MEB, a state-owned bank, and a Japanese think tank. The MSEC initiated activities to raise public awareness about the need to foster share trading (such as underwriting, buying and selling, notifying, and over-the-counter trading) rather than negotiation-based share transactions.[3] Such measures created an expectation among foreign countries that further liberalization would follow, and foreign banks were motivated to submit to the government proposals regarding joint ventures in collaboration with Myanmar's private banks in 1996 (five proposals were submitted, including one by the Fuji Bank-Yoma Bank).

Stagnation

The situation changed in the late 1990s. There was increasing tension within the sphere of domestic politics, and the Asian financial crisis in 1997 had an adverse impact on Myanmar's foreign trade that resulted in the expansion of the trade deficit and a sharp decrease in the amount of foreign reserves. The military government responded by halting the open-door policies and adopting an inward-looking perspective; the financial reforms stagnated or were even reversed. In 1998, the government expropriated the licenses to conduct foreign exchange held by nine private banks, thereby creating a monopoly for the state-owned banks. Joint venture proposals submitted by the foreign banks were rejected by the government. Moreover, the interest rate policies and control of the banking business lines by the financial authorities remained rigid, the expansion of the bank branches was severely restricted, and competition was curtailed.

The highly inflated economy limited opportunities for long-term development in the banking sector. The financial authorities did not provide a road map for developing the financial infrastructure and there were no policy measures, such as the development of the money markets or the creation of an environment, to promote the modernization of the banking industry. No explicit measures for developing the expertise of the central bankers or building capacity for monitoring and supervision were undertaken, although prudential regulations and guidelines about maintaining healthy banks developed to some degree.

The stagnation of the financial reforms since the late 1990s appears to be a consequence of the strong precautions taken by the military government against the risk of destabilizing the domestic financial sector, as the supervisory capacities of the financial authorities remained weak. The government seemingly stalled the financial reforms due to the perception that further liberalization and open-door policies would substantially increase this risk, but the policy reversal coupled with mismanagement of the macroeconomy produced the opposite of the desired effect by increasing systemic risks in the financial sector. This was the context of the bank run in February 2003 (see Section: The February 2003 Bank Run).

State-Owned Bank Reforms

This section describes the status of the banking sector, which is a central institution in Myanmar's financial system, focusing on its evolution until the bank run in February 2003. The state-owned banks, private banks, and other financial organizations are discussed in turn. Figure 1 illustrates the organizations within Myanmar's financial system and their interrelationships.

Under the Financial Institutions Law, the MEB, the Myanma Investment and Commercial Bank (MICB) and the MFTB are state-owned banks. Their presidents are nominated by the Ministry of Finance and Revenue, and their employees are regarded as civil servants. The same law places bank management in the hands of a Board of Directors in each organization, although in practice important managerial decisions are always made in consultation with the Governor of the CBM or the Minister of Finance and Revenue. The Myanma Agricultural Development Bank (MADB), another state-owned bank, is overseen by the Ministry of Agriculture and Irrigation rather than

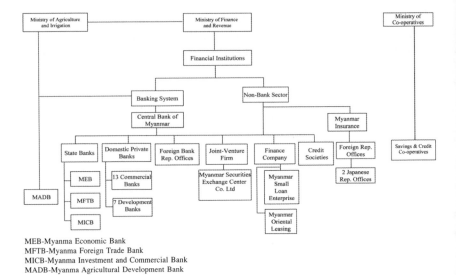

MEB-Myanma Economic Bank
MFTB-Myanma Foreign Trade Bank
MICB-Myanma Investment and Commercial Bank
MADB-Myanma Agricultural Development Bank

Figure 1   Myanmar's Financial System

Source: Fukui (2004).

the CBM, and from a purely legal viewpoint, the CBM neither supervises nor monitors the MADB.

The Myanma Economic Bank (MEB)

The MEB, a commercial bank established in 1976, has 311 branches and offices and is the largest banking network in Myanmar. Services include taking deposits and making loans, as well as handling transactions involving government funds, such as transfers of public money. After the books of the state-owned banks were merged with the SFA in 1989, MEB's main loan customers were private companies, about 30,000 of them altogether. Private companies accounted for 96 per cent of the total loans outstanding, with cooperatives and SEEs each holding 2 per cent. About 65 per cent of the loans were made to the commercial and service sector, about 25 per cent to the industrial sector, and about 10 per cent to the transportation and construction sector. The MEB also provided "policy-based directed credit", with a lower interest rate and a government guarantee, to projects undertaken by private firms for infrastructure development, such as road and bridge construction and telecommunications.[4] The criteria for granting this directed credit were undocumented, however, and the policies blurred regarding the selection of projects that are eligible for the lower interest rates or government guarantee. Therefore, it may be reasonably assumed that the government was influential in decision making, and that project selection was to some extent arbitrary. In fact, even in the broader sphere of loan making, the MEB does not appear to have established credit policies.

The total assets of the MEB at the end of March 2000 were 698.9 billion kyat, including 66.7 billion kyat of loans outstanding and 103.4 billion kyat of deposits outstanding. A large portion of these assets involved public money transactions — dealings with the government funds controlled by the SFA — amounting to 569.4 billion kyat, with equivalent liabilities. At the end of March 1998, the deposits in the MEB constituted 56 per cent of total deposits outstanding in all banks in Myanmar.[5] After 2000 the MEB decreased its weight in the deposits market, as deposits in the private banks, such as the Asia Wealth Bank (AWB), sharply increased. The MEB seemingly recovered and became the biggest deposit taker following the bank run in 2003, when the major private banks substantially reduced their assets. The financial standing of the MEB is very weak: deficits of 2 billion kyat and 0.6 billion kyat were recorded for fiscal years 1996/97 and 1997/98 respectively, and the profit for the fiscal year 1999/2000 was close to zero. The nonperforming loan (NPL) ratio was estimated to be 28 per cent at the end of March 1999 (actual figures were not disclosed).[6] Although the credit policies have been tightened since then (the deposits to loan ratio decreased from 79 per cent in fiscal year 1997/98 to 65 per cent in fiscal year 1998/99), the NPL is estimated to remain high. The efficiency of the MEB's banking services and its capacity to conduct credit analysis are considered poor, and there is little in the way of human resource development or modernization of banking services.

The Myanma Investment and Commercial Bank (MICB)

The MICB was established, firstly, as a subordinate organization of the MEB in 1989, based on the Foreign Investment Law that was promulgated in 1988, becoming an independent financial organization in 1990 under the Financial Institutions Law. Its major businesses include mid- to long-term financing for domestic or foreign companies and their joint ventures, related financial services, and foreign exchange. The MICB has a branch in Mandalay. The assets of the MICB are very small: at the end of March 2000, its total assets, loans outstanding, and deposits outstanding were 8.8 billion kyat, 3.3 billion kyat, and 7 billion kyat, respectively. Long-term loans are estimated to amount to approximately a quarter of the total loan portfolio. Nevertheless, the MICB claims to be the only bank to offer "comprehensive" financial services, including short- to long-term loans and foreign exchange. The presence of the MICB in the banking system remains marginal.

The Myanma Foreign Trade Bank (MFTB)

The MFTB has its beginnings in an entity established under the National Commercial Banks Law in 1954. The MFTB itself was established in 1976, with the launch of the monobank system, succeeding the department of foreign exchange of the People's Bank of the Union of Burma. The major role of the MFTB is to provide foreign exchange services for the government, SEEs, and private companies with a virtually monopolistic status, given that the private banks are not allowed to engage in foreign exchange. Its other business lines include deposit taking in foreign currencies and the provision of credit to trade business. However, the MFTB's financial services remain fairly limited in their support of foreign trade, except for the provision of letters of credit to private companies. This restriction seems to reflect the influence of the Ministry of Commerce. Moreover, it is often noted that the MFTB does not serve the needs of private companies because the bank only provides letters of credit to firms that place deposits with it in a foreign currency equivalent to the credit claimed. Thus, the MFTB's financial operation is not a true banking operation, as it does not take credit risks.

The Myanma Agricultural Development Bank (MADB)

The predecessor of the MADB was the Myanma Agricultural Bank, established in 1976, which grew out of the Agricultural Finance Division of the monolithic People's Bank system. The Myanma Agricultural Bank was renamed as the Myanma Agricultural Development Bank in 1990, and further reconstituted in 1997 under the Myanma Agricultural Development Bank Law. The MADB has been overseen by the Ministry of Agriculture and Irrigation since 1996.

The MADB's loan portfolio consists mainly of seasonal crop production loans and term loans. Loans are extended without taking collateral. According to the MADB annual report, it has as many as 1.5 million clients. Seasonal crop production loans are short-term loans, normally for 12 to 34 months. During the 2000/01 financial year, the bank disbursed 9.9 billion kyat for monsoon crops, 2.1 billion kyat for winter crops, and 159 billion kyat for pre-monsoon crops. There were two types of term loan: short-term loans of up to four years, and long-term loans of five years or more. As of November 2001, the total term loans outstanding amounted to 6.2 billion kyat. The interest rate for both the seasonal loans and term loans was 15 per cent per annum. The MADB is not under the supervision of the CBM, and in principle it could apply higher interest rates than those permitted under CBM regulations — but in practice it has followed the regulated interest rates.

MADB was based on a village banking system (the number of village banks across the nation exceeded 12,000) but in 1998 it began shifting to a network of branches that deal directly with farmers' groups. This transition was completed by 2000. There were about 300,000 groups nationwide, each made up of five to ten farmers, and these groups borrowed from the MADB with a mutual guarantee by the group members. The MADB had 216 branches, with, on average, 15–20 employees per branch. The average loan size is relatively small, ranging from 10,000 kyat to 15,000 kyat.

Although the MADB began attempting to mobilize savings in 1993, when the "Rural Savings Promotion" was launched (permitting the amount of loans to exceed the deposit amount by several times), total deposits were as little as 2.1 billion kyat as of March 2000. As demand for loans far exceeded deposits, the MADB took out short-term loans from the CBM at an interest rate of 10 per cent to fund seasonal crop production loans.[7] According to the MADB's annual reports, the loan recovery ratio was almost 100 per cent, and the nonperforming loan ratio was very low, at 0.1 per cent (nonperforming loans are defined as those with arrears extending beyond a month). This good performance was due to several facts: (i) the organization of communities in rural areas was successful following the period of village banking; (ii) the quality of information about individuals' credibility in rural communities remained high even after the ending of the "Burmese Way to Socialism"; and (iii) the loan size was so small that repayment was not difficult for farmers if they gave priority to repayment.

Thus, in contrast with other state-owned banks, the MADB played an important role in rural Myanmar as the sole public finance organization supporting farmers. The MADB also avoided poor performance in terms of loan collection and the consequent danger of bankruptcy, a common problem among state-owned agricultural banks in other countries. The problems faced by the MADB were: (i) the scale of funds was small and the loans had only a limited impact on the expansion of production or promotion of efficiency in the agricultural sector; (ii) autonomous and sustainable financial models were not in place because the savings mobilization is weak; and (iii) the rural development banking functions are insufficient, as the MADB does not support nonagricultural business or agribusiness in rural areas.

The Characteristics of the Private Banks

According to statistics from the Asian Development Bank, private banks had total deposits of 334 billion kyat and total outstanding loans of 207 billion kyat as at March 2001. There are 20 private banks in total, 10 of which were established by the government for various purposes, including banks for civil servants and military personnel or for specific industrial development; for example, Myawaddy Bank provides financial services for military personnel; The Myanma Industrial Development Bank (MIDB) was established by the Myanma Industrial Development Committee to finance companies in industrial parks; and the Myanma Livestock and Fishery Development Bank specializes in financing livestock and fishery businesses. These banks are called "semi-governmental banks". The government or military personnel have substantial influence over the management of these banks through shareholding or political power, although the government does not exert direct control, as it does with the state-owned banks; for example, all shares in the Myawaddy Bank are held by Myanma Economic Holding (UMEHL), which is dominated by the government and the military. The Inwa Bank is wholly held by the Myanma Economic Corporation (MEC), which is in turn 100 per cent owned by the government, and the military authorities control the bank's management.[8] In the case of the MIDB, 70 per cent of the shares are owned by funds established by civil servants (who belong to the Ministry of Industry (1), the Ministry of Industry (2), or the Ministry of Agriculture and Irrigation) and 30 per cent by private investors (totaling about 380 individuals).[9] These "semi-governmental banks" hold few assets compared with private commercial banks.

With the exception of the Myawaddy Bank, the top seven private banks in terms of asset size are commercial banks that are "purely" held by the private sector. These banks make up 70 per cent of the private banks in the deposits market (see Table 1). The aggregate financial standing of the seven banks are shown in Table 3. In the Myanmar's entire banking sector, the First Private Bank and the Myanma Citizen Bank are the only two public banks whose shares are traded in the public. Investors in the private banks are largely in the trade, real estate, or other service sectors; typical examples are the Asia Wealth Bank (AWB), the Yoma Bank, and the Myanma Mayflower Bank. These entities were established by businesspeople of Chinese descent who achieved success in real estate or construction (the AWB, the Yoma Bank, the Myanma Mayflower Bank) or trade (the Myanma Oriental Bank).[10] The AWB and the Yoma Bank belong to powerful conglomerates: the Olympic Group and the Serge Pan Associates and First Myanmar Investment (SPA-FMI) Group respectively. The SPA-FMI group is one of the biggest private conglomerates in Myanmar, with over 40 affiliated companies.[11] The central function of the AWB and the Yoma Bank appears to be to raise funds to finance their affiliates within each conglomerate. In fact, the weight of loans to the real estate and service sectors is high in

Deposits

	1998	1999		2000		2001 (preliminary)	
	mill. kyat	*mill. kyat*	*annual growth*	*mill. kyat*	*annual growth*	*mill. kyat*	*annual growth*
Total deposits	145,789	210,360	44.3%	319,518	51.9%	485,000	52.0%
of which demand deposit	35,818	47,751	33.3%	83,135	74.1%		
of which time deposit	109,971	162,609	47.9%	236,383	45.4%		
Deposits of private banks	66,039	115,826	75.3%	204,831	76.8%	334,000	63.0%
Market share of private banks in percent of total deposits	45%	55%		64%		68%	
Market share of 7 largest private banks in percentage of deposits of private banks	–	83%		88%		90%	

Credits

	1998	1999		2000		2001 (preliminary)	
	mill. kyat	*mill. kyat*	*annual growth*	*mill. kyat*	*annual growth*	*mill. kyat*	*annual growth*
Total Credits	114,543	142,318	24.2%	188,728	32.6%	279,000	48.0%
to State-owned enterprises	17	17	–	7	–		
to private firms and cooperatives	114,526	142,301	24.2%	188,728	32.6%		
to cooperatives	5,502	3,249	–4.1%	1,826	–43.8%		
to private firms	109,024	139,052	27.5%	186,895	34.4%		
to private banks	51,207	71,367	39.4%	114,732	60.8%	207,000	80.0%
Credit to deposit ratio of private banks	78%	62%		56%		62%	
Market share of private banks in percentage of total credits	45%	50%		61%		74%	
Market share of 7 largest private banks in percentage of credits of private banks	78%	78%		83%		87%	

Note: Top seven private banks refer to AWB Yoma Bank, Myanma Mayflower Bank, Myawaddy Bank, Myanma Oriental Bank, Kanbawza Bank and Myanma Universal Bank.

Sources: ADB (2001), Fukui (2004).

Table 2 Selected Indices of 20 Private Banks

Name of institution	License issued	Commencement	Ownership	No. of branches			No. of employees		Scale of operation				Notes
				1998	2002	2003	2002	2003	Paid-up capital 1998	Deposits 1998	Total assets 2003	Deposits 2003	
1 Asia Wealth Bank	11/21/94	4/30/95	private	13	39	39	3,346	3,005	664	20,345	251,394	212,140	
2 Yoma Bank	7/26/93	8/14/93	private	21	42	41	2077	2016	268	6,131	4,200	N/A	
3 Kanbawza Bank	8/6/94	7/1/94	private	0	22	23	1,465	1,400	15	180	7,650	N/A	
4 Myanma Mayflower Bank	3/17/94	6/9/94	private	10	24	24	1,213	1,031	480	9,320	156,680	50,642	
5 Myanma Universal Bank	11/21/94	1/24/95	private	7	25	26	1,088	1,500	80	1,550	19,104	21,000	
6 Myanma Oriental Bank	7/26/93	11/18/93	private	8	14	15	604	603	170	4,739	23,881	20,477	
7 First Private Bank	5/25/92	10/6/92	private	9	15	15	459	477	507	2,105	N/A	6,498	Public limited company
8 Myawaddy Bank	1/1/93	1/4/93	semi-gov.	0	6	6	330	N/A	300	7,934	N/A	15,406	Subsidiary of the Myanmar Economic Holding Ltd. (MEH)
9 Cooperative Bank	8/3/92	8/21/92	semi-gov.	0	8	8	309	282	50	866	10,277	6,961	Specialized in financial services for cooperatives
10 Myanma Livestock and Fisheries Development Bank	2/9/96	2/15/96	semi-gov.	3	7	8	258	N/A	680	1,858	N/A	3,262	
11 Innwa Bank	5/15/97	11/28/96	semi-gov.	N/A	8	10	181	N/A	N/A	N/A	N/A	4,849	Subsidiary of the Myanmar Economic Company Ltd. (MEC)
12 Yangon City Bank	3/19/93	4/1/93	semi-gov.	0	1	0	167	N/A	450	5,003	N/A	3,994	

Table 2 continued

Name of institution	License issued	Commencement	Ownership	No. of branches			No. of employees		Scale of operation				Notes
				1998	2002	2003	2002	2003	Paid-up capital 1998	Deposits 1998	Total assets 2003	Deposits 2003	
13 Tun Foundation Bank	6/8/94	6/14/94	private	0	5	1	151	N/A	70	941	N/A	N/A	
14 Myanma Industrial Development Bank	1/12/96	2/15/96	semi-gov.	1	2	2	141	150	1,208	1,930	6,000	2,350	Specialized in financial services for firms in industrial zones
15 Myanma Citizens Bank	5/25/92	6/2/92	private	1	1	1	107	105	110	2,364	5,849	3,578	Public limited company
16 Cooperative Promoters Bank	3/22/96	7/6/96	semi-gov.	N/A	0	2	85	N/A	N/A	N/A	N/A	554	Specialized in financial services for cooperatives
17 Cooperative Farmers Bank	3/22/96	7/6/96	semi-gov.	N/A	2	1	83	N/A	N/A	N/A	N/A	417	Specialized in financial services for cooperatives
18 Sibin Tharyaryay Bank	6/26/96	7/4/96	semi-gov.	0	1	0	55	60	650	250	2,297	961	Under the supervision of the Ministry of Progress of Border Area and National Races and Development Affairs
19 Asian Yangon International Bank	3/17/94	10/18/94	private	0	0	0	28	30	40	189	414	215	
20 Yadanabon Bank	8/27/92	9/11/92	semi-gov.	0	0	0	22	N/A	100	130	N/A	102	

Notes: Number of employees in 2002 is as of October 2002. The indices of scale of operation are in million of kyats, and the indices for Bank 10, 11, 12 are as of September 2000.

Sources: Wang (2004: Table1, Table 2), Fukui (2004: Table 3).

Table 3 Financial Statement of Banks

Income Statements

	1999/00		2000/01	
	mill. kyat	*% of total income*	*mill. kyat*	*% of total income*
Interest income	18,463	92.1	27,167	90.7
Other income	1,594	7.9	2,796	9.3
Total income	20,057	100.0	29,963	100.0
Interest expenses	13,319	66.4	18,810	62.8
Other expenses	2,891	14.4	6,087	20.3
Total expenses	16,210	80.8	24,897	83.1
Income before tax	3,847	19.2	5,066	16.9
Net income	1,452	7.2	1,098	3.7
Dividend	1,454	7.2	1,074	3.6
Net interest income	5,144	25.6	8,357	27.9

Statements of Balance Sheet

	1999		2000		2001	
	mill. kyat	% of total assets	mill. kyat	% of total assets	mill. kyat	% of total assets
Cash and deposits	23,364	19.9	26,712	13.2	40,585	11.6
Cash	12,812	10.9	19,325	9.5	29,155	8.4
Balance with Central Bank	4,641	4.0	3,244	1.6	4,440	1.3
Balance with other banks	5,912	5.0	4,143	2.0	6,990	2.0
Loans	58,895	50.2	96,772	47.7	171,25	49.1
Treasury Bonds	29,180	24.9	68,390	33.7	122,608	35.1
Other investments	224	0.2	323	0.2	324	0.1
Fixed assets	2,844	2.4	4,861	2.4	6,655	1.9
Other assets	2,444	2.1	4,694	2.3	6,469	1.9
Guarantees etc.	462	0.4	952	0.5	1,170	0.3
Total assets	117,413	100.0	2202,704	100.0	349,062	100.0
Deposits	102,385	87.2	180,210	88.9	291,701	83.6
Demand deposits	34,459	29.3	60,288	29.7	103,043	29.5
Time deposits	67,925	57.9	119,922	59.2	188,655	54.0
Borrowings from Central Bank (collateralized with Treasury bills)	4,900	4.2	6,450	3.2	35,006	10.0
Other liabilities	3,982	3.4	5,303	2.6	6,139	1.8
Guarantees etc.	462	0.4	952	0.5	1,170	0.3
Total liabilities	111,729	95.2	192,915	95.2	334,016	95.7
Paid–up capital	3,145	2.7	5,745	2.8	7,954	2.3
Reserves	2,322	2.0	3,804	1.9	6,746	1.9
Earnings in current period	218	0.2	242	0.1	346	0.1
Equity items	5,685	4.8	9,791	4.8	15,046	4.3

Note: Top seven banks refer to the same banks as in Table 1.

Source: Fukui (2004).

Table 4   Bank Branch Network and Access to Banks

	no. of branches	no. of branches/ millions of people	Regional disparities
Whole banking sector	778	18	13.3 (Mon State)~46.7 (Kayin State)
of which MEB	311	7.2	5.4 (Mandalay Division)~20.0 (Kayin State)
of which MADB	216	5.0	2.1 (Shan State)~13.3 (Kayin State)
of which private banks	251	5.8	0.0 (Chin State)~17.8 (Yangon Division)

Note: MEB: Myanma Economic Bank, MADB: Myanma Agricultural Development Bank.
Source: Fukui (2004).

both banks — those sectors are the core business for each conglomerate — whereas the industrial sector, including manufacturing, is a relatively small component of their loan portfolios. Both banks are aggressive in expanding their consumer banking, which is not only a natural business development of commercial banks pursuing economies of scale, but also supports various service businesses and real estate development and sales in each conglomerate.

The private banks in Myanmar have a track record of less than two decades and the aggregate value added is less than 0.1 per cent of GDP, which shows that banking remains a relatively small industry. With approximately 12,000 aggregate employees, the banking sector makes little impact in terms of employment. There are 251 branches in total, which is less than the number of MEB branches (311) and only slightly more than the number of MADB branches (216) (see Table 4). The penetration of the private banks is also low: the average number of private bank branches per million inhabitants is 5.8 nationwide and 17.8 in Yangon (the largest number across all states). Even including the MEB and MADB, the total number of bank branches per million habitants in Myanmar is as low as 18.0 (the same indicator in Kayin State is 46.7, the largest number across all states), which shows that people's access to banking services is relatively limited.

Other Financial Institutions

The foreign banks

Foreign banks are allowed to open representative offices but do not have authority to engage in banking operations. Starting in 1992, 49 foreign banks opened offices, but many subsequently closed them as a result of the sluggish economic growth, stagnating inward direct investment, and the discontinuation of the open-door policies. The number of foreign bank offices had decreased to 36 by 2003. Three Thai banks and one Korean one withdrew in 1998. The Japanese banks repeatedly downsized their operations and closed their offices: UFJ Bank virtually withdrew in 1998 and the last remaining Japanese bank, Tokyo Mitsubishi Bank, transferred management to its local employees. The foreign banks submitted six joint venture projects with Myanmar's private banks[12] in 1995, but none received government approval.

Insurance, leasing and the financial company sectors

The Myanma Insurance Corporation, a SEE that sells life and accident insurance, is the only insurance company operating nationwide in Myanmar. As in the banking sector, the foreign presence in the insurance industry is very limited. There are a few Japanese operations: Mitsui Marine and Fire Insurance and Yasuda Fire and Marine Insurance opened representative offices in 1996, and a joint venture with a Japanese corporation was established in 1997 (the Myanma International Insurance Corporation), the only joint venture with foreign capital in Myanmar.

The financial and leasing companies also remain underdeveloped. The only known institutions are a state-owned finance company and a leasing company. The Myanma Small Loans Enterprise, which provides small-scale loans to small private companies and individuals, was hived off from the MEB in 1992. The Myanma Oriental Leasing Company, owned by the Myanma Oriental Bank, provides leasing services for appliances, cars, and heavy electrical machinery.

The small-scale finance institutions

Apart from banks, Saving and Credit Cooperative Societies and microfinance businesses are small-scale financial systems operating in Myanmar. The former were developed with government encouragement to support farming activities, and operated through the 1980s. The New Cooperatives Law was promulgated in 1992 in accordance with the financial reforms. As of fiscal year 2001/02, 1,942 associations were reported to be operational under this law, with a total membership of 431,000 individuals, a total amount of savings of 3.9 billion kyat, and loans of 6.3 billion kyat. Statistics from the Ministry of Cooperatives indicate that savings increased by 707 per cent and loans 1,184 per cent during the decade after 1995, forming an active financial sector, while the number of cooperative societies and members declined. Most Saving and Credit Cooperatives have a restricted membership, limited

Table 5   Development of Saving-Credit Co-operatives

Year	No. of co-operatives	No. of member	Capital	Deposits	Loans
1988–89	2,641	7,240	19.6	477.55	493.54
1989–90	2,372	6,110	15.25	421.98	667.17
1990–91	2,372	5,990	15.89	492.77	835.88
1991–92	2,374	5,870	15.39	544.47	988.09
1992–93	2,346	5,500	19.07	654.69	1,044.50
1993–94	2,347	5,520	102.87	655.86	1,283.03
1994–95	2,188	5,240	280.53	1,433.66	2,411.38
1995–96	2,249	5,050	465.44	918.11	2,690.93
1996–97	2,212	4,960	500.35	1,223.83	4,013.48
1997–98	2,042	4,240	1,176.89	1,754.74	3,639.59
1998–99	2,038	4,180	1,316.56	4,487.88	16,466.93
1999–00	2,098	4,530	1,232.54	3,354.71	9,270.48
2000–01	1,964	4,160	1,104.43	3,696.54	8,483.07
2001–02	1,942	4,310	1,072.17	3,851.41	6,336.45

Note: Number of members in thousands of people, capital, deposits and loans in million of kyat.

Source: Fukui (2004).

to, for example, employees or factory workers. There are also societies open to anybody, regardless of their sector or company. As of 2001, there were reportedly 139 open-type Saving and Credit Cooperative Societies, with a total membership of approximately 10,000 individuals. Fukui (2004) reported that open-type societies provided small-scale, short-term loans (mainly to micro entrepreneurs or vendors for 12 months or less) that average 5,000–10,000 kyat per recipient with interest rates ranging from 25 to 60 per cent per annum.[13] The Saving and Credit Cooperative Societies are highly concentrated in the Mandalay and Sagaing areas, where societies have performed well.

Microfinance, increasingly prevalent in developing countries, operates on a limited scale in Myanmar. The United Nations Development Programme (UNDP) initiated microfinance as part of a humanitarian project in cooperation with international NGOs that have expertise in microfinance. These NGOs provided small-scale finance to the poor in rural areas with designated UNDP projects. As of 2001, the international and local NGOs were implementing 23 microfinance projects in 40 townships. There were 110,000 loan recipients in all, and loans amounting to 1.6 billion kyat, which demonstrates fast growth in a short period.[14]

The Development Mechanisms of the Private Commercial Banks

The Operational Environment of the Private Commercial Banks

The newly established private commercial banks grew rapidly after the liberalization of entry into the banking industry, a contrast to the relative decline of the state-owned commercial banks (SOCBs). Obstacles faced by private commercial banks included limited branch networks and repressive regulations, such as interest rate controls. Private commercial banks had about 80 branch offices as of 1998, whereas the MEB alone had more than 300 branches. Controls on interest rates limited the deposit interest rate and the lending interest rate, both of which were negative in real terms. The annual inflation rate ranged from 10 to 50 per cent, while the nominal lending interest rate was fixed at around 15 per cent.

Nevertheless, private commercial banks attracted deposits and expanded rapidly, overtaking the SOCBs in terms of their share of deposits in 1998. Their growth is striking when compared with the Lao PDR and Vietnam. While the entry of the private commercial banks commenced in these countries at approximately the same time as in Myanmar, the SOCBs still account for more than 70 per cent of deposits and loans in both countries.

Table 6 summarizes changes in the consolidated balance sheet of the private commercial banks. It shows that equity capital did not catch up with the expanding deposits. The ratio of deposits to equity, the focal ratio at the start of the bank run in February 2003, jumped from 1.5 in 1992 to 17.9 in 2001. The surge in deposits was accompanied by a marked increase in treasury bond (TB) holdings, which grew from 7.3 per cent of total assets in 1998 to 30.6 per cent in 1999 even though the bonds bore very low interest. While the regulated interest rate on fixed deposits (nine months) was 9.75 per cent per annum during 2000/01, the five-year bonds bore interest of only 9 per cent.

One interpretation is that the banks had to increase their holdings of TB in order to comply with the prudential regulations. In fact, the ratio of equity to loans and advances plus investments fell to 11 per cent in 1998, while the rules required the banks to maintain a risk-weighted capital adequacy ratio of above 10 per cent.

The Background to the Development of the Private Commercial Banks

Despite the relatively unfavourable operational conditions, private commercial banks recorded marked growth until the bank run took place in February

Table 6 Consolidated Balance Sheet of Domestic Private Commercial Banks (million kyat)

	1992	1993	1994	1995	1996	1997	1998	1999	2000	2001
Number of Banks	4	8	13	15	21	20	20	20	20	20
Liquid Assets	273	881	2,188	6,884	13,810	17,655	33,190	36,246	52,725	82,290
Cash	114	322	581	3,339	4,599	8,913	15,838	19,691	31,358	54,101
Balance with the Central Bank	154	547	1,584	2,397	8,093	6,258	11,027	8,233	10,616	16,297
Investments	14	14	35	220	1,799	1,920	19,864	973	1,466	2,089
Loans and Advances	180	1,294	3,516	9,719	26,223	50,488	60,866	97,066	159,807	309,561
Bonds and Securities	14	49	374	809	1,535	5,081	10,209	70,374	102,091	133,903
Total Assets	522	2,373	6,557	20,034	48,393	84,339	139,240	229,716	382,650	590,987
Deposits	230	1,578	4,840	15,705	37,014	58,156	110,784	186,169	324,580	487,101
Equities	152	415	842	1,546	4,731	7,363	8,913	13,325	19,053	27,238
Equities/(Loans and Advances + Investments)	78.2%	31.8%	23.7%	15.6%	16.9%	14.0%	11.0%	13.6%	11.8%	8.7%
Deposits/Equities	1.5	3.8	5.7	10.2	7.8	7.9	12.4	14.0	17.0	17.9
Loan to Deposit ratio	78.1%	82.0%	72.6%	61.9%	70.8%	86.8%	54.9%	52.1%	49.2%	63.6%
Reserve Ratio (Liquid Assets/Deposits)	118.6%	55.8%	45.2%	43.8%	37.3%	30.4%	30.0%	19.5%	16.2%	16.9%
Liquidity Ratio (Liquid assets + Bonds and Securities)/ Total liabilities)	77.4%	47.5%	44.8%	41.6%	35.1%	29.5%	33.3%	49.3%	42.6%	38.3%

Notes: as of December 31.
"Bonds and Securities" are mostly Treasury Bonds. "Equities" are the sum of "Paid–up capital" and "Retained earnings".

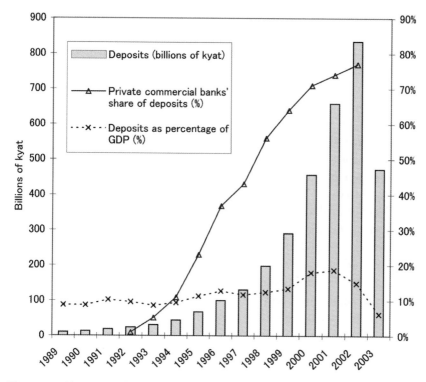

Figure 2 Changes in the Deposits of the Consolidated Commercial Banks and the Share of Private Commercial Banks

Notes: Values of Deposits and Private commercial banks' share of deposits as at year end. Values of Deposits as percentage of GDP are calculated by dividing deposits as at year end with GDP for the corresponding fiscal year (April–March). For the calculation of the Share of private banks' deposits, the sum of the savings deposits of consolidated private commercial banks (from *Selected Monthly Economic Indicators*) Central Statistical Organization (CSO) (various issues, a) and the demand deposits of the consolidated commercial banks (from *Statistical Yearbook*) is divided by the total deposits of deposit money banks (from IMF *International Financial Statistics*).

Sources: IMF (various issues), Central Statistical Organization (CSO) (various issues, a) CSO (various issues, b).

2003. This subsection focuses on the incentives for depositors and bank owners that lay behind this growth.

For depositors, the primary question is why they increased their deposits in the private commercial banks despite the negative real deposit interest rate. One explanation for this is that, at the time of the entry of these banks, the economic reform had stimulated the real economy, which in turn provided an impetus to the latent demand for banking facilities as a means of savings and settlements. In contrast to the inconvenient services of the existing SOCBs,[15] their services, such as swift money remittance to the rural areas, arguably increased the demand for deposits.[16]

The real interest rate elasticity of deposits is generally low in developing countries, where alternatives are scarce (Giovannini, 1985). For example, compared with cash, a bank deposit is an advantageous asset that bears interest, albeit at a low rate. In addition to this basic property of deposits, the convenience of the banking services in Myanmar improved along with the expansion of the branch network, which in turn promoted the shift towards deposits.

What caused owners of banks to enter the banking industry? The management bodies of the private commercial banks include business groups that originated from businesses engaged in trade, real estate, and construction, and their motives relate to the overall logic governing the expansion of private commercial banks. When information asymmetry between a creditor and a borrower causes high agency costs, a business group can save such costs by establishing a bank within its group and utilizing mobilized savings as internal funds.[17] It is possible that the banks invested aggressively in their branch networks despite the low profitability of the banking business in nominal terms in order to gain access to this source of finance. The prohibition of borrowing by SEEs created favourable conditions for the bank owners. In contrast to other transition economies, the insulation of the SEEs from the banking sector protected the banks from any losses associated with directed lending to SEEs.

In addition, the operational environment may have forced the banks to augment their leverage (debt/equity ratio) in order to maintain profitability. Regardless of the negative real interest rate, more deposits lead to a higher return on equity capital (ROE) for banks as long as the interest margin between the lending and deposits interest rates remains positive. In fact, at the end of 2002, the ratio of deposits to equity reached 57 per cent for the largest private commercial bank, the AWB, and 30 per cent for the second largest, the Yoma Bank (Wang, 2004).

The slump in the SOCBs is also noteworthy. Because the SEEs were insulated from the banking sector and are an integral part of the national budget, the SOCBs were not required to mobilize savings to finance them. As a result, the SOCBs became obsolete, allowing profit-seeking private banks to exploit the latent demand for banking services and to mobilize savings.

The February 2003 Bank Run

The growth of Myanmar's banking sector was due largely to the autonomous development of private commercial banks in a repressive business environment; from a policy perspective the government did little to promote the industry. In this context, the bank run in February 2003 can be regarded as a turning point, since the private sector-led growth could no longer maintain stability in the financial sector. This section reviews the chronology of the bank run, and evaluates the government's response.

The Chronology of the Bank Run

The bank run was started by a rumour about a scandal in the largest private commercial bank, the AWB, at the beginning of February 2003, and as early as 6 February, long queues for the withdrawal of deposits at AWB branches were reported. The rumour was preceded by the bankruptcy of several informal financial companies, the so-called "general service companies (GSCs)". The AWB made the following announcement at its annual meeting on 8 February, stressing the difference between the informal GSCs and the formal financial institutions:

> Private banks including the AWB bank, unlike economic services (GSCs), are organized systematically according to rules and regulations of the Central Bank of Myanmar and the Financial Institutions of Myanmar Law. They are firmly performing financial services under close supervision and with the backing of the Central Bank of Myanmar according to law (*The New Light of Myanmar*, 9 February, 2003).

On 10 February, the governor of the Central Bank issued a similar statement, and on 16 February the prime minister gave further assurances that private banks were safe.

These announcements, however, did not stem the outflow of deposits, and the tide of withdrawal spread to other private commercial banks. Individual banks reacted to the withdrawal requests by setting a limit on either the withdrawal amount per depositor or the number of depositors handled per day. On 17 February, the Central Bank ratified the suspension of convertibility, and instructed all banks to limit withdrawals to 5,000,000 kyat per week per deposit account; the limit was further reduced to 100,000 kyat on 24 February. In the meantime, it was reported that the shortage of kyat cash in circulation led to an appreciation of the kyat *vis-à-vis* the US dollar from 1,000 to 900 kyat/US$ in the parallel currency market.[18]

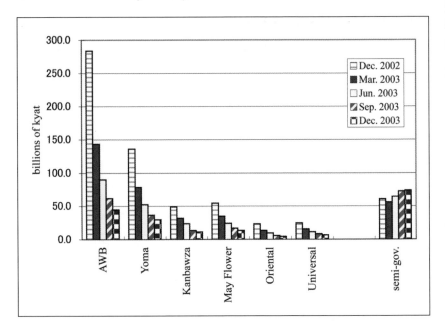

Figure 3   Changes in Deposits of Private Commercial Banks Before and After the Crisis (by Ownership)

Note: Semi-government banks comprise five banks (Myawaddy, Innwa, MLFDB, MIDB, Co-operative).

Sources: Fukui (2004: Table 3), Wang (2004: Table 6).

The banks requested liquidity support from the Central Bank at the outset of the bank run. It was not until 21 February that the Central Bank announced liquidity assistance of a total of 25 billion kyat to the three largest private commercial banks, including the AWB.[19] However, this liquidity assistance amounted to less than 10 per cent of the deposits of the AWB alone (250 billion kyat as at the end of 2002). On the other hand, in the middle of February, the Central Bank ordered banks to recover 20 to 50 per cent of their loans to borrowers by the end of March by forcibly altering the repayment terms.

Figure 3 illustrates the change in the deposits of the major private commercial banks. The outflow of deposits had slowed by September 2003, but three quarters of the deposit holdings of the AWB were gone. Private commercial banks were prohibited from issuing new loans or accepting new deposits, whereas the compulsory collection of loans, scheduled for completion by the end of March, was extended until the end of May 2003. It was not until February 2004 that three of the crisis-ridden banks were permitted to resume normal operations.

In response to the bank run, the government drastically tightened the prudential regulations. Notably, to cope with the deficiencies in equity capital in relation to deposits, the capital adequacy ratio regulation was replaced by an "equity to deposit ratio regulation". Under the former regulation, although the banks were required to maintain the risk-weighted capital adequacy ratio at above 10 per cent, there was no ceiling on the amount of savings that they could mobilize. The new regulation, however, compelled the banks to restrict their deposits to no more than seven times their paid-up capital.

Various Views on the Origin of the Bank Run

The primary view of the causes of the bank run is that the bankruptcies of the informal financial companies, the GSCs, implanted the bank run in the depositors' minds.[20] In addition, various rumours and reports circulated about the AWB, suggesting that the bank was suffering financial distress. One rumour suggested that the bank had suffered a huge loss from a speculative business deal with a Chinese company.[21] Another possibility is that the governor's remark about the AWB "going public" was mistakenly interpreted as meaning the bank was to be nationalized (Fukui, 2004). An article in the business magazine, *Living Color*, published in early February[22] is also considered significant, since it critically reported that the AWB's deposit to equity ratio was over 50. These rumours and reports caused doubts among the depositors regarding the solvency of the banks, especially the AWB.

Apart from these rumors, various events are also frequently associated with the bank run. One was the creation of the Control of Money Laundering Law in June 2002; another was the boom and bust in real estate speculation, although this is not regarded as the trigger of the bank run (Fukui, 2004). Third, the replacement of the Minister of Finance and Revenue on 1 February and the associated uneasiness in the financial market was also noted.

The General Service Companies (GSCs)

While causal relationships between the bank run and the incidents described in the previous section are not necessarily evident, it is certain that the bankruptcy of general service companies (GSCs) from late 2002 was an unprecedented event that changed people's perception of Myanmar's financial sector and influenced the bank run in 2003. The following facts are known about the bankruptcy of the GSCs and its implications.

Many companies categorized as GSCs and offering informal financial services were established in the late 1990s; no new private banks were founded during this period, after the establishment of the Inwa Bank in 1997.[23] The GSCs were constituted under the Company Act or Cooperative Law. Their main business was fields such as real estate, hotels, tourism, mining, manufacturing, and fisheries, but they also extended financial services to investors whom they attracted by promising high returns. The objects for the GSCs' investment were diverse: real estate, precious metals, US dollars, FEC, cars, and phones. To raise funds, the GSCs sold financial products, which they called "deposits" or "shares", to private companies and individuals. They said that the interest rates for these "deposits" were as high as 2–6 per cent per month (lasting from a month to two years), which by far exceeded the regulated interest rates of the banks. It was evident that the GSCs were failing to comply with the Financial Institutions Law or regulation by the CBM, under whose jurisdiction they fell. Investment in US dollars was obviously illegal.

Despite their informal nature, the financial services of the GSCs rapidly became very popular among the general public in Myanmar. Their products were offered for sale to the public through word-of-mouth communication and newspaper advertising. There were at least 20 GSCs, mainly in the Yangon and Mandalay areas. Some of them created enterprise groups with affiliated companies. "Deposits" were mobilized not only in the Yangon and Mandalay areas but also in other cities and even rural areas. Moreover, the GSCs apparently raised funds from the private banks to increase investments. Although the total number of GSCs is unknown, it has been estimated that the funds mobilized by them were equivalent to a quarter of the total funds mobilized by the formal banks.

Following their rapid growth, the GSCs suddenly went bankrupt in quick succession in 2002. Thitsar Pan Kin, Maha Danan, Naing Aung Myay, which were major GSCs, stopped business or announced liquidation from late 2002. They announced to the investors that they would pay back only the "principals" against the "deposits" or "shares" of the investors. Other GSCs were forced into liquidation, and by March 2003 the financial businesses of almost all of the GSCs had vanished. It is plausible that the fragility of Myanmar's financial sector was revealed to people through the bankruptcy of the GSCs, which, essentially, was an indirect cause of the bank run.

Two factors largely influenced the rapid growth and sudden failure of the GSCs. The first was demand for savings or investment spontaneously increased by both corporations and households. The second was the fact that the market price of assets peaked in the late 1990s. In her analysis of real estate market price trends, Wang (2004) reported that the plateau in the price of assets damaged the illegal investment of the GSCs, which pursued high returns through speculative investments.[24]

The Control of Money Laundering Law, and Recent Developments

The Control of Money Laundering Law was one of the most significant changes in the financial sector. Following rumours about a relationship between some of the major private commercial banks and the illegal drug business, the government of Myanmar faced pressure to act from the international community, including the Financial Action Task Force on Money Laundering (FATF) of the Organization for Economic Co-operation and Development (OECD). This pressure intensified following the terrorist attack in the US in September 2001, and the legislation was created in June 2002. When investigations of the large deposit account holders were initiated, considerable amounts of drug-related funds were withdrawn in anticipation of a possible freeze on withdrawals.[25] To stem the sudden outflows of deposits, the legislation was modified to narrow the subject of investigation to only new accounts following the enactment of the Law, which calmed the situation.

A further change occurred in November 2003 when the US government instructed American banks that they should not enter into transactions with the AWB and the Myanma Mayflower Bank due to a suspicion that these banks were involved in money laundering. The government of Myanmar finally enacted the law in the following month, December 2003, and established an investigation committee to scrutinize the two banks. By the end of 2004, both banks had suspended business.[26] The law not only placed a brake on the sort of expansion of deposits that had preceded the bank run, but also hindered the recovery after the bank run.

For the banking sector as a whole, there have been signs of recovery since the beginning of 2004. Steps have been taken towards the reorganization of the banking industry; two small cooperative banks merged to become the Cooperative Bank. Kanbawza Bank and the Myawaddy Bank, which had been relatively unharmed by the banking crisis, recovered as leading private banks. Other banks, such as the AWB, the Myanma Mayflower Bank, and the Yoma Bank continued to face difficulties. As of July 2004, the three largest private commercial banks were the Kanbawza Bank (with a total deposit above 50 billion kyat), the Myawaddy Bank (43.2 billion kyat), and the Cooperative Bank (24 billions kyat).[27]

Evaluation

The steps taken by the government to deal with the bank run were not adequate. When the crisis began, the Central Bank and the government merely announced that the banks were sound, but the assistance given to maintain liquidity was both inadequate and too late. It has been argued that the resulting suspension of the convertibility of deposits aggravated the situation (Turnell, 2003; Zaw Oo, 2003), and the notification of the changing collection terms of the loans exacerbated the damage. The series of government measures suggests that the development of the banking sector had reached a stage where the private sector-led banking system could no longer sustain stability in relation to the financial sector policies.[28]

Turning to the transmission process of the crisis, all six of the hardest-hit private commercial banks, including the AWB, originated from private business groups and experienced rapid growth. Figure 3 shows that these major private commercial banks lost more than half of their deposits, whereas the outflow of deposits from the so-called "semi-government banks" was minimal. Given this contrast between the two types of bank, the following characteristics of the major private commercial banks can be made. First, there may have been a concern among the depositors regarding the opaque financial condition of the large private commercial banks; and, second, given the lower government involvement with these banks, the depositors may have anticipated that the probability of a bailout was small.

With regard to tightening the prudential regulations after the crisis, the "equity to deposit ratio regulation" limiting the amount of deposits to within seven times the bank's paid-up capital is noteworthy. Given the difficulties of raising capital, this regulation effectively hampered the mobilization of savings, and probably suppressed the development of the private commercial banks.

A Comparison of the Financial Systems in Cambodia, Lao PDR, Myanmar and Vietnam (CLMV Countries)

All of the CLMV countries were formerly socialist economies and implemented the reorganization of their banking sectors concurrently. A comparative analysis will shed light on banking sector development in Myanmar. The principal points of comparison include: (i) the introduction of the two-tier banking system and the entries of the non-state banks; (ii) the instability of the banking system and its reconstruction; and (iii) the financial condition of the banks.

The Two-Tier Banking System and the Entry of the Non-state Banks

In the CLMV countries, economic reform in the real sector influenced the banking sector reorganization that began in the late 1980s. For the Lao PDR and Vietnam, the approach was through gradual reform of the SEEs. The SOCBs supplied credit to the SEEs, and constituted the core of the banking sector. In Myanmar, the government prohibited the SEEs from taking out bank loans to prevent the accumulation of nonperforming loans, and introduced a State Fund Account (SFA) to compensate for the deficits of the SEEs through the national budget. Given the government's fiscal balance, the deficits of the SEEs were actually financed by printing money. This was effectively a retreat from SEE reform, and left the SOCBs without any clear role to play. In Cambodia, the SEEs were scarcely operational due to the unstable political conditions, and their privatization progressed relatively smoothly, resulting in a limited role for the SOCBs.

Table 7 outlines banking sector development. The two-tier banking system was introduced almost simultaneously in the four countries, as was liberalization of the entry of non-state banks. In Cambodia, Myanmar, and Vietnam, private commercial banks were launched successively in the first half of the 1990s. In Cambodia, small banks established by overseas Cambodians sprang up like mushrooms. In Vietnam, the banking regulation required that at least 10 per cent of the equity of a bank should be held by SEEs, so no banks were wholly held by the private sector. In the Lao PDR, there were no private commercial banks except those established as joint ventures with foreigners, implying that few private entrepreneurs could afford to establish a bank. Except in Myanmar, entry liberalization also meant the entry of foreign banks and foreign banks branches. In contrast, foreign banks were not allowed to operate in Myanmar.

Table 8 summarizes the shares of the SOCBs along with the indices for financial deepening. The SOCBs maintain large market shares in Lao PDR and Vietnam but not in Cambodia and Myanmar. In Vietnam, four SOCBs together accounted for approximately 70 per cent of the loans of the consolidated commercial banks in 2000. The share of the foreign banks (26 banks) was 15 per cent, while private commercial banks (43 banks) and joint-venture banks (4 banks) had market shares of 12 and 3 per cent, respectively (World Bank, 2002). In Cambodia, there was only one SOCB, the Foreign Trade Bank, and it had no branches. Its market share was small, and it was scheduled to be privatized.

The above comparison implies that the Myanmar government's lack of concern regarding the role of the banking sector as a financial source for the

Table 7 Outline of the Banking Sector Reform in CLMV Countries

	Myanmar	Cambodia	Lao PDR	Vietnam
Start of reorganization				
Introduction of two-tier banking system	1976/1990	1989	1988	1988
Amendment of Laws associated with the Central Bank and financial institutions	1990	1989	1990	1990
Entry of private and foreign banks	1992	1991	1989	1991

Number of banks	Dec. 1997	Dec. 2002	Dec. 1997	Jul. 2004	Dec. 1997	Dec. 2002	Dec. 1998	Dec. 2002
State-owned commercial banks	3	3	1	1	7	3	4	5
Other state banks	1	1	0	0	1	1	0	0
Private commercial banks	20	20	20	8	0	0	51	39
Joint-venture banks	0	0	2	2	2	3	4	4
Foreign banks incorporated	0	0	2	2	0	0	0	0
Foreign bank branches	0	0	7	3	7	7	23	27

Notes: Other state banks refer to the public financial institutions that are not under the jurisdiction of the Central Bank. The ones in Myanmar and Lao PDR are both agricultural development banks. For the introduction of a two-tier banking system in Myanmar, three state banks were superficially separated from the central bank in 1976, but the substantial reorganization started in 1990. In the table, for Cambodia, private commercial banks and joint-venture banks are categorized in one group.

Sources: Myanmar: Wang (2004), Cambodia: IMF (1999c), (2004), Lao PDR: Economic Research Department (2001), Bank of the Lao PDR (2003), Vietnam: IMF (1999a), State Bank of Vietnam (2003).

Table 8 Selected Indices of Financial Deepening in CLMV Countries

	Myanmar	*Cambodia*	*Lao PDR*	*Vietnam*
	as of end 2001	*as of end 2003*	*as of end 2003*	*as of end 2002*
M2/GDP	34.3%	21.2%	18.2%	61.4%
Deposits/GDP	18.7%	15.4%	17.0%	47.5%
Credit/GDP	11.0%	8.6%	7.9%	43.1%
Credit to SEEs/GDP	n.a.	0.0%	2.0%	16.7%
Share of SOCBs				
Credit	20.1%	9.5%	53.5%	75.9%
Credit to SEEs	n.a.	0.0%	73.4%	91.2%
Deposits	26.0%	19.3%	73.6%	74.3%
SOCBs credit to SEEs/ Total credit of SOCBs	n.a.	0.0%	25.4%	38.7%

Sources: Myanmar: Central Statistical Organization (2002b), Cambodia: IMF (2004), Unteroberdoerster (2004), Lao PDR: IMF (2005), Vietnam: IMF (2003).

SEEs resulted in the decline in the SOCBs. The government's introversion or caution towards the foreign banks gave private banks room to develop autonomously. This (non)competitive market condition, which benefitted local private banks, resulted from the government's heavy reliance on printing money as a financing tool.

The Instability of the Banking System and its Reconstruction

The CLMV countries, as transition economies, shared the experience, although to differing degrees, of the instability of the banking system.[29] This instability stemmed from two factors: the government's weak regulatory and supervisory capacity, and the relationship between the banking sector and the SEEs.

For transition economies, such as those of the CLMV countries, commercial banking is a new form of economic transaction that was absent during the period of the planned economies. Without proper government regulation and supervision, inexperienced banks would easily fall into financial distress. However, the governments also lacked experience in the regulation and supervision of the banking industry, so the banking sector often faced instability during the transition process. The situation was exacerbated by the entry of an excessive number of small banks into the industry, as

occurred in Cambodia. The financial distress in Cambodia was also associated with the business recession caused by the Asian economic crisis in
1997. To reconstruct the banking system, the financial authorities rein-
forced the prudential regulations. All banks had their banking license revoked
and, to regain them, were required to comply with the minimum paid-up
capital within three years, an amount that was increased from US$5 million
to US$13 million. As a result, 14 banks had closed by 2002.

The lending of the SOCBs to the SEEs is another source of instability
in the banking sector of the Lao PDR and Vietnam. Under the sluggish
reform of the SOCBs and the SEEs, the continued supply of credit to the
SEEs led to the accumulation of nonperforming loans. In the Lao PDR,
while the SOCBs underwent capital injection for the disposal of impaired
assets, the nonperforming loans to the SEEs continued to increase. As a
further reform, the additional lending to SEEs with overdue loans was, in
principle, prohibited. In Vietnam, the SOCBs' nonperforming loans to the
SEEs were a serious problem, reaching, according to an estimate by the IMF,
an average of 30 to 35 per cent of the total loans as at 1997, and the bulk
of these loans had been made to the SEEs (IMF, 1999a). The government
repeatedly injected capital into the SOCBs to dispose of nonperforming
loans, but improving their credit risk management remains a challenge.

The banking instability in Myanmar is attributable to the government's
weak regulatory and supervisory capacity. While the trigger of the banking
crisis in 2003 was arguably the collapse of the informal financial institutions
or various rumors, the public was suspicious about the financial fragility of
the private banks under the government's weak supervisory capacity. The
government's weak capacity also aggravated the banking crisis. As a counter-
measure to the banking sector distress, all of the CLMV countries tightened
their prudential regulations, in particular by strengthening the banks' equity
capital requirements. Myanmar's "equity to deposit ratio regulation" that
limits deposits to no more seven times the paid-up capital is particularly
restrictive. While an increase in the minimum paid-up capital had the effect
of stabilizing the banking business through the expansion of the bank's scale,
the equity rule caused the bank's balance sheet to contract and retarded the
recovery of the private banks in Myanmar.

The Financial Condition of the Banks

Table 9 compares the balance sheets of the consolidated commercial banks.[30]
It shows that equity capital in relation to assets is extremely low in Myanmar.
The shortage of equity capital partly reflects the rapid expansion of deposits.

Table 9 Comparison of the Balance Sheets of the Consolidated Commercial Banks in CLMV Countries

	Myanmar	Cambodia	Lao PDR	Vietnam
	billion kyat	*billion riel*	*billion kip*	*trillions VND*
Reserve	70.4	1,331.0	1,101.0	20.2
Foreign assets	0.0	834.0	1,717.0	70.7
Credit to the economy	309.6	1,347.0	1,778.0	231.1
of which to SEEs	n.a.	0.0	451.0	89.5
of which to private sector	n.a.	1,347.0	1,327.0	141.6
Balance with the government (net)	n.a.	91.0	243.0	–2.3
Others (net)	143.5	24.0	151.0	–4.7
of which Treasury Bonds	132.7	n.a.	n.a.	n.a.
Total asset	523.4	3,627.0	4,990.0	315.0
Deposits	487.1	2,412.0	3,833.0	254.8
of which foreign currency deposits	n.a.	2,301.0	2,634.0	93.6
Foreign liabilities	n.a.	318.0	790.0	9.9
Balance with the central bank (net)	9.1	58.0	166.0	19.3
Equities	27.2	840.0	201.0	30.9
Credit/Deposits	63.6%	55.8%	46.4%	90.7%
Equities/Credit	8.8%	62.4%	11.3%	13.4%
Reserve/Deposits	14.5%	55.2%	28.7%	7.9%
Foreign currency deposits/Deposits	n.a.	95.4%	68.7%	36.7%
exchange rate (local currency/US$)	450	3,980	10,467	15,368
Total assets in US$ (million US$)	1,163	911	477	20,497

Notes: Myanmar, as of end 2001, Vietnam, as of end 2002, Cambodia and Lao PDR, as of end 2003. The balance sheet for Myanmar is that of the consolidated private commercial banks, and does not include the state-owned commercial banks.

Sources: Myanmar: Central Statistical Organization (2002b), Cambodia: IMF (2004), Lao PDR: IMF (2005), Vietnam: IMF (2003).

The capital adequacy ratio of the Cambodian banks is high because of restructuring during 1999–2002, but its high capital adequacy ratio also reflects the sluggish growth of deposits.

The proportion of foreign assets is high in all of the CLMV countries except Myanmar.[31] It is especially high in Lao PDR, and suggests inactive financial intermediation and capital flight via the formal banking sector.

Similarly, the deposit to loan ratio is low in Cambodia, the Lao PDR, and Myanmar, although the low deposit to loan ratio and the high liquidity ratio in these three countries may be associated with provisions by individual banks against liquidity shocks. As the financial markets in these countries are shallow and the interbank loan market limited, each bank has to prepare for liquidity shocks. It might be for this reason that the banks in Myanmar keep TBs, while the banks in Cambodia and the Lao PDR maintain a high liquidity ratio with deposits in banks abroad.

For CLMV countries other than Myanmar, the "dollarization" of the banks' balance sheets is a notable phenomenon. In Cambodia, 95 per cent of deposits are denominated in US$. In the Lao PDR, the proportion of foreign currency deposits denominated in US$ and the Thai baht to the total deposit rose from 65 per cent in 1996 to 83 per cent in 1999 due to high inflation in 1998/99. In Vietnam, deregulation of the opening of foreign currency deposit accounts by individuals in 1999 heralded an influx of dollar cash into the banking system, and the proportion of foreign currency deposits in the total deposits reached 40 per cent. From the viewpoint of the currency risk, such a high proportion of foreign currency deposits on the liability side partially accounts for the shift towards foreign assets on the asset side. Dollarization is a matter of concern for the financial authorities because it weakens the capacity of the Central Bank to act as the lender of last resort.[32]

A couple of factors account for the low extent of dollarization in Myanmar. First, the openness to trade is low in Myanmar compared with that in other CLMV countries. Secondly, foreign exchange transactions have been severely regulated in Myanmar. In principle, the public is prohibited from holding foreign currency; only exporters with formal export earnings can open foreign currency deposit accounts. Furthermore, although foreign currency is circulated informally and is used for smuggling, these funds cannot be used for official imports. The aim of strict foreign exchange regulations appears to be to control informal foreign exchange earners, such as drug traders. As a result, the dollarization of the bank balance sheet has been largely avoided in Myanmar.

Section Summary

This comparison of the banking systems in the CLMV countries has shed some light on the characteristics and development of the banking sector policies in Myanmar. First, the prohibition on the borrowing from banks by SEEs is a notable reason for the growth of private commercial banks. Myanmar is different from the Lao PDR and Vietnam, where the SOCBs have financed the SEEs and occupy the core position in the banking sector. Banks in Vietnam and Laos have made large loans to SEEs. These are nonperforming loans, and finding a way to dispose of them and to prevent other loans from becoming nonperforming are important challenges in Vietnam and Laos. In Myanmar the deficits of the SEEs are shouldered by the whole economy through the inflationary finance of the government. In Cambodia the development of the banking sector is also led by private commercial banks, but liberalization has progressed throughout the economy in Cambodia, whereas the reform of the SEEs remains an unresolved issue in Myanmar.

Second, the government's regulatory and supervisory capacity with regard to the banking sector has been weak in Myanmar, as in the other CLMV countries, and this was a cause of the banking crisis of 2003. To restore stability to the banking sector in the aftermath of the crisis, the government opted to narrow the scope of the banks' operations rather than providing better regulation and supervision. Such a policy is possibly a reflection of the policy-formation of the government that prefers the stability and controllability of the economy to economic growth.

Third, the closed nature of Myanmar's banking sector is noteworthy. As a result of the strict foreign exchange regulations, dollarization in the bank balance sheet, which is prominent in the other CLMV countries, has been largely avoided, although such foreign exchange regulations are definitely not intended to encourage stability in the banking sector. Again, policy-formation may be oriented, not towards economic growth, but towards the discretion of the government.

Concluding Remarks

This chapter has examined the history of the financial sector and the features of the state and private banks in Myanmar. In Myanmar's financial system, the state banks have stagnated and their role remains ambiguous. This is partly because the reforms of the early 1990s bar SEEs from borrowing money from banks. As a paradoxical result, the mechanism whereby the growth of the financial system is obstructed by the burden of the SEEs — a common phenomenon in transition economies — is substantially restricted in the case of Myanmar, but the SEEs have become a major cause of the fiscal deficit through their low productivity and profitability, and consequently of macroeconomic instability.

Following the partial liberalization of the banking business, private banks experienced autonomous growth under adverse conditions. The private banking sector grew rapidly owing to the strong investment by domestic private capital over a short period, and until 2003 the industry was stable. This situation could be seen as a notable characteristic of Myanmar's financial system and contrasts with the situation in Cambodia. There the banking sector was extensively liberalized, both domestically and overseas, and Cambodian private capital faced serious threats of bankruptcy within five years of liberalization. Myanmar's experience could be understood as a consequence of an uncompetitive environment characterized by the stagnation of the state banking sector and protection from foreign capital in the financial sector. Simultaneously, however, it reflected the strength of domestic capital, magnified by the newly-opened foreign trade opportunity, which survived both political and administrative turmoil.

Myanmar's bank run of 2003 and the persistent ensuing turmoil imply that the private sector-led growth of the financial system has reached the stage where growth is no longer sustainable or stable. This means that proper, drastic restructuring is required. In particular, supervision and prudential regulation measures are extremely inconsistent and still in a primitive state, as demonstrated by the administrative response to the bank run.

For a long time, the direction of future development in the closed banks and re-building of the private banks remained relatively ambiguous. It appears to be too early to tell how the financial system and financial administration will be restructured in the future; as such, the restructuring is closely related to the political environment and the recovery of the real sectors.

Annex Table 1. Changes in Myanmar's Banking Sector

1988	Transition to a market-based economy started.
1990	Promulgation of the Central Bank of Myanmar Law, the Financial Institutions of Myanmar Law, and the Myanma Agricultural and Rural Development Bank Law. Establishment of private commercial banks permitted.
1992	Private commercial banks started. Representative offices of foreign banks opened (49 banks at peak).
1994	Foreign exchange transactions liberalized to private commercial banks.
1995	The Mayflower Bank introduced automated teller machines (ATMs) (November).
1995	Joint venture banks between foreign and local private commercial banks banks planned (December); six projects applied for approval.
1997	Asian Financial Crisis.

Annex Table 1. continued

1998	Suspension of new banking licenses. Growth of informal financial institutions, general service companies (GSCs). Foreign exchange licenses for private commercial banks revoked, and concentrated among state-owned commercial banks (June).
2002	Legislation of the Control of Money Laundering Law (June). Continual bankruptcies of GSCs (late 2002).
2003	Bank run on six major private commercial banks (February). The Central Bank ordered repayment of loans before maturity (February).
2004	Three crisis-ridden banks permitted to resume normal operations (February).

Notes

The views and opinions presented in the chapter belong to the authors personally and not to the organizations with which they are affiliated.

[1]   The banking sector in Myanmar prior to the revolution in 1962 was dominated by foreign commercial banks, particularly English banks, which seemingly controlled all industry. The nationalization of the banks in 1963 aimed at crowding out the foreign banks.

[2]   SFA is, in practice, administered by MEB; SFA accounts constitute part of the balance sheets of MEB.

[3]   Myanmar Securities Exchange Center Ltd transacts shares in public companies. Its transactions are, however, extremely limited, as there are very few public companies. Laws to develop stock markets were drafted in 1992, but their promulgation has not been considered, so the stock markets have remained underdeveloped.

[4]   According to an interview with MEB officials by one of the authors in April 2000, "policy-based directed credit" to private projects in the infrastructure sector constituted about 10 per cent of the total loans outstanding (64 billion kyat) at the end of 1999. The conditions for the directed credit were an interest rate of 10 per cent per annum and a government guarantee.

[5]   Computed from Mya Than and Myat Thein, ed. (2000: 88).

[6]   The NPL ratio was obtained during an interview with the senior management of the MEB in April 2000. It includes the defaulted housing loans that were extended to civil servants as housing construction programmes promoted by the government from 1990–93.

[7]   The MADB used to borrow from the Asian Development Bank and United Nations Development Programme before 1988.

[8]   This description of the structure of shareholdings of the Myawaddy Bank and the Inwa Bank is based on interviews conducted by one of the authors in February

2001 as part of the field research. MEC and UMEHL function as windows to foreign companies when the government negotiates for the establishment of joint ventures.

[9] The description of MIDB is based on an interview conducted by one of the authors in June 2000 during field research.

[10] Among the top seven private banks at the end of 2001, Kanbawza Bank is an exception, which is owned by a Burmese successful in the mining industry, not a person of Chinese descent.

[11] The 27 affiliated companies belonging to the SPA group include: four companies engaged in finance; five companies in real estate; eight companies in manufacturing or construction; and ten in service.

[12] Joint venture projects include: the Tun Foundation and Maybank (Malaysia); the Myanma Mayflower Bank and Siam City Bank (Thailand); Yoma Bank and Fuji Bank (Japan); the Myanma Citizens Bank and Public Bank Malaysia (Malaysia); AWB and the Thai Farmers Bank (Thailand); and the Myanma Livestock and Fishery Development Bank and the Global Commercial Bank (Cambodia) (Wang, 2004).

[13] According to the Japan International Cooperation Agency (JICA) study conducted in 2002, 70 per cent of the open-type Saving and Credit Cooperative Societies surveyed were paying dividends (ranging from 3 to 4 per cent per annum), which indicates that these societies absorbed their operational and capital costs through interest rate revenue.

[14] As for the lending methodology of the microfinance NGOs, every organization adopted group lending with peer groups guaranteeing loans and no collateral. Half of them also provide loans to individuals. The duration of the loans ranges from 6 to 12 months. Interest rates can be on a cost-recovery basis but in most cases are set at "market"-based rates of the moneylenders. The minimum loans range from 1,500–50,000 kyat, and the maximum from 50,000–300,000 kyat. The financial performance of the NGOs engaged in the UNDP project encourages aggregate "operational self-sufficiency", which ranges from 117 to 227 per cent, and "financial self-sufficiency", which is an indicator of the degree to which the capital costs are covered, from 47 to 76 per cent; for further details, see Fukui (2004).

[15] During interviews conducted with several private commercial banks in September 2004, it was often stated that the poor information processing facilities of the SOCBs inhibited prompt deposit withdrawal and money transfer at their branches.

[16] The newly introduced services include automated teller machines (ATMs) and bank-issued credit cards.

[17] For a general discussion of information asymmetry and agency costs, see Frexias and Rochet (1997).

[18] As of 20 February 2003 (*Irrawaddy* online, 6 Dec. 2003).

[19] There is another report that at the start of the bank run the AWB requested the withdrawal of its deposits, amounting to 52 billion kyat, from the Central Bank, and that the Central Bank accepted this request (Zaw Oo, 2003). Furthermore, it is also reported that the Central Bank approved t1he liquidity assistance scheme to provide loans from the Myanmar Economic Bank to three banks: the AWB, the Yoma Bank, and the Kanbawza Bank (Wang, 2004), although the reliability of these reports cannot be confirmed.

[20] This includes Myat Thein (2003), Turnell and Vicary (2003) and Zaw Oo (2003).

[21] According to Zaw Oo (2003), there are several versions of the rumours regarding the scandal in the AWB, including one that the AWB's vice-governor made a huge loss while gambling in Macau, and another that the vice-governor was arrested on suspicion of engaging in illegal financial transactions.

[22] Dr. Ko Ko, "New Year for the Private Banks", *Living Color* No. 92 (in Burmese), quoted in Myat Thein (2003).

[23] GSCs established under the Company Act include: Thabarwa, Ngwe Zone, Thitsar Pan Kin, Ei Myintmo, Green Myanmar, and Ayeyarmyae. GSCs registered as cooperatives include: Maha Danan, Mudita, and Lin Thitsar (Wang, 2004).

[24] See Chapter 1 for the trends in real estate prices.

[25] Zaw Oo (2003) reported that the AWB faced panic-driven withdrawals.

[26] Later, in April 2005, the banking licenses of these two banks were revoked.

[27] *The Myanmar Times*, 19–25 July 2004.

[28] Barth *et al.* (2004) discuss the importance of the regulatory and supervisory capacity of the government in the development of the financial sector.

[29] For a general analysis of banking crises in transition economies, see Berglof and Bolton (2000), and Enoch *et al.* (2002).

[30] Due to data availability, the figures for Myanmar are as of 2001 and do not include the SOCBs.

[31] These foreign assets consisted mainly of deposits with banks abroad that are used for foreign exchange settlements. In Myanmar, only the SOCBs have permission to engage in foreign exchange transactions. It should be noted again that, as the figures for Myanmar in Table 8 do not include the SOCBs, the amount of foreign assets is zero for Myanmar.

[32] Watanabe (2004) discusses various problems that dollarization poses for financial development. Earlier contributions to the analysis of dollarization include that of Balino *et al.* (1999).

PART TWO

The Economy of Agriculture and Labour

CHAPTER 5

Overview of Agricultural Policies and the Development in Myanmar

Koichi Fujita and Ikuko Okamoto

Introduction

Before 1988 Myanmar's economy was characterized by isolation from the outside world. This chapter reviews the development process of the agricultural sector after 1988, with special reference to the extent to which the economy was involved in and influenced by international markets. This involves exploring how Myanmar succeeded in optimizing the sub-sectors in which it enjoyed a comparative advantage, and the extent to which it overcame, or failed to overcome, the demerits of the sub-sectors in which there was no comparative advantage. An analysis carried out from this perspective makes it possible to examine the significance and role of the agricultural sector in Myanmar's economic development.

Many analysts agree that Myanmar's economic policy during the socialist period (1962–88), especially up to the early 1970s, was essentially one of agricultural exploitation, with a heavy emphasis on rice production (Tin Soe and Fisher, 1990; Takahashi, 2001; Myat Thein, 2004). A policy of agricultural exploitation generally implies the following two elements: first, food prices are repressed and wages kept low in order to promote industrialization; and, second, export crops are purchased at below the international price, with the resulting revenue used to promote industrialization. Myanmar's rice policy during the socialist period was typical of agricultural exploitation. The government introduced a compulsory paddy procurement system at below-market prices and a system of rationing the supply of cheap rice to consumers through people's shops and cooperatives,[1] and it monopolized rice exports, which became the largest source of foreign exchange earnings at that time.

In itself, a system of procurement and rationing does not necessarily constitute an exploitative policy. Consider, for example, the case of edible oil. The socialist regime adopted a policy of self-sufficiency with regard to edible oil production, even though Myanmar enjoyed no comparative advantage in this sub-sector. It was very likely that the domestic price of edible oil would be well above its international price and thus farmers were "protected" by limiting imports, even though a procurement and rationing system similar to that applied to rice production was adopted in respect of oilseed crops, such as sesame and groundnuts.

As will be described later, imports of edible oil increased dramatically after 1988. As a result, the domestic edible oil price was lowered to a level close to that of the international price. On the other hand, there was a remarkable increase in exports of pulses and beans, which became Myanmar's largest export item. In due course the domestic price of pulses increased rapidly as pulses and beans underwent a rapid process of adjustment to the international market price. In this sense, the largest change that Myanmar agriculture has experienced since 1988 has been a departure from the closed trade regime that had isolated the domestic market from the international market.

By contrast, in the case of rice, after 1988 the domestic price was continuously limited to about half the international price, although the disparity narrowed somewhat over time. On the other hand, the inputs indispensable for rice cultivation (chemical fertilizer and diesel oil) became more closely linked to the international market, and finally began to be imported on a purely commercial basis. This means that Myanmar's rice sector has strengthened its linkage with the international market, albeit in a rather asymmetric way. This process created difficulties for farmers and for the Myanmar government alike.

Even after 1988 the farmers in Myanmar were controlled by "three internal major agricultural systems" inherited from the socialist period; namely, the procurement system, the planned cropping system and the state ownership of farmland, as stressed by Takahashi (Takahashi, 2001). It could even be argued that, after 1988, the government tightened these systems in order to control the farmers. At the same time, Myanmar agriculture was forced to come to terms with the current wave of internationalization. Given that internationalization is inevitable, making the best use of its merits while at the same time minimizing its demerits is the key to the successful reform of the domestic control systems. In analyzing trends in the agricultural sector after 1988, this chapter examines the transition to an open economy, rather than to a market economy in general. For this reason, the chapter focuses on broader measures rather than simply the domestic factors in an attempt to fill the gap in the previous research.

We group Myanmar's major agricultural products into the following four categories: export crops, crops for import competition, crops for the domestic market and crops for the state-owned economic enterprises. We believe that this is the most appropriate classification for analyzing the problems encountered with regard to Myanmar's crop production in the course of internationalization.

Specifically, the categories comprise the following: export crops (rice and pulses), crops for import competition (oilseeds), crops/products for the domestic market (vegetables, fruit, meat and fishery products), and crops for state-owned economic enterprises (sugarcane and cotton).[2]

The contents of the chapter are as follows. Section 1 reviews the development of the agricultural sector since 1988 within the context of the trends in the national economy as a whole. Section 2 discusses performance, analyzing the factors that have determined performance for each of the major agricultural products contained in the four main categories of crop production. By way of conclusion, the nature of Myanmar's agricultural policies and agricultural development that can be attributed to these policies will be summarized briefly.

The Performance of the Agricultural Sector in the National Economy

Let us first look at the performance of the agricultural sector and its role in Myanmar's overall economic development. Table 1 indicates the changes in the composition of GDP by sector and the annual growth rates since the early 1980s. The agricultural sector was surprisingly slow to lose its relative importance in terms of its contribution to GDP, accounting for more than 40 per cent of GDP even in recent years (at 1985/86 constant prices). This suggests that the agricultural sector has been growing at a pace equal to that of the other sectors of the economy.

The table also shows that agriculture's share of GDP is significantly higher at current prices than at 1985/86 constant prices. The discrepancy widened sharply between 1985/86–1990/91 and the divergence increased further until 1994/95. This means that agricultural prices, which in the socialist period had been highly suppressed compared to non-agricultural prices, had become "normalized" by the mid-1990s.[3] In general, the rate of increase in agricultural retail prices was higher than that of the Consumer Price Index (CPI).

Table 1 Agriculture in Myanmar: Contribution to GDP and Growth Rates, 1980–2006

		1980/ 81	1985/ 86	1990/ 91	1995/ 96	1996/ 97	1997/ 98	1998/ 99	1999/ 2000	2000/ 01	2001/ 02	2002/ 03	2003/ 04	2004/ 05	2005/ 06
Contribution to GDP (at constant price)	Agriculture	47.9	48.2	48.0	45.1	44.4	43.6	43.0	43.2	42.7	55.9	52.9	51.9	50.7	50.1
	Crop	39.4	39.7	38.7	37.1	36.2	35.2	34.5	34.4	33.6	47.4	44.3	42.5	41.2	40.2
	Livestock and Fishery	7.0	7.1	7.9	6.8	7.2	7.3	7.5	7.9	8.3	8.0	8.1	8.9	9.1	9.5
	Forestry	1.5	1.4	1.3	1.1	1.1	1.0	1.0	1.0	0.9	0.5	0.5	0.5	0.4	0.4
	Manufacturing	9.6	9.9	7.7	9.3	9.1	9.1	9.1	9.4	10.1	7.8	9.0	9.7	10.6	11.4
Contribution to GDP (at current price)	Agriculture	46.5	48.2	57.3	60.0	60.1	58.9	59.1	59.9	57.3	57.1	54.5	50.6	48.2	46.7
	Crop	38.8	39.7	46.3	53.2	53.2	52.1	52.3	52.2	48.8	49.0	48.3	44.9	40.9	38.4
	Livestock and Fishery	6.3	7.1	9.2	6.0	6.1	6.2	6.3	7.2	7.9	7.5	5.8	5.4	6.9	7.7
	Forestry	1.5	1.4	1.8	0.8	0.8	0.6	0.5	0.5	0.6	0.5	0.4	0.4	0.3	0.6
	Manufacturing	9.5	9.9	7.8	6.9	7.1	7.1	7.0	6.5	7.2	7.7	9.2	9.8	11.6	12.8
Real Growth Rate	GDP	7.9	2.9	2.8	6.9	6.4	5.7	5.8	10.9	13.7	11.3	12.0	13.8	13.6	13.6
	Crop	12.6	2.2	2.0	5.5	3.8	3.0	3.5	10.5	11.1	8.1	4.7	9.3	10.2	10.7
	Livestock and Fishery	4.0	2.0	-0.6	3.0	11.9	7.1	9.3	16.8	18.9	12.6	14.0	25.3	15.5	18.8
	Forestry	1.9	-0.1	8.3	-4.5	2.1	2.8	3.2	4.6	3.3	7.7	6.2	6.4	-5.9	4.0
	Manufacturing	6.9	2.9	0.1	7.6	4.6	5.0	6.2	14.5	23.0	21.8	28.7	22.0	24.7	21.9

Note: Constant price at 1985/86 for 1980/81 to 2000/01, at 2000/01 for 2001/02 to 2005/06.

Sources: CSO, *Statistical Yearbook* (1997, 2002, 2006).

Table 2 shows the differences in the rate of price increase among crops in this respect. First, for export crops, the rate of price increase was generally relatively high. Domestic prices, held at a very low level, rose dramatically because of the stimulus provided by international prices, and the result was a sharp increase in production and exports. Second, the price of import competition crops increased only slightly, because the expansion of imports prevented a surge in domestic prices. Third, the price of crops destined for the domestic market rose fairly sharply, probably due to the high income elasticity of items such as vegetables, meat and fishery products.

In sum, the agricultural sector played a prominent role in Myanmar's economic recovery and growth after 1988, and continued to do so until the mid-1990s. This was made possible largely by the price incentives given to the farmers. The agricultural marketing reforms of 1987 were, in general, relatively effective in achieving an adjustment between the hitherto highly suppressed agricultural prices and international prices. The rate of price increase was very high, not only for a few (but important) export crops but also for a variety of crops intended for the domestic market. Farmers responded quickly to the new economic opportunities.

Increases in agricultural production can be achieved by either an expansion of the sown area or a rise in the crop yields per unit area of land. How did Myanmar increase its farm output?

Table 3 sets out changes in the sown acreage of major crops. The total sown acreage, which was 24 million acres in the late 1980s, increased rapidly to 40 million acres.[4] Since the land frontier disappeared long ago in Myanmar, this expansion of sown acreage can be mostly attributed to the intensification of land use, or in other words, to a rise in cropping intensity. The sown acreage expanded in the case of almost every crop, except for oil seeds, which is a typical crop for import competition. Rice, pulses, vegetables (chillies, onions and garlic), cotton, sugarcane and rubber all merit particular attention in this regard.

Table 4 shows the changes in yield for major crops. A notable feature revealed in Table 4 is that, except for rice and rubber, yields have not shown any upward trend since 1988. We can conclude that development of the agricultural sector during the period was achieved through expansion of the acreage sown rather than through improvements in land productivity.

Finally, the contribution of agriculture to total exports over the same period is briefly reviewed (Table 5). According to Table 5, in the early years, agricultural exports (here defined broadly to include livestock, fishery products and timber) had a dominant share, accounting for more than 85 per cent of total exports. Rice and teak, the two major agricultural export products,

Table 2 Changes in Price of Major Agricultural, Livestock and Fishery Products, 1987–2005 (1986=100)

	Crop	1987	1988	1989	1990	1991	1992	1993	1994	1995	1996	1997	1998	1999	2000	2001	2002	2003	2004	2005
1 Export Crops/ Products	Rice (Emata)	112	191	339	266	306	503	864	796	1132	1286	1389	1907	2817	2548	2489	4898	7031	5536	6981
	Pigeon Pea	100	859	895	1286	2308	2677	2969	3693	6459	7049	7186	14643	15787	10355	13614	22933	24475	23833	36720
	Black Gram	100	463	579	699	1480	1547	1065	2154	3578	3390	3434	6157	7060	9773	13227	13680	28832	16200	22000
	Prawns	158	138	193	241	364	410	539	731	1121	1919	2444	4168	3926	3936	3943	1875	4571	4740	8209
2 Crops for Import Competition	Sesame Oil	127	135	143	165	232	365	328	434	585	572	912	1572	1772	1474	1904	3671	4654	4165	4729
	Groundnut Oil	130	144	144	170	228	365	325	422	552	545	875	1472	1620	1487	1795	4061	4729	4465	4813
	Palm Oil	100	100	100	125	174	296	250	332	404	399	650	1114	1185	936	1373	3054	3229	2914	3275
	Sesame	121	145	145	193	260	354	337	520	657	655	1010	1397	1499	2435	2677	2894	6564	4706	5142
	Groundnut	112	139	148	150	198	304	382	460	661	598	1075	1498	1848	1683	1893	2141	2829	4469	5345
3 Produce for the Domestic Market	Chilli	202	128	159	298	444	386	598	587	1072	1861	1434	2031	2854	2923	4243	6809	7666	6902	9758
	Onion	131	178	119	313	340	319	612	515	514	1646	1296	1762	1278	1156	3608	6809	7666	6902	9758
	Garlic	228	189	143	201	594	613	385	561	779	1406	1098	1473	2214	1977	2772	3125	3995	4138	6974
	Potato	163	209	255	361	466	469	739	898	1017	1222	1396	2589	2460	2571	2730	4949	85324	8576	10356
	Fish	137	129	173	238	304	325	459	638	787	821	1179	1328	1543	1974	2624	4200	5868	7074	9204
	Chicken	135	141	195	281	348	399	645	781	966	1051	1303	1583	1702	1937	2709	4223	5279	6599	8198
	Pork	127	137	162	280	331	336	487	663	704	705	1064	1638	1675	1990	2826	4001	4844	5356	8996
	Beef	221	149	177	281	363	386	478	565	615	619	696	1217	1603	1763	2063	4312	5677	5939	10250
4 Crops for State-owned Economic Enterprises	Sugar	183	198	198	248	395	458	432	631	930	1024	1003	1458	1638	1877	3163	4751	5511	5049	6902
	CPI	127	155	192	234	302	369	493	604	736	883	1182	1578	1825	1794	2422	3830	4784	4965	5498

Notes: 1–3 are calculated based on the prices in Yangon. The figures for rice and palm oil are retail prices and the rest are wholesale price.
The palm oil figure was also the official price until 1989.
For pigeon pea and black gram, as there was no domestic demand for these pulses, the official price was used in this table.

Sources: CSO, *Statistical Yearbook* (1993, 1995, 2001, 2002, 2006).

Table 3 Major Agricultural Crops: Changes in the Sown Acreage, 1970–2005 (Thousand acres)

	1. Export Crops		2. Crops for Import Competition		3. Crops for the Domestic Market				4. Crops for State-owned Economic Enterprises			Total Sown Acres
	Rice	Pulses	Sesame	Groundnut	Vegetable	Chilli	Onion	Garlic	Cotton	Sugarcane	Rubber	
1970/71	12,294	1,576	2,510	1,735	186	145	47	18	466	108	217	22,338
1980/81	12,668	1,995	3,231	1,271	301	170	47	21	546	118	200	24,805
1987/88	11,531	1,863	2,933	1,327	391	146	46	26	425	133	193	23,870
1988/89	11,807	1,642	2,994	1,355	342	179	64	27	443	123	192	23,802
1989/90	12,057	1,934	3,158	1,380	342	182	57	27	379	113	190	24,344
1990/91	12,220	2,281	3,271	1,369	343	170	57	26	386	118	191	25,024
1991/92	11,935	2,945	3,184	1,261	391	202	60	28	424	136	188	25,426
1992/93	12,684	3,500	3,379	1,220	389	220	65	33	416	187	193	27,200
1993/94	14,021	3,553	3,211	1,204	391	194	57	30	356	154	205	28,134
1994/95	14,643	4,117	3,288	1,252	416	172	62	28	505	130	220	30,005
1995/96	15,166	4,808	3,153	1,303	445	158	66	29	937	165	259	31,837
1996/97	14,518	4,584	2,830	1,184	463	203	60	29	824	204	294	30,422
1997/98	14,294	4,967	2,430	1,111	514	190	69	35	659	266	333	30,336
1998/99	14,230	5,729	2,738	1,241	524	169	115	34	804	311	369	32,882
1999/2000	15,528	6,209	3,173	1,400	657	220	146	41	842	333	419	36,582
2000/01	15,713	6,725	3,308	1,458	732	249	145	46	801	343	446	38,177
2001/02	15,940	7,372	3,210	1,405	740	280	139	47	730	402	460	39,153
2002/03	16,032	7,556	3,325	1,436	809	293	136	51	747	367	457	39,896
2003/04	16,168	7,734	3,414	1,617	952	273	144	52	721	373	468	41,318
2004/05	16,946	8,099	3,496	1,690	1,036	318	155	59	756	361	503	43,073
2005/06	18,259	8,662	3,122	1,805	1,094	323	179	60	820	330	558	46,342

Sources: MAS (1994), CSO, *Myanmar Agricultural Statistics* (2001), CSO, *Statistical Yearbook* (2006).

Table 4 Major Agricultural Crops: Changes in Yields, 1970–2002 (Tons per acre)

	1. Export Crops				2. Crops for Import Competition		3. Crops for the Domestic Market		4. Crops for State-owned Economic Enterprises		
	Rice	Black Gram	Green Gram	Pigeon Pea	Sesame (Rain)	Groundnut (Dry)	Chili	Onion	Cotton	Rubber	Sugarcane
1970/71	0.69	0.18	0.11	0.17	0.07	0.38	0.16	1.80	0.19	0.56	11.61
1980/81	1.13	0.29	0.13	0.16	0.07	0.44	0.19	2.37	0.25	0.67	15.50
1985/86	1.25	0.39	0.23	0.26	0.10	0.50	0.22	4.20	0.31	0.73	21.53
1990/91	1.19	0.29	0.23	0.26	0.07	0.46	0.19	3.05	0.28	0.72	15.50
1992/93	1.19	0.29	0.26	0.23	0.44	0.10	0.21	2.80	0.33	0.74	15.50
1993/94	1.23	0.29	0.26	0.26	0.10	0.48	0.22	2.79	0.29	0.75	15.50
1994/95	1.27	0.33	0.29	0.26	0.10	0.50	0.20	2.75	0.31	1.03	15.50
1995/96	1.21	0.33	0.29	0.23	0.12	0.56	0.22	2.87	0.24	1.04	17.23
1996/97	1.23	0.33	0.29	0.26	0.15	0.55	0.22	3.19	0.27	1.11	17.23
1997/98	1.23	0.36	0.33	0.29	0.15	0.56	0.24	3.30	0.31	1.11	17.23
1998/99	1.27	0.36	0.29	0.26	0.10	0.54	0.26	4.15	0.25	0.95	15.50
1999/2000	1.32	0.33	0.26	0.26	0.10	0.52	0.23	3.26	0.25	0.99	14.64
2000/01	1.38	0.36	0.29	0.36	0.12	0.58	0.23	4.09	0.24	1.13	15.50
2001/02	1.38	0.33	0.29	0.36	0.10	0.59	0.26	4.66	0.26	1.15	14.64
2002/03	1.38	0.36	0.33	0.39	0.60	0.12	0.27	4.88	0.26	1.16	15.50
2003/04	1.42	0.39	0.33	0.36	0.62	0.10	0.28	4.96	0.27	1.08	15.50
2004/05	1.46	0.46	0.36	0.39	0.64	0.12	0.32	5.25	0.31	1.13	17.23
2005/06	1.48	0.49	0.39	0.43	0.65	0.12	0.34	5.65	0.33	1.17	18.95

Sources: MAS (1994), CSO, *Statistical Yearbook* (2002, 2006).

made up more than 65 per cent of all exports. However, after 1988, this mono-culture export structure underwent a major transformation.

First, pulses increased markedly as an important export item. The export of pulses by value had overtaken rice and teak combined by the mid-1990s, and came to account for 20–25 per cent of total exports. Second, exports of fishery products increased after the mid-1990s, just as the momentum in the increase of pulse exports was beginning to slow. The main item was prawns. Third, exports of non-agricultural commodities increased after the late 1990s. The expansion of garment exports in the late 1990s and subsequent increases in natural gas exports have been prominent features of Myanmar's changing export structure.

To summarize, Myanmar's export structure departed from a mono-culture pattern dominated by rice and teak, and diversified, first into a variety of agricultural commodities and then into non-agricultural commodities, a category that has become increasingly important in the last few years. It should be noted, however, that exports of non-agricultural commodities have been dominated by two items, garments and natural gas, and that agricultural exports remain important to Myanmar's economy.

The Nature and Determinants of the Production Performance of the Major Crops

This section will analyze and identify the main determinants of the production performance of Myanmar's major crops after 1988.

Export Crops

Export crops are defined here as those in which Myanmar enjoys a comparative advantage. Whether Myanmar has always succeeded in taking advantage of its comparative advantage in these categories is, of course, another issue. Although typical of its agriculture, rice is a crop whose production potential Myanmar has failed to exploit. By contrast, the cultivation of pulses and beans has been a notable success story. The critical difference between the two is that rice is a staple food, enjoying a significant position in people's diet, and any price hike therefore affects consumers badly. This is not the case for pulses in Myanmar.

Rice

Rice is the key crop in Myanmar's agriculture and has great significance for the national economy. Since several observers have already undertaken

Table 5 Major Agricultural Commodities: Changes in Exports, by Value, 1980–2002 (Million kyat, percentages)

Export Value (Million kyat)	1980/ 81	1985/ 86	1990/ 91	1995/ 96	1996/ 97	1997/ 98	1998/ 99	1999/ 2000	2000/ 01	2001/ 02	2002/ 03	2003/ 04	2004/ 05	2005/ 06
Agricultural Products	**1761**	**1126**	**942**	**2321**	**1981**	**1952**	**1890**	**1602**	**2312**	**3021**	**415**	**2343**	**1828**	**2536**
Rice	1355	763	172	440	126	38	167	65	208	754	633	131	180	214
Pulses	152	238	515	1358	1272	1403	1135	1179	1658	1898	1760	1731	1283	1876
Maize	11	15	13	46	107	45	116	54	92	59	139	93	165	64
Oil Cake	46	32	11	12	4		1	2						
Rubber	82	56	3	180	171	134	100	75	67	76	88	99	87	205
Cotton	4	18		1	3	26	21	10	11	1				
Jute	99			6	5	8			5	37	10	5		
Other	12	4	228	278	293	298	350	217	271	196	178	284	113	177
Livestock Products	**13**	**11**	**5**	**7**	**9**	**8**	**34**	**28**	**37**	**42**	**22**	**13**	**17**	**21**
Fishery Products	**82**	**94**	**165**	**615**	**887**	**945**	**941**	**807**	**934**	**861**	**1116**	**966**	**1036**	**1147**
Fish	58	13	36	159	219	289	307	229	291	310	445	328	387	512
Prawns	24	76	114	407	560	559	569	529	598	519	623	589	597	576
Other		5	15	49	108	97	65	49	45	32	48	49	52	59
Timber	**793**	**1046**	**999**	**1048**	**985**	**853**	**789**	**925**	**803**	**1880**	**1871**	**2049**	**2242**	**2750**
Teak	721	982	740	903	855	698	640	727	651	1423	1388	1493	1515	1723
Hard Wood	72	64	259	145	130	155	149	198	152	457	483	556	727	1027
Sub-Total	**2649**	**2277**	**2111**	**3991**	**3862**	**3758**	**3654**	**3362**	**4086**	**5804**	**3424**	**5371**	**5123**	**6454**
Precious Stones & Metals	295	188	158	207	192	237	223	508	687	415	531	697	1163	2005
Natural Gas							5	31	1110	4247	5919	3478	5812	6235
Garment		6	8	300	402	436	471	2722	3785	2985	2976	1965	1238	1586
Other	281	183	685	546	1032	2016	2403	2324	3068	3680	4712	2608	3361	4367
Grand Total	**3225**	**2654**	**2962**	**5044**	**5488**	**6447**	**6756**	**8947**	**12736**	**17131**	**17562**	**14119**	**16697**	**20647**

Export Value	1980/81	1985/86	1990/91	1995/96	1996/97	1997/98	1998/99	1999/2000	2000/01	2001/02	2002/03	2003/04	2004/05	2005/06
Share (%)														
Agricultural Produce	**54.6**	**42.4**	**31.8**	**46.0**	**36.1**	**30.3**	**28.0**	**17.9**	**18.2**	**17.6**	**2.4**	**16.6**	**10.9**	**12.3**
Rice	42.0	28.7	5.8	8.7	2.3	0.6	2.5	0.7	1.6	4.4	3.6	0.9	1.1	1.0
Pulses	4.7	9.0	17.4	26.9	23.2	21.8	16.8	13.2	13.0	11.1	10.0	12.3	7.7	9.1
Maize	0.3	0.6	0.4	0.9	1.9	0.7	1.7	0.6	0.7	0.3	0.8	0.7	1.0	0.3
Oil Cake	1.4	1.2	0.4	0.2	0.1	0.0	0.0	0.0	0.0	0.0	0.0	0.0	0.0	0.0
Rubber	2.5	2.1	0.1	3.6	3.1	2.1	1.5	0.8	0.5	0.4	0.5	0.7	0.5	1.0
Cotton	0.1	0.7	0.0	0.0	0.1	0.4	0.3	0.1	0.1	0.0	0.0	0.0	0.0	0.0
Jute	3.1	0.0	0.0	0.1	0.1	0.1	0.0	0.0	0.0	0.2	0.1	0.0	0.0	0.0
Other	0.4	0.2	7.7	5.5	5.3	4.6	5.2	2.4	2.1	1.1	1.0	2.0	0.7	0.9
Livestock Products	**0.4**	**0.4**	**0.2**	**0.1**	**0.2**	**0.1**	**0.5**	**0.3**	**0.3**	**0.2**	**0.1**	**0.1**	**0.1**	**0.1**
Fishery Products	**2.5**	**3.5**	**5.6**	**12.2**	**16.2**	**14.7**	**13.9**	**9.0**	**7.3**	**5.0**	**6.4**	**6.8**	**6.2**	**5.6**
Fish	1.8	0.5	1.2	3.2	4.0	4.5	4.5	2.6	2.3	1.8	2.5	2.3	2.3	2.5
Prawns	0.7	2.9	3.8	8.1	10.2	8.7	8.4	5.9	4.7	3.0	3.5	4.2	3.6	2.8
Other	0.0	0.2	0.5	1.0	2.0	1.5	1.0	0.5	0.4	0.2	0.3	0.3	0.3	0.3
Timber	**24.6**	**39.4**	**33.7**	**20.8**	**17.9**	**13.2**	**11.7**	**10.3**	**6.3**	**11.0**	**10.7**	**14.5**	**13.4**	**13.3**
Teak	22.4	37.0	25.0	17.9	15.6	10.8	9.5	8.1	5.1	8.3	7.9	10.6	9.1	8.3
Hardwoods	2.2	2.4	8.7	2.9	2.4	2.4	2.2	2.2	1.2	2.7	2.8	3.9	4.4	5.0
Sub-Total	**82.1**	**85.8**	**71.3**	**79.1**	**70.4**	**58.3**	**54.1**	**37.6**	**32.1**	**33.9**	**19.5**	**38.0**	**30.7**	**31.3**
Precious Stones	9.1	7.1	5.3	4.1	3.5	3.7	3.3	5.7	5.4	2.4	3.0	4.9	7.0	9.7
Natural Gas	**0.0**	**0.0**	**0.0**	**0.0**	**0.0**	**0.0**	**0.1**	**0.3**	**8.7**	**24.8**	**33.7**	**24.6**	**34.8**	**30.2**
Garments	**0.0**	**0.2**	**0.3**	**5.9**	**7.3**	**6.8**	**7.0**	**30.4**	**29.7**	**17.4**	**16.9**	**13.9**	**7.4**	**7.7**
Other	8.7	6.9	23.1	10.8	18.8	31.3	35.6	26.0	24.1	21.5	26.8	18.5	20.1	21.2
Grand Total	100.0	100.0	100.0	100.0	100.0	100.0	100.0	100.0	100.0	100.0	100.0	100.0	100.0	100.0

Sources: CSO, *Statistical Yearbook* (2002, 2006).

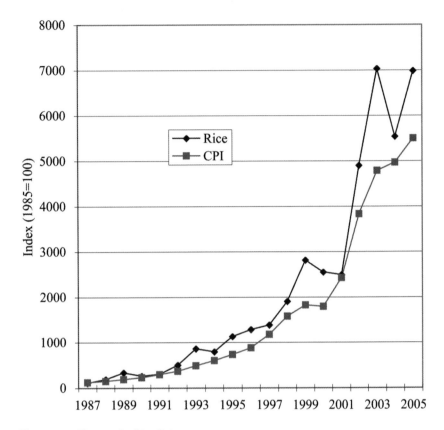

Figure 1　Changes in Rice Price

Sources: CSO, *Statistical Yearbook* (2002, 2006).

research on rice cultivation in Myanmar (Takahashi, 2000; Garcia *et al.*, 2000; Fujita and Okamoto, 2000; Fujita, 2003; and Kurosaki *et al.*, 2004), we will confine ourselves to a concise summary.

Changes in the rice price

A sharp increase in the rice price, far exceeding the rise in the CPI, occurred immediately after liberalization of the agricultural market in 1987 (Table 2). Figure 1 indicates the trends in the rice price and in the CPI. The rice price was 1.77 and 1.27 times that of the CPI in 1989 and 1993, respectively, a situation that caused considerable anxiety for the government. A widespread sense of crisis forced the government to adopt corrective measures, such as the exclusion of rice from the marketing liberalization in 1988[5] and the

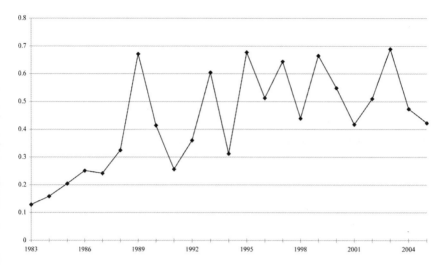

Figure 2 Myanmar Rice Price: Ratio of Domestic Retail Price to International Price, 1983–2005

Sources: International Rice (Thai rice): IMF, *International Financial Statistics*; Domestic Wholesale Rice (Yangon) *Statistical Yearbook* (1997, 2003, 2006). Market Exchange Rate: 1988/89–1996/97 ADB (2001); 1997/98–2002/03 Tokyo-Mitsubishi Bank Yangon Representative Office; 2003/04–05/06 Author's Survey.

introduction of the summer paddy programme, initiated in 1992–93 to boost rice production. Despite such measures, another emergency regarding the rice price occurred around 1999 (Figure 1), and the rice price remained relatively high until 2001, when it finally converged with the CPI.

Let us now examine the surge in the rice price from a different angle. Figure 2 illustrates the ratio of the domestic to the international price of rice between the mid-1980s and the early 2000s.[6] According to Figure 2, the domestic price was between a seventh and an eighth of the international price in 1983/84, which shows that the domestic rice price was kept at an extremely low level during much of the socialist period, but the ratio then increased rapidly and was around 25–33 per cent by the end of the socialist period. After 1988 it further increased, reaching a peak of 70 per cent in 1989. Thereafter, it fell to 25 per cent in 1991 before again rising to 60 per cent in 1993. From then on, with wide fluctuations, it averaged at around 50 per cent, meaning that the domestic price was half the international price.

To summarize, despite the government's intention and efforts, Myanmar's rice market could not be protected from internationalization. Although the price disparity has been reduced compared to the socialist period or the early

1990s, the gap remains large, and the disparity continues to be the main factor hampering the development of Myanmar's rice sector.

What made the situation worse for Myanmar's rice farmers was the fact that they did not receive the already low domestic market price in full owing to the existence of a government paddy procurement system. The paddy procurement system was abolished in 1987/88, but was reintroduced only a year later, in 1988/89. The lowering of the quota to the level of 10–12 baskets per acre (1 basket of paddy equals 20.9 kg) reduced the farmers' burden, and summer paddy was exempted from the procurement obligation in order to provide an incentive to farmers to expand their summer paddy cultivation. These changes were possible because of a reduction in the scale of the rice rationing system, which now provided rice only to targeted groups including civil servants.

Although it was scaled back, the paddy procurement system was a heavy burden for rice farmers. First, the procurement price was set far below the (domestic) market price, and the price disparity was as large as 50–60 per cent.[7] Second, it is possible that the burden borne by the farmers was even heavier than is indicated by official statistics. If the yield was around 60 baskets per acre, as claimed in the official statistics, the burden on farmers would be less than 20 per cent of total production, but the official figures may overstate production.[8] If the actual yield was only 40–45 baskets per acre, the farmers' burden was more onerous, constituting as much as 25–30 per cent of production.

The system kept the price paid to producers far below the market price, which was already quite low in comparison with the international price levels.[9] It was finally abolished in 2003/04.

Changes in rice production

As stated earlier, the main element of rice production policy after 1988 was the summer paddy programme initiated in 1992/93.[10] To promote summer paddy production, investment in irrigation was indispensable not only in the dry zone in Upper Myanmar, but also in Lower Myanmar. In this sense, the programme was essentially one of irrigation development.

Let us now consider Table 6. The irrigated area was stagnant at about 2.48 million acres until 1991/92, but then expanded rapidly, reaching 4.55 million acres by 1999/2000. It should be stressed here that, out of the increased irrigated area of 2 million acres, the area under pump irrigation, which amounts to no less than 1.65 million acres, accounts for the dominant share.[11] Table 7, which gives the sown acreage of summer paddy by region, clearly shows that the increase in summer paddy acreage was prominent in

Table 6 Irrigated Acreage, by Type of Irrigation, 1974–2000 (Thousand acres)

		1974/ 75	1984/ 85	1989/ 90	1990/ 91	1991/ 92	1992/ 93	1993/ 94	1994/ 95	1995/ 96	1996/ 97	1997/ 98	1998/ 99	1999/ 2000
Canal	Government	855	893	614	613	593	638	651	701	685	668	726	761	806
	Farmer	700	691	664	665	651	645	601	618	608	636	634	600	611
Tank	Government	130	98	394	388	378	416	418	389	350	435	455	408	462
	Farmer	111	75	82	92	82	95	70	89	94	95	74	44	34
Tubewell		31	44	53	53	65	69	75	92	99	123	135	164	199
Pump		267	470	322	310	323	469	1,051	1,551	2,057	1,511	1,545	1,865	2,076
Other		318	411	354	358	375	411	437	403	448	378	363	340	362
Total		2,412	2,682	2,483	2,479	2,467	2,743	3,303	3,843	4,341	3,846	3,932	4,182	4,550

Source: CSO, *Agricultural Statistics* (2001).

Table 7 Paddy Land in Myanmar: Changes in the Sown Acreage, by Region, and Type of Rice Sown (by season), 1993–2005

Monsoon Paddy	States and Divisions	1993/94	1995/96	1997/98	1998/99	1999/2000	2001/02	2003/04	2005/06
Delta	Ayeyarwaddy	3,232	3,279	3,229	3,224	3,323	3,372	3,403	3,600
	Yangon	1,165	1,174	1,131	1,135	1,162	1,176	1,185	1,200
	Bago	2,160	2,167	2,094	2,114	2,347	2,378	2,414	2,760
	Mon	646	649	641	641	659	670	674	831
	Total	**7,203**	**7,268**	**7,095**	**7,114**	**7,491**	**7,595**	**7,676**	**8,391**
Dry Zone	Sagaing	1,102	1,144	1,260	1,257	1,404	1,331	1,414	1,602
	Magwe	379	439	468	383	437	505	510	669
	Mandalay	551	608	648	524	552	616	610	841
	Total	**2,033**	**2,190**	**2,376**	**2,164**	**2,392**	**2,451**	**2,534**	**3,112**
Coastal Area	Rakhine	859	856	854	864	913	940	957	1,100
	Tanintharyi	208	213	208	208	215	233	279	375
	Total	**1,067**	**1,069**	**1,062**	**1,072**	**1,128**	**1,173**	**1,236**	**1,475**
Mountainous Area	Shan	859	866	793	787	874	954	1,047	1,310
	Kachin	251	269	292	329	365	388	396	412
	Kayah	61	68	67	44	51	68	69	97
	Kayin	325	327	326	326	326	330	362	492
	Chin	88	90	93	93	105	107	109	120
	Total	**1,584**	**1,620**	**1,571**	**1,579**	**1,721**	**1,847**	**1,983**	**2,431**
	Grand Total Area	**11,886**	**12,148**	**12,104**	**11,928**	**12,732**	**13,066**	**13,429**	**15,409**

Table 7 continued

Summer Paddy	States and Divisions	1993/94	1995/96	1997/98	1998/99	1999/2000	2001/02	2003/04	2005/06
Delta	Ayeyarwaddy	1,120	1,613	1,277	1,412	1,597	1625	1,320	1,200
	Yangon	155	334	172	197	253	222	214	167
	Bago	291	317	174	141	210	195	272	321
	Mon	72	105	73	85	127	113	101	101
	Total	**1,638**	**2,369**	**1,696**	**1,836**	**2,187**	**2,155**	**1,907**	**1,789**
Dry Zone	Sagaing	150	203	124	95	134	243	299	269
	Magwe	30	56	42	45	67	79	94	140
	Mandalay	150	145	137	123	174	165	190	160
	Total	**330**	**404**	**303**	**263**	**375**	**487**	**583**	**569**
Coastal Area	Rakhine	7	14	9	9	10	13	17	17
	Tanintharyi	8	23	10	15	14	17	17	17
	Total	**15**	**37**	**19**	**25**	**25**	**30**	**34**	**34**
Mountainous Area	Shan	33	36	35	49	59	56	61	56
	Kachin	8	24	13	14	16	16	15	19
	Kayah	4	8	10	3	8	8	9	4
	Kayin	122	140	114	112	126	128	119	113
	Chin	0	0	0	0	0	0	0	0
	Total	**167**	**208**	**172**	**178**	**209**	**209**	**204**	**192**
Grand Total Area		**2,150**	**3,018**	**2,190**	**2,302**	**2,796**	**2,880**	**2,728**	**2,584**

Sources: Ministry of Agriculture and Irrigation Documents (1999/2000–2005/06), CSO, *Myanmar Agricultural Statistics* (1997, 2001).

the Delta, especially in the Ayeyarwaddy Division, where pump irrigation is used.

The development of pump irrigation in the Delta area was achieved on the basis of: (1) the construction of sluice gates by the Irrigation Department in order to adjust the water level of rivers and canals; (2) the construction of drainage channels for dry season irrigation using the voluntary labour of village residents; and (3) the farmers' private investment in water pumps (Fujita and Okamoto, 2000; Fujita, 2003). The government's financial support for pump irrigation was relatively small.[12]

By contrast, the government invested hugely in canal irrigation projects, including the construction of reservoirs. In addition, by keeping the water charge at a nominal rate (10 kyat per acre), the government provided a generous de facto subsidy towards maintenance costs. Nevertheless, as shown in Table 6, the contribution of canal irrigation to overall irrigation development has been rather limited.

Table 7 shows that the acreage of summer paddy expanded dramatically until 1995/96 but plunged in 1996/97, recovering only moderately thereafter. The slowdown in summer paddy production was the main cause of the sluggish expansion of paddy production in Myanmar after the mid-1990s. Why was the summer paddy programme thwarted? The answer lies in the decline in the profitability of summer paddy cultivation. Since pump irrigation was introduced by private investment and depends on large amounts of expensive diesel oil, farmers are very sensitive to profitability.

Table 8 summarizes the data from various surveys, showing the trend of profitability. The data for Kyaukse in 1993/94 and Htantabin in 1998/99 relate to a time when the rice price was high. In Kyaukse, the share of operators' surplus increased to as much as 60 per cent of gross revenue. Reflecting, amongst other things, the low cost of canal irrigation, the high profitability of summer paddy cultivation was, at this time, notable. Despite its relatively higher cost structure, arising from the local usage of pump irrigation, the case of Htantabin also shows that the high rice prices allowed the farmers to obtain reasonably good profits from summer paddy production.

Once the rice price fell, however, the intrinsically expensive nature of pump irrigation emerged as a serious drawback for farmers. In Myaungmya in 2000/01, for example, there arose a literally disastrous situation for farmers growing summer paddy, and the operators' surplus was almost nil. By contrast, the profitability of summer paddy production in the canal irrigation area of Kyaukse did not deteriorate to the same extent.[13]

The vulnerability of pump-irrigated summer paddy production caused some friction between the farmers and the government once the rice price

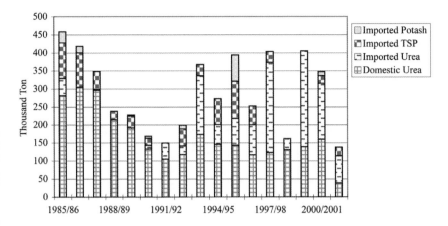

Figure 3 Changes in the Supply of Chemical Fertilizer, 1985–2000

Sources: CSO, *Statistical Yearbook* (1995, 1997, 2002), MOAI (2000b), MAS Documents.

declined.[14] While government pressure had penetrated deeply into the rural areas, the farmers persistently attempted to resist such influences. This was especially evident in 2000–1, when the rice price collapsed.[15]

Generally speaking, rice production became unattractive to farmers after the mid-1990s, not only because of the low rice prices, but also because of the high input prices.

Changes in the input supply

The decline in the profitability of summer paddy cultivation was not merely the outcome of the sluggish rice prices. Hikes in the prices of inputs, such as chemical fertilizer, diesel oil and agricultural machinery had a seriously negative effect. Farmers had no alternative but to depend on these inputs, which are mostly imported on a purely commercial basis. It is relevant to note here that foreign assistance stopped after 1988,[16] and the government was obliged to abolish subsidies for these inputs.

Figure 3 shows changes in the supply of chemical fertilizers, both imported and domestically produced. The supply of domestic fertilizer declined because of the degradation of the producing factories and the difficulty of obtaining raw materials for these factories.[17] This fall in supply had to be compensated for by imports, and the dependence on imports increased after 1993/94.

The figures for imports are the sum of imports by the government (Ministry of Agriculture and Irrigation and Ministry of Commerce) and

Table 8 Rice Production in Myanmar: Cost and Revenue Structure, by Major Regions

Area	Delta						Dry Zone			Mountainous Area	
Location of Study Village (Township)	Hlantabin (1998/99)		Myaungmya (2000/01)		Kyaukse (1993/94)		Kyaukse (2000/01)		Taundwingyi (2000/01)	Taunggyi (1993/94)	Nyaung Shwe (2000/01)
Season	Monsoon	Summer	Monsoon	Summer	Monsoon	Summer	Monsoon	Summer	Monsoon	Monsoon	Monsoon
Type of Irrigation	Rainfed	Pump	Rainfed	Pump	Canal	Canal	Canal	Canal	Rainfed/Tank	Rainfed	Rainfed
Number of Farmers in Sample	9	9	67	66	68	52	33	25	13	14	9
Sown Acres	17.4	8.1	8.6	6.5	4.4	3.3	4.1	2.7	5.2	4.2	2.4
Yield per Acre (Basket/Acre)	46.8	86.8	45.4	67.7	45.1	66.8	56.2	69.0	25.4	35.1	44.5
① Gross Revenue (Kyat/Acre)	29,427	53,324	17,615	27,526	10,042	15,128	29,171	42,093	11,865	13,904	31,238
② Current Input Cost	6,064	20,210	4,736	13,765	1,390	1,715	10,273	12,686	3,003	1,682	12,001
Seed	1,883	4,701	1,558	2,375	502	515	2,827	2,806	1,407	391	2,009
Manure	0	0	144	39	0	0	528	327	891	1,291	1,186
Chemical Fertilizer	3,704	9,438	2,702	8,599	888	1,200	6,405	8,813	640	0	5,923
Other Chemicals	53	600	39	174	0	0	240	594	65	0	2,519
Diesel Oil	424	5,471	293	2,578	0	0	271	145	0	0	365
③ Labour Cost	8,629	7,410	7,884	6,400	2,750	3,339	5,937	8,178	3,107	5,336	15,395
Hired Labour	5,238	4,543	5,023	2,881	2,323	3,089	5,072	6,887	2,063	3,661	10,194
Family Labour (a)	3,390	2,867	2,861	3,519	427	250	865	1,292	1,044	1,675	5,201

Table 8 continued

Area	Delta				Dry Zone					Mountainous Area	
Township in which Study Villages Locate	Htantabin (1998/99)		Myaungmya (2000/01)		Kyaukse (1993/94)		Kyaukse (2000/01)		Taundwingyi (2000/01)	Taungyi (1993/94)	Nyaung Shwe (2000/01)
Season	Monsoon	Summer	Monsoon	Summer	Monsoon	Summer	Monsoon	Summer	Monsoon	Monsoon	Monsoon
Type of Irrigation	Rainfed	Pump	Rainfed	Pump	Canal	Canal	Canal	Canal	Rainfed/Tank	Rainfed	Rainfed
④ Capital Cost	5,277	8,336	3,963	7,271	822	846	5,927	8,493	3,591	2,532	5,682
Agricultural Machinery	1,696	4,980	983	5,017	186	178	2,488	3,471	162	104	1,906
Bullocks	3,284	3,264	2,564	1,791	636	668	3,430	4,256	3,166	2,428	3,335
Interest Payment	297	92	416	464	0	0	10	766	264	0	441
⑤ Total of Production Cost (②+③+④)	19,970	35,956	16,582	27,436	4,962	5,900	22,137	29,357	9,701	9,550	33,079
⑥ Operator's Surplus (①–⑤)	9,457	17,368	1,033	90	5,080	9,228	7,034	12,737	2,164	4,354	–1,840
⑦ Income (⑥+a)	12,847	20,235	3,894	3,609	5,507	9,478	7,899	14,028	3,208	6,029	3,360
Share of Each Cost and Operators' Surplus in Gross Revenue (%)											
Current Input Cost	20.6	37.9	26.9	50.0	13.8	11.3	35.2	30.1	25.3	12.1	38.4
Labour Cost	29.3	13.9	44.8	23.3	27.4	22.1	20.4	19.4	26.2	38.4	49.3
Capital Cost	17.9	15.6	22.5	26.4	8.2	5.6	20.3	20.2	30.3	18.2	18.2
Operator's Surplus	32.1	32.6	5.9	0.3	50.6	61.0	24.1	30.3	18.2	31.3	–5.9

Notes: Year in brackets is the survey year.

The survey for Htantabin was done Fujita and Okamoto, and the Kyaukse (1993/94), and the Kyaukse (2000/01), and Taungyi surveys were by Takahashi's Survey.

The remainder relate to surveys by srelate to surveys by survey by Kurosaki and others.

Water charge is not available for every survey, and it is generally quite nominal (10–20 kyats per acre). It is not included in the current cost.

Summer paddy produced in Kyaukse is generally called "Mo-Kyaw Zaba" (pre-monsoon paddy) and has been produced for very many years.

One basket equals 20.9 kg in the case of paddy.

Sources: Takahashi (2000), Fujita and Okamoto (2001), Kurosaki et al. (2004).

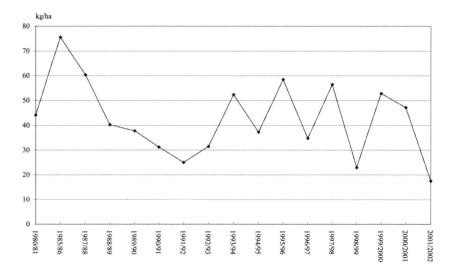

Figure 4   Estimated Changes in Chemical Fertilizer Application in Rice Cultivation, 1980–2001

Sources: CSO, *Statistical Yearbook* (1995, 1997, 2002), MOAI (2000b), MAS Documents.

by private enterprises. Government attempts to boost private imports by exempting them from import duty, this proved unsuccessful, and the government continued to be the main importer (Takahashi, 2000: 39–40). Fluctuations in import volume after 1993/94 may have resulted from the insufficient allocation of foreign exchange to government agencies for importing fertilizer. The government distributed chemical fertilizers to farmers through the Myanma Agriculture Service (MAS), which operates a broad network of agencies in rural areas. Among all the crops of Myanmar, rice has a dominant share insofar as the receipt of fertilizer is concerned, accounting for more than 80 per cent of the total volume of fertilizer made available for cultivation (CSO, 1997, 2000).

Figure 4 provides an estimate of the volume of chemical fertilizer used for paddy, assuming that 80 per cent of the total supply was allocated to paddy cultivation. Fertilizer application reached 75 kg per hectare in the peak year (1985/86) but fell to 30 kg in the early 1990s, and subsequently fluctuated widely between 30 and 60 kg. The fertilizer application per hectare was low in Myanmar compared with the international average.[18]

In the late 1980s, the price of chemical fertilizer increased sharply. As noted earlier, the rice price also increased steeply in the mid-1980s.

Table 9   Ratio of Rice Prices to Fertilizer (Urea) Prices, 1986–2005

Year	*Official Paddy Procurement Price/ Official Fertilizer Distribution Price*	*Market Paddy Price/ Market Fertilizer Price*
1986	1.3	–
1994	0.6	–
2000	–	0.7
2001	0.3	0.3
2003	0.1	0.3
2005	–	0.2

Notes: The paddy price for 2000–2003 has been obtained from the authors' survey.
  Fertilizer prices are from the MIS Bulletin.
  For 2005, both rice and fertilizer prices have been obtained from Okamoto's survey.
Sources: 1986, 1994 are based on Takahashi (2000: 40).

Nevertheless, the rice/fertilizer price ratio deteriorated rapidly (Table 9), meaning that fertilizer prices increased at an even faster pace than rice prices.

The government's official price for fertilizer was kept low for 15 years until 1987/88 (FADINAP, 1987: 14), but in the 1990s, it rapidly increased to a level close to the international price. Since the government was obliged to withdraw its subsidies, the official price was raised frequently[19] in accordance with rises in the market price. Owing to difficulties in securing adequate supplies, the government distribution of fertilizer shrank considerably in 2005.[20]

Changes in the diesel oil supply also influenced paddy cultivation in Myanmar. Diesel oil is indispensable in summer paddy cultivation using pump irrigation. As with fertilizer, most of Myanmar's diesel oil is imported and the domestic price has risen quite rapidly. In order to support summer paddy production, the government provided diesel oil at a lower cost to those farmers who cultivate summer paddy using pump irrigation. In 2001, for example, the market price per gallon was 350–600 kyat but the government price was 160 kyat. In 2004, the market price was 1,500–1,600 kyat, while the government price was 760 kyat, although the supply remained insufficient. According to our surveys,[21] one acre of pump irrigation required 6–10 gallons, but the government distribution remained at around 3.5–4 gallons.

Pulses

The production of pulses in Myanmar underwent a remarkable development in terms both of output and of exports after the liberalization of agricultural

Table 10 Pulse Exports, by Major Destinations, 1991–2000 (%)

Country	1991/92	1993/94	1995/96	1997/98	1999/2000
India	55.7	66.4	71.5	73.6	67.5
Pakistan	16.3	8.3	6.5	4.8	2.1
Bangladesh	0.0	3.4	0.1	0.2	0.7
Singapore	14.4	7.6	8.6	4.7	5.7
Indonesia	0.4	7.1	5.9	7.2	11.7
Malaysia	2.4	4.0	3.5	4.0	4.1
Japan	8.9	2.9	1.9	1.4	1.4
Philippines	0.3	0.1	1.1	1.2	0.8
Other	1.6	0.2	0.9	2.8	5.9
Total	100.0	100.0	100.0	100.0	100.0

Sources: CSO, *Myanmar Agricultural Statistics* (1997, 2001).

marketing in 1987.[22] It should be emphasized, however, that from the outset, the success of this sector was never really the government's intention. Indeed, the government showed relatively little interest in this matter and the expansion of the production of pulses was led exclusively by the private sector. The government appreciated the sector's success in later years and attempted to reap some of the benefits of expansion by introducing a procurement system at the end of the 1990s, albeit without success.[23]

Among the 17 varieties of pulses produced in Myanmar, the three varieties of black gram, green gram and pigeon pea are particularly important. These three pulses account for between 80 and 90 per cent of total exports by value. The main export destination is India (Table 10), and the emergence of the large Indian market was a key factor underlying the development of pulse cultivation in Myanmar.

In India, following the Green Revolution in the mid-1960s, production shifted to rice and wheat at the expense of pulses. The increase in pulse imports from Myanmar was the result of the stagnation in the domestic production of pulses as well as the relaxation of import regulations by the Indian government after 1991, when economic liberalization began (UN, 1997: 41, Rao, 1994: 146). By 2002/03, pulses from Myanmar accounted for about 40 per cent of India's total pulse imports.

Since there is no government regulation over exporting pulses from Myanmar (except for the 10 per cent export tax), the import demand of India was transmitted directly to Myanmar's market, pushing the domestic

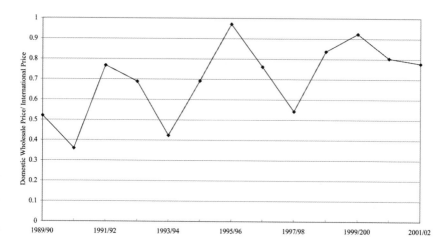

Figure 5   Myanmar Black Gram (Pulse) Prices Compared: Ratio of Domestic Wholesale Price to International Price, 1989–2002

Sources: International Price: Government of India, *Agricultural Statistics at a Glance* (2003).

Domestic wholesale price: CSO, *Statistical Yearbook* (1991, 1997, 2002).

Market exchange rate: 1988/89–1996/97 ADB (2001), 1997/98–2001/02 Tokyo-Mitsubishi Bank Yangon Representative Office.

pulse prices in Myanmar upwards (Table 2). The close linkage between the domestic and international prices of pulses is clearly shown in Figure 5.

The increase in the acreage sown with pulses has been striking. The total acreage under the major three pulses increased four-fold in ten years in the 1990s (Table 11). Figures 6, 7 and 8 show the growth of production in black gram, green gram and pigeon pea, by region. The following points emerge from these figures. The expansion of the acreage under black gram and green gram first occurred in the Lower Myanmar region and was particularly conspicuous in Ayeyarwaddy and Bago. While the production of black gram remains concentrated in Lower Myanmar, green gram cultivation started to increase in Upper Myanmar, with Sagaing and Magwe becoming important production regions in the mid-1990s, and these two regions came to account for a larger acreage of green gram cultivation than Lower Myanmar. Pigeon pea is dominant in Upper Myanmar, in regions such as Sagaing, Magwe and Mandalay.

In Lower Myanmar, pulses were introduced everywhere as a second crop after monsoon paddy, a new development, as there was virtually no second

Table 11 Changes in the Sown Area of Pulses, 1980–2005 (Thousand acres)

		1980/81	1989/90	1991/92	1993/94	1995/96	1997/98	1999/2000	2001/02	2003/04	2005/06
Area	Black Gram	210	255	725	693	1,172	1,215	1,371	1,785	1,809	2,014
	Green Gram	102	227	434	721	1,137	1,349	1,839	1,845	1,902	2,345
	Pigeon Pea	169	155	280	571	617	622	761	1,197	1,296	1,319
	Soy Bean	63	83	85	114	177	195	267	291	334	385
	Cow Pea	154	148	210	241	392	364	509	660	711	764
	Penauk	125	176	218	316	289	270	385	355	346	387
	Garden Pea	66	63	69	91	90	92	92	104	116	110
	Chick Pea	408	392	459	329	410	297	323	485	512	553
	Total of the above pulses	1,297	1,499	2,480	3,076	4,284	4,404	5,547	6,722	7,026	7,877
	Total of pulsese	1,995	1,934	2,945	3,553	4,808	4,967	6,209	7,372	7,734	8,662
Share of the Total Area of Pulses (%)	Black Gram	11.0	13.2	24.6	19.5	24.4	24.5	22.1	24.2	23.4	23.3
	Green Gram	7.2	11.7	14.7	20.3	23.6	27.2	29.6	25.0	24.6	27.1
	Pigeon Pea	9.7	8.0	9.5	16.1	12.8	12.5	12.3	16.2	16.8	15.2
	Total	27.9	32.9	48.9	55.9	60.9	64.1	64.0	65.5	64.7	65.6

Note: The cow pea acreage is the sum of the acreages under Pelun and Bokait.

Sources: CSO, *Statistical Yearbook* (1995, 2002, 2006).

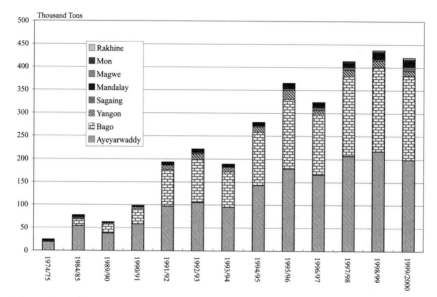

Figure 6 Changes in Production of Black Gram by States and Divisions, 1974–2000
Source: CSO, *Myanmar Agricultural Statistics* (2001).

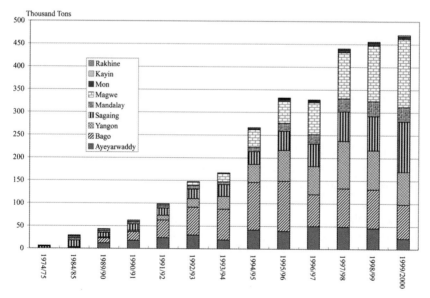

Figure 7 Changes in Production of Green Gram by States and Divisions, 1974–2000
Source: CSO, *Myanmar Agricultural Statistics* (2001).

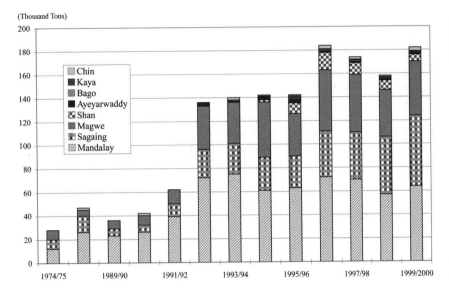

Figure 8   Changes in Production of Pigeon Pea by States and Divisions, 1974–2000

Source: CSO, *Myanmar Agricultural Statistics* (2001).

crop before 1988. In the dry season, idle land suddenly came to be utilized in the production of pulses. In order to cultivate rice during the dry season, as noted earlier, irrigation is indispensable. But because it is unnecessary for pulses, the introduction of pulses was relatively undemanding.

Table 12 illustrates the profitability of pulses under different cropping patterns, based on various field surveys, and also shows the changes in cropping systems that have come about as a result of the introduction of pulses.

To illustrate trends in Lower Myanmar, the examples of Yangon Division in 1999/2000 and Bago Division in 2000/01 were examined. In both cases, farmers obtained a larger operator's surplus and income from pulses than from monsoon paddy. The figures in Table 8 show that pulses generally yield a higher profit than summer paddy. It is well known that in monsoon Asia as a whole, the cultivation of un-irrigated second crops following the main rice crop usually yields only a marginal profit. This is not true, however, of the cultivation of pulses in Myanmar,[24] which have had a huge impact on the farm economy.

In sum, the development of pulses in Lower Myanmar in the 1990s can be characterized in terms of the so-called "vent for surplus" (Hla Myint, 1971). With the sudden emergence of export demand, idle resources (land

Thousand Tons

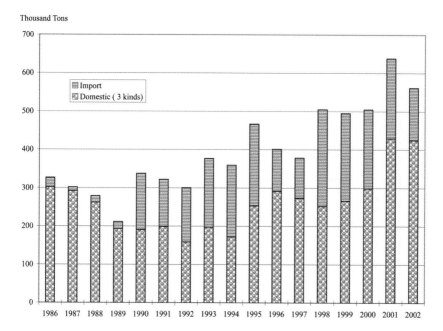

Figure 9   Changes in the Supply of Edible Oils, 1986–2002 (Thousand tons)
Source: FAO, *FAOSTAT.*

and labour in the dry season) came to be utilized effectively and production expanded rapidly without any need for substantial investment (such as irrigation).[25]

Crops for Import Competition

Oilseed is the second most important crop after paddy in people's diet in Myanmar. The edible oils traditionally consumed are groundnut oil and sesame oil.[26] The latter is estimated to account for 5–10 per cent of total edible oil consumption, while the former accounts for the remaining 90–95 per cent.[27]

As has already been noted, even though Myanmar enjoys no comparative advantage regarding the production of oilseed crops, the import of oilseeds was strictly regulated and thus it is probable that, during the socialist period, the domestic price was higher than the international one, although after the 1990s, the full-scale import of edible oils flourished (see Figure 9). Almost all (99 per cent) imported edible oil is palm oil, mainly from Malaysia, Singapore and Indonesia.

Table 12 Cost and Revenue Structure of Cropping Patterns that Include Pulses and Beans

	Lower Myanmar (Delta)					Upper Myanmar (Dry Zone)				
	Paddy + Pulses					Sesame/Pigeon Pea + Green Gram			Magve (2000/01)	(Reference) Groundnut + Sorghum
	Bago (2000/01)			Yangon (1999/2000)						
	Monsoon Paddy	Black Gram	Green Gram	Monsoon Paddy	Green Gram	Sesame	Pigeon Pea (Mix cropped with Sesame)	Green Gram	Groundnut	Sorghum
Number of Samples	36	15	14	43	43	13	3	8	3	3
Sown Acres	9.4	5.6	3.7	11.8	8.0	4.2	8.2	4.1	4.3	2.4
Yield per Acre (Basket/Acre)	40.0	6.3	4.1	46.7	8.0	6.6	1.0	3.8	40.6	–
① Gross Revenue (Kyat/Acre)	18,071	30,648	20,630	25,405	27,240	32,563	3,035	12,052	56,890	19,067
② Current Input Cost	2,956	5,467	4,630	4,075	4,870	9,489	93	4,657	14,497	4,382
Seed	1,224	4,660	3,676	2,218	3,384	2,019	93	1,798	7,053	1,163
Manure	741	67	72	0	0	2,093	0	0	1,721	0
Chemical Fertilizer	805	159	357	1,853	778	4,185	0	1,808	5,723	3,038
Other Chemicals	125	417	525	4	707	1,193	0	1,051	0	181
Diesel Oil	61	165	0	0	1	0	0	0	0	0
③ Labour Cost	7,486	6,156	4,846	8,478	3,385	4,772	1,554	4,836	7,313	2,163
Hired Labour	5,406	3,550	1,934	6,930	2,536	3,733	1,144	3,991	6,824	834
Family Labour (a)	2,080	2,606	2,912	1,548	849	1,039	410	844	489	1,329

TABLE 12 continued

	Lower Myanmar (Delta)					Upper Myanmar (Dry Zone)				
	Paddy + Pulses					Sesame/Pigeon Pea + Green Gram			(Reference) Groundnut + Sorghum	
	Bago (2000/01)			Yangon (1999/2000)			Magwe (2000/01)			
	Monsoon Paddy	Black Gram	Green Gram	Monsoon Paddy	Green Gram	Sesame	Pigeon Pea (Mix cropped with Sesame)	Green Gram	Groundnut	Sorghum
Number of Samples	36	15	14	43	43	13	3	8	3	3
④ Capital Cost	4,433	4,488	4,085	7,343	5,025	3,132	49	1,947	2,330	2,292
Agricultural Machinery	637	344	148	67	3,357	0	0	157	0	0
Bullocks	3,607	4,144	3,891	5,648	1,570	2,299	44	1,449	2,224	2,292
Interest Payment	190	0	46	1,628	98	833	5	342	106	0
⑤ Total of Production Cost (②+③+④)	14,875	16,111	13,561	20,217	13,598	17,393	1,696	11,440	24,140	8,837
⑥ Operator's Surplus (①−⑤)	3,197	14,537	7,069	5,188	13,642	15,170	1,339	612	32,750	10,230
⑦ Income (⑥+a)	5,277	17,143	9,981	6,736	14,491	16,209	1,749	1,456	33,239	11,559
Share of Each Cost and Operator's Surplus in Gross Revenue (%)										
Current Input Cost	16.4	17.8	22.4	16.0	17.9	29.1	3.1	38.6	25.5	23.0
Labour Cost	41.4	20.1	23.5	33.4	15.5	14.7	51.2	40.1	12.9	11.3
Capital Cost	24.5	14.6	19.8	28.9	18.8	9.6	1.6	16.2	4.1	12.0
Operator's Surplus	17.7	47.4	34.3	21.7	48.9	46.6	44.1	5.1	57.6	53.7

Notes: All data is based on field surveys in townships in each Division.

The year of the survey is given in brackets

In Bago, either black gram or green gram is cultivated after monsoon paddy.

In Magwe, sesame mixed with pigeon pea + green gram is the major cropping pattern.

Formerly, the main pattern was ground nut followed by sorghum or cow pea or soy bean.

Sources: Kurosaki *et al.* (2004), Okamoto (2008).

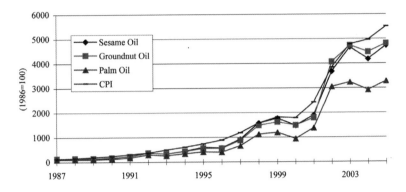

Figure 10 Changes in the Price Index of Edible Oils, 1988–2005

Sources: CSO, *Statistical Yearbook* (1993, 1995, 2001, 2006).

As can be seen in Figure 9, in some years imports exceeded domestic production. The private sector began to import edible oils at an early stage, but after 1999 their importation fell under the monopoly of the Union of Myanmar Economic Holdings Ltd (UMEHL, which is a military-affiliated company). This suggests that the shortage of foreign exchange available to the government, rather than overall foreign exchange constraints, was the main factor restricting the volume of palm oil imports.

The huge quantity of palm oil imports was the main determinant of the trends in edible oil prices (Figure 10). The prices of sesame oil and groundnut oil are kept in line with the price of imported palm oil[28] and consequently they have increased at a lower rate than the CPI.

It is hardly surprising that, in the absence of technological progress, this weak price trend for edible oil worked against the domestic production of oilseed crops. The sluggish expansion of the sown acreage of sesame and groundnut cultivation, as shown in Table 3, is a clear manifestation of this reality. Self-sufficiency in edible oil supplies is one of the three major goals of Myanmar's agricultural policy[29] but, despite this being the government's stated intention, no clear trend towards an increase in production has materialized.

Given that the country suffers from a serious balance of payment deficit, curbing the volume of palm oil imports has become a major issue for the government. Figure 11 shows that the import value of edible oil is almost equal to the export value of pulses. The gap between the two after 1995 clearly indicates the difficulties experienced by the Myanmar government as the foreign exchange constraint grew more severe.[30] This is

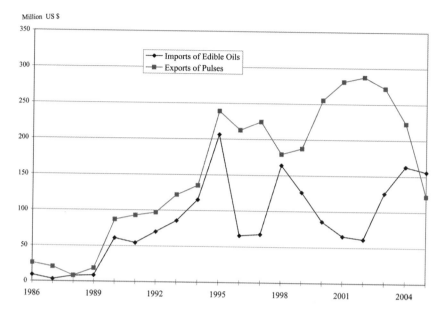

Figure 11   Imports of Edible Oils and Exports of Pulses, 1986–2005 (Million US dollars)

Source: FAO, *FAOSTAT.*

also evident in Figure 12, where the domestic and international prices of palm oil are compared. The price gap widened after the mid-1990s, revealing the probability of constraints operating so far as imports are concerned.

Edible oil is essential for the people of Myanmar and any rapid increase in its price could cause the government considerable anxiety, although less so than in the case of a rise in the price of rice. The government could attempt to keep the domestic price low by increasing imports. Occasionally, surges in the domestic price occur, and the wide fluctuations in palm oil import volumes in recent years may represent a kind of "swing" in the government's attempts to deal with the problem.

A similar problem occurs with rice since the stabilization of prices at a low level is regarded as a priority, but Myanmar enjoys a comparative advantage in rice, and price stabilization can be achieved through various internal "regulative" policies. Such is not the case for oilseed crops. If imports are barred, there is no possibility of compensating for this by raising the efficiency of domestic production.[31] The alternative, whereby Myanmar's oilseed supplies would depend entirely on high-handed policy decisions, is fraught with difficulties.

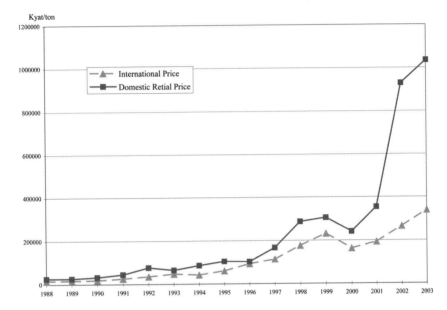

Figure 12   Changes in the International and Domestic Retail price of Palm Oil, 1988–2003

Sources: CSO, *Statistical Yearbook* (1997, 2002). *Monthly Economic Indicators* (April 2003), International Price, *International Financial Statistics* (Malaysian Export Price)

Market exchange rates: 1988/89–1996/97 ADB (2001): 1997/98–2002/03 Tokyo-Mitsubishi Bank Yangon Representative Office.

Crops for the Domestic Market

In this section, the crops/products that are produced essentially for the domestic market, such as vegetables, fruit, meat and fishery products, are dealt with briefly. As already noted, the price of these crops has increased at a rate slightly higher than the CPI (see Table 2).

The output of crops that are indispensable to the Myanmar people's diet, such as garlic, onion, and chillies, did not undergo any significant change, but the production of other types of vegetable and fruit increased sharply after the mid-1990s (Figure 13). A similar trend can also be observed regarding meat (especially chicken and pork;[32] see Figure 14) and fishery products (Figure 15). Per capita meat consumption doubled from 4.8 kg in 1987/88 to 9.2 kg in 2001/02. As far as fishery products are concerned, the increase rate during the same period amounted to about 50 per cent, from 17.5 kg to 25.9 kg.[33]

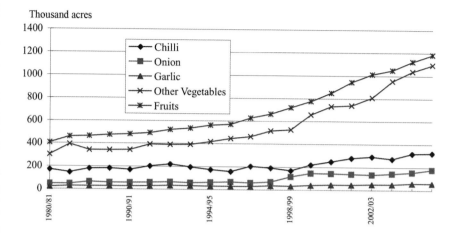

Figure 13 Changes in the Sown Area of Vegetables and Fruit, 1980–2005
Sources: CSO, *Statistical Yearbook* (1997, 2002, 2006).

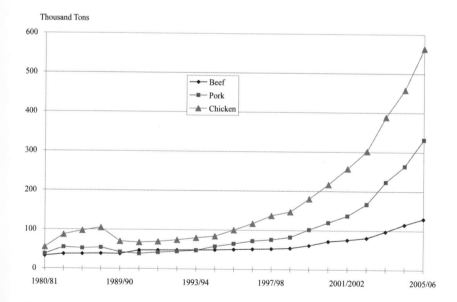

Figure 14 Production of Meat, 1980–2005
Sources: CSO, *Statistical Yearbook* (1997, 2002, 2006).

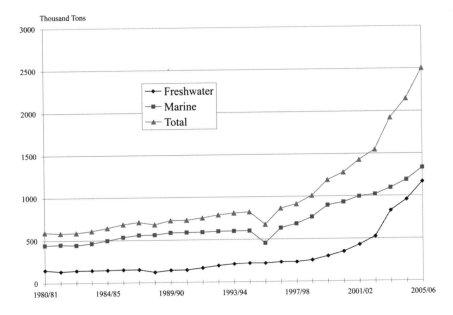

Figure 15   Fishery Products: Changes in Output, 1980–2005

Sources: CSO, *Statistical Yearbook* (1997, 2002, 2006).

To summarize, the production of crops/products for the domestic market increased in response to the expansion in domestic demand as part of the process of economic development, especially after the mid-1990s. Fishery products (especially prawns) were an exception, however, since increases were partly led by export demand. In recent years, onion and chili production has also begun to be stimulated by overseas demand.

In general, the profitability of vegetable and fruit production is high,[34] and expansion of these crops contributed substantially to the stimulation of the rural economy. Although it may sound obvious, a key factor that facilitated the marketing of these perishable crops over a wide area was improvement in Myanmar's infrastructure, including improvement of the road network. Table 13 clearly shows a sharp increase in the mileage of roads and the number of lorries during the 1990s. Before development of the road network, railways and waterways were the most common means of transportation. In those days, transportation was far more time consuming and the area that rural commodities (especially perishable ones) could reach was more limited. As this constraint was reduced, it became possible to produce perishable crops even in areas that were remote from the main centres of consumption.

Table 13 Changes in Modes of Transportation, 1980–2005

(%)

	1980/81	1985/86	1990/91	1995/96	2000/01	2005/06	80/81–85/86	85/86–90/91	90/91–95/96	95/96–2000/01	2000/01–05/06
Road (Miles)	7,620	10,490	10,943	11,962	14,145	15,754	37.7	4.3	9.3	18.2	11.4
Bituminous	3,138	5,485	5,608	5,979	8029	9,296	74.8	2.2	6.6	34.3	15.8
Metalled	1,069	1,457	1,639	1,889	2991	3,487	36.3	12.5	15.3	58.3	16.6
Surface	3,413	3,548	3,696	4,094	3125	2,971	4.0	4.2	10.8	-23.7	-4.9
Small Trucks (Number)	3,818	6,527	10,355	19,629	24,229	23,364	71.0	58.6	89.6	23.4	-3.6
Yangon	2,587	3,874	2,386	10,196	13,845	13,630	49.7	-38.4	327.3	35.8	-1.6
Other Areas	1,231	2,653	7,969	9,433	10,384	9,734	115.5	200.4	18.4	10.1	-6.3
Large Trucks (Number)	30,863	34,064	22,188	23,199	29,663	31,437	10.4	-34.9	4.6	27.9	6.0
Yangon	11,490	12,651	10,032	10,039	8,112	9,102	10.1	-20.7	0.1	-19.2	12.2
Other Areas	19,373	21,413	12,156	13,160	21,551	22,335	10.5	-43.2	8.3	63.8	3.6

Sources: CSO, *Statistical Yearbook* (2002, 2006).

Crops for the State-Owned Economic Enterprises

Cotton, sugarcane, rubber and jute are industrial crops procured by the government as raw materials for state-owned economic enterprises (SEEs). The sown area of these four crops accounts for approximately only 3 per cent of the total (average for 1987/88–2000/01). Industrial crops are important, however, as their production and marketing affects not only farmers and traders but also the management of the SEEs and national fiscal conditions. In this section, the examples of sugarcane and cotton are briefly discussed.

Sugarcane

The sugar industry is characterized by a few state-related, large-scale sugar factories and numerous small-scale private factories. The state-related sector has undergone many changes of ownership.[35] In 1994, the state sugar factories under the Ministry of Industry (1) were transferred to the Ministry of Agriculture and Irrigation. The state-owned institution, Myanma Sugarcane Enterprise (MSE), which became the Sugarcane Development Department of Myanma Industrial Crops Development Enterprise (MICDE) in 2003, was made responsible for the management of these factories. Under the MSE, nine new sugar factories were constructed using foreign aid in 1997.[36] After 1998, some 18 factories came into operation, and the total production capacity doubled, from 8,600 tons to 17,500 tons per day. Some of these factories were transferred to the Union of Myanma Economic Holdings Ltd (UMEHL) and the Myanma Economic Corporation (MEC) (both military-affiliated companies), in the 2000s.

One characteristic of sugarcane is that the sugar content decreases rapidly unless the crop is processed shortly after being harvested. Furthermore, a modern sugar processing factory generally requires substantial capital investment, so it follows that its performance is heavily influenced by the rate of capacity utilization. What this means in practice is that, to ensure their supply, state-owned sugar factories prescribe procurement zones around the mills and require farmers to grow and sell all of their sugarcane output to the factory handling their particular zone.

The problem lies not in the physical procurement of the crop but in the price prescribed by the government, which, for a long time, was far lower than the market price (Takahashi, 2002: 141–44). For example, the market price in 2000 was 5,270–6,100 kyat per ton, while the government procurement price was only 2,500 kyat (Kudo, 2003: 41). Since the sugarcane farmers outside the procurement zones could sell freely in the market, the question

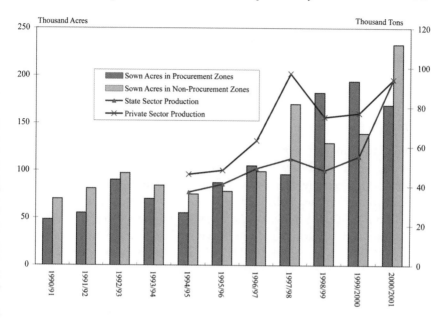

Figure 16 Changes in the Sown Area of Sugarcane and in Sugar Production, 1990–2001

Source: Kudo, ed. (2003: Table 1, 265).

of whether or not a sugarcane farmer's fields fell within a procurement zone determined his fate.

Figure 16 indicates changes in the total sown acreage of sugarcane, as well as in the acreage of the procurement and non-procurement zones. The sugarcane procurement zones began to expand in 1996/97 and then increased further in 1998/99, when the new factories mentioned above were coming into operation.

The non-procurement zones became more extensive from around 1996/97 onwards. Underlying this trend were three background factors. The first was the indirect effect of the expansion of the procurement zones. Because of the establishment of the new state factories, local private sugar processors began to find it difficult to purchase raw materials, and the price of sugarcane increased accordingly, stimulating sugarcane production in other areas (Kudo, 2003: 40; U Tin Htut Oo and Kudo eds., 2003: 262–63). The second was a general increase in domestic sugar demand after about the mid-1990s, arising from diversification of the diet of the Myanmar people that caused demand to increase for sugar and also for vegetables, fruit, meat, and fishery products. Third, the relocation of the small sugar factories from the sugar marketing centre (Mandalay) to the sugarcane producing areas encouraged the further expansion of sugarcane production. This relocation was mainly due to the impact of inflation, that is, increased input and transportation costs in the early 2000s (San Thein and Kudo, 2008).

Cotton

Cotton must undergo a ginning process before yarn can be produced by spinning. There are 20 state-owned spinning mills run by the Ministry of Industry (1). The state-owned cotton ginning factories that the supply raw material to the spinning mills used to be run by the Ministry of Industry (1) as well, but in 1994/95, some factories were transferred to the Ministry of Agriculture and Irrigation, and the Myanma Cotton and Sericulture Enterprise (MCSE) was established. The MCSE also became responsible for procuring the cotton required by the state owned factories.

The MCSE procures cotton directly either from farmers or cotton traders. Cotton traders formerly supplied cotton exclusively for the private cotton ginning factories (the number reached 370 in 2000/01), but after

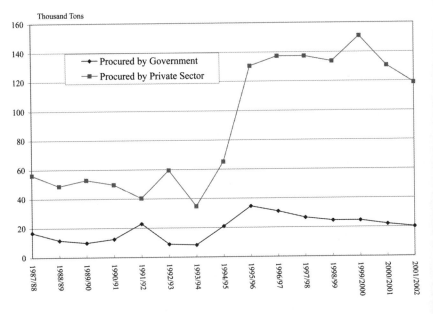

Figure 17   Cotton Production, 1987–2002 (Thousand tons)

Source: U Tin Htut Oo & Kudo eds. (2003: 320).

1998 were required to sell a proportion of their cotton to the government (50 per cent in 1998, and 25 per cent after 1999).

Figure 17 indicates the trends in cotton supply, classified by governmental and private procurement. The big jump in production in 1995/96 was the result of an aggressive policy to promote the expansion of the sown acreage of cotton immediately after the transfer of the responsible authority, as described above. The objective was to ensure the supply of raw material for the state-owned cotton industry, but the figures show a rise in private procurement. It is obvious that the MCSE did not succeed in acquiring the planned amount. The application of the procurement system to cotton traders in 1998 was a last resort in the drive to ensure adequate supplies, but it failed to produce any significant results. On average, the state sector succeeded in procuring only 52 per cent of its needs during 1998/99–2001/02 (U Tin Htut Oo and Kudo eds., 2003: 323).

The problem is, obviously, the low procurement price; for example, in the case of 2001/02, the market price was 370–375 kyat per viss (1.6 kg), whereas the government procurement price was only 180 kyat (U Tin Htut Oo and Kudo eds., 2003: 315).

Conclusion

How can we best characterize Myanmar's agricultural policies after 1988? In the light of the narrow technical definition of the concept of an agricultural exploitation policy (that is, a policy that absorbs the surplus from agriculture and uses it as a base for economic development through industrialization), it would be inappropriate to state that an agricultural exploitation policy was pursued, even after 1988. Rather, if examined dispassionately, the genuine policy objective of the government appears to consist of the following two elements: avoiding social unrest and sustaining the regime.

These objectives required that the agricultural policy achieve two subordinate aims: to stabilize prices at a low level for commodities that are indispensable to ordinary diets, and to sustain the SEEs in the agro-processing sector, which depends for its raw materials on domestically produced agricultural commodities.

The stabilization of essential agricultural prices at a low level conforms with the main objective, which is to avoid social unrest. This explains why Myanmar's agricultural policies are strongly inclined towards production increases for their own sake, while paying rather less attention to the farmers' income and welfare. The impact of such policies on the agricultural sector's performance is summarized below.

The key crops that are most important in the people's diet are rice and oilseeds. When the present regime was established in 1988, its first challenge was a surge in the rice price. A wholesale return to the system under the socialist period was not an option for the government. Instead, they adopted two measures. The first was to restrain the agricultural marketing reforms with respect to rice, with the rice procurement and ration systems being maintained, although on a smaller scale than before, and rice exports continuing to operate under a government monopoly. The second was to implement an aggressive policy aimed at stimulating rice production, as exemplified in the summer paddy programme.

As mentioned above, even though it slowed down midway, the summer paddy programme proved successful overall. Further, thanks to the restrictions on rice exports, the regime almost succeeded in controlling the rice price. The domestic rice price remained about 40 per cent lower than the international one. As Myanmar enjoyed a comparative advantage with regard to rice production, it was possible for it to achieve price stabilization, simply by strengthening its "inwards" policy.

A similar phenomenon can also be observed with regard to crops other than rice. Recently, onions and maize have provided good examples. In January 2004, exports of these commodities were suddenly prohibited in order to prevent a rise in the domestic prices.

To ensure supplies of another important commodity, edible oils, the government began importing palm oil, and starting in the mid-1990s, imports were somewhat constrained by strict foreign exchange conditions, and the government has also promoted cultivation of new oilseed crops. Examples are the attempt to introduce sunflower and the development of large private oil palm plantations in the south. This policy is an aggressive initiative and not entirely rational in economic terms. Moreover, it was not always welcomed by the farmers or private companies, and the prospects of it becoming a self-sustaining success seem rather remote. Above all, it remains a fact that, without the benefit of a comparative advantage, achieving self-sufficiency in crops is a difficult task.

As for sugarcane and cotton, cultivation has inevitably been heavily influenced by the government's policy of compelling farmers and traders to sell their produce at low prices in order to fulfill the goals of the state-owned processing enterprises.

In summary, in recent years, rice, oilseed crops, industrial crops, onions and maize have been government priorities. The avoidance of social unrest and the maintenance of SEEs have been two key imperatives. The farmers, traders and processors dealing with these crops struggle daily to find ways of avoiding, or at least reducing, the negative impact of government policies. The effect of the government's role has been to limit exports (of rice, onions, and maize, for example) and to promote the cultivation of crops under disadvantageous conditions (rice, oilseed crops and industrial crops).

On the other hand, the government has been relatively indifferent towards crops that lie outside the objectives of the state (in other words, crops that have no role to play in the avoidance of social unrest or the maintenance of the SEEs). Particularly surprising has been the government's lack of interest in pulses, which have become a major export crop for Myanmar. Even in the major pulse-producing areas, the main task of the government officials has been to take care of the politically important crops, especially rice.

A similar tendency may be observed with regard to some crops that are profitable for farmers and are grown for the domestic market. Examples include tomatoes in the vicinity of Inle Lake and chillies in Kyaukse. In these areas, too, the agricultural administration has focused mainly on rice, seeking either to expand the area under rice or achieve an increase in yields, and paying scant attention to the cultivation of tomatoes or chillies.

In fact, Myanmar's agricultural development after 1988 owed a great deal to self-sustaining growth pioneered by the private sector in crop categories that fell outside the main concerns of the government. In this respect, the role of the government has been minimal. Another notable feature is the fact that development has not been supported by improvements in productivity. In particular, the success of pulses was due to the possibility of using land that had formerly lain unused during the dry season. In this sense, the development pattern has been a typical example of providing a "vent for surplus".

The Myanmar government has been highly fortunate, since the country had room for development under the "vent for surplus" process. At the same time, however, a challenge will inevitably occur once the development potential of this path has been exhausted.[37] Opening up a development path through improvements in productivity would have been a far more difficult task.

Finally, mention must be made of changes in Myanmar's rice policy. There can be no doubt that the policy of keeping the domestic rice price substantially lower than the international one was a major constraint on the development of Myanmar's rice sector. As the experience of Thailand and Vietnam shows, however, a low rice price policy adopted for a substantial period of time, while encouraging rice exports.[38] At the initial stage of economic development, when the majority of the population remains poor, the risks accompanying a policy of exporting the staple food should not be underestimated. This indicates that the liberalization of rice exports, even if unavoidable, should be undertaken with extreme caution.[39]

Notes

1   The transportation cost for rice distribution was subsidized by the government, and this resulted in a lower rice price even in border districts that were far removed from the major rice-producing areas. This nationwide distribution of rice supported by the government, promoted a shift in the consumption pattern of staple food, and resulted in a huge increase in rice consumption throughout the country.

2   There are, of course, exceptions to the categorization that we have employed; for example, sesame is an export crop, and some of the crops that we have classified as crops/products for the domestic market are also exported (e.g., prawns and fish, and garlic and onions).

3   A similar development also occurred in China between 1978 and the mid-1980s.

4   There is, of course, the possibility that the rapid increase in the sown acreage in the late 1990s is the result of some statistical adjustment.

5   The paddy procurement system was revived, although surplus paddy could be sold in the market, while the entry of the marketing agents (traders and rice millers) was practically free. In this sense, it is more appropriate to say that rice was only partly liberalized; see Chapter 6 for further discussion.

6   We took the retail price, not the wholesale price, as the domestic price, simply because of the lack of wholesale price data for the socialist period.

7   See Chapter 6 for details.

8   There are two grounds for authors recognizing this possibility: first, it is reported that there was a huge gap in the yield of rice between the official record and the estimates conducted in the field; and, second, the per capita supply of rice is unrealistically high if we rely purely on the official production statistics.

9   Under the system whereby the quota obligation is uniformly fixed per acre, the average effective price will be lower for small farmers with less marketable surplus.

10   After the mid-1990s, the policy also stressed the self-sufficiency in rice of each locality, including rice deficit areas, such as the mountains and the dry zone. This conflicts starkly with the promotion of production based on the principle of comparative advantage.

11   The number of irrigation pumps was 46,000 in 1990/91, 72,000 in 1995/96 and reached 155,000 in 2000/01 (CSO, *Statistical Yearbook*, 2002). These pumps were mainly imported from China.

12   Some water pumps (especially the large ones that extract water directly from the Ayeyarwaddy River) are owned and maintained by the Water Resources

Utilization Department, although, in this type of irrigation too, there is almost no subsidy for farmers, as opposed to canal irrigation. According to the author's survey conducted in Magway in July 2001, the water charge was 1,500 kyat per acre for summer paddy, 1,200 kyat for monsoon paddy, 750 kyat for monsoon oilseed crops and cotton, and 1,200 kyat for summer oilseed crops and cotton. There is a huge discrepancy between the water charges for canal irrigation, which amounts to only 10 kyat per acre.

[13] It should be noted, however, that the difference between productivity in Myaungmya and Kyaukse was partly due to the fact that the rice price fell to a lesser extent in Upper Myanmar than in Lower Myanmar.

[14] For the interaction between the state policy and agencies and the farmers, including the summer paddy programme, see Thaungmung (2003).

[15] See Fujita (2003), for further discussion.

[16] After the late 1970s, there was a big flow of chemical fertilizers almost free of cost, mainly due to the official development assistance provided by Japan (Saito, 1987: 181).

[17] There are three urea factories in Myanmar: two were constructed in the 1970s, with a daily production capacity of 200–260 tons; the other was constructed with the official assistance of Germany in 1985, and has a daily capacity of 1,200 tons (FANDINAP, 1987: 2–3).

[18] Since data for fertilizer input per hectare for rice cultivation alone is unavailable, we have used the average figure in kilograms for the total cultivated area in 2000/01. It was 285 kg in Vietnam, 90 kg in Thailand, 130 kg in the Philippines and 256 kg in China. The increase in fertilizer application in Vietnam is quite prominent: it was only 88 kg per hectare in 1990/91, but jumped by almost 3.2 times over a period of 10 years.

[19] The price was increased from 600 kyat per bag (1 bag contains 50 kg) to 1,200 kyat in 1995/96 and then to 2,000 kyat in 1996/97. The market price for urea was 2,300 kyat in 1999, which was almost the same as the government's official price of 2,200 kyat (Fujita and Okamoto, 2000: 37).

[20] The official fertilizer price was maintained at 6,000 kyat per bag in 2004/05 (the market price was 12,000–15,000 kyat), the same level as in the previous year, although the amount distributed was reduced to only 1 bag per 4–5 acres (Authors' survey in Bago Division in 2005).

[21] Based on surveys in the Ayeyarwaddy Delta in 2001 and 2004.

[22] See Okamoto (2008), for a discussion of marketing liberalization and its effect on the production and export of pulses.

[23] Although the procurement system for pulses was revived, together with sesame in 1999/2000, gathering the required amounts proved difficult. The system was finally abolished after two years of trial (Okamoto, 2008: 38–39).

[24] The explanation for this lies in Myanmar's rice policy. Since the rice price is kept far below the international price, the profitability of rice and pulses were reversed at the farmers' level. If the rice price was close to the international

level, pulse acreage could not have expanded to present levels. In this sense, the success of pulses can be regarded as an unintentional fruit of Myanmar's rice policy; see Kurosaki *et al.* (2004), and Okamoto (2008), for further discussion.

[25] The increase in rice production through the rapid reclamation of the Delta in colonial Burma was also regarded as development by way of providing a "vent for surplus", although, strictly speaking, the development of the Delta required investment in flood control and drainage. In contrast, the development of pulses in the 1990s required no investment at all, so it complied fully with the theory of providing a "vent for surplus".

[26] The preference of edible oil differs according to region. In Upper Myanmar, sesame oil is preferred, while more groundnut oil is consumed in Lower Myanmar.

[27] This is based on an interview with a large edible oil trader in Yangon in January 2005. Other domestically produced edible oil, such as sunflower oil, is generally sold after having been mixed with groundnut oil and sesame oil (MOAI, 2000a). However, based on figures from *FAOSTAT*, the market share of sesame oil could be larger than reported; sesame oil takes about 30 per cent, groundnut oil 40–50 per cent, and the rest consists of sunflower oil and others. The discrepancy may occur because of a large volume of illegal exports of sesame oil through cross-border trade.

[28] In rural areas, where low-income groups predominate, only palm oil is consumed, while in urban areas, some consumers avoid it because of its taste.

[29] The other goals are to generate a surplus in rice and to step up the production of exportable pulses and industrial crops (Ministry of Information, 2000: 87).

[30] Needless to say, Figure 11 does not mean that the import of palm oil is constrained by the amount of export earnings obtained from pulses.

[31] Since 1998/99, oil palm plantations have been established by 17 large private companies in Tanintharyi, especially in the Kautaung region. Domestic palm oil will be supplied in large quantities in the future, although the cropped area was only 133,000 acres in 2004 and is likely to remain at a low level; 500,000 acres would be required in order to replace all of the imports by domestic production. In addition, sunflower production is being vigorously promoted by the Ministry of Agriculture and Irrigation in various parts of Myanmar, although the economic viability of these programmes for private companies and farmers remains unclear.

[32] Generally speaking, beef is not preferred by consumers, so its increase was less evident than that of other categories of meat.

[33] Calculated based on the CSO, *Statistical Yearbook* (2002).

[34] On the high profitability of vegetable production, see Kurosaki *et al.* (2004: Table 12).

[35] For further details about the industrial structure by the mid 2000s, see San Thein (2006: Table 8), and San Thein and Kudo (2008).

[36] Among these nine factories, eight were constructed with Chinese assistance, and the remaining one with Thai assistance.

[37] According to interviews held at the Union of Myanmar Federation of Chambers of Commerce and Industry (UMFCCI) in January 2005, pulses can be expanded up to 10 million acres from the present sown acreage of 8 million.

[38] According to Choeun *et al.* (2004), the domestic rice price in Thailand (the wholesale price in Bangkok) was 40 per cent lower than the international price until the early 1980s, mainly due to the adoption of a special export taxation system called the "rice premium". It was only after the mid-1980s that the gap was narrowed to about 10 per cent. In the case of Vietnam also, the gap remained at 20–30 per cent in the first half of the 1990s, through imposing an export quota system (Nicholas and Goletti, 2000). Note that the same indicator for Myanmar during the 1990s and early twenty-first century was, on average, 50–60 per cent.

[39] On the consequences of the rice marketing reforms announced in April 2003, see Chapter 6. A review of the entire process reveals that the preparations were highly insufficient, taking into account that such a drastic reform might have such a huge social impact.

Transformation of the Rice Marketing System after Market Liberalization in Myanmar

Ikuko Okamoto

Introduction

Creating a marketing system for rice[1] to serve the national interest has been one of the central policy issues for the Myanmar government since independence. The importance of rice for food security and as a source of government revenues and foreign exchange earnings have been the major reasons for the historical priority placed on rice. It is the leading staple food in Myanmar, and the dependency of Myanmar people on rice is quite high even when compared with neighbouring Asian countries. The average amount of rice consumed is around 130–160 kg per person per year, and the cost of rice amounts to 16–20 per cent in the household expenditure accounts (based on figures for 1997) (CSO, 1997). For this reason, agricultural policy in Myanmar has been virtually synonymous with rice policy.

Under the socialist government that was in power for more than 25 years starting in 1962, a comprehensive system of controls over rice marketing was established for the first time. The system included rice rationing for consumers along with a compulsory delivery system for procuring paddy directly from farmers to support the rationing system.[2] At the same time the exportation of rice became a state monopoly and served as the regime's main source for earning foreign exchange.

Agricultural marketing liberalization began in the late 1980s, starting with the domestic agricultural market in September 1987. This move signaled the start of Myanmar's transition to a market economy. A year later, in October 1988, the ban on the private export of agricultural produce was lifted, and thereafter the marketing of some crops enjoyed full liberalization. However, the marketing of rice, which was basically the main target of agricultural reform, remained under state control. The rice ration system was maintained for civil servants, and the paddy procurement system, which had been stopped in 1987, was revived in 1989. Further, rice exporting remained a government monopoly with responsibility taken over by Myanma Agricultural Produce Trading (MAPT).[3] This sequence of reforms can be called the first liberalization.

In April 2003, a further liberalization of rice marketing was suddenly announced. Under this second liberalization the rice ration system for the public servants and the paddy procurement system were finally abolished. Initially, the private export of rice was also incorporated into the reform plan, but this part of the plan was removed when abolition of the rice rationing system was announced in January 2004. The second liberalization shows that the government was not ready to undertake full-scale rice export deregulation.

Research on the institutional changes and current state of Myanmar's rice marketing system has been very limited. Takahashi (2000), Okamoto (1993), MOAI (2000a) and U Tin Htut Oo and Kudo eds. (2003) provide overviews of the rice marketing system after the first liberalization, while Theingyi Myint (2007) has examined the rice market integration based on price causality. However, these studies do not specifically analyze the development process of the marketing system or the interrelationship between the state and the private marketing sector. By examining the transformation of Myanmar's rice marketing system closely, this study seeks to bring into clearer focus the rationale of the government's rice policy and how it influenced the rice marketing sector. The following discussion will show that the government has a strong belief that losing control over the rice sector to any extent might shake the regime in some way or other. The frequent policy changes can be seen as a manifestation of their fear of losing control, and the mid- and long-term development of the rice sector has been kept apart from the reform process.

In this chapter, Section 1 describes the features of the state marketing sector after the first liberalization along with presenting the background and underlying factors of the reform and its problems. Section 2 explores the development of the private marketing sector and the problems it has faced. Section 3 examines the significance of the second liberalization, and the findings of this study are summed up in the concluding section.

The First Liberalization: Background

Two problems led to the first liberalization. One was the government's growing fiscal deficit. As noted earlier, the rationing system of the socialist period applied to consumers generally. As the population increased over the years, the fiscal burden of rationing continued to expand. This can be seen in MAPT's balance sheet figures, which registered a peak surplus in 1982/83 of 200 million kyat but dropped sharply thereafter, recording a deficit in 1985/86 of 220 million kyat (MAPT, 1991).[4] This fall suggests that it was impossible for the government to increase its procurement price in response to the rising discontent of rice farmers against the procurement system.

The second problem was a growing disinclination of farmers to produce rice. The paddy procurement system created a huge disincentive for farmers. The system had been revised several times during the socialist period and by the mid-1980s it had become a very great burden for the farmers because the state absorbed their entire marketable surplus. Adding to their woes was the low procurement price, which remained unchanged from 1980/81 to 1986/87 while the free market price doubled during the same period. Takahashi (1992: 93) saw this paddy procurement system as resting on the "good will" (*seidana*) of the farmers and "pressure" from the state, but from the beginning of the 1980s there was only "pressure", which drove up farmer discontent and made them reluctant to cultivate rice.

The result of this discontent and reluctance was that the government failed to procure a sufficient supply of paddy at its low procurement price in 1986/87. This triggered government moves to reform Myanmar's rice marketing policy. To deal with the skyrocketing free market rice price, the government introduced another procurement scheme that handled purchases of paddy through cooperatives in an effort to assure a sufficient supply of rationed rice to consumers. Along with this the government issued yet another prohibition against the sale of rice on the black market in an effort to keep the rice price under control. However, neither of these moves achieved their aims, and it was starkly clear to everyone that the socialist rice marketing system with its reliance on pressure and price controls had reached a dead end.

Despite the fact the paddy/rice was the main target of the broad-ranging liberalization of agricultural marketing in 1987, the system was soon modified. Why? The reason was closely related to the underlying rationale for the rice policy, which was to assure a stable supply of rice at a low price for the stability of the regime. The regime had bitter experiences with social unrest associated with increases in the price of rice in 1967 and 1974.[5] To avoid any repetition of these events, even though the rice rationing system for general consumers was abandoned, that for the civil servants was maintained to secure the political base of the regime. Initially it was planned to collect paddy for the rice ration as land revenue from farmers and commercial taxes from traders. However, the new collection system became caught up in the political turmoil in 1988 and did not function well, with the result that the quantity collected fell far short of the amount required. In 1988/89 the government revived the paddy procurement system, which had a very strong institutional base under the Socialist government. In a determined effort to achieve its procurement goals, the government sought to placate farmers by reducing the "pressure" of procurement while making efforts to obtain their "good will". A clear indication of the government's new approach was the initial labeling of paddy collected under this revised system as "good will paddy (*seidana zaba*)" (Okamoto, 1993: 107).

Along with this, the government monopoly over rice exporting was utilized to control the price of rice for general consumers, who were excluded from the rice rationing system after the first liberalization. A general deregulation of private exports was announced in the midst of the tense situation. Due to fear of further instability, the government very much wanted to keep a stable rice price for general consumers and it regarded its monopoly of rice exports as one means to this end. Consequently, the decision to allow private rice exporting was shelved.

The First Liberalization and Changes in State Marketing Sector

The main objective of the rice policy after the first liberalization continued to be maintenance of a stable supply of rice at a low price for the domestic market. This goal was pursued both from the production and from the marketing side. The government aggressively promoted expansion of paddy sown acreage by introducing double cropping as well as extending cultivation in marginal areas.[6] The government also maintained tight control over the state rice marketing sector, while intervening in the private market whenever it seemed necessary.

This section will look at the changes that occurred as well as the problems experienced by the state rice marketing sector after the first liberalization in attempting to achieve this goal. The discussion will follow the flow of paddy/rice from farmers to consumers (rationing and export), analyzing procurement, milling, rationing and export of paddy/rice by state sector will be analyzed in turn.

Procurement of Paddy

With the decline in the volume of rationed rice, the paddy procurement system that supplied rice was scaled back. The procurement quota set for paddy produced in the monsoon season (monsoon paddy) was decreased to

Table 1 Estimation of Domestically Marketed Volume of Rice (In Terms of Paddy) (Thousand Tons)

| | A Production | B Deduction | | | | | C=A-B Marketed Volume | | | | | D Export |
| | | Procurement | Ratio | Seed | Waste | Home Consumption | Volume | Ratio (%) | Milled Rice | Converted to Paddy | Share in Procurement (%) | Share in Production (%) |
		b	b/A					C/A		d	d/b	d/A
1980/81	13,340	4,259	31.9	530	530	7,384	637	4.8	703	1,049	24.6	7.9
1985/86	14,341	4,156	29.0	506	506	7,354	1,818	12.7	594	887	21.3	6.2
1987/88	13,658	564	4.1	482	482	7,402	4,728	34.6	320	478	84.7	3.5
1988/89	13,186	1,672	12.7	494	494	7,447	3,080	23.4	48	72	4.3	0.5
1989/90	13,826	1,482	10.7	504	504	7,551	3,785	27.4	169	252	17.0	1.8
1990/91	13,748	1,851	13.5	511	511	7,579	3,296	24.0	134	200	10.8	1.5
1991/92	12,993	2,095	16.1	499	499	7,589	2,312	17.8	183	273	13.0	2.1
1992/93	14,603	2,222	15.2	530	530	7,648	3,672	25.1	199	297	13.4	2.0
1993/94	15,500	1,939	12.5	587	587	7,694	4,693	30.3	261	390	20.1	2.5
1994/95	17,908	2,034	11.4	613	613	7,737	6,911	38.6	1,041	1,554	76.4	8.7
1995/96	17,669	1,934	10.9	634	634	7,772	6,695	37.9	354	528	27.3	3.0
1996/97	17,397	1,522	8.7	607	607	7,810	6,852	39.4	93	139	9.1	0.8
1997/98	16,391	1,601	9.8	597	597	7,829	5,765	35.2	28	42	2.6	0.3
1998/99	16,808	2,200	13.1	607	607	7,869	5,524	32.9	120	179	8.1	1.1
1999/2000	20,159	2,212	11.0	649	649	7,908	8,741	43.4	55	82	3.7	0.4
2000/01	21,359	2,126	10.0	657	657	7,948	9,972	46.7	251	375	17.6	1.8
2001/02	21,569	2,119	9.8	666	666	7,987	10,131	47.0	939	1,401	66.1	6.5
2002/03	21,461	2,066	9.6	670	670	7,987	10,067	46.9	793	1,184	57.3	5.5
2003/04	22,770	0	0.0	676	676	8,027	13,391	58.8	168	251	–	1.1
2004/05	24,361	0	0.0	708	708	8,067	14,877	61.1	182	272	–	1.1
2005/06	27,246	0	0.0	763	763	8,108	17,612	64.6	180	269	–	1.0

Notes 1: Seed and waste is assumed to be 2 baskets per acre.
2: Home consumpion is calculated as the number of households × 5.5 (the average numbers per houhsehold in 1999) × 15 baskets. For 1998/99–1999/2000, since the data for farm households are not available, it is estimated using the average increase rate of households.
3: Export includes bot white rice and brokend rice.
4: The paddy conversion rate for export is assumed as 67%.

Sources: Number of farm households *RFES*, up to 1997/98, various issues.

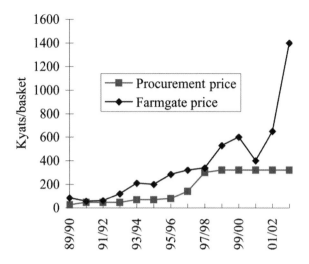

Figure 1   Changes in Procurement and Farmgate Prices

Sources: MAPT, Author's survey, Takahashi (2000).

10–12 baskets[7]/acre (0.5–0.6 tons per hectare) from the 30–40 basket/acre (1.5–2.1 tons per hector) of the socialist period. Consequently, the quantity of rice procured by the government as a share of total rice production decreased from 30 per cent to 12 per cent on average (Table 1). Despite the official assertion that the burden of the paddy procurement system on farmers had eased, there were various problems with the procurement process.

First, the amount procured was fixed on a per acre basis; thus farmers with lower productivity or less marketable surplus were at a disadvantage. Unlike the system in the socialist period that absorbed the farmers' entire marketable surplus, the new system had the merit of inducing farmers to increase production. However, it did not reflect the disparity in the productivity of individual farmers or fluctuations in yield owing to weather conditions.

Second, as Figure 1 shows, the procurement price was only revised after the disparity between the market and official price became an obstacle to procuring paddy from farmers.

This widening disparity in price suggests that the real burden on farmers was not lessened to the extent that official statistics indicate. While farmers received payments 3 to 4 month in advance, the procurement price was kept at 40–60 per cent of the prevailing free market price as in the socialist period.

A third issue is the likelihood of an upward bias in the production statistics as a negative consequence of the policy of aggressively increasing

Table 2 Area-wise Share of Paddy Procurement (%)

	1991/ 92	1992/ 93	1993/ 94	1994/ 95	1995/ 96	1996/ 97	1998/ 99	1999/ 2000
Rice Deficit Area	12.9	11.0	21.2	16.6	22.4	28.1	18.7	25.0
Rice Surplus Area	87.1	89.0	78.8	83.4	77.6	71.9	81.3	75.0
Ayeyarwaddy	47.5	55.1	38.9	42.4	37.5	40.8	42.7	35.5

Note: Rice deficit area includes Kachin, Sagain, Mandalay, Kyin, Kaya and Shan, Magwe, Rakhine and Tanintharyi.
Surplus areas includs Ayeyarwaddy, Bago, Mon and Yangon.
This categorization is base on MOAI (2000).

Source: MAPT documents.

rice production. The real rice production level in some areas could have been less than the figures that appeared in the statistics since there was a tendency for local administrators to overstate production, and the real burden borne by farmers may have been much heavier than officially reported.

A fourth problem was a rise in the cost transportation for farmers (Takahashi, 2000: 191). Normally procurement took place at procurement depots set up by MAPT. Farmers had to deliver paddy to designated depots at their own cost. However, after liberalization the number of procurement depots decreased, and many farmers had to deliver their paddy to more distant locations.

An additional cost faced farmers at the procurement depots (Takahashi, 2000: 56, 191). Sometimes they were asked to supply more than was initially demanded. To avoid this situation, some farmers entrusted their deliveries of procured rice to special brokers who could better handle bargaining with staff at purchasing depots. The cost of this service in 1999 for farmers in a township in Yangon Division was 8 baskets for the delivery of 100 baskets of procured paddy, a fee of 8%. This suggests that farmers may have had to bear even greater costs if they delivered their paddy to procurement depots on their own.

A sixth problem was the enlargement of the areas targeted for the procurement of paddy, which added to the burden of farmers in general. Looking at the percentage of procurement by area (Table 2), one would expect rice surplus areas (Ayeyarwaddy, Bago and Yangon Divisions and Mon State) to account for the larger share. However, rice deficit areas (the rest of the divisions and states) also had their shares increased, especially from around 1993/94. Even though the procurement rate per farmer in the rice deficit areas was set lower than for the surplus areas, their share in actual terms increased in the 1990s as a result of government pressure to increase rice production nationwide, not only in the major rice producing areas.[8] Procurement quotas were raised even for places where rice production was basically for home consumption with little marketable surplus.

A seventh problem was that it was virtually impossible to adjust procurement quotas according to the real condition of each area. In principle, official quotas were determined at the township and district level based on the performance of the previous year and actual production conditions. However, it was extremely difficult to set a target lower than the previous year without special reasons. There was continuous pressure from the top authorities to increase or at least maintain the total volume of procurement for each location.

An eighth problem, apart from the effect on the farm economy, was that the system entailed excessive administrative effort. The procurement process in the villages involved not only MAPT staff but also all administrative bodies in a local area. Whenever local authorities found procurement operations falling short of the target, all the government officials in the township were sent out to the villages to encourage farmers to meet their procurement obligations. In this way, local administration was greatly biased toward maintaining the procurement system, a posture that impeded the functioning of the administration.

Finally, there was the problem of the quality of procured paddy. This issue also affected the rice rationing system and export. In response to the government's low procurement price, farmers tended to deliver to the depots their lower quality paddy (including grain that was not fully dried or had been intentionally mixed with foreign matter) and sold their better paddy on the free market. Another factor affecting quality was that paddy delivered to the depot was supposed to be separated into varieties, but in practice this separation was loosely controlled and different varieties became intermixed. Thus good quality paddy could become mixed with poor quality paddy, leading to a lower grade of milled rice. The quality of procured paddy became a big problem, as it had been in the socialist period (Takahashi, 1992: 93–94).

The Milling of Procured Paddy

The paddy collected from farmers was either milled at MAPT-owned rice mills or contracted to private mills. As of 2000/01, MAPT owned 68 mills, mainly in the major rice producing areas. Most had been constructed in the 1980s with official development assistance (ODA) from Japan or other international organizations. Many MAPT mills were large, with a capacity of

Table 3 Changes in the Milled Rice by MAPT Owned and MAPT Contracted Mills (Million)

Fiscal Year	Procurement (basket)	MAPT Mills		MAPT Contract Mills		Share of MAPT Mills (%)	Share of Milled Rice in the Total Procured Amount (%)
		Paddy (basket)	Milled Rice (ton)	Paddy (basket)	Milled Rice (ton)		
1988/89	85.1	14.7	0.2	46.1	0.6	24.2	71.4
1989/90	63.0	19.1	0.2	59.2	0.8	24.4	124.3
1990/91	72.1	19.6	0.2	40.4	0.5	32.7	83.2
1991/92	74.7	20.3	0.2	45.9	0.6	30.7	88.6
1992/93	76.5	25.0	0.3	57.7	0.7	30.2	108.1
1993/94	92.3	27.0	0.3	50.9	0.7	34.7	84.4
1994/95	97.3	32.1	0.4	76.5	1.0	29.6	111.6
1995/96	92.9	27.4	0.3	67.1	0.9	29.0	101.7
1996/97	73.0	22.6	0.3	49.9	0.7	31.2	99.3
1997/98	44.7	21.7	0.3	37.2	0.5	36.8	131.8
1998/99	105.3	26.2	0.3	46.0	0.6	36.3	68.6
1999/2000	105.8	30.9	0.4	53.3	0.7	36.7	79.6
2000/01	101.7	28.1	0.4	51.8	0.7	35.2	78.5

Source: U Tin Htut Oo and Kudo eds. (2003: 114).

100 tons of milled rice per day, while most private mills had a capacity of less than 50 tons per day. There was far more paddy procured than MAPT could handle at its own mills, so it contracted with private mills. Table 3 shows the share of milling by MAPT and by private mills after liberalization began in 1987. The share for MAPT mills was only 32 per cent on average, indicating the government's great dependency on private mills.

One reason for the high dependency on private rice mills after liberalization, even with the decrease in the volume of procured rice, was the run-down condition of MAPT mills. These facilities could not be maintained or repaired after the halt of ODA after 1988. Also the chronic shortage of electricity greatly lowered their rate of operation as most of MAPT mills were powered by electricity. Some mills operated only 6–10 hours a day because of blackouts, although they had the capacity to operate around the clock.[9]

The biggest problem with the milling of procured paddy was the low milling fee paid to contracted private mills, which was half to one-third of the prevailing free market milling rate. For example, in 1998/99 the market milling fee was 20–30 kyat per basket while MAPT paid only 10 kyat per basket. The government kept this milling fee low in order to curb the growing expenditures incurred by the state marketing sector. This meant that the rice rationing system created a burden both for the farmers and for private millers.

Rice Rationing for the Budget Group

The rice rationing system targeting general consumers was abolished with the first liberalization, and the system was limited to the so-called Budget Group made up of civil servants, including military personnel. This substantially lowered the number of people receiving rice rations and reduced the volume of rationed rice to 0.6–0.8 million tons in normal years, a decrease of 1 million tons compared to the volume rationed in the socialist period (Table 4). Sixty per cent of the total rationed rice went to civil servants, 30 per cent to the military, and the rest to special institutions such as hospitals.

Under the rice rationing system of the socialist period, every household was eligible to receive 12.6 kg (6 pyi[10]) monthly per adult and 6.3 kg (3 pyi) per child under 12 years old (Mya Than and Nishizawa, 1990: 104).[11] Assuming that the monthly per capita consumption for an adult was 6.2 pyi, as it was in 1997 (CSO, 1997), 97 per cent of consumption would have been covered by the ration system, which can be regarded as quite a sufficient amount. Moreover, the average price of rationed rice remained at about

Table 4   Changes in the Volume of Rationed Rice (Thousand tons)

	Procurement Volume of Paddy	Rationed Rice Rice	Rationed Rice Converted from Paddy	Share of Rationed Volume in the Procurement Volume (%)
1980/81	4,259	1,618	3,236	76.0
1983/84	4,145	1,709	3,418	82.5
1987/88	564	574	1,148	203.5
1988/89	1,672	568	1,136	68.0
1989/90	1,482	195	390	26.3
1990/91	1,851	747	1,494	80.7
1991/92	2,095	635	1,270	60.6
1992/93	2,222	779	1,558	70.1
1993/94	1,939	751	1,502	77.5
1994/95	2,034	843	1,686	82.9
1995/96	1,934	804	1,608	83.1
1996/97	1,522	848	1,696	111.4
1997/98	1,601	793	1,586	99.0
1998/99	2,200	672	1,344	61.1
1999/2000	2,212	685	1,370	61.9
2000/01	2,126	590	1,180	55.5
2001/02	2,119	578	1,137	53.7
2002/03	2,066	678	1,137	55.0

Note: The conversion rate from rice to paddy is 50%.

Sources: Procurement volume: CSO, *REFS*. Various issues and MAPT (2003).
       For 1980/80–1994/95, it includes the procurement by the cooperative.
       Rationed volume: MAPT (2003).

50 per cent of the free market price for the period of 1962/63–1986/87, and for a decade after 1978, the price was kept unchanged.[12] This means that consumers were sufficiently protected in terms of food security.

After the first liberalization, the volume of rationed rice (for the Budget Group) was reduced to 25 kg (12 pyi) per month for an unmarried adult and 28 kg (14 pyi) for a married adult, regardless of the number of family members. This amount was sufficient for an individual adult, but depending on the size of a household, the amount of rationed rice decreased compared to the socialist period. The price of rationed rice was kept at 21 per cent of the free market price on average for the period of 1988–2001,[13] and some ministries and organizations even provided the rice to their personnel for free.[14] Therefore, it can be said that the price was kept low in order to compensate for the decrease in the amount of rationed rice compared to that of the socialist period for this targeted group.

The inferior quality of procured paddy affected the rationing system in the 1990s. Although the rice ration system benefitted recipients in terms of volume and price, this was not sufficient enough to overcome the inferior quality of the rice, which led recipients to sell it to traders as feed for livestock rather than consume it at home. The increasing availability of a wide variety of rice at varying prices on the free market, as will be seen later, contributed to this trend. Consequently, the rice ration system no longer provided the benefit to recipients that the government intended.

The Rice Export System

Although the ban on the private export of agricultural produce such as pulses was lifted in 1988, rice exports remained the monopoly of MAPT. The government's priority was on securing rice for rationing, and only the rice remaining in government hands after rationing was released for export. Consequently, the amount of rice exported was extremely small when compared with the socialist period (Table 2).

In order to monopolize exports, the government separated the domestic and international markets. This led to a huge disparity between the domestic and international price of rice. The domestic price at the free market foreign exchange rate averaged 50 per cent of the international price after the first liberalization. It even fell to 40 per cent when the domestic price collapsed in 2000–01.[15] The international price of rice had been trending downward over the previous two decades, but the Myanmar government kept the price of domestic rice well below even the declining international level.

A further reason that the government wanted to maintain a monopoly over rice exports was they provided a direct source of foreign exchange earnings, as was true in the socialist period as well. Even though the amount exported was sharply reduced, the foreign exchange earned per unit was substantial because the rice had been procured at 40–50 per cent below the market price.

The inferior quality of the paddy procured by the government hampered efforts to increase exports, and limited the destinations that would accept Myanmar rice. A breakdown of Myanmar's rice exports (Table 5) shows that most go to South Asia, Africa and Southeast Asia, areas with low-income countries where there is demand for poor quality rice. Myanmar rice has failed to generate stable export demand because its export regime depended greatly on the state marketing sector. Because the state attached importance to the quantities supplies rather than quality, Myanmar was not

Table 5 Direction of Myanmar Rice Exports (Volume) (%)

	1990/91	1992/93	1994/95	1996/97	1998/99	2000/01	2001/02	2003/04	2005/06
Southeast Asia	11.2	2.0	61.0	50.5	55.0	18.3	39.1	46.4	27.2
South Asia	49.3	37.7	9.5	21.5	15.8	69.3	5.3	23.2	16.1
The rest of Asia	0.0	0.0	0.0	0.0	0.8	0.0	0.0	0.0	0.0
Africa	29.9	57.3	26.5	26.9	25.8	10.0	0.0	0.0	5.0
Middle East	2.2	3.0	0.0	0.0	0.0	0.0	39.1	19.6	50.0
North and South America	7.5	0.0	1.4	0.0	0.0	0.0	0.9	0.0	0.0
Europe	0.0	0.0	1.5	1.1	2.5	2.4	6.1	2.4	0.6
Oceania	0.0	0.0	0.0	0.0	0.0	0.0	9.1	0.0	0.0
Total	100.0	100.0	100.0	100.0	100.0	100.0	100.0	100.0	100.0
Total Exported Amount	134	199	1041	93	120	251	939	168	180
(Thousand Tons)	134	199	1041	93	120	251	939	168	180

Sources: CSO, *Statistical Yearbook* (1997, 2001, 2006).

able to meet demands for wide range of qualities and therefore could not increase exports.

The Private Rice Marketing Sector after the First Liberalization

The development of private marketing

The rice rationing system and its supporting procurement system were scaled back after the first liberalization, and the private sector began to play a larger role in supplying rice to the general consumer. The first liberalization removed restrictions on private millers and traders, and the geographical limits on rice trading that existed in the socialist period.

The shrinking of the state marketing sector along with the government's efforts in the 1990s to raise rice production brought a steady increase in the volume of rice on the free market. The amount reached 30–40 per cent of total production by the end of the 1990s (Table 2).[16] This section will examine how the private marketing sector developed in this context, focusing on qualitative changes in the marketing system.

One important change was the spread of marketing over wide areas of the country. The rice flows are shown in Figure 2.

The major commodity flows are from Lower to Upper Myanmar and from Lower Myanmar to coastal areas. Rice is transferred via Upper Myanmar to the mountainous frontier areas. Yangon, the former capital, functions as the central marketing point and the flow of rice there reaches 3–3.4 million tons annually (based on figures for 2000–02) (MOAI, *MIS*, various issues), accounting for 34 per cent of the total marketed volume per year indicated in Table 2. The rice assembled in Yangon is transferred to markets in Upper Myanmar and in coastal areas while also feeding the capital's four million people. During the socialist period, the only milled rice marketed was small quantities that slipped through the mesh of government regulations, but now rice is traded in large volumes over wide areas of the country, supported by the development of transport infrastructure.

The price trends of rice in different parts of the country are another indication that rice is now marketed over a wide area. Figure 3 shows the change in the price of rice of similar quality in six different areas. Yangon, Mawlyamyaing and Pyay are in rice surplus areas; Mandalay and Pakkoku are in rice deficit areas, while Taunggyi is an important collection/transfer market in a rice deficit mountainous area. Figure 3 shows that the prices in the six areas moved in tandem, although the prices in deficit areas were higher than those of surplus areas, as would be expected.

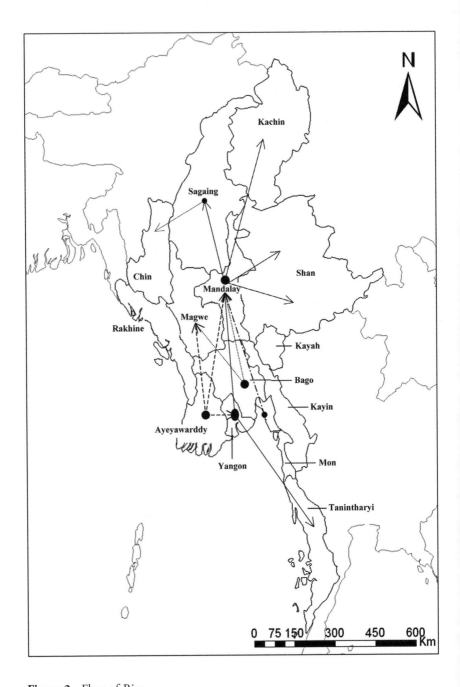

Figure 2 Flow of Rice

Source: Made by author, based on MOAI (2000).

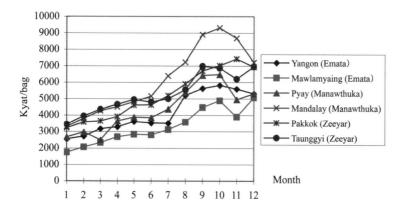

Figure 3 Changes in the Rice Prices in Different Areas (2002)

Sources: MIS (various monthly issues).

A second change was the involvement of private rice millers and traders. In response to the increased market surplus, many private millers and traders enter the rice marketing sector.

The number of private rice mills increased throughout the 1990s, mainly due to a sharp rise in the number of small mills in the villages (often called huller mills, with a capacity of less than 15 tons per day). The exact number of these small rice mills is not available, but there are normally one to five of them in each village tract. Assuming that there are two rice mills in a village tract in the major rice producing areas (for example, Ayeyarwaddy, Bago, Yangon and Mandalay Divisions and Mon State), the total number of these small mills could be as high as 14,240. However, it is not unusual for a village tract to have more than 2 rice mills, so the above figure is a rather conservative estimate. The establishment of small rice mills was first permitted officially from around 1992/93, and the number of these mills quickly increased dramatically after that. Most of these mills handle paddy for home consumption in the villages, while only a few engage in milling for sale on the free market. The owners of these small mills are often farmers who do not have sufficient capital to invest in high quality machines. Thus, their efficiency is often low, and the quality of their milling poor.

In addition to rice millers, a large number of traders entered the rice market. According to the author's survey of 47 wholesalers in eight major rice markets (Pathein, Pyapon, Mawlamyaingyun, Myaungmya, Yangon, Pyay, Mandalay, Pakkoku), 39 wholesalers (85%) began rice trading after liberalization in 1987, and only five (11%) were doing so before then.[17] By

Table 6   Number of Private Mills Registered with MAPT

State·Division	1998/99	2000/01	1998/99 (%)	2000/01 (%)
Ayeyarwaddy	489	369	47.2	53.7
Bago	208	133	20.1	19.4
Yangon	123	69	11.9	10.0
Mon	66	32	6.4	4.7
Rakhine	5	4	0.5	0.6
Sagaing	49	41	4.7	6.0
Mandalay	68	11	6.6	1.6
Magwe	6	0	0.6	0.0
Kachin	8	10	0.8	1.5
Tanintaryi	2	2	0.2	0.3
Kaya	11	16	1.1	2.3
Total	1035	687	100.0	100.0

Sources: MAPT documents, U Tin Htut Oo & Kudo eds. (2003: Annex 7).

far the greater share of rice traders entered the market after liberalization. The formation of marketing networks over wide areas of the country as well as the increase in the volume of marketed rice produced by farmers encouraged the entry of traders, especially in the late 1990s.

Problems that Private Rice Marketing Sector Has Faced

In the previous section we noted various positive aspects of private rice marketing in Myanmar after the first liberalization. However, there were also problems in the development process and these were closely bound with the official rationale of the rice marketing system, which was to maintain a stable rice supply at a low price. The private rice marketing sector did not dare to interfere with this rationale. Consequently, the sector had to limit the scope of its transaction activities to the government's procurement operations (for the Budget Group) and the domestic rice market.

Problems Facing Rice Millers

It was pointed out earlier that there was a remarkable rise of small rice mills in rural areas in Myanmar. However, mid- and large-scale rice mills (mills with a capacity of more than 16 tons of rice per day) decreased in numbers. Table 6 indicates the changes in the number of MAPT registered mid- and large-scale rice mills.

The figures show that the number of these rice mills decreased greatly in just two years. Another example of this big drop comes from the author's 1999 survey. There were 13 mid- and large-scale rice mills in a township in Yangon Division but only seven of the mills were actually operating. The other six had closed down.

The great majority of these big rice mills had been established during the British colonial period or the socialist period. Those opened during the colonial period had played a primary role in making Myanmar one of the giant rice exporters of the world. However, when rice exporting became a government monopoly in the socialist period, these rice mills were required to mill the government procured paddy at the official fixed rate, though they were not nationalized in the strict sense. After the first liberalization in 1987, these mid- and large-scale mills also started operating in the private rice market, but business was difficult because of their large capacity. The main reason that the rice mills closed down in the township mentioned above was capacity underutilization.

One reason for this underutilization was the decreasing demand for milling at mid- and large-scale rice mills. The rapid increase in the number of small mills in the villages following the first liberalization reduced the need to transport paddy to the distant big mills, and their rate of operation declined. Before liberalization, the rice for rural household consumption was milled at the big mills located in towns, but during the 1990s this rice came to be processed mostly at the newly established village mills, and the big town mills lost business. Competition also arose from some rice traders, especially from those in Pathein and Myaungmya in Ayeyarwaddy Division, who procured paddy over a wide area, and set up their own rice mills. As noted earlier, the rice price can fluctuate widely on the Yangon market, and the timing of transactions has a big impact on profits. If the rice sent to Yangon has to be milled at one of the big mills, traders sometimes have to wait their turn, which can cause them to miss the best timing for a sale. It was to avoid this problem that some traders set up their own mills, even if these were small. Given the downward trend in the demand for milling at mid- and large-scale rice mills, some big mills decided to turn away from custom milling in favour of normal milling in an effort to increase their rate of operation. In this case, the mills purchased and milled paddy at their own expense and then sold the rice.

A second problem for mid- and large-scale rice mills was that the milling of MAPT paddy often became a burden, both financially and physically. Even though MAPT bore the cost of labour for the milling of its paddy, big mills under contract with MAPT often found that milling for the organization

Table 7   The Number of Private Mills Contracted to Process Procurement Paddy

Division/State	1991/92	1995/96	1998/99	2000/01
Ayeyarwaddy	220	208	144	138
Bago	173	136	100	51
Yangon	75	61	49	38
Mon	40	37	30	43
Rakhine	19	15	12	0
Sagaing	101	81	78	68
Mandalay	56	66	38	39
Magwe	32	19	20	15
Kachin	20	25	14	14
Tanintaryi	19	14	12	17
Kayin	9	1	1	0
Kaya	1	1	1	0
Total	765	664	499	423

Sources: MAPT documents, U Tin Htut Oo & Kudo eds. (2003: Annex 5).

did not pay. The mills also needed to follow a set of cumbersome procedures satisfy MAPT requirements.[18] There were also cases where MAPT required mills to store its paddy or milled rice for medium to long periods but did not pay storage charges. These mills were then hard pressed to find space to store their own rice or paddy. Statistics show government dependency on the private sector for rice storage to be less than 10 per cent (Okamoto, 2004: 170), but it was very likely more than that. All these difficulties made the big rice mills reluctant to contract with MAPT. Table 7 shows the decline in the number of mills contracted by MAPT to mill government procured paddy, a change that reflects the general reluctance of private rice mills to contract with MAPT.[19]

While the long-term trend of private rice mills has been away from MAPT, some mills that found benefits in contracting to mill MAPT's procured paddy. One reason is that they can at least secure a certain amount of paddy to continue operating. With general demand decreasing for milling at mid- and large-scale mills, they needed to find ways to keep themselves running. It is a rather passive response. But they have workers to pay, and they see it as better to get whatever paddy they can to keep operating. Another reason is the deterioration and obsolescence of their milling facilities, which made it difficult for some mills to achieve the quality required to sell rice on the free market. When milling for MAPT, the quality is less important.

Rice mills that are less inclined to expand their business or improve quality are willing to contract with MAPT. Most of the rice mills that have closed down in recent years have been run by passive operators who relied mainly on MAPT paddy for their business.

The biggest problem facing the mid- and large-scale mills is the dilapidated condition of their milling facilities and equipment. Important parts of these mills, such as engines, are now very old and have been in use since the 1930s; the most recent are from the 1960s. A survey by the author of mid- and large-scale mill in Ayeyarwaddy Division in 2002 found that even millers who started business after the 1987 liberalization often did not construct completely new mills, but made use of second-hand equipment or purchased old mills. The survey covered 22 mid- and large-scale mills; seven were new entrants into the business but only two of these constructed new facilities. The other five purchased mills second-hand. Even with new ownership, the cost and maintenance of running old mills with worn-out equipment can be very high. But no support or assistance for maintenance or improving efficiency has been forthcoming from the government despite its dependence on the big mills for milling state procured paddy.

In the view of most of the old big rice mills, any substantial investment to upgrade facilities and improve quality will not pay given that the market is still dominated by medium and low quality rice.[20] Replacing their old steam engines with electric motors would in all likelihood lower their rate of operation because of the chronic shortage of electricity. The limited supply of spare parts at reasonable cost and adequate quality has also detracted from the willingness of millers to invest. The great majority of mid- and large-scale millers say that they are ready to undertake new investment once private rice exporting is allowed and the market for high quality rice expands. This clearly indicates that the present condition of Myanmar's rice market, characterized by government restrictions on exports and the dominance of low and medium quality rice has narrowed the business opportunities for big rice millers, and this in turn has shaped their business perspective.

Problems Facing Rice Traders

The first liberalization gave rice traders the freedom to deal in the domestic rice market, and this new market environment encouraged the entry of new rice traders. However, this new freedom was only on the condition that their dealings did not jeopardize the government's rice policy. Herein lay the nature of the first liberalization. Rice traders were not entirely free from government intervention. There were three situations where the government intervened in the domestic rice market.

One was when rice transactions were done with remote regions. In general after the first liberalization, there were no longer any restrictions on the marketing of rice over a wide area of the country. However, transactions with regions bordering neighbouring countries were an exception. These regions were Shan, Chin and Rakhine States, and Tanintharyi Division. For any rice transactions with these regions, it was necessary to get permission from the local authorities. For some regions, there was a monthly quota for the volume of rice purchased. The rationale of this regulation was to keep the domestic rice price stable. With Myanmar's internal rice price kept far below the international price, exporting sizable amounts of rice (even informally) to the neighbouring countries of Thailand, China, India and Bangladesh would inevitably cause upward pressure on the domestic rice price. To prevent this, the authorities made every effort to strictly regulate the volume of rice traded in these remote regions, an arrangement that meant the people in these regions, which are rice deficit areas, paid a relatively high price for the rice they consumed.[21] Nevertheless, the government put tight controls on the transactions of rice involving these remote regions because it placed top priority on maintaining a stable price for the domestic rice market as a whole.

The second situation was when the volume of procured rice fell below the government's target. There was an unwritten rule, even when the harvest was normal, that traders could not buy paddy or rice from farmers who had not met their procurement quotas for that year. However, when procurement was not progressing well in an area, the government often prohibited all private sales of paddy or rice in that area. In the remote rice deficit regions discussed above, the government generally did not permit such sales during the procurement season.

The third situation was when an abrupt rise took place in the rice price. The government was noticeably wary about depending on the private sector for marketing rice. This was because it basically viewed traders as evil,[22] and often blamed the private sector for hikes in the price of rice. Whenever the authorities judged that the rice price had gone above the level they could tolerate, orders were issued to start inspecting rice traders in various parts of the country, in both rural and urban areas. Compared to the situation for other commodities, the rice market in Myanmar faced a much higher risk of sudden, unexpected intervention by the government. One rice trader commenting on the government's stance on rice said, "If you want to make a profit, don't go into rice trading; choose some other business."[23] Rice traders have to accept such intervention because the government has not changed its stance against an unstable rice price.

The Second Liberalization and Its Consequence

During the second liberalization in April 2003, there were three policy agendas. One was to open rice exports to the private sector. The second was to abolish the paddy procurement system, and the third was to retain the rice rationing system for the Budget Group by procuring rice from traders instead of farmers. However, in January 2004 private rice exports were suddenly halted when the rice rationing system ended. Eventually, the second liberalization only applied to the domestic market.

What was the background and objective of the second liberalization?

The government's original objective in the second liberalization was probably to earn additional foreign exchange by exporting rice. As pointed out earlier, it appears that from the late 1990s, the government sought to export larger quantities of rice by increasing procurement from the farmers. However, it seems that this effort did not work as planned, and the government apparently decided to try another way, which was to earn more foreign exchange by increasing rice exports, utilizing the private sector. This stance is evident in the fact that private rice millers and wholesalers also became members of the Rice Trading Leading Committee, which was in charge of this reform. The inclusion was something of a surprise since there was a tendency that the more important the policy, the more reluctant the government was to allow other parties to be involved in setting policy.

The original reform plan for rice export was as follows. The government would open rice exporting to private traders by issuing export licenses. Those who obtained licenses could export rice within a quota set annually by the government, and the government would take half of the foreign exchange earnings, in fact 45 per cent of total earnings after deduction of the 10 per cent export tax. In turn, the government repaid marketing costs (such as transportation and labour cost) incurred by the traders for 45 per cent of the rice exported but in local currency. The government issued export licenses covering 0.5 million tons of rice, out of which 0.27 million tons were actually exported.

Behind this increased emphasis on exports was the government's feeling that the domestic rice price was more or less under control. Thanks to its aggressive rice production policy during the 1990s, the supply of rice in the domestic market had steadily increased, although the profitability of rice trading had deteriorated over the same period. The direct result of this was a collapse of the rice price in 2000–01. In 2002 the price started to rise again, but this was a temporary phenomenon caused by the farmers' strong reluctance to sow paddy in response to the price collapse, as well as by a fall in production due to unfavourable weather. By 2003 the rice price had started to stabilize, and it is very possible that the government saw this as a good time to start deregulating private rice exporting.

Second, the paddy procurement system was abolished as it no longer yielded sufficient benefits to justify the cost of retaining it. This was an indirect effect of the low rice price as a result of increased rice production. Because of the depressed domestic market price, rice production in general suffered a decline in profitability. This increased the difficulty of sustaining the procurement system because the government had to procure paddy at a price even lower than the repressed market price. While the government was able to sustain the procurement system by reducing the burden for farmers after the first liberalization, it was reaching a deadlock, though not in the form of the discontent from farmers observed in the mid-1980s. Worse still, the recipients were finding little merit in greater government efforts to secure rationed rice because of the poor quality of the grain, a problem hampering the expansion of exports as well. Added to this was MAPT's deficit, which had begun to widen again from the late 1990s.

Soon after the first liberalization, the procurement system deficit shrank remarkably when compared to that in the socialist period. According to MAPT, the deficit was 350 million kyat in 1986/87, but this was turned into a surplus of 310 million kyat by 1989/90. However, it appears that the deficit increased again from the mid-1990s and especially at the end of the 1990s. It was 4.7 billion kyat in 1997/98 and then rose to more than 10 billion kyat from 1998–2000, followed by a slight decline to 9.8 billion in 2001/02 (MAPT, 2003). It is possible that this increase was the result of a rise in the quantities acquired under the procurement scheme. The situation was beginning to resemble the adverse conditions for the rice sector at the end of the socialist period.

As opposed to the liberalization in export and procurement of paddy/ rice, the rice rationing system for the Budget Group was retained. It was a manifestation of the government's efforts to consolidate its political base. Since the procurement system was to be abolished, rice had to be procured from commercial traders by paying market prices. However, just before procurements began, the government realized that it would be difficult to cover the whole cost of rice purchased at prevailing market prices, and in the early 2004, it suddenly announced that the rice rationing system was to be abolished. To compensate government personnel for the loss of rationed rice, each person would receive a payment of 5,000 kyat per month.[24]

This decision to abolish rice rationing and replace it with fixed cash payments had various ramifications. If these payments were the only compensation for the cost of rice, very likely discontent would break out among public servants if the price of rice went up even just a little. This was a real concern because there were signs that price increases would accompany export liberalization. This possibility unnerved the government, which decided to freeze private rice exports.[25] The reform plan was then modified without discussions with the private sector, causing great disappointment, but ultimately the stable supply of rice at a low price had top priority. The fundamental rationale of government rice policy prevailed over the prospect of earning a larger amount of foreign exchange.

As with the first liberalization, the second liberalization went through twists and turns as it progressed. However, the significance of the second liberalization in deregulating domestic rice marketing cannot be overemphasized, as the domestic rice market was finally completely liberalized 42 years after the establishment of Myanmar's socialist government. MAPT, long the main organization responsible for the rice procurement and rationing systems, lost its purpose for existing. Sizable reduction began in its personnel, and its rice mills were put up for sale.

The second liberalization was expected to have three effects. First, the profitability of rice production was expected to benefit. With an appropriate level for the price of rice on the market, the profitability of rice production, and thus farmers' incomes, could be expected to improve. In marginal rice producing areas where rice is grown mainly for home consumption, the change was expected to lead to a reduction in the amount of rice purchased on the market. At the same time, the sale of rice on the market was expected to increase by 10–20 per cent and rice production would become more market oriented. This would make farmers more concerned about the quality of the rice they produced.

The second effect of this liberalization was a reduction in the number of situations where the government would abruptly intervene in the market. This would reduce transaction costs for private rice traders and inefficiencies in the rice marketing system arising from heavy-handed government intervention. The procurement system carried with it numerous political and economic costs and also was a breeding ground for corruption. Its abolition was expected to lead to improvements in economic efficiency as a whole.

However, the failure to open rice exporting to private traders following the second liberalization was a big setback for the rice marketing sector in Myanmar from a mid- to long-term perspective. Rice traders were eagerly anticipating export deregulation and were greatly disappointed when it failed to take place. More than 20 export companies had been set up in preparation for liberalization, and these efforts were completely wasted. Though the government said the freeze on exporting was only temporary, the issue was not restored to the policy agenda. Its handling of rice exports intensified mistrust of the government within the commercial sector, leading traders to adopt a risk adverse attitude toward new investment in facilities and the expansion of business. Without doubt this is very much dampening the future outlook for the rice marketing sector in Myanmar.

Conclusion

The stable supply of rice at a low price continued to be the principal objective of the rice marketing system in Myanmar even after the two liberalizations. The transition from comprehensive state control over rice marketing that began with the first liberalization and continued with the second can be seen as an ad hoc transformation of the marketing system. Despite the various problems that had occurred throughout the state marketing sector, the government did not abandon its rationale and attempted to keep the direct control of the marketing system. Consequently, the transformation proceeded with twists and turns in response to the changing economic and political situation, and eventually took the form of a gradual deregulation of rice prices. The consequence of the two liberalizations was to shift Myanmar's rice marketing system from one supported by the rice procurement and ration systems and export controls to one solely dependent on export controls to achieve the policy objective of a low price for rice. From the experience of neighbouring rice exporting countries, such as Thailand and Vietnam, the policy objective of keeping low domestic rice price is not always incompatible with increasing rice exports, if the liberalization proceeds properly and in a timely fashion (Choiyang Chuchart and Sopin Tongpan, 1965; Tsujii, 1975; Nicholas and Goletti, 2000). However, in the case of Myanmar, the government continued to have strong fears of losing control over the rice sector.

Consumers in Myanmar have benefitted from the low rice prices, which are about 40–60 per cent of the international price, but at the cost of sacrificing the potential for Myanmar to be one of the world's major rice exporters. Restraining exports would surely benefit the poorest segment of the economy, such as the many landless agricultural labourers in rural areas and net buyers of rice,[26] but the government's policy of giving the highest priority to maintaining low domestic rice prices has shaped the development of private rice marketing. Exports could only take place in the remaining sphere of the rice marketing sector and on condition that they did not jeopardize the stable supply of rice at a low price. This was the inevitable consequence of the rationale for Myanmar's rice marketing policy.

In the liberalization process, however, the private rice marketing sector was able to achieve self-sustaining development. The government's policy of promoting rice production and cutbacks in the volume of rice procured by the government increased the amount of rice sold in the market and induced more traders to enter the rice marketing business. At the same time there was improvement in infrastructure in the areas of transportation, market facilities and financial services, which are indispensable for an efficient marketing system. These improvements made possible the establishment of a rice marketing system that extended over a wide area of the country, clearly demonstrating the latent willingness of Myanmar's traders to grasp whatever small opportunities arose to increase profits, something denied to them during the socialist period. The rice traders who expanded their business while avoiding conflicts with the government's rice policy were the ones who survived during the 1990s.

By the end of the decade, however, the private rice marketing sector had reached a crossroads as the domestic rice market approached the point of total saturation. This problem was most evident in the tough business conditions facing mid- and large-scale rice millers. The decrepitude and worn-out state of their mills grew apace, but they could not risk making any new investments under the existing market structure, where low and medium quality rice was in most demand. Even in the milling of lower quality rice, the big mills were losing out to the growing number of small-scale rice mills in the villages. Thus, by the time of the second liberalization, mid- and large-scale rice mills were facing a crisis in their business operations.

The commercial and processing industries of Myanmar's rice marketing sector continue to be based on the rural economy of the country. In neighbouring Thailand, rice millers turned to exporting, and with the capital they accumulated expanded their business to other industries with great success (Usui and Mishima ed., 1994: 98). In Myanmar as well, the same scenario seems possible for the private rice traders and millers. However, there is little prospect that full-scale private rice exporting will be allowed in the near future.[27] The present government is unlikely to change the rationale of its rice policy, which prioritizes a low price for the sake of political stability. If export controls are the sole direct policy tool that the government has for keeping the price of rice low, the government will remain reluctant to undertake any rapid deregulation of rice exports. This means that the private rice marketing sector will have to survive within the confines of the present domestic market, which limits the demand largely to low and medium quality rice. Thus the government's rice policy and its primary rationale have again thwarted the development of Myanmar's private rice marketing sector and its potential to stimulate growth in the economy as a whole.

Notes

1   In this paper both paddy and milled rice are referred to as rice. When a distinction is necessary, the terms paddy or milled rice are used.

2   See Saito (1981), Takahashi (1992), Tin Soe and Fisher (1990) for analyses of the procurement system in the socialist period.

3   The government institution responsible for rice marketing has been reorganized and renamed several times. MAPT came into being following reorganization of the AFPTC (Agricultural Farm Produce Trading Corporation) in 1989.

4   The figures were not only for rice. However, due to the overwhelming share of rice in the ration system, any increase/decrease in the volume of rationed rice had a substantial impact on MAPT's balance sheet. Tin Soe (1994: 21) pointed out that the deficit for rice procurement and rationing increased five-fold during the nine years from 1978/79 to 1986/87.

5   In 1967, demonstration led by housewives demanding larger amount of rice distribution occurred throughout the country. The inefficiency of the rice rationing system introduced by the Ne Win government was the fundamental cause of the shortages. Again in 1974, because of the abrupt increase of rice price due to the worldwide food price surge, demonstrations by the workers of state-owned factories spread across the country (Steinberg, 1981).

6   For details of the government's policy to increase rice production (via expansion of sown acreage) in the 1990s, see Chapter 5 of the present volume, Takahashi (2000) and Fujita (2003) and Kurosaki *et al.* (2004), Thawnghmung (2003). One extreme example of the inefficient expansion of the sown acreage was the large scale reclamation of land in deep water areas in Ayeyarwaddy and Yangon divisions in the late 1990s. The government invited private companies to reclaim the land by providing privileged access to fuel and machinery at subsidized prices and by allowing half of the rice produced to be exported. These companies (mostly construction and export firms with no experience of cultivation) were supposed to reclaim 3,000–5,000 acres on average. However, no companies actually exported rice because the programme was not economically viable to begin with, and most of the participating companies sought the "privileges" such as cheap fuels and machineries rather than the potential income from rice cultivation and export.

7   1 basket of paddy equals 20.9 kg.

8   This policy emphasized the self-sufficiency in rice of each locality since the mid-1990s.

9   Based on the author's interviews in Myaungmya in January 2002.

10 1 pyi equals 2.1 kg.

11 Interviews with a civil servant. Rice farmers did not receive rationed rice but were allowed to deduct paddy for home consumption from their paddy procurement quota. However, anyone farming less than three acres was eligible for rationed rice. Civil servants were eligible for a special ration known as "Project rice" if they were part of any government project.

[12] Saito and Lee Kin Kiong (1998: 98). The price of rationed rice differed depending on whether a location was categorized as a rice deficit or rice surplus area. For example, the difference in the price charged for rationed rice in Mandalay and Yangon was formerly 10 per cent (MAPT, 2003: 222, 225). The difference in free market prices for rice in these two cities was in the range of 30–80 per cent (Okamoto, 2003: 174). This indicates that deficit areas were given special consideration for the supply "cheap" rice through the rationing system compared to the rice surplus area.

[13] Calculated based on *Monthly Economic Indicators* (various issues) and MAPT (2000: 260).

[14] Some ministries having a relatively good financial footing provided their own subsidies for rice.

[15] See Chapter 5 for detail discussion.

[16] This estimate is based on official statistics. As Fujita points out there can be some upward bias in yields in official figures, especially after the late 1990s (Fujita, 2003: 310). The volume percentage shown here is based on the officially estimated average yield of around 60–65 baskets per acre since 1995–96. However, according to field surveys, the average yield for monsoon paddy was around 50 baskets per acre, which is 20 per cent lower than the official figures. If the estimate is based on this 20 per cent lower figure, the marketed volume of rice for 2000–01 decreases from 46 per cent to 27 per cent. In this estimation, however, the calculation of home consumption does not differentiate between adults and children. Thus, the volume for home consumption could be less than these figures suggest, and the marketed volume for 2000–01 could have been between 27 per cent and 46 per cent.

[17] Author's survey in 2002–03. There was no pertinent information on the remaining two traders.

[18] In some instances, even though contracts prescribed a rate of 25 per cent for broken rice, millers were required to meet a rate of 15 per cent at the time of quality inspections.

[19] The year 2001–02, although showing a decline, was not an ordinary year. MAPT increased rice exports that year, and it had to contract with more private mills for these exports. To provide incentives for mills, the milling fee was raised to 30 kyat per basket, close to the market rate. This attracted even those mills that had never contracted with MAPT before. Thus the figure for contracted mills in 2001–02 was higher than it otherwise would have been. MAPT also resorted to coercive methods. In some areas it notified mill owners that their milling licenses would be revoked if they refused to contract with MAPT.

[20] The share for rice classified as *Emata* and *Ngasein*, which are two groups of low- and medium-grade rice, accounted for a high share (70–80 per cent on average) of total production even in the 1990s; thus their share of marketed volume was also large. Nevertheless, it may worthwhile noting that demand for higher quality rice (such as Pawsan Hmwe belonging to *Midon* group) is increasing, especially

in urban areas like Yangon. Along with these changes in consumer preference, some big wholesalers started to sell their rice in bags printed with their logos. This made consumers more conscious of the "brand" of the rice they eat, especially from the late 1990s.

[21] According to the author's survey in 2001, the retail rice price in these remote regions was 10–20 per cent higher than in the average rice deficit area in Upper Myanmar.

[22] This is the persistent perception shared among the authorities (Tin Maung Maung Than, 2007: 353). The following quotes from a speech by a high ranking official clearly show the stance of the present government on the marketing of rice. "… The price of rice should not be raised because of the scarcity of rice or exporting. The central authorities sent directives to the concerned local authorities to ensure that rice is transported freely, that the transport and flow of rice are not controlled, and that rice mills and hullers are not closed down …. There was instability in the price of rice in February [2002]. That was because of paddy being stored by some private rice mills in the townships, the manipulation of market [rice] price and rumors about government purchases of rice for export, and the storage of rice by those who are not rice merchants. There are some conditions in which the purchase and sale of rice cannot be regarded as merely a business undertaking. An unstable or soaring rice price is sometimes linked to unscrupulous instigations. Stability in the price of rice is linked to the need of the people for food, clothing and shelter, and to the stability of the State. Therefore, it can be assumed that there will always be the danger of destructionist existing in the paddy and rice trade (sic). Moreover, whenever there has been an unusual occurrence and instability, some merchants in Myanmar, who have no scruples about the interests of the nation and the people, have taken advantage of the situation and have served their own self-interests by exorbitantly hiking the prices of rice, edible oil, gold, silver and other commodities. The manipulation of commodity prices is harmful and a burden on the grass-roots-level workers who live hand to mouth, on the poor and government personnel; and it must be prevented." *New Light of Myanmar*, 24 March 2002.

[23] Interviews with rice wholesalers in Yangon in 2002.

[24] If we calculate the cost using the market rice price for *Emata* in January 2004, this amount of compensation would be equivalent to 16 pyi (33.6 kg), more than the 12 pyi civil servants received under the rationing system. However, January is normally the time of the year when the rice price is lowest, so this amount of compensation would not necessarily assure them of the same amount of rice throughout the year. Moreover, some ministries also halted the rationing of other items, such as eggs and edible oil. Therefore, it has been argued that this monetary compensation in place of the ration system was actually a reduction in the real salaries of public servants.

[25] Along with rice, the export of chillies, onions, maize and sesame was also banned. This also reflected the high priority that the government put on self-sufficiency in important crops.

[26]   See Chapter 7 of the present volume, Takahashi (2000) and Okamoto (2008) for discussions of agricultural labourers in Myanmar.

[27]   It is reported that some companies obtained export license in 2005. However, the number of companies and the quantities exported were small. It should be regarded that they were allowed to export in line with the decrease of rice exports through MAPT. At the end of 2007, the government signaled that it would allow about 400,000 tons of rice to be exported by 22 private companies in 2008. However, after cyclone Nargis hit the country in May 2008, the government suspended licenses owing to fears that domestic rice prices would rise (*Myanmar Times*, 4–11 February 2008 and 5–11 May 2008).

CHAPTER 7

Agricultural Labourers in Myanmar during the Economic Transition: Views from the Study of Selected Villages

Koichi Fujita

Introduction

One of the most prominent features of Myanmar's agrarian structure is the presence of a large number of agricultural labourers who are excluded from the farm management. In the agricultural research field of Myanmar in Japan, the problems of the agricultural labourers has been paid due attention (see, for example, Saito, 1980; Saito, 1982; Takahashi, 1992; Takahashi, 2000; and Okamoto, 2004).

Even the number of agricultural labourers in Myanmar is unknown, however, and there is no data on the agricultural wage rate, not to mention the other statistical data related to the socio-economic conditions of agricultural labourers. Thus, the research on agricultural labourers conducted so far could not go beyond case studies based on individual field surveys undertaken in a limited number of villages. Systematic research on the structure of the rural labour market surrounding the agricultural labourers and the direction of its changes has been neglected and we cannot draw even a rough picture of such important issues.

This chapter is also hindered by these limitations, given that the above-mentioned scarcity of labour-related official statistics remains unchanged today. By adding some original data based on recent field surveys after 2001, however, this chapter aims to consolidate the existing research, and construct a common framework of understanding about the socio-economic conditions of agricultural labourers in Myanmar as well as the direction of its changes. In particular, it seeks to clarify the changes under the economic transition to a market economy after 1988.

The major objectives of this chapter are three-fold. First, it tries, as far as possible, to estimate the number of agricultural labour households in

Myanmar whose livelihood depends mainly on agricultural wage incomes. Second, it attempts to clarify how the conditions of their employment, particularly the wage rate and the mode of wage payment, have changed. It not only deals with the changes during the economic transition after 1988, but also traces them back to the mid-1970s or even earlier, depending on the data availability. In the course of the analysis, the long-term changes in the other key price indicators, such as the prices of rice, agricultural land, draft cattle, and chemical fertilizers, will also be examined. Third, it seeks to illustrate various aspects of the "poverty" of the agricultural labourers. Specifically, we discuss income disparity with regard to farm households, debt situations, non-land asset holdings, and the education of the members of agricultural labour households. Part I deals with the first topic, while the second and the third topics are discussed in Parts II and III, respectively. Finally, concluding remarks are presented in the final section.

An Estimate of the Number of Agricultural Labourers

The existence of a large number of agricultural labourers in rural Myanmar is evident. The evidence indicates that, during the British colonial period, agricultural labour households already existed in approximately the same proportion as today (approximately 40 per cent of the total number of rural households). Shortly after gaining independence, in 1948, the Myanmar government nationalized agricultural land by passing a Land Nationalization Act and, in the latter half of the 1950s, a land reform was implemented. Myanmar's agrarian structure, however, with its many agricultural labourers, experienced almost no change, due to the insufficient implementation of the land reform programme, which covered only 17 per cent of the targeted area and only 6 per cent of the total area.[1] Moreover, priority was given to tenant farmers and small farmers rather than landless agricultural labourers as the beneficiaries of the land redistribution programme, because the government believed that agricultural productivity might decline through the creation of inefficient farms smaller than "*da don htun*".[2] It may be unnecessary to repeat here that, after 1962, when Myanmar became a socialist country, the collectivization of agriculture was not introduced, as happened in China and Vietnam, but the peasant farming system was maintained. No further land redistribution programme has yet been implemented. In this way, there has been a clear demarcation in Myanmar between farmers with the tillage right of land (under the nationalized land tenure system) and non-farmers without it. In a situation where land tenancy and mortgages are prohibited, the latter have lived mainly as landless agricultural labourers.

Non-farm households as a proportion of total rural households in Myanmar were, according to Saito's (Saito, 1982: 238) estimates based on the population census data, were 41.7 per cent in 1931, 46.5 per cent in 1953/54, and 42.0–44.5 per cent in 1973. Village studies conducted after 1988 indicate, almost without exception, that the proportion of non-farm households was approximately the same as in the above estimates.[3] The problem is that, for more recent years, we cannot obtain even a rough estimate, because no population census has been carried out since 1983.

At the lowest local administrative unit, such as the village tract and township, however, data exists regarding the total number of households and farm households, from which we can calculate the number of non-farm households as residuals. The problem we encountered was that there were no aggregated data about this at the national level. Scattered data needed to be assembled and aggregated, which proved extremely costly.

Table 1 shows some of the results of a government pilot project to gather and aggregate these local level statistics. Eight districts (Kyaukse, Magwe, Taungdwingyi, Taunggyi, Myaungmya, Bago, Thaton, and Myeik) were selected as the pilot area, which consisted of 41 townships in total. As the table shows, the share of non-farm households for 38 of the townships (three were excluded because of the non-availability of data) ranged from 12.7 per cent (minimum) to 85.6 per cent (maximum), with a weighted average of 41.3 per cent. The more detailed distribution was as follows; 10.0–19.9 per cent in five townships; 20.0–29.9 per cent in six townships, 30.0–39.9 per cent in eight townships, 40.0–49.9 per cent in nine townships, 50.0–59.9 per cent in two townships, 60.0–69.9 per cent in four townships, 70.0–79.9 per cent in two townships, and 80.0–89.9 per cent in two townships.

Table 1   Estimates of the Number of Non-Farm Households

Township	Total Households	Farm Households	Non-Farm Households	Share of Non-Farm Households (%)
Myeik	33,259	n.a.		
Kyunsu	18,055	2,598	15,457	85.6
Palaw	22,797	7,004	15,793	69.3
Tanintharyi	13,440	n.a.		
Bago	59,645	32,243	27,402	45.9
Thanatpin	30,721	18,013	12,708	41.4
Kawa	30,947	20,957	9,990	32.3
Waw	40,580	16,593	23,987	59.1

Table 1 continued

	Total Households	Farm Households	Non-Farm Households	Share of Non-Farm Households (%)
Nyaunglebin	30,718	20,467	10,251	33.4
Kyauktaga	33,778	22,434	11,344	33.6
Daik-U	38,587	22,833	15,754	40.8
Shwegyin	14,244	10,714	3,530	24.8
Magwe	49,433	29,189	20,244	41.0
Yenanachaung	31,452	17,456	13,996	44.5
Chauk	36,381	28,516	7,865	21.6
Taundwingyi	39,898	31,918	7,980	20.0
Myothit	24,318	18,575	5,743	23.6
Natmauk	36,800	21,333	15,467	42.0
Kyaukse	31,863	16,721	15,142	47.5
Sintkaing	22,473	11,034	11,439	50.9
Myitthar	29,453	18,165	11,288	38.3
Tada-U	24,355	15,697	8,658	35.5
Thaton	36,384	10,264	26,120	71.8
Paung	42,248	11,325	30,923	73.2
Kyaikhto	24,248	9,446	14,802	61.0
Bilin	25,671	22,419	3,252	12.7
Taunggyi	52,968	16,614	36,354	68.6
Hopong	14,016	10,059	3,957	28.2
Nyaungshwe	22,585	16,760	5,825	25.8
Hsihseng	13,609	n.a.		
Kalaw	22,498	11,801	10,697	47.5
Pindaya	11,242	9,286	1,956	17.4
Ywangan	15,109	5,027	10,082	66.7
Lawksawk	11,832	1,848	9,984	84.4
Pinlaung	39,249	25,916	13,333	34.0
Hpekon	10,445	8,972	1,473	14.1
Myaungmya	59,118	36,052	23,066	39.0
Einme	32,093	27,416	4,677	14.6
Laputta	43,858	25,156	18,702	42.6
Wakhema	47,066	40,544	6,522	13.9
Mawlamyainggun	45,455	31,471	13,984	30.8
Total	1,142,938	670,593	472,345	41.3

Source: Internal data from the GIS Project of the Department of Agricultural Planning, Ministry of Agriculture and Irrigation, Myanmar .

The results of the pilot study, in sum, support Okamoto's (Okamoto, 2008) statement that non-farm households in Myanmar with no tillage right of land constitute 30–50 per cent of the total rural households on average, if we confine our view to the plains (excluding the mountainous and coastal areas). It should be noted, however, that the non-farm households here defined include households other than agricultural labour households, such as tenant farm households[4] and households with non-agricultural jobs. If our target is the "pure" agricultural labour households, the above estimate of the number of non-farm households is clearly too high. Furthermore, given the multi-occupational structure of the members of the rural household, especially the non-farm household members (both among different members of the household and the same member of the household in different seasons), the definition of agricultural labour households itself is unclear. Here, therefore, we define agricultural labour households as those in which more than 50 per cent of the total household income depends on agricultural wages.

Table 2 presents the results of the estimates of the agricultural labour households defined as such for eight village tracts (hereinafter simply referred to as villages) that were surveyed by our study team in 2001.[5] Five villages were selected from the plains, two from the mountainous area (Shan State) and the last from the coastal area (Taninthayi Division).

According to the table, the share of the non-farm households (column [C]) ranged from 34.5–55.0 per cent, with the exception of Kalaw (15.1 per cent), which is consistent with Okamoto's summary statement (30–50 per cent). Moreover, the share of the agricultural labour households (as defined above) of total non-farm households (column [F]) was 59.4 per cent on average for eight villages, and 62.7 per cent for the five villages on the plains. As a result, the share of the agricultural labour households of total households (column [G]=[C]×[F]) ranged from 22.4 per cent (minimum) to 40.0 per cent (maximum), with exceptions of 5.0 per cent (Kalaw) and 15.6 per cent (Myeik).

In sum, we can now roughly conclude that non-farm households and agricultural labour households constitute 30–50 per cent and 20–40 per cent respectively in rural Myanmar, although these are still estimates, based on fragmented and limited data. Now, estimates in 2002/3 indicate that Myanmar's total population was 52.17 million, at least 70 per cent of which (36.52 million) can be considered a rural population. If we assume that the share of non-farm households and agricultural labour households was 40 and 25 per cent, respectively, the size of each category of household would be 14.61 million and 9.13 million. In other words, it can be said that nearly ten million people live on agricultural labour incomes in Myanmar.

Table 2 An Estimate of the Number of Agricultural Labour Households

Location of Study Village	Total Households [A]	Farm Households	Non-Farm Households [B]	[C] = [B]/[A]	Sample Non-Farm Households [D]	Tenants	Agricultural Labourers [E]	With Non-Agricultural Jobs	[F] = [E]/[D]	Ratio of Agricultural Labour Households [G] = [C] × [F]
Ayeyarwaddy Division, Myaungmya Township	515	232	283	55.0	33	1	17	15	51.5	28.3
Bago Division, Waw Township	456	213	243	53.3	40	0	30	10	75.0	40.0
Mandalay Division, Kyaukse Township	219	118	101	46.1	37	6	18	13	48.6	22.4
Magwe Division, Magwe Township	662	326	336	50.8	16	0	12	4	75.0	38.1
Magway Division, Taundwindgyi Township	510	334	176	34.5	16	2	12	2	75.0	25.9
Shan State, Nyaungshwe Township	842	544	298	35.4	12	0	9	3	75.0	26.5
Shan State, Kalaw Township	497	622	75	15.1	6	0	2	4	33.3	5.0
Tanintaryi Division, Myeik Township	1,167	647	520	44.6	20	5	7	8	35.0	15.6

Source: Based on surveys conducted in 2001 by the author.

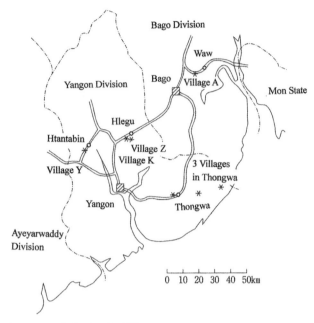

Figure 1   Location of the Study Villages

Source: Prepared by the author.

This estimate is based on a relatively narrow definition of agricultural labour households and we should not forget that agricultural hired labour income is important for more rural people in Myanmar than these results indicate.

Changes in the Employment Conditions of Agricultural Labourers

Let us next investigate the employment conditions of agricultural labourers in Myanmar. The most critical point is the real wage rate, which largely determines the level of economic welfare of the labour households. As already mentioned, however, there are no statistics regarding wages available for Myanmar. Therefore, this chapter seeks to approach the issue by synthesizing data from the existing literature based on intensive fieldwork that has been conducted from the mid-1970s until recently. Case studies on four villages close to Yangon are selected here. We assumed that, by confining ourselves to such relatively narrow geographical areas, the wage rate and other employment indicators of agricultural labourers may be comparable.

As shown in Figure 1, "Village K" (Saito, 1979; Saito, 1980) and "Village Z" (Takahashi, 1992; Takahashi, 2000) are both located in Hlegu Township (Yangon Division), while "Village Y" (Fujita and Okamoto, 2000) and "Village A" (surveyed by the author in 2001 and 2003) are located in Htantabin Township (Yangon Division) and Waw Township (Bago Division) respectively. In addition, the results of the case studies in three villages in Thongwa Township (Yangon Division) reported by Okamoto (2004) are occasionally used as supplementary data.

Changes in Economic Indicators other than Agricultural Wages

Table 3 presents a summary of the changes in the various economic indicators from the mid-1970s until recently. In this section, let us first briefly examine the movement of the economic indicators other than agricultural wages (and related employment indicators), because these are closely interrelated.

First, one of the commonly observed facts among the four villages is that farm households with the tillage right of land accounted for approximately 50 per cent and the average farm size was 10–14 acres per household, which is more or less equivalent to the "*da don htun*" for the area.[6] It is also found that the share of agricultural labour households was low (about 30 per cent) in Villages K and Z, both of which are adjacent to Hlegu town and thus blessed with abundant non-agricultural jobs, whereas it was relatively high (40 per cent) in Village A.

Second, for many years the four villages have been economically dependent on monsoon paddy cultivation. The average yield of monsoon paddy per acre was about 40 baskets in Village Z (in the late 1990s) and 40–47 baskets in Villages Y and A (around 2000), and these amounts are far lower than the national average of nearly 60 baskets.[7] A notable change after 1988 was the progress of double cropping in each village. The additional crops introduced in the dry (summer) season were summer paddy (Village Y), summer paddy and pulses (Village A) and groundnuts (Village Z).

Third, let us consider the movement in the rice (paddy) price. The government procurement price for paddy, fixed at 9.55 kyat per basket during the socialist period since the late 1970s, was rapidly raised after 1988, reaching about ten times the original price by the latter half of the 1990s, and further tripling by the late 1990s or early twenty-first century. On the other hand, the market price was 1.5–2 times greater than the procurement price for paddy in the latter half of the 1970s, and rose to about 3 times greater by the latter half of the 1980s, but fell again thereafter and has fluctuated in the range of 1.5–2 times in recent years. From the table, we can also confirm that, after 1988, the rice price in Myanmar increased faster than the general inflation, as discussed in Chapter 5.

Fourth, a surge in the price of chemical fertilizers is also evident. The use of chemical fertilizers began in Myanmar in the latter half of the 1970s with a heavy government subsidy supported mainly by Japanese ODA, but,

Table 3 Changes of Yangon's Sub-Urban Villages during the Last 30 Years

	1970	Late 1970s	Late 1980s	1994	1999	2001	2003
		Kyungale (K)	Zepinwe (Z)		Yorktua (Y)	Acarick (A)	
Number of households		550	138	170	130	456	
Composition of households		F42%, AL28%, NFL30%	F49%, AL32%, NFL19%	F44%, AL31%, NFL25%	F50%, Others50%		F47%, AL40%, NFL13%
Major cropping pattern of paddy fields		MP	MP	MP (–Groundnut)	MP-SP		MP-Pulses/SP
Average yield of monsoon paddy (bsk/ac)		30–35	26–36	37–41	47		40 (VT average: 65)
Average size of paddy field per farm household		13.5	12.4		10.2		12.0
Da don htun (ac)		15	10–14				
Ratio of procured paddy (%)		33	50–60	30	26		Abolished
Timing of payment for procurement		Advance two times yearly			Advance when transplanting	Advance when transplanting	
Official paddy price (K/bsk)	4.15	9.55	9.55	10 times of late 1980s	320	320	NA
Market paddy price (K/bsk)		1.5–2 times official rate	30		630	420	1,200–2,200
Land rent		5–10bsk/ac					
Land price of paddy field (K/ac)		100–500	300–400	3,000–4,000	30,000–50,000	30,000	40,000–150,000
Price of adult bullock (kyat/head)		1,500–2,500	2,500–3,000	15,000	30,000–60,000	40,000–50,000	
Rental fee of bullocks (/pair)			30–50bsk		3,000K/ac (600K/D)	700K/D	1,000K/D
Wage rate							
Ploughing & Harrowing (with bullocks born by farmers)	2K/D	1bsk/6h	10K/5h	100K/5h	200K/D+1ml		500K/D+3ml
Transplantation		5K+ml or 6K/8–10h	6K/7h	50K/D	150K/D	200K/D	300K/D
Uprooting of seedlings		10K/6h (4K/100bdle)	3K/100bdle	70K/2M		480K/D	150K/100bdle
Harvesting		4bsk/ac (4md)	4bsk/ac	1,800K/2M	2,000K/ac(5–6md)	2,000K/ac	4,000–5,000K/ac
Threshing		1bsk/6h	n.a.	n.a.			
Permanent labourers		125bsk+2ml		n.a.	15,000–20,000K/Se+3ml	18,000–20,000K/Se+3ml	15,000K/M+3ml
Seasonal labourers (Monsoon)		100bsk/9M+2ml	40–50bsk/4M+3ml	50bsk/4M+3ml	15,000–20,000K/Se+2ml	18,000–20,000K/Se+3ml	15,000K/M+3ml
Seasonal labourers (Summer)		5–10bsk/M+2ml	40–50bsk/4M+3ml	50bsk/3M+3ml	15,000K/Se+2ml		
Seasonal labourers (Intermediate)			20–30bsk/3M+3ml	n.a.			

Table 3 continued

	1970	Late 1970s	Late 1980s	1994	1999	2001	2003
		Kyungale (K)	Zepinue (Z)		Yoekua (Y)	Acarick (A)	
Price of fertilizers (Kyat/bag)							
N (official)		9.5	18				
N (market)		30<	65		2,300	4,800	
P (official)		62.2	60				
P (market)		NA	130		3,450	4,200	
K (official)		29.9	35				
K (market)		NA	65		1,650	3,200	
Average income (K)							
Agricultural labourers (Daily)			2,357	29,906		115,922	
Agricultural labourers (Seasonal)		2,606	3,230	31,686	82,000–85,000	154,399	
Non-agriculturalists		n.a.	n.a.	n.a.	n.a.	125,477	
Small-scale farmers (<7.9 ac)		5,023	3,897	36,000–58,000	90,000–250,000	103,190	
Medium-scale farmers (8.0–15.9 ac)		7,966	3,614	67,000–75,000	400,000–600,000	167,213	
Large-scale farmers (≥16.0 ac·)		8,701	7,560	81,000–200,000	500,000–800,000	211,458	
Index of rice price (1970s–80s=1)	1	1	1	10	30	Slightly declined	90

Note: K: kyat. D: day. M: month. Se: season. Ml: meal. Bsk: basket. H: hour. Bdle: bandle. Ac: acre. F: farm households. AL: agricultural labour households. NAL: non-agricultural households. NA: not available. MP: monsoon paddy. SP: summer paddy. Md: Man days. N: nitrogen. P: phosphorus. K: potassium.

Sources: Prepared by the author based on Saito (1979)·(1980), Takahashi (1992)·(2000), Fujita and Okamoto (2000), etc.

after 1988, such subsidies were lifted gradually and have almost vanished in recent years. As a result, by the late 1990s, the price of urea, for instance, had increased to approximately 35 times the original price in ten years, which was faster than the rise in the rice price (20–30 times). Moreover, even when the rice price collapsed in 2001, chemical fertilizers continued to surge and further doubled within a short period.[8] The deterioration in the terms of trade for rice production, at least in terms of the rice/fertilizer price ratio, continued until recently.

Fifth, the price of land (paddy fields) experienced the fastest rise, and, by the late 1990s, had increased by over 100 times during the last 10 years or so, which was far higher than the rise in the rice price (20–30 times) or chemical fertilizers (35 times). It should be noted here that, if the progress of double cropping after 1988, mentioned above, is reflected in the price of land, it is natural for land to rise in price more than rice. The pace of the rise in land prices, however, was more than theoretically expected, which may indicate that agricultural land was beginning to have some asset value other than being for purely agricultural purposes. At any rate, it may be concluded that the situation made it more difficult for agricultural labourers to become farmers through purchasing land.

Sixth, in sharp contrast with the surge in land prices, the price of draft cattle showed a relative decline in the long term. As a result, the relative price of draft cattle *vis-à-vis* land declined substantially over time; i.e., the price of one draft animal, which was equivalent to the price of 6–10 acres of paddy field in the latter half of the 1970s, declined sharply to only that of one acre by the late 1990s. The cost of holding draught cattle diminished greatly, although the price of a pair of draught cattle, indispensable for cultivation,[9] remains equivalent to the price of two acres of land in Myanmar. For comparison, note that in Bangladesh, for example, one draught animal is worth only a fifteenth of an acre of land.[10] It is not easy for agricultural labourers in Myanmar to become farmers in this sense also.

Summing up this section, the economic environment surrounding Myanmar's agriculture, especially its paddy cultivation, has undergone a drastic change during the last two decades or so. The introduction of secondary crops in the paddy field, including the progress of the double cropping of rice, accelerated. Land prices, however, surged more than the value derived from the increased agricultural land rents. The rice price also increased more rapidly than general inflation, but lagged behind the rise in the price of chemical fertilizers, thus causing a deterioration in the terms of trade for rice production. The real price of draft cattle declined, especially compared to the price of land. However, along with the high price of land, cattle are still too expensive for agricultural labourers to buy them and become cultivators. The possibility for the agricultural labourers to become farmers is smaller than before. Furthermore, the surge in the rice price above the general inflation rate hit the poor most, including agricultural labour households, who are the net buyers of rice and whose food expenses constitute the largest share of household expenditure.

Changes in Agricultural Wages and Related Employment Indicators

Let us now investigate the movement of various indicators related to the employment conditions of agricultural labourers, especially real agricultural wages. Owing to data constraints, what we examine here as the real wage is the "rice wage", which is defined as the amount of rice that can be purchased with an individual's (daily) wages. As mentioned earlier, after 1988, the rice price in Myanmar rose faster than the general inflation rate. Therefore, even if the rice wage declined sharply, the degree of decline in the "genuine" real wage may be less. Revisions in line with this consideration will be discussed later in this chapter.

Changes in the mode of employment and the mode of wage payment

Before discussing the wage level, let us first explore briefly the changes in the mode of employment and wage payment (Table 3).

First, it is noted that the hire period for seasonal labourers has been shortened gradually. In earlier years, as the case of Village K in the latter half of the 1970s shows, seasonal labourers used to be hired for 9 months continuously,[11] but, gradually, a demarcation between monsoon season labourers (four months) and summer season labourers (four months) emerged, the hire period for summer season labourers was then shortened to three months and, finally, labourers were increasingly being paid on a monthly basis, such as in Village A in 2003. It seems that factors relating to both parties to the contract caused the hire period to be shortened; the farmers (employers) wanted to save the cost of providing meals for the labourers and the labourers wanted to seek additional employment when they were not hired.

Second, in-kind payments, which had long been prevalent for harvesting wages and wages for seasonal labourers, were rapidly replaced by cash payments after 1988. According to Table 3, in-kind payments to seasonal labourers were made during the socialist period without exception and continued up until in 1994 (in Village Z), but thereafter vanished. The gradual change in harvesting wages from in-kind to cash payments can also be observed in the table.

It may be hypothesized that such a monetization of in-kind wages[12] was an institutional adjustment to the sharp increase in the rice price after 1988. In Village Y, for instance, interviews conducted by the author (in August 2000) with several farmers and agricultural labourers revealed the process of the change from in-kind to cash payments as follows: the harvesting wages in the village used to be paid by a share (three out of every 23 bundles of paddy was paid to the labourers) for many years, and the share received by the labourers was equivalent to about six baskets of paddy per acre under prevailing yields. At some point in 1992 or 1993, however, this payment-in-kind began to be replaced gradually by a cash payment of 700–800 kyat per acre. The value of six baskets of paddy and 700–800 kyat was equal at that time, according to the respondents. By the year 1995, the in-kind payment system had disappeared, after which, the rate of the cash wages, originally 700–800 kyat per acre, increased annually according to changes in the economic environment (mainly inflation), although it gradually lagged behind the rise in the rice price. It was finally observed that the rate in 1999 (2,000 kyat per acre) was equivalent to only 3.2 baskets of paddy, much lower than the six baskets of a few years previously. Thus, the "rice wage" declined sharply to nearly half within only 6–7 years. It should be added here that 1993 (when the change of payment system started) was the year when the rice price increased sharply (see Chapter 5).

It may be difficult for us to conclude, however, that such a sharp decline in the rice wage happened in accordance with the change in demand and supply conditions in the rural labour market. Instead, it may be hypothesized that the decline in real wages had already started during the socialist period, although the existence of the traditional, in-kind payment systems prevented the realization of this for many years. It took place only after the payment system changed to a cash system.

Changes in real wages

Seasonal labourers

The rice wage for seasonal labourers also declined sharply, especially during the change in the wage system from in-kind to cash payments. Note here that in-kind payments other than in the form of paddy, such as daily meals and clothes, are excluded from the discussion.

The amount of paddy paid to the seasonal/permanent labourers in the latter half of the 1970s — 100 baskets for nine months' and 125 baskets for 12 months' work, respectively, as observed in Village K — was almost the same as during the colonial period,[13] and the rate appears to have been kept at the same level until 1994, as observed in Village Z, where 50 baskets of paddy were paid to both monsoon season and summer season labourers.

Following the change in the payment system from in-kind to cash, however, if we convert the cash wages into paddy, it appears that the rice wage declined very rapidly; for example, the total payment to the monsoon and summer season labourers in Village Y (in 1999) and/or Village A (in 2001) (30–40,000 kyat) can be converted to only 48–63 baskets of paddy (in the case of a high paddy price in 1998) or 71–95 baskets (in the case of a low paddy price in 2001), which is far lower than 100 baskets in both cases. In the case of Village A in 2003, cash wages paid for seven months' labour (105,000 kyat) was equivalent to only 48–87 baskets (68, on average) of paddy and, in the case of the three villages in Thongwa, the cash wages paid for 8.6 months' labour (4.2 months during the monsoon season plus 4.4 months during the summer season) was of the same value as only 45–92 baskets (69, on average) of paddy (Okamoto, 2004).

In sum, the rice wage for seasonal labourers declined rapidly, constituting as little as 50-60 per cent (at most 70 per cent) of the amount paid in earlier years, when the in-kind payment system still prevailed.

Daily labourers

There is also evidence of a decline in the rice wage for daily labourers. First, regarding the daily wages for male labourers, the customary rate was one basket of paddy per day, as typically observed in land preparation and threshing in Village K in the latter half of the 1970s. This rate was equivalent to a payment of four baskets of paddy per acre that was observed for harvesting in the same village, because four man-days were necessary to harvest one acre of paddy field, on average. If we consider the recent daily wage rates for male labourers, however, 0.5 baskets of paddy per day (or 2.5 per acre for harvesting) can be observed in villages where the in-kind payment system remains. Moreover, in Village Y in the late 1990s, the harvesting wage rate was 2,000 kyat per acre, which could be converted into 3.2 baskets of paddy at the prevailing rice price. Given that 5–6 labourers can harvest an acre of land, it was found that the daily wage was only 0.5–0.6 baskets of paddy per day. In either case, the daily wage rate for male labourers declined to only 50–60 per cent of the previous rate.

Assuming 0.6 to be the standard milling rate (paddy to milled rice), and taking into account the necessary milling costs, a basket of paddy can be converted into approximately 9 kg of rice. The rice wage for daily male labourers in rural Myanmar declined sharply, from 9 kg in the 1970s and 1980s to a mere 4–5 kg after 2000, a reduction of 40–50 per cent.

Second, let us consider the wage rate for paddy transplantion, which is exclusively a task for female labourers and has been paid for in cash since the early years. The rate was 6 kyat per day during the socialist period, at least after the latter half of the 1970s, but had increased to 50 kyat (8 times the earlier rate) by the early 1990s, and further to 150–200 kyat (more than 3 times) by the late 1990s or early twenty-first century. Namely, the rate of increase was almost the same as that of the rice price, which means that the rice wage for female labourers remained largely unchanged,[14] although it should be noted that it remained at an extremely low level, at only slightly more than 2 kg of rice.[15]

Summary and discussion

The real wage rate in rice terms (rice wage) declined to 50–60 per cent in Myanmar for both seasonal and daily labourers during the last two or three decades. The daily wage rate for male labourers, for instance, declined substantially, from 9 kg in the latter half of the 1970s to 4–5 kg. The rice wage for female labourers (engaged in paddy transplantation) appeared to undergo no such rapid decrease, but was stagnant at a very low level (2 kg per day). On the other hand, it is highly plausible that the rice wage for seasonal labourers remained at almost the same level for a long period, but declined rapidly during the process of monetization of the in-kind payment system after 1988, falling to only 50–60 per cent of the previous rate within the last ten years or so.

It should be noted, however, that, in recent years, the rice price showed a higher rate of increase than that of general consumption goods. The decline in real wages is exaggerated, at least to some extent, if measured in rice terms.

As shown in Table 2 in Chapter 5, the relative value of the rice price index *vis-à-vis* the CPI (=100) recorded the following movements:

1987	88
1988	123
1989	177
1990	114
1991	101
1992	136
1993	175

1994	132
1995	154
1996	146
1997	118
1998	121
1999	154
2000	142
2001	103
2002	128
2003	147
2004	112
2005	127

The average for the index during this period was, therefore, 131, which means that, on average, the rice price increased about 30 per cent more than the CPI, so it can be concluded that the 40–50 per cent decline in the rice wage was equivalent to a decline in the "genuine" real wage of about 10–20 per cent.[16]

Figure 2 illustrates the long-term movement of the rice wage (for male labourers) in Myanmar. Its sharp decline in the last ten years or so cannot be considered as a movement according to the changes in demand and supply conditions in the rural labour market, however, and it can be hypothesized that the traditional in-kind payment system prevented the wage rate from declining for a long time, a fall occurring only after the change in the payment system after 1988. The dotted line in the figure attempts to trace this hidden movement.

The figure shows the long-term movement of the rice wage in Bangladesh also,[17] which ranged between 4–6 seers (1 seer = 0.93 kg) per day in the early twentieth century but, due to the stagnation of agriculture and the population growth, declined gradually and bottomed out (at 2–2.5 seers) for several years just after the gaining of independence in 1971. The success of the "Green Revolution" since the 1980s, however, has affected the rice wage, which recovered to approximately 4 kg recently. As a result, the rice wage in both countries converged to a similar level of 4–5 kg per day.

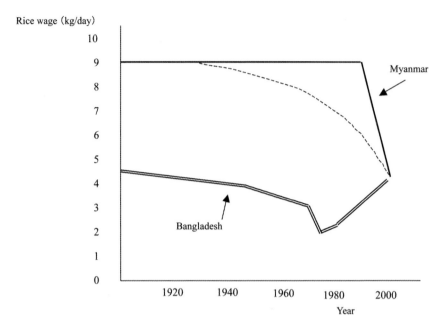

Figure 2   Long-term Changes in "Rice Wage" in Bangladesh and Myanmar

It should be noted here that the 4–5 kg daily rice wage is the minimum level among contemporary Asian countries.[18] If we recall that, during the British colonial period, many labourers came to Myanmar from India, attracted by the high wages available in the development frontier at that time, it is significant that the real wage rate (the rice wage) in both areas has finally converged in recent years.

Another notable point is that, due to the success of the "Green Revolution", the real price of rice in Bangladesh showed a steady decline since the late 1970s from 16–20 taka per kg in the late 1970s to 13 taka in the early 1990s, and 10 taka in the late 1990s (at constant prices in 1998; see Ahmed, Haggblade, and Chowdhury ed., 2000: 33), and the rate of decline during the 20 year period reached 40–50 per cent. By contrast, the real price of rice showed an increase of about 30 per cent in Myanmar during the same period, as mentioned above. The rapid reduction in the wage gap (rice wage) between the two countries was attributed to the reduction in the gap not only between money wages but also the rice price.

There remains, however, a wide difference between the rice price in these two countries. Whereas the rice price in Bangladesh is almost the same as the international price, it remains nearly half of it in Myanmar (Chapter 5). In other words, agricultural labourers in Myanmar can only purchase 4–5 kg of rice with their daily wages, exactly the same amount as their counterparts in Bangladesh, although the domestic rice price in Myanmar is suppressed at an extremely low level.

The Multi-dimensions of the "Poverty" of Agricultural Labourers

The previous section clarified how the real wage rate for agricultural labourers in Myanmar declined by 40–50 per cent in rice terms and 10–20 per cent in "genuine" real terms during the last two decades or so. It was also found that the decline occurred during the process of the monetization of the in-kind (paddy) payment system following the economic liberalization in 1988.

Let us here illustrate the economic meaning of the 4–5 kg rice wage received by the agricultural labourers. The declining share of food expenditure during a process of economic development is known as Engels Law. This experiential law can also be observed among different income strata at the same time; that is, the poorest spend the largest percentage of their total expenditure on food and beverage items. According to a household expenditure survey conducted in Bangladesh in the year 2000, for instance, the Engel's coefficient for the poorest stratum reached 67 per cent, of which rice occupied approximately 70 per cent. This means that expenditure on rice as a share of total household expenditure was nearly 50 per cent. Considering the severe economic conditions of the poorest people in Bangladesh, this indicates a situation of bare subsistence.

Now let us assume that the average per capita rice consumption is 180 kg per year in Myanmar. For a nuclear family with five members, the total rice requirement would be 900 kg per year. Under the assumption that rice expenditure constitutes a 50 per cent share of total household expenditure, in order to secure a subsistence livelihood, the combined household members must earn annual wages equivalent to 1,800 kg of rice. The number of man-days required per year in the case of a 4 kg rice wage is 450, and in the case of a 5 kg rice wage, 360 man-days. Even if an adult male member could obtain employment all year round (say, 340 man-days), it would be insufficient to meet even the minimum requirement.

We may, therefore, conclude that, in general, the agricultural labourers in Myanmar were reduced to a bare subsistence level during the last two or three decades, and are now suffering "absolute poverty". In this section, let us further show this severity faced by the agricultural labourers from a multi-dimensional viewpoint, under the headings: (1) rural income distribution; (2) debt; (3) non-land asset holdings; and (4) education.

Rural Income Distribution

There is some evidence to indicate the worsening trend in rural income distribution in recent years in favour of farm households, *vis-à-vis* agricultural labour households. According to Table 3, as typically observed during the socialist period, in Village Z, agricultural labourers used to enjoy almost the same income level as small-scale farmers (below 8 acres) and medium-scale farmers (8–16 acres). Note that, in Village K, there were no large differences observed between the agricultural income of agricultural labourers and small/medium-scale farmers, mainly because "in the socialist period, paddy production was not profitable and the realized labour income in the production of paddy was less than the agricultural wage level" (Saito, 1979: 13). The government's low rice price policy suppressed the income level of farmers substantially, although the income disparity between the two categories of rural household started to widen after 1988. Although agricultural labourers were successful in increasing their income at almost the same pace as the rise in the rice price, mainly due to the increase in employment opportunities brought about by the progress of double cropping, the farm households increased their income 1.5–3 times faster than the households of agricultural labourers.

Several factors caused this widening income disparity. First, the agricultural labourers also benefited from the double cropping-led agricultural development process, but labour demand for non-rice secondary crops was, in general, far smaller than that for monsoon rice. A typical case was pulses for export.[19] Second, the farmers benefited from the surge in the agricultural commodities prices, in contrast with the disadvantageous situation faced by the agricultural labourers (the decline in the real wage rate). Thirdly, it is plausible that the disparity also widened in terms of non-agricultural income, because some farmers re-invested their profits in non-agricultural ventures, which the poor agricultural labourers could not afford to do.[20]

Debt

The impoverishment and absolute poverty of agricultural labourers in Myanmar can best be observed in their debt situation. Rural Myanmar is well known for the widespread informal credit practices with their exorbitantly high interest rates. Lenders include goldsmiths, pawnbrokers, traders, and wealthy farmers, plus relatives, friends and neighbours. The monthly interest rate usually ranges between 4 and 6 per cent with collateral (such as gold), or ten per cent or more without collateral. The agricultural labourers, in general, lack sufficient credibility to obtain even such usurious informal credit, so their sole source of credit is, as a last resort, advance payment of wages from their employers (the farmers).

Let us briefly review the most striking cases in the three villages in Thongwa (Okamoto, 2008). According to Okamoto, the proportion of agricultural labourers who received advances of wages was 21.4, 65.6, and 58.8 per cent (per village) for daily labourers, and 43.5, 46.7, and 46.2 per cent for seasonal labourers. The range of money borrowed was 6,250–16,630 kyat (for daily labourers) and 12,546–35,900 kyat (for seasonal labourers), which corresponds to 4.5–12.0 per cent and 3.3–9.5 per cent of their annual household income, respectively.

The problem is the high interest rate involved in these transactions;[21] for example, when seasonal labourers under an in-kind payment contract received an advanced wage, they had to repay it under either the "double repayment" system or the "sale at discounted price". In the former case, if they received 20 baskets of paddy as an advance, 40 baskets would be deducted when they were paid their remaining wages. In the latter case, when they borrowed cash, the amount was converted to paddy at a disadvantageous rate; for example, a basket of paddy is valued at 400 kyat rather than the prevailing market rate (1,540 kyat). In this case, labourers can only borrow 8,000 kyat and need to repay 20 baskets of paddy. According to Okamoto's estimates, the effective rate of interest (per month) involved in such transactions was 20 per cent and 40–50 per cent for each repayment system. For example, in the case of daily labourers, they were paid 150 kyat (per day) instead of 200 kyat or, for harvesting paddy, they were paid 1,500 kyat (per acre) instead of 4,000 kyat. The effective interest rate (per month) ranged from 25–80 per cent in two villages, but just 10–12 per cent in the remaining village.

The frequent reliance of the agricultural labourers on such usurious informal credit from their employers indicates that, increasingly, they fail to receive even the very low wages which have been rapidly deteriorating in recent years.

Non-land Asset Holdings

"In terms of income earnings, there was certainly a gap between farm households and agricultural labour households, but it was not so large. Particularly, only a very small difference could be observed in the earnings of

Table 4 Disparity in Assets Ownership between Farmers and Agricultural Labourers in the Eight Study Villages

	Total Values (kyat)		
	Livestock	Production and Transportation Assets	Consumer Durables
Farm Households	157,640	195,320	25,646
Non-farm Households			
Tenant farmers	56,725	7,143	3,580
Agricultural Labourers	10,077	4,764	1,383
Others	315,000	32,744	7,152

Note: Production assets include agricultural implements such as ploughs, pumps, power tillers, threshers, etc. Transportation assets include bullock carts, cars, bicycles, boats, motorbikes, etc.

Source: The author arranged Table 6 of Kurita *et al.* (2004: 13), adapted by the author.

agricultural income. However, in terms of asset holdings there was a huge gap between the two, which indicates a large difference in the accumulation from the past. Agricultural labourers are completely lacking such an accumulation and they are pure proletariats who must rely on their naked labour." (Saito, 1980: 83)

This is a very important aspect regarding the household economy of agricultural labourers in Myanmar, as Saito noted from her intensive survey of Village K during the latter half of the 1970s. Such a huge gap in asset holdings persists even today.

As an example, let us consider the results of our own survey of eight villages, conducted in 2001. The average value of the various non-land assets is estimated in Table 4, which shows a huge disparity between farm households and agricultural labour households, at 15.6 times (livestock), 41.0 times (production and transportation assets), and 18.5 times (consumer durables), respectively. As already pointed out, in situations where the income disparity is widening and the price of agricultural land is increasing rapidly, there is no possibility of narrowing the disparity between non-land assets, and it will probably widen, in fact.

Education

Finally, let us consider the situation with regard to investment in human capital (education). Tables 5–8 summarize the educational background of the labour force from both farm and non-farm households from diversified areas in Myanmar, based on the author's survey conducted in 2001. As the tables show, the majority of farm household members were engaged in cultivation, while the majority of non-farm household members were engaged in agricultural wage labour. Several important facts related to educational attainment can be drawn from these tables.

First, a rather clear regional difference can be observed between Upper Myanmar (Kyaukse and Magwe) and Lower Myanmar (Myaungmya and Bago). For example, the ratio of the labour force with more than 5 years' education (secondary school or higher education, including secondary school drop-outs), is 26.0 per cent for Kyaukse and 30.5 for Magwe, but only 11.7 per cent in Myaungmya and 14.6 per cent in Bago.

Second, a large disparity can also be observed between farm households and agricultural labour households in each area. Again, if we calculate the ratio of the labour force with more than 5 years' education, we obtain 35.0 per cent (farmers) vs. 10.1 per cent (labourers) in Kyaukse, 39.2 per cent (farmers) vs. 14.5 per cent (agricultural labourers) in Magwe, and 20.0 per cent (farmers) vs. 5.3 per cent in Bago. The exceptional case was Myaungmya, where the farmers attained 12.9 per cent, which was little more than the 9.2 per cent attained by the agricultural labourers.

Third, it is notable that a large gap between the different generations in each area is not observed. The ratio of the labour force with more than 5 years' education (the total for the four regions) was 32.8 per cent (10–19 years), 32.7 per cent (20–29 years), 30.7 per cent (30–39 years), 14.9 per cent (40–49 years), and 14.5 per cent (50–59 years) in the case of farm households, while, for agricultural labour households, the figures were 8.5 per cent (10-19 years), 6.0 per cent (20–29 years), 15.8 per cent (30–39 years), 3.5 per cent (40–49 years), and 14.3 per cent (50–59 years). It should be noted here, however, that among the younger generation, especially those aged 10–19, many would still be studying and thus do not appear in the tables.

Additional tables were prepared in the lower part of Tables 5–8 respectively, in order to address this issue. As the tables show, with the exception of Myaungmya, few students were included in the 10–19 age group in Kyaukse, Magwe and Bago. After graduating from school and starting work, they will contribute towards raising the ratio of the labour force with more than 5 years' education in the 10–19 and 20–29 age groups. The third finding above should be revised in the light of this.[22]

In either case, however, because of the remarkable progress made in education by the surrounding Southeast Asian countries, like Thailand, during the last two or three decades, a large difference between the educational achievement of those from different generations is observable in

Table 5 Education of Rural Population in a Village in Myaungmya in 2001

Farm Households (67 households)

Age	Population			Labour force			Engaged mainly in farming	Nil	Monastery	Education for the labour force						
	Male	Female	Total	Male	Female	Total				0–3	4 (Primary school)	5–7	8 (Middle school)	9	10 (High school)	11–
0–9	39	31	70	1	0	1	0	1								
10–19	48	51	99	20	19	39	35		2	9	20	6		1	1	
20–29	19	26	45	19	17	36	34		2	8	20	5		1	1	
30–39	21	27	48	21	12	33	30		13	7	9	2		1		1
40–49	27	28	55	26	19	45	40	3	29	3	6		1	1	2	
50–59	6	8	14	6	1	7	7		5							
60–69	8	6	14	8	2	10	10	1	9		2					
70 and above	2	5	7	0	0	0	0									
	170	182	352	101	70	171	156	5	60	27	57	13	1	4	3	1

Non-farm Households (33 households)

Age	Population Male	Female	Total	Labour force Male	Female	Total	Engaged mainly in farming	Nil	Monastery	0–3	4 (Primary school)	5–7	8 (Middle school)	9	10 (High school)	11–
0–9	26	20	46	0	0	0	0									
10–19	25	15	40	8	8	16	11	2	3	8	2	1				
20–29	5	13	18	5	10	15	12	2	2	8	3					
30–39	12	15	27	12	10	22	18	2	9	6	2	2				
40–49	9	5	14	9	4	13	10	1	8	3		1			1	
50–59	6	4	10	6	3	9	6	2	5	1		1				
60–69	1	1	2	1	0	1	0					1				
70 and above	0	1	1	0	0	0	0									
	84	74	158	41	35	76	57	9	27	26	7	6	0	0	1	0

Education of students

Age	Population Male	Female	Total	Labour force Male	Female	Total	Monastery	0–3	4 (Primary school)	5–7	8 (Middle school)	9	10 (High school)	11–
Farm														
10–19	48	51	99	25	21	46	1	21	8	13	1		1	
20–29	19	26	45	0	1	1								1
Non-farm														
10–19	25	15	40	14	4	18		12	4	1		1		
20–29	5	13	18	0	0	0								

Source: Prepared by the author, based on his survey in 2001.

Table 6 Education of Rural Population in a Village in Bago in 2001

Farm Households (60 households)

Age	Population			Labour force			Engaged mainly in farming	Education for the labour force								
	Male	Female	Total	Male	Female	Total		Nil	Monastery	0–3	4 (Primary school)	5–7	8 (Middle school)	9	10 (High school)	11–
0–9	28	34	62	0	0	0	0									
10–19	40	58	98	17	19	36	34	2	2	12	13	6	1			
20–29	32	24	56	28	16	44	39		4	16	14	5	3		2	
30–39	22	21	43	21	13	34	32		4	8	10	7	1	1	3	
40–49	19	18	37	19	6	25	25		4	7	13	1				
50–59	14	11	25	13	6	19	18		6	6	6	1				
60–69	8	7	15	3	3	6	5		3		1	2				
70 and above	5	4	9	1	0	1	1		1							
Total	168	177	345	102	63	165	154	2	24	49	57	22	5	1	5	0

Non-farm Households (40 households)

Age	Population			Labour force				Education for the labour force								
	Male	Female	Total	Male	Female	Total	Engaged mainly in farming	Nil	Monastery	0–3	4 (Primary school)	5–7	8 (Middle school)	9	10 (High school)	11–
0–9	36	25	61	0	0	0	0	4	7	6	5					
10–19	34	26	60	13	9	22	20	1	7	8	9					
20–29	19	17	36	17	10	27	21		7	8	9	2				
30–39	14	16	30	14	10	24	20	4	5	4	6		1			
40–49	11	7	18	11	5	16	6		4	4	8					
50–59	7	4	11	4	2	6	3	2	2			1		1		
60–69	1	0	1	0	0	0	0									
70 and above	0	0	0	0	0	0	0									
Total	122	95	217	59	36	95	70	11	25	26	28	3	1	1	0	0

Education of students

Age	Population			Labour force			Education of students							
	Male	Female	Total	Male	Female	Total	Monastery	0–3	4 (Primary school)	5–7	8 (Middle school)	9	10 (High school)	11–
Farm														
10–19	40	58	98	23	31	54	1	8	11	18	7	2	7	1
20–29	32	24	56	0	1	1							1	1
Non-farm														
10–19	34	26	60	15	8	23	3	7	3	7	3		3	
20–29	19	17	36	0	3	3	3	1	2				3	

Source: Prepared by the author, based on his survey in 2001.

Table 7 Education of Rural Population in a Village in Kyaukse in 2001

Farm Households (65 households)

Age	Population			Labour force			Engaged mainly in farming	Education for the labour force								
	Male	Female	Total	Male	Female	Total		Nil	Monastery	0–3	4 (Primary school)	5–7	8 (Middle school)	9	10 (High school)	11–
0–9	28	34	62	0	0	0	0									
0–9	26	28	54	0	0	0	0									
10–19	35	34	69	6	8	14	14			3	5	3		3		
20–29	27	24	51	25	16	41	36			2	22	10	3	3		
30–39	26	30	56	25	16	41	38		5	3	18	12	1	2	1	
40–49	15	17	32	14	9	23	21		2	4	10	3		2	2	
50–59	13	12	25	11	6	17	14		2		11	1		2		1
60–69	6	7	13	3	1	4	4		3		1					
70 and above	1	6	7	0	0	0	0									
	149	158	307	84	56	140	127	0	12	12	67	29	4	12	3	1

Non-farm Households (37 households)

Age	Population			Labour force				Education for the labour force								
	Male	Female	Total	Male	Female	Total	Engaged mainly in farming	Nil	Monastery	0–3	4 (Primary school)	5–7	8 (Middle school)	9	10 (High school)	11–
0–9	22	24	46	0	0	0	0									
10–19	17	24	41	3	11	14	14	1	2	6	4	1				
20–29	8	14	22	7	12	19	15		2	4	11	2				
30–39	17	17	34	17	11	28	17		3	4	16		1	2	1	1
40–49	10	12	22	10	6	16	9		3	5	8					
50–59	2	2	4	2	0	2	1		1		1					
60–69	0	2	2	0	0	0	0									
70 and above	0	0	0	0	0	0	0									
	76	95	171	39	40	79	56	1	11	19	40	3	1	2	1	1

Education of students

Age	Population			Labour force			Education of students							
	Male	Female	Total	Male	Female	Total	Monastery	0–3	4 (Primary school)	5–7	8 (Middle school)	9	10 (High school)	11–
Farm														
10–19	35	34	69	24	25	49		6	7	19	7	2	8	
20–29	27	24	51	1	2	3							1	2
Non–farm														
10–19	17	24	41	10	9	19		7	1	7	1	1	2	
20–29	8	14	22	0	0	0								

Source: Prepared by the author, based on his survey in 2001.

Table 8 Education of Rural Population in Two Villages in Magwe in 2001

Farm Households (48 households)

Age	Population			Labour force			Engaged mainly in farming	Education for the labour force								
	Male	Female	Total	Male	Female	Total		Nil	Monastery	0–3	4 (Primary school)	5–7	8 (Middle school)	9	10 (High school)	11–
0–9	28	34	62	0	0	0	0									
0–9	15	17	32	0	0	0	0									
10–19	41	29	70	16	11	27	26		1	1	8	11	3	1	2	
20–29	22	28	50	22	19	41	34		1		20	9	1	3	5	2
30–39	15	21	36	15	17	32	31		5	3	12	7		1	3	1
40–49	13	23	36	13	15	28	27	2	2	2	16	3	2		1	
50–59	14	12	26	12	7	19	19		2	4	9	2		2		
60–69	2	6	8	1	1	2	2		1		1					
70 and above	8	9	17	3	1	4	4	1	2			1				
Total	130	145	275	82	71	153	143	3	14	10	66	33	6	7	11	3

Non-farm Households (32 households)

Age	Population			Labour force			Engaged mainly in farming	Education for the labour force								
	Male	Female	Total	Male	Female	Total		Nil	Monastery	0–3	4 (Primary school)	5–7	8 (Middle school)	9	10 (High school)	11–
0–9	17	20	37	1	0	1	1		1	1						
10–19	18	24	42	6	13	19	16		1	1	13	3	1			
20–29	8	16	24	8	14	22	17	2	8	5	6		1			
30–39	13	11	24	12	9	21	18	1	3	4	8	2	1	2	1	
40–49	7	7	14	7	5	12	11		2	2	6	1				
50–59	3	3	6	2	2	4	1		1	1	2					
60–69	6	5	11	3	1	4	3		1	1	2					
70 and above	1	4	5	0	0	0	0									
Total	73	90	163	39	44	83	67	3	16	15	37	6	3	2	1	0

Education of students

Age	Population			Labour force			Education of students							
	Male	Female	Total	Male	Female	Total	Monastery	0–3	4 (Primary school)	5–7	8 (Middle school)	9	10 (High school)	11–
Farm														
10–19	41	29	70	22	16	38	7		3	16	6		6	
20–29	22	28	50	0	3	3			3	5		1	2	
30–39	15	21	36	0	1	1								1
Non–farm														
10–19	18	24	42	8	4	12	4		3	5				
20–29	8	16	24	0	0	0								

Source: Prepared by the author, based on his survey in 2001.

general, while our data from Myanmar indicate a stagnant situation regarding education.

A sharp decrease in the government's budget for education can be observed in Myanmar after 1988. Government expenditure on education accounted for approximately 2.5 per cent of GDP until 1990, but decreased thereafter, falling to only 1.0 per cent by 1995 (Khin Maung Kyi *et al.*, 2000: 148). The government's neglect of education in terms of budget expenditure is evident, which lead to the serious situation mentioned above. The very low educational attainment of children from agricultural labour households remains a major problem; the majority of them do not even attend primary school, with a very small proportion going on to attend secondary school. In such a situation, even if Myanmar attains favourable economic growth and employment opportunities in its expanding urban sectors, it may prove very difficult for children from agricultural labour households to obtain jobs there.[23]

Concluding Remarks

In Chapter 5, we concluded that Myanmar's agricultural policies are characterized by a strong bias towards increased production and, therefore, the orientation towards the increased income or economic welfare of the farmers remains relatively weak. A similar logic can be applied to agricultural labourers. Even the existence of such labourers is almost totally neglected by policy makers, as well as by the various agricultural officials working in rural areas. For instance, when we visited the local offices under the Ministry of Agriculture and Irrigation, it proved easy to obtain data on acreage, production, and the per acre yield of various crops, but difficult to determine the number of farm households and impossible to obtain data related to the socio-economic conditions of the agricultural labourers. Even the number of non-farm households (including agricultural labourers) is nothing but a residual figure.

Many agricultural labour households do make a living in rural Myanmar, however, and this is a significant fact. Moreover, they are usually the poorest group in rural areas. Under the current situation, whereby poverty alleviation is one of the most important policies on the agenda for development assistance, if Myanmar were to receive such assistance from abroad, certainly assistance for landless agricultural labourers would be the primary target.

For a long time, the agricultural labourers in Myanmar enjoyed a relatively high living standard, especially compared to their counterparts in

India and Bangladesh, mainly because of plentiful natural resources (including land) and their high productivity. During the British colonial era, Lower Myanmar was an attractive frontier, and many unskilled labourers emigrated there from the Indian sub-continent. During the socialist period, agricultural labourers enjoyed almost the same income level as small- and medium-scale farmers.

It seems that the economic stagnation that lasted for many years, however, finally consumed all of these advantageous pre-conditions. As the economic reforms and liberalization started in 1988 and the rice price increased rapidly, the real wage rate (in rice terms) for agricultural labourers declined by 40–50 per cent, reaching 4–5 kg per day, almost the same level as in India and Bangladesh. By contrast, farm households enjoyed a far more rapid increase in earnings, mainly because of the progress of double cropping in agriculture ("vent-for-surplus") as well as participation in non-farm business activities. The result was a widening income disparity among the rural population. Moreover, it was also pointed out that agricultural labour households lagged behind in terms of their asset holdings (both land and non-land).

To make things worse, in general the agricultural labour households are suffering due to the poor educational attainment of their children, and we are obliged to admit that the possibility of escaping from poverty in the future is lower for them. To date, there have been no serious signs of them moving to urban areas to seek work, and helping create slums. The labour absorptive power of Myanmar's agriculture has been very high, at least so far, and it seems that people can access sufficient employment opportunities in the rural areas, despite the declining trend in the real wage rate. The potential for agricultural development that is in line with a "vent-for-surplus" has been rapidly disappearing and there is little reason for optimism regarding the future. The possibility cannot be denied that a large number of uneducated labourers may relocate to the urban areas and fail to get jobs, which will ultimately lead to various serious social problems.

Lastly, we should mention another serious potential problem, which is also related to the existence of a large number of agricultural labourers, in that they are especially vulnerable to rice price increases. If Myanmar liberalizes its rice exports in the future, the domestic rice price will rise, providing an incentive for farmers to increase production. This will hurt consumers, however, especially the poor, including agricultural labourers living in rural areas. Even in Thailand, where virtually no such labourers exist in the rural areas, the government adopted a policy of maintaining the domestic rice price far below the international one for a long time, until the mid-1980s,[24] due to the severity of the problems related to the export of the national staple food. It can be stated that the dilemma posed by tensions between economic development and the rice price level in Myanmar is far more serious.

Notes

1   On the details and the results of the land reform, see Takahashi (1992: 72–81).
2   The literal meaning of "*da don htun*" in Myanmar is "a piece of harrow", from which it came to mean "a unit of land area which can be cultivated by a set of agricultural implements and a pair of draft cattle, and from which it is sufficient for a farm household (nuclear family) to make a living" (Takahashi, 1992: 73).
3   According to Takahashi (2000: 104), the share of non-farm households was 46–53 per cent in Tindaungyi village (Kyaukse, Mandalay), 44 per cent in Kantale village (Magwe, Magwe), 38 per cent in Gukain village (East Pathein, Ayeyarwaddy), 21 per cent in South Tande village (Taunggyi, Shan), 70 per cent in Einsyay village (Pakokku, Magwe), and 72 per cent in West Payeichen village (somewhere close to Mandalay and Kyaukse); see also some additional cases in Tables 2 and 3 of this chapter.
4   As already mentioned, the transfer of the tillage right of land through tenancy and/or mortgage is illegal in Myanmar. In fact, it can only be sometimes observed among relatives and is rare, except in Upper Myanmar, where it is relatively developed, among non-relatives.
5   See Kurosaki *et al.* (2004) for details.
6   Needless to say, it is too hasty for us to conclude that, in every village, the "*da don htun*" was maintained over time without the fragmentation of farms occurring.
7   According to the government statistics, the per acre yield of monsoon paddy in Myanmar underwent a rapid increase, from 30 to 60 baskets, during the late 1970s and early 1980s, when the "All Township High Yielding Varieties Paddy Production Programme" was implemented, and it maintained this level until recently. It is plausible, however, that it has been overstated to a substantial degree. As evidence for this, we obtained the figure of 65 baskets as the official average yield from Village A from the Myanma Agricultural Service (MAS), while our estimates based on interviews with sample farmers showed only 40 baskets. Note that 1 basket of paddy equals 20.9 kg.
8   On the serious economic hardship experienced by the rice farmers in Myanmar during 2000 and 2001, see Fujita (2003).
9   The recent rapid diffusion of power tillers in Myanmar, however, is altering this situation.
10   According to a survey conducted by the author in a village in the Tangail district in 1992, the price of one draft animal and one acre of agricultural land were 3,500–5,000 taka and 45,000–75,000 taka, respectively (1 US$ = 40 taka at that time).

11 In the British colonial period too, seasonal labourers were generally employed for 10–12 months and paid 100–140 baskets of paddy as wages (Mizoguchi, 1958: 143).

12 Some exceptional cases were reported from diverse areas, however; for instance, Okamoto (2004) reported in-kind payments being made to seasonal labourers in three villages in Thongwa (50–60 per cent of the total, if cases of in-kind and cash payments combined are included). For the harvesting wage also, the Asian Population and Development Association (2001: 119–24) suggests the existence of an in-kind payment of 0.5 baskets of paddy per day in Pateingyi Township, Mandalay Division, and seven basket of paddy per acre (threshing is obligatory in this case) in Danubyu Township, Ayeyarwaddy Division. The latter case is interesting because, before 1997, it constituted a ten per cent share of the harvest, so that the system changed there from one sort of in-kind payment to another. Among the eight villages surveyed by the author in 2001, we also observed a case of 2.5 baskets of paddy per acre as the harvesting wage in Kyaukse Township.

13 See note 11.

14 Some evidence exists, however, to indicate a decline in the rice wage for female labourers, as observed in Village A in 2003, when the rice price increased rapidly (see also the case of three villages in Thongwa by Okamoto, 2004). In 2003, in fact, the rice wage for female labourers fell below 2 kg. Taking into account that their rice wage was 2.8–3.2 kg in Village K, it is possible that the rice wage for female labourers also underwent a decline in the long term.

15 Why was the wage rate for female labourers so low in Myanmar? Takahashi (2000: 247) suggested that this may be due to the scarcity (with high seasonality, concentrating only on the transplanting and harvesting seasons) of demand for female labourers.

16 We should take into account, however, that the share of expenditure for rice is substantially higher than the average for the poor agricultural labourers. Hence, the decline in the "genuine" real wage for the agricultural labourers must be higher than 10–20 per cent, as here estimated.

17 See Fujita (2005: 31) for details.

18 The (daily) rice wage in Laos and Vietnam is 6–7 kg, while it is 10–12 kg in Thailand.

19 See, for example, Table 12 (Chapter 5). The labour income share of green gram ranged between14–20 per cent in Lower Myanmar, compared to 33–41 per cent for monsoon rice.

20 As Takahashi (2000: 278–305) put it, "In an agricultural country like Myanmar, land holding size is the most influential determinant of the economic welfare of each rural household. However, the influence of land holding is not confined to the agricultural sector, but through the channel of re-investment of agricultural income to some self-employed non-agricultural businesses, the income disparity between farmers and agricultural labourers can be much more."

21 As Saito (1980: 84) put it, "The relation between farmers and agricultural labourers (in Myanmar) is very businesslike, characterized as a pure employer-employee relation." The usurious interest rate involved in the advance payment of wages can be understood well here.

22 We should note, however, that those with a higher education tend to leave their original village to seek work in urban areas, which may reduce the necessity to revise the previous research findings.

23 It is well known that, in developing countries, education is a decisive factor in obtaining non-agricultural jobs; see Kurosaki (2005) on the case of Myanmar.

24 See Hong *et al.* (2004).

CHAPTER 8

Urban Informal Sector Labourers in Yangon

Nang Mya Kay Khaing and Koichi Fujita

Introduction

No population census has been conducted in Myanmar since 1983. Estimates by the Central Statistical Organization's estimates indicate that the population had reached 52.17 million by 2002/03 (CSO, 2002: 14). According to the 1983 census, the total population was 34.13 million, of which the urban population was 8.47 million and the remaining 25.66 million the rural population. Therefore, the share of urban population was 24.8 per cent in 1983, but the urban population has been growing rapidly in recent years and may have exceeded 30 per cent of the total.

The population of the former capital city, Yangon, increased particularly fast in the 1980s and 1990s, growing from 2.51 million in 1983 to 3.1 million in 1993 (as estimated by the Ministry of Home Affairs, 1993), and to 4 million in 2000 (according to a survey by Myanmar Marketing Research and Development, a Yangon-based think-tank), with an average growth rate of 2.12 per cent per annum during 1983–93 and 3.65 per cent during 1993–2000. If the fact that the area of Yangon was expanding into rural areas, with an increase from 27 townships to 33, is considered, the actual population growth rate during 1993–2000 may have been slightly lower. The conclusion that the growth rate of Yangon's population accelerated after the economic transition, however, appears to be unaltered.

Myanmar's economy largely stagnated during the socialist period, especially in the late 1980s. During that period, since people's economic activities were restricted and/or monopolized by the state sector, the development of the non-agricultural sector, such as manufacturing, trade and transportation, was hampered. The agricultural sector continued to absorb an overwhelming share of the labour force. After the introduction of the market economy in 1988, however, the economy recovered and began to develop, as private enterprises, including foreign companies, started to flourish in urban areas, along with the rapid growth in the urban informal sector. Against such a background, an explosion in the size of the population and the labour force occurred in Yangon.

On the other hand, however, the evidence shows that the urban-rural income disparity in Myanmar is only 1.2 times (CSO, 1999), which is far smaller than that in other Asian countries.[1] This may be one of the reasons why there are fewer, smaller slums in Yangon, especially if we consider the existence of the immense pool of landless agricultural labourers in the rural areas. The urban economy, although it grew relatively quickly, had relatively little power to attract labourers from the rural areas into the cities. As this chapter will discuss in detail below, the wage rate for unskilled labourers in Yangon is apparently no higher than that in rural areas. Instead, we can say that it is almost the same between the two regions. The lack of any development of labour-intensive, export-oriented manufacturing sectors, except for the garment industry, which flourished in the late 1990s as discussed earlier in this book, may be the most important factor underlying such a phenomenon.

Regarding the labour situation, however, there are very few statistics or survey records; for example, there is only one labour force survey, and that was undertaken by the Ministry of Labour in 1990 (Ministry of Labour, 1993). Moreover, there is no wage data available at all for Myanmar, although this information should be available every year. Regarding labour migration too, the only statistics available relate to population changes and fertility (Ministry of Immigration and Population, 1995).

Given this desperate situation, this chapter is the first attempt to study urban labourers in Yangon empirically, with a focus on the so-called urban informal sector labourers.[2] This is for two main reasons: first, we hypothesize that there is some connection between the agricultural labour market in the rural areas (discussed in Chapter 7) and the urban informal labour market; and, second, it is relatively easy for the authors themselves to conduct a survey among informal labourers, since there is no need for formality. There will be some limitations to this paper, mainly because of the vagueness of the definition of the "urban informal sector" (see note 2) and some arbitrariness in the sampling of the labourers, which is in a sense "fatal" when dealing with informal sectors. It is hoped, however, that this paper will at least shed some light on an aspect of the urban labour market in Myanmar.

More concretely, based on the surveys conducted in Yangon in September 2003, we will explore several typical urban informal jobs, and present the profile, employment status, income structure, and financial situation of the workers. Finally, the conclusions and implications will be described.

A Profile of Labourers

A total of 181 labourers from the urban informal sector from various locations in Yangon were selected and interviewed in September 2003, including 17 shop owners, 6 shop employees, 4 restaurant waiters, 28 vendors, 31 taxi drivers, 35 trishaw (*hsai car*) drivers, 24 skilled labourers, 13 unskilled labourers, 12 waste collectors, 5 refuse collectors and 6 slipper/umbrella repairers. It should be noted that those selected for interview do not necessarily represent all urban informal sector labourers in Yangon. Selection was made with some arbitrariness, which is more or less inevitable in the case of informal sectors,[3] and the number sampled for each job does not necessarily reflect the number of labourers involved in each sphere. This paper can at least provide some information about the informal sector labourers in Yangon, however, classified into 11 types of job, through clarifying their profiles, employment conditions, and livelihood.

The profiles of 181 informal sector labourers are shown in Table 1, where individual details, such as age, sex, marital status, educational background, birth place, and migration, are illustrated. Some notable points arise, as follows.

First, regarding composition by gender, jobs dominated by female labourers are shop employees (67 per cent), vendors (46 per cent), and shop owners (29 per cent). On the other hand, jobs as taxi drivers, trishaw drivers, skilled labourers, waste collectors and restaurant waiters are completely dominated by male labourers.

Second, looking at the age structure, those in their twenties and thirties constitute the largest group, with a 37 and 26 per cent share respectively, followed by those in their forties (17 per cent), fifties (9 per cent), and teens (7 per cent). If we call labourers over 40 years old "elders", the share of "elders" is high among slipper/umbrella repairers (67 per cent), taxi drivers (65 per cent), shop owners (41 per cent), vendors (36 per cent), and trishaw drivers (29 per cent). On the other hand, "youths" (those under 40 years old) are dominant among restaurant waiters (100 per cent), refuse collectors (100 per cent), shop employees (83 per cent), unskilled labourers (69 per cent), and skilled labourers (54 per cent).

Third, with regard to marital status, 124 (69 per cent) of the labourers were married, and the remaining 31 per cent unmarried. The unmarried

Table 1 Profile of Labourers in Yangon's Informal Sector

Occupations	Total	Sex and Marital Status				Age						
		Male		Female		15–19	20–29	30–39	40–49	50–59	60–69	70–74
		Married	Unmarried	Married	Unmarried							
Shop Owners	17	7	5	2	3		6	4	5	1	1	
Taxi Drivers	31	29	2				4	7	11	6	3	
Vendors	28	10	5	10	3	2	10	6	7	3		
Skilled Labourers	24	14	10			3	10	8	2	1		
Trishaw Drivers	35	28	7				13	12	4	4	1	1
Waste Collectors	12	8	4			1	5	5		1		
Slipper/Umbrella Repairers	6	3	2	1			1	1	1	1	1	1
Refuse Collectors	5	3	1	1		1	4					
Unskilled Labourers	13	4	7	2		2	7	3	1			
Shop Employees	6	1	1	1	3	2	3	1				
Restaurant Waiters	4		4			1	3					
Total	181	107	48	17	9	12	66	47	31	17	6	2
Percentage	100%	59.1%	26.5%	9.4%	5.0%	6.6%	36.5%	26.0%	17.1%	9.4%	3.3%	1.1%

Table 1 continued

| | | | Educational Background (Education Years) | | | | | | | | Migration Status[1] | | | |
| | | | | | | | | | | | New Migrants from | | Rural areas | |
	None	Monastery	Primary School Dropouts (0-3)	Primary School Graduates (4)	Middle School Dropouts (5-7)	Middle School Graduates (8)	High School Dropouts (9)	High School Graduates (10)	University Students	University Graduates	Yangon Inhabitants	Regional Cities/Towns	Farm Households	Non-farm Households
Shop Owners			1		1	1	2	5	2	5	13	3		1
Taxi Drivers		1		1	4	6	3	8		8	26	5		
Vendors	1		4	5	6	2	4	5	2	1	14	9	4	1
Skilled Labourers			2	3	6	3	3	2		3	10	3	5	6
Trishaw Drivers		2	3	7	9	8	3	2	1		27	3	3	2
Waste Collectors		2	5	1	2	2					11			1
Slipper/Umbrella Repairers		1	1	3					1		3	3		
Refuse Collectors		1	3		1						5			
Unskilled Labourers		2	3	2	3			2	1		1		5	
Shop Employees								3		2	4	2		7
Restaurant Waiters				1		1	1					1	3	
Total	1	9	22	23	33	23	16	27	8	19	114	29	20	18
Percentage	0.6%	5.0%	12.2%	12.7%	18.2%	12.7%	8.8%	14.9%	4.4%	10.5%	63.0%	16.0%	11.1%	10.0%

Note: [1] Migrants who arrived before 1988 are counted as Yangon inhabitants.

Source: Based on the authors' survey conducted in September 2003.

labourers are dominant among restaurant waiters (100 per cent), shop employees (67 per cent), unskilled labourers (54 per cent), shop owners (47 per cent), and skilled labourers (42 per cent).

Fourth, regarding educational background,[4] the majority (70 per cent) are middle school dropouts or higher and the remaining 30 per cent are primary school graduates or less. This clearly indicates the relatively high level of educational background among urban informal sector labourers, compared to Myanmar's average.[5] Especially notable is the fact that the share of high school graduates or more is high among shop employees (100 per cent), shop owners (71 per cent), and taxi drivers (52 per cent). By contrast, labourers with a low educational background (primary school graduates or less) predominate among slipper/umbrella repairers (100 per cent), refuse collectors (80 per cent), waste collectors (67 per cent), and unskilled labourers (54 per cent).

Finally, regarding their birth place and migration status, the labourers who were living in Yangon before 1988 account for 63 per cent, while 37 per cent migrated to Yangon after 1988. In particular, there are very few new migrants in jobs such as refuse collectors (0 per cent), waste collectors (8 per cent), taxi drivers (19 per cent), trishaw drivers (23 per cent), and shop owners (24 per cent). On the other hand, many migrants are found working as restaurant waiters (100 per cent), unskilled labourers (92 per cent), skilled labourers (58 per cent), vendors (50 per cent), slipper/umbrella repairers (50 per cent), and shop employees (33 per cent).

Furthermore, if we look at the birth place of new migrants, "regional city/town" accounts for 43 per cent, and "rural village" for 57 per cent. There are unexpectedly few migrants from the rural villages, which may indicate the difficulty they face in finding jobs even in the urban informal sectors, especially high-income jobs, such as shop owners and taxi drivers.

In Table 1, various jobs are arranged, from the highest income (top) down to the lowest (bottom). At a glance, it is evident that older and more highly educated labourers tend to get higher income jobs. This is natural, because labourers with a higher educational background have a higher probability of obtaining high-income jobs and, also, older labourers may enjoy the advantage of having accumulated capital savings and experience.

The Employment Conditions and Income Structure of the Labourers

We will proceed to analyze the employment conditions and income earnings of the labourers interviewed (Table 2). To promote our understanding, we processed a matrix table (Table 3), which classified 11 jobs according to two criteria. The first criterion is the working status of the labourers, i.e., self-employed or employed. Most of the taxi/trishaw drivers are not owner-drivers, but rent vehicles, pay a rental fee, and work under the supervision of the owners. Therefore, they are not purely employed, nor are they purely self-employed, so we classified them in an intermediate position. Regarding skilled labourers as well, sometimes they should be categorized as self-employed, but, for our samples, it was found that all of the labourers should be classified as employed. The second criterion is the level of income earnings. The details of the estimated income are shown in Table 2, according to which, we classified income into three levels (high, low, very low) in Table 3.

Shop Owners

Included here are the owners of various shops, such as car workshops (two persons), electrical equipment shops (one person), paint shops (one person), tea/coffee shops (one person), general stores (three persons), and various shops in shopping malls, such as handbag shops (two persons), CD shops (two persons), clothes shops (one person), cosmetics shops (two persons), and watch shops (two persons). Altogether, 17 persons were selected to be interviewed. The average sales amount per month was estimated at 620 thousand kyat, with a net profit of 250 thousand kyat on average. The net income per month was highest for the car workshop owners (850 thousand kyat = 867 US$), and lowest for the general store owners (110 thousand kyat = 112 US$), depending on the size of the business.

Table 2 indicates a large gap between the income earnings of the shop owners and other informal sector labourers. The shop owners are actually the owners of small- and medium-scale enterprises, and it may sometimes be more appropriate to exclude them from the analysis of urban informal sector labourers.

A huge amount of capital, both for initial investment and everyday operations, is necessary for the shop owners. The initial investment of a car workshop owner was estimated at one hundred million kyat (= 102,000 US$), which was an exceptional case. The average amount for the other 16 shop owners was 2 million kyat (= 2,040 US$) for their initial investment and 370 thousand kyat (= 378 US$) for their everyday operations.

Taxi Drivers

Of the total 31 taxi drivers interviewed, there were six owner-drivers and 25 non-owners. Non-owner drivers usually need to deposit some money to the

Table 2 Income Estimates by Occupation in Yangon's Informal Sector

Occupations	No. of Samples	Initial Investment/ Deposit	Gross Income (1)	Rental Fees (2)	Costs other than Rental Fees (3)	Net Income (1)-(2)-(3)	Monthly Income (US$)	Rice Wage (kg/day)	Remarks
				Amount per day[1]					
Shop Owners	17	7,704,000	621,000	–	368,000	253,000	258	52.8	
Taxi Drivers									
Owner-Drivers	6	692,000	6,333	–	1,433	4,900	140	28.7	
Rental (depositors)	11	422,000	9,273	4,318	1,364	3,591	103	21.0	–
Rental (non-depositors)	14	–	9,000	4,750	1,279	2,971	85	17.4	–
Vendors									
Fruit	5	109,000	13,200	–	9,900	3,300	94	19.2	
Betel Cigarettes	3	19,333	11,500	–	8,450	3,050	87	17.8	
Sweets and Fried Snacks	3	33,333	8,667	–	5,900	2,767	79	16.8	
Daily Necessities	6	70,000	5,167	–	3,117	2,050	59	12.0	
Vegetables and Eggs	6	24,417	8,318	–	7,280	1,038	30	6.1	
Hawkers	5	2,440	3,480	–	2,120	1,360	39	8.0	
Skilled Labourers									
Construction Site Managers	4	–	21,250	–	–	21,250	22	4.4	with shelters/meals [2]
Construction Site Managers	2	–	2,000	–	–	2,000	57	11.7	with shelters
Construction Site Artisans	12	–	1,292	–	–	1,292	37	7.6	with shelters/meals [3]
Car Mechanics	3	–	2,300	–	–	2,300	66	13.5	with shelters/meals [3]
Managers/Crane Drivers at Port	3	–	40,000	–	–	40,000	41	8.4	with shelters
Trishaw Drivers									
Depositors	32	13,156	1,809	480	85	1,244	36	7.3	
Non-depositors	3	–	2,033	433	85	1,515	43	8.9	

Table 2 continued

Occupations	No. of Samples	Initial Investment/ Deposit	Amount per day[1]				Monthly Income (US$)	Rice Wage (kg/day)	Remarks
			Gross Income (1)	Rental Fees (2)	Costs other than Rental Fees (3)	Net Income (1)–(2)–(3)			
Waste Collectors	12	1,983	3,692	–	2,575	1,108	32	6.5	
Slipper/Umbrella Repairers	6	–	983	–	–	983	28	5.7	
Refuse Collectors	5	–	1,460	500	–	960	27	5.6	
Unskilled Labourers									
Construction Site Manual Labourers	7	–	757	–	–	757	22	4.4	with shelters
Trainee Car Mechanics	3	–	5,000	–	–	5,000	5	1.0	with shelters/meals
Manual Labourers at Port	3	–	21,667	–	–	21,667	22	4.5	with shelters
Shop Employees	6	–	10,417	–	–	10,417	11	2.2	
Restaurant Waiters	4	–	9,250	–	–	9,250	9	1.9	with shelters/meals

Notes: [1] Data highlighted by grey colour indicates the amount per month.
[2] Only 2 persons were provided with meals.
[3] Only one persons was provided with meals.
[4] Retail rice price was 171 kyat/kg (Emata), and 1 US$ = 980 kyat in September 2003.

Source: Survey by the authors.

290 Nang Mya Kay Khaing and Koichi Fujita

Table 3 Classification of Urban Informal Sector Labourers

		Employment Conditions		
		Self-employed	*Intermediate Position*	*Employed*
Income	High	Shop Owners	Taxi Drivers	–
	Low	Vendors	Trishaw Drivers	Skilled Labourers
	Very Low	Waste Collectors Slipper/Umbrella Repairers Refuse Collectors	–	Unskilled Labourers Shop Employees Restaurant Waiters

Source: Prepared by the authors.

owners as security, although several exceptional cases were observed where they were the close relatives and/or friends of the owners. Of the 25 rental taxi drivers, 11 deposited some money (with an average of 420 thousand kyat (= 429 US$); from a minimum of 90 thousand kyat to a maximum of 1 million kyat, and the most frequent amount was 500 thousand kyat; see the table), whereas 14 did not. Note however, that, the daily rental fee is slightly higher for non-depositors than depositors. The contract with the taxi owners is basically a verbal agreement, without any written form.

A special driving license, to obtain which one must have held a general license for at least five years, is necessary to be a taxi driver in Myanmar. The license fee (approximately 2,500 kyat = 2.6 US$) must be paid every two years. The taxi owners usually bear the cost of the annual automobile inspection, but not necessarily the cost of other repairs; it was found that about half of the renting drivers had to bear the cost of the automobile repairs.

The average monthly income is estimated to be 130 thousand kyat (= 133 US$) for owner-drivers and 80–100 thousand kyat (= 82–102 US$) for renting drivers. The latter is 30–40 per cent less than the former, and the income level of owner-drivers is almost equivalent to that of the poorest shop owners in our survey.

Vendors

Out of 28 vendors interviewed, five were so-called hawkers, with no fixed place for sale, who sold sweets and fried snacks (four persons) and flowers (one person). Their average daily net income was estimated at 1,360 kyat (= 1.4 US$), which was found to be very low.

On the other hand, the remaining 23 vendors, with a fixed sales location, were found on the streets outside some public (municipality-run) markets, on the streets of some residential areas, in the Central Business District (CBD) area of Yangon, etc. They stated that they had to pay a bribe of 60–150 kyat per day to the local police and staff of the Yangon City Development Committee (YCDC). They sold fruit (five persons), vegetables and eggs (six persons), betel cigarettes (three persons), sweets and fried snacks (three persons) and daily necessities, such as clothes, glasses, hair accessories, and jewelry (six persons).

A large difference was observed between their respective daily income levels, depending on what they sold and the size of their business; 5,000 kyat (daily necessities) to 13,000 kyat (fruit) for the gross revenue, and 1,000 kyat (vegetables and eggs) to 3,300 kyat (fruit) for the net income. If converted into monthly terms, the net income ranges between 29,000 kyat (= 29.6 US$) (vegetables and eggs) and 92,000 kyat (= 93.9 US$) (fruit). Even the richest vendors can only earn as much income as the renting taxi drivers, although, if we compare them with the daily wage rate for unskilled construction labourers (800–900 kyat = 0.8–0.9 US$ for males and 600 kyat = 0.6 US$ for females), the vendors' earnings are much higher.

Needless to say, vendors and hawkers need some capital both for their initial investment and their everyday operations, although their initial investment, ranging from 2,400 kyat (= 2.4 US$) (hawkers) to 110 thousand kyat (= 112.2 US$) (fruit vendors), is far smaller than that of the shop owners (2 million kyat on average), and their necessary working capital, ranging from 2,100 kyat (= 2.1 US$) (hawkers) to 10 thousand kyat (= 10.2 US$) (fruit vendors), is also relatively small, although certainly not negligible for such small-scale, self-employed workers.

Skilled Labourers

We surveyed a total of 24 skilled labourers, including 6 construction site managers, 12 artisans, such as carpenters, plasterers, welders, and electrical engineers, three car mechanics, and three managers and crane drivers in Yangon port.

Some of the construction site managers were found to have been promoted from among the labourers working at the same construction site, although others were recruited as university students/graduates, who lived in Yangon after graduating. It was found that they come from the same native place as the contractors and were all employed through this connection. The site managers are responsible for such tasks as the employment/management of unskilled labourers and the procurement of building materials. Therefore, unskilled labourers also tend to be recruited from the same native place as the site manager. The wage payment system for the managers can be classified into two types; daily payment (1,500–2,500 kyat = 1.5–2.6 US$) and monthly payment (15,000–25,000 kyat = 15.3–25.5 US$).

Skilled and unskilled labourers live together and share meals at the construction site, by pooling money (in some cases, the contractors bear the total cost of the meals). The daily wage rate for skilled labourers varies between 1,000, 1,200, 1,300, 1,500 kyat (= 1.0, 1.2, 1.3, 1.5 US$),[6] depending upon their skill. Note that the wage rate for the mechanics was found to be considerably high (2,200–2,500 kyat), and they were paid on a monthly basis, but have to work as trainee mechanics for two to three years for very low wages before they acquire this position. The skilled labourers who were working at the port on the transshipment of logs, were also paid monthly (40,000 kyat = 40.8 US$ per month).

In conclusion, the average wage rate of the skilled labourers, if in-kind payment in the form of shelter and meals is included, was almost the same or slighly lower than that of the vendors mentioned above.

Trishaw Drivers

All 35 of the trishaw (*hsai car*) drivers interviewed were rental drivers, without exception. Like the taxi drivers, some of them deposited money with the owners as security while others did not, although the latter case was relatively rare, applying to only three of the drivers.

A considerable variation was observed between both the deposited amount and the rental fee for the trishaw. The deposited amount varied between 3,000–30,000 kyat (most paid 10,000 kyat = 10.2 US$), while the daily rental fee varied from 300–700 kyat (in most cases 500 kyat = 0.5 US$, with an average of 480 kyat with a deposit and 433 kyat without one).[7] The trishaw owners, just like taxi owners, take responsibility for bearing the costs of registration (which is renewable annually) and major repairs (such as re-painting) when necessary,[8] but the drivers have to bear the cost of minor repairs (such as punctured tyres), not to mention any fines imposed on them for violating the traffic regulations.[9] Furthermore, the trishaw drivers also have to bear the renewal cost of their drivers' license every year.[10] The average net income per day was estimated at 1,244 kyat (with a deposit) (= 1.3 US$) and 1,515 kyat (without a deposit) (= 1.5 US$),[11] which is more or less equal to the vendors of the lowest stratum.

Waste Collectors

Waste collectors purchase such items as old newspapers, used cans and bottles from households, and sell them to scrap merchants. The necessary equipment is only a weight measure and cloth bags for carrying the collected waste. Of the 12 collectors surveyed, 10 live in the poor residential areas of the suburbs of Yangon, including Ywa Thar Gyi (5 persons), South Dagon (4 persons), and Hlaing Thar Yar (one person) and commute every day to the middle class residential areas, such as Kyauk Myaung, by city-loop trains in order to collect waste. The level of net income per day was found to be equal to the lowest stratum of vendors and hawkers.

Slipper/Umbrella Repairers

Usually, the repairers of slippers and umbrellas can be found on the streets near the municipality-run markets or CBD, and can be categorized as the kinds of hawker analyzed already but, considering that they need some skills, and are socially despised (for doing a "dirty" job), we decided to deal with this group separately. Their net daily income is estimated to be slightly less than 1,000 kyat (= 1.0 US$), which is lower than that of waste collectors.

Refuse Collectors

Refuse collectors visit households, collect rubbish and throw it away. Sometimes, they find items (such as opened cans and PET bottles) among the rubbish that can be recycled. Like the waste collectors, they usually live in the suburbs of Yangon where the poor are concentrated, and commute to the middle class residential areas, such as Kyauk Myaung and San Gyaung, where six to seven storey buildings were built during the 1990s' construction boom. They earn a small amount of money, depending on their workload; 20–50 kyat for the lower floors and 50–100 kyat for the higher floors of the buildings.

Basically the poorest class of people is involved in this job, due to its easiness to make a start; the requirement is to own a barrow. The net daily income is lower than that for waste collectors and almost the same as that of slipper/umbrella repairers.

Unskilled Labourers

The unskilled labourers whom we interviewed include manual labourers (probationary carpenters, probationary plasters, sand carriers, and brick carriers) working at construction sites (seven persons), trainee car mechanics working in workshops (three persons), and manual labourers working on the transshipment of logs at Yangon port (three persons).

The daily wage rate on the construction sites was 800–900 kyat (= 0.8–0.9 US$) for the male labourers and 600 kyat (= 0.6 US$) for the female ones (light tasks, such as carrying sand and bricks),[12] who were the spouses of the male labourers in most cases. Most of the unskilled labourers were also provided with shelter and meals. When such in-kind payment is taken into account, the wage rate is close to that of the waste collectors, refuse collectors, and slipper/umbrella repairers.

Shop Employees

We interviewed six shop employees in total, who worked in sundry goods shops, cosmetics shops, a clothes shop in a shopping mall, etc. The majority of them were sales assistants and they were paid only around 10,000 kyat (= 10.2 US$) as a monthly salary without any additional in-kind payment, which is definitely far lower than the wages for unskilled labourers or waste collectors. However, their actual working hours are short and the work intensity is also relatively slight. Consequently, despite the extremely low salary, people such as students taking correspondence courses, young single women living with their parents, or housewives prefer this kind of job, and earn some money for their personal use and/or to supplement the household income.

Restaurant Waiters

The interviews were extended to four restaurant waiters. In most cases, their employers provide them with shelter and meals, although, even if such in-kind payment is taken into account, their salary is lower than that of unskilled labourers. Moreover, the task itself is very difficult and takes many hours. The employees are young people, mostly teenagers and in their early twenties. From the viewpoint of the households that dispatch such a young workforce, it seems that to "reduce the number of mouths" to feed was their prime objective.

The Household Economy of the Labourers

So far, we have concentrated on analyzing the economy of the urban informal labourers from the individual point of view. Now, let us consider the household economy as a whole, to which the labourers belong.

Table 4 classifies the labourers according to their marital status and their status in their households in terms of being the major/supplementary income earners. Of the total of 181 labourers, slightly less than 70 per cent were married and 30 per cent were unmarried. Of the 122 married persons (excluding two migrants whose family members live separately in their place of origin), 99 persons (81 per cent) were household heads, while 23 (19 per cent) were not. Of these, 114 persons (93 per cent) were the major income earners, whereas only ten persons (8 per cent) were supplementary earners. This means that there were some cases in which the non-household heads were the major income earners.

Typical cases can be found among vendors (all nine of the non-household heads were the major earners) and taxi drivers (all three of the non-household heads were the major earners). The former were wives working as vendors, while the latter were sons or sons-in-law working as taxi drivers while their aged parents remained the household heads.

On the other hand, 67 per cent of the unmarried persons live with their parents and/or siblings' family, and the remaining 33 per cent live alone in Yangon as migrant workers. It should be noted that 53 per cent (20 persons) of the unmarried persons living with their families are the major income earners. Such people can be found mainly among vendors and taxi drivers, as expected, but also among shop owners and skilled labourers.

Table 5 shows the number of household members in the labour force and the structure of income earning, only for the 122 married labourers (except for the two married migrants, who lived alone).

According to the table, the average number of household members was slightly less than five, two of whom had a job. The typical nuclear family is dominant, although a tendency was observed for the number of workers to be smaller among low-income households, reflecting the fact that the category includes young families with wives who cannot work due to their need to look after small children.

The fact that a household has two workers on average means that there is another worker besides the informal sector labourers whom we interviewed, although the contribution of the interviewed labourers to the household income reached 74 per cent on average, which implies that the income of the other worker in general was small.

By contrast, the cases of a low contribution by the informal sector labourers include shop employees (a contribution of 29 per cent), refuse collectors (38 per cent), trishaw drivers (46 per cent), and unskilled labourers (53 per cent), and so this is particularly notable in the case of trishaw drivers. A typical case would be where the wife is a vendor and her unmarried son

Table 4 Household Characteristics of Yangon's Informal Sector Labourers

Occupations	Total	Married				Unmarried			Married[1]		Unmarried[2]	
		Household Heads	Non-household Heads	Migrants (Family members live in native places)	Total	Living with parents and/or siblings', family	Living alone	Total	Major Income Earners	Supplementary Income Earners	Major Income Earners	Supplementary Income Earners
Shop Owners	17	7	2	0	9	8	0	8	8	1	5	3
Taxi Drivers	31	26	3	0	29	2	0	2	29	0	2	0
Vendors	28	11	9	0	20	7	1	8	20	0	7	1
Skilled Labourers	24	12	2	0	14	6	4	10	13	1	4	6
Trishaw Drivers	35	24	2	2	28	4	3	7	23	5	1	6
Waste Collectors	12	8	0	0	8	4	0	4	8	0	0	4
Slipper/Umbrella Repairers	6	4	0	0	4	2	0	2	4	0	0	2
Refuse Collectors	5	2	2	0	4	1	0	1	4	0	1	0
Unskilled Labourers	13	4	2	0	6	1	6	7	4	2	0	7
Shop Employees	6	1	1	0	2	3	1	4	1	1	0	4
Restaurant Waiter	4	0	0	0	0	0	4	4	0	0	0	4
Total	181	99	23	2	124	38	19	57	114	10	20	37

Notes: [1] Migrants whose family members live in native places are included in the major income earners.
[2] Labourers living alone are included in the supplementary income earners.

Source: Based on the authors' survey conducted in September 2003.

Table 5 Household Economy of Married Labourers in Yangon's Informal Sector

Occupations	Total Married Labourers			Average Household Member	Average Labor Force	Household Income per month (A)	Per Month Income of the Labourers Interviewed (B)	Contribution (%) (B)/(A)	(Ref.) Per Capita Monthly Income (kyat)	(Ref.) Per Capita Monthly Income (US$)
	Household Heads	Non-household Heads	Total							
Shop Owners	7	2	9	4.2	2.0	336,474	303,333	90	80,113	81.7
Taxi Drivers	26	3	29	5.0	2.0	125,363	100,897	80	25,073	25.5
Vendors	11	9	20	4.5	2.3	71,932	55,902	78	15,985	16.3
Skilled Labourers	12	2	14	4.6	1.9	67,374	40,960	61	14,647	14.9
Trishaw Drivers	24	2	26	6.2	2.3	78,939	36,615	46	12,732	13.0
Waste Collectors	8	0	8	4.3	1.4	36,750	29,400	80	8,547	8.7
Slipper/Umbrella Repairers	4	0	4	2.3	1.3	27,300	27,300	100	11,870	12.1
Refuse Collectors	2	2	4	6.5	2.8	78,400	29,400	38	12,062	12.3
Unskilled Labourers	4	2	6	3.7	1.7	36,400	19,133	53	9,838	10.0
Shop Employees	1	1	2	3.0	1.5	31,500	9,000	29	10,500	10.7
Total	99	23	122	4.9	2.0	99,150	72,904	74	20,289	20.7

Source: Based on the authors' survey conducted in September 2003.

Table 6 Household Economy of Unmarried Labourers in Yangon's Informal Sector

Occupations	Total Unmarried Labourers (Living with Family only)	Average Household Member	Average Labor Force	Household Income per month (A)	Per Month Income of the Labourers Interviewed (B)	Contribution (%) (B)/(A)	(Ref.) Per Capita Monthly Income (kyat)	(Ref.) Per Capita Monthly Income (kyat)
Shop Owners	8	6.0	3.9	305,325	71,750	23	50,888	51.9
Taxi Drivers	2	5.5	2.5	172,200	140,000	81	31,309	31.9
Vendors	7	5.0	2.4	114,840	74,340	65	22,968	23.4
Skilled Labourers	6	4.8	3.3	130,667	42,700	33	27,222	27.8
Trishaw Drivers	4	10.8	3.5	223,300	49,700	22	20,676	21.1
Waste Collectors	4	5.8	3.0	118,244	34,300	29	20,387	20.8
Slipper/Umbrella Repairers	2	5.5	4.0	178,668	28,000	16	32,485	33.1
Refuse Collectors	1	4.0	2.0	58,800	30,800	52	14,700	15.0
Unskilled Labourers	1	5.0	3.0	165,200	25,200	15	33,040	33.7
Shop Employees	3	6.3	4.0	199,160	10,833	5	31,613	32.3
Total	38	6.0	3.3	182,102	55,555	31	30,337	31.0

Source: Based on the authors' survey conducted in September 2003.

or son-in-law a trishaw driver (or an unskilled labourer working at Yangon port). Their household economy is supported by the labour contributions of all of the members who can work.

Finally, Table 6 shows the same data as Table 5 for the 38 unmarried labourers (except for the single household). The notable facts, especially when compared to married labourers, are as follows.

First, the number of household members was 6.0 persons, with 3.3 workers on average. Compared to the married labourers' households, both the household members and workforce are larger by one. This suggests that one labourer (our sample interviewee) is added to the average married labourers' household. There may be various cases but, in these cases, the earnings of the unmarried labourer are small and not necessarily transferred to the household income. This is the case of unmarried shop employees, in particular.

Second, the contribution of the labourers' income to the total household income was very low, at 31 per cent on average. This was particularly true for shop employees (5 per cent), unskilled labourers (15 per cent), slipper/umbrella repairers (16 per cent), trishaw drivers (22 per cent), and waste collectors (29 per cent). The opposite case was observed among taxi drivers (81 per cent) and vendors (65 per cent), even though they were unmarried.

The Financial Situation of the Labourers

Finally, let us examine the debts and savings of the informal sector labourers. Table 7 shows the situation regarding savings. Of the interviewees, 45 persons (25 per cent) stated that they have savings, with an average amount of slightly more than 60,000 kyat (= 61.2 US$). Those with the largest amount of savings are shop owners and taxi drivers, who are the highest income earners.

The debt situation, on the other hand, is shown in Table 8, indicating the following points. First, only a third of the urban informal sector labourers have some degree of debt, with an average amount of slightly more than 75,000 kyat (= 76.5 US$). This amount almost equals the monthly household income of vendors, skilled labourers, and trishaw drivers, which are classified as the low income group (Table 5). The job groups with a high percentage of debt are trishaw drivers (83 per cent), refuse collectors (60 per cent), vendors (43 per cent), and waste collectors (42 per cent). On the contrary, the job groups with a large amount of loans (although the percentage of debt is relatively small) are taxi drivers and shop employees.

Table 7   The Savings of Yangon's Informal Sector Labourers

| Occupations | Total | Persons with Saving | | Average Saving Amount (Only for Persons with Savings) |
		Number	Percentage	
Shop Owners	17	4	24%	202,500
Taxi Drivers	31	7	23%	127,143
Vendors	28	8	29%	27,750
Skilled Labourers	24	10	42%	54,300
Trishaw Drivers	35	8	23%	17,500
Waste Collectors	12	2	17%	12,500
Slipper/Umbrella Repairers	6	1	17%	40,000
Refuse Collectors	5	1	20%	12,000
Unskilled Labourers	13	2	15%	7,000
Shop Employees	6	0	0%	0
Restaurant Waiters	4	2	50%	7,000
Total	181	45	25%	60,222

Source: Based on the authors' survey conducted in September 2003.

Turning to the purpose of borrowing, 26 cases (43 per cent) are for production purposes, while 34 cases (57 per cent) are for consumption purposes, including education, medical treatment and marriage. The job groups borrowing mainly for production purposes are taxi drivers, vendors,[13] trishaw drivers, and waste collectors. Production purposes here include working capital for running businesses (vendors, waste collectors), the payment of repair costs and fines (taxi/trishaw drivers), and sometimes initial investment money for purchasing vehicles or providing a deposit to the owner of the vehicles. It is interesting to note that they are the middle income groups, with an intermediate status between self-employed and employed, because there is no need to borrow in the case of high income groups, such as shop owners, and also it is rare and difficult for really low income people to borrow for production purposes. Another interesting point that emerges from the table is that, of the three cases of borrowing by refuse collectors (the lowest income group), two were for the purpose of gambling.

Regarding the relationship between the borrowers and lenders, friends or those from the same area are the largest group (50 per cent), followed by relatives (15 per cent) and those engaging in the same business (8 per cent). Money lenders (22 per cent) and authorized pawnshops[14] (5 per cent)

are not common but not negligible. In particular, it was found that trishaw drivers, waste collectors, and refuse collectors depended more on money lenders. They usually faced high interest rates: many trishaw drivers were charged a 20 per cent monthly interest rate, while the waste collectors and refuse collectors were charged a 4–6 per cent daily interest rate.

When the trishaw drivers borrow money from their friends, those from the same area, relatives, those engaging in the same business, etc., a high interest rate appears to be imposed in many cases, as among the money lenders, which is very common in Myanmar.[15]

Returning to the interest rate, the vendors' interest rate remains slightly lower than that of the trishaw drivers, but the average monthly interest rate is 20 per cent. On the other hand, it can be seen clearly that the taxi drivers' interest rate is lower than that of the trishaw drivers and the vendors, and the monthly interest rate of the taxi drivers ranges between 3 and 10 per cent.

Conclusion

In Myanmar after 1988, when the policies for economic transition were implemented on a full scale, the inflow of population into the big cities accelerated, especially for the capital, Yangon. On the other hand, there was no large-scale emigration from the rural areas, even from the suburban villages, although there was a large pool of poverty-struck landless agricultural labourers in every village and the income disparity was widening between the farmers and landless labourers (see Chapter 7 of this book for a more detailed discussion). How should we understand these apparently contradictory phenomena?

Based on the detailed discussion regarding the employment/livelihood conditions of certain selected urban informal sector labourers in this chapter, lastly, we summarize some important points and try to answer the above question.

(1)   It is quite natural that there is a large gap in earnings depending on the jobs involved, even within the urban informal sector in Yangon. People who differed in terms of sex, age, educational background, native place and social class, were working under various conditions.

(2)   Slightly more than 60 per cent of labourers in Yangon were living there before 1988. Such people came mainly from the self-employed high income groups (shop owners and taxi drivers) and self-employed low income groups (waste collectors, refuse collectors, slipper/umbrella repairers). On the other hand, new migrants were dominant among

Table 8 The Debts of Yangon's Informal Sector Labourers

Kind of Occupations	Total	Persons with Debts		Average Debt (Only for the Persons with Debts)	Relationship with Lenders				
		Number	Percentage		Friends in the Native Place	Relatives	Same Business	Money Lenders	Authorized Pawnshops
Shop Owners	17	0	0%	0					
Taxi Drivers	31	9	29%	264,444	3	5	1		
Vendors	28	12	43%	74,450	7	2	1	1	1
Skilled Labourers	24	1	4%	20,000	1				
Trishaw Drivers	35	29	83%	37,024	15	2	2	8	2
Waste Collectors	12	5	42%	9,400	2		1	2	
Slipper/Umbrella Repairers	6	0	0%	0					
Refuse Collectors	5	3	60%	5,667	1			2	
Unskilled Labourers	13	0	0%	0					
Shop Employees	6	1	17%	100,000	1				
Restaurant Waiters	4	0	0%	0					
Total	181	60	33%	75,518	30	9	5	13	3

Table 8 continued

	Interest Rate											Purpose of Borrowing						
	Without Interest	With Interest (monthly rate)					With Interest (daily rate)				Unknown	Production Purpose	Consumption Purposes					
		3–5%	6–10%	15%	20%	25–30%	4%	5%	6%	11%			Supplement of Household Needs	Repair of Residence	Medical Treatment	Education	Marriage	Others
Shop Owners																		
Taxi Drivers	2	4	2								1	5	1	1	2			
Vendors	2	1	2	1	4	1				1		7			3	1		1
Skilled Labourers	1														1			
Trishaw Drivers	4	3		4	15	2					1	11	11	3	1	2		1
Waste Collectors								3	1		1	3	1	1				
Slipper/Umbrella Repairers																		
Refuse Collectors							1	1			1				1			2
Unskilled Labourers																		
Shop Employees	1																1	
Restaurant Waiters																		
Total	10	8	4	5	19	3	1	4	1	1	4	26	13	5	8	3	1	4

Note: Vendors and refuse collectors borrowed for gambling, and trishaw drivers borrowed to purchase alcohol.

Source: Based on the authors' survey conducted in September 2003.

the low-income hired labourers, such as restaurant waiters, and skilled and unskilled labourers, and were mainly recruited through blood and regional connections with their employers. Otherwise, it is difficult in general for rural residents to migrate to Yangon and get jobs.

(3) Furthermore, it should be noted that 43 per cent of the new migrants to Yangon (after 1988) came from the regional cities/towns, and not from purely rural areas, and such people came mainly from the high-income groups, such as shop owners, taxi drivers, and vendors, who needed a fairly large amount of capital. This may indicate that capital is one of the major constraints for the purely rural residents.

(4) Another remarkable fact is the unexpectedly high educational level of the urban informal sector labourers. The educational situation in rural Myanmar is under-developed, especially for the children of agricultural labour households, who tend to fail to graduate even from primary school (see Chapter 7). One of the reasons there are few new migrants from non-farm households (most of them are agricultural labour households) may be this educational factor. In other words, even if there exist factors to "push out", they cannot be a sufficient condition for the landless agricultural labourers to decide to migrate to the urban areas.

(5) However, if there really are push factors, rural/urban labour migration may increase rapidly in the future, should the social problems arising from unemployment/underemployment become very serious in Yangon. In order to prevent such a situation, it is necessary to understand precisely the nature of the labour market in both the urban and rural areas, among others. Further research on the labour market in Myanmar, and an improvement in the statistics, is indispensable.

Notes

[1] The urban-rural income disparities are 1.5–1.7 in Bangladesh, 1.9 in India, 1.7–2.9 in Thailand (Bangkok), about 3.0 in China, and so on; see Fujita (2007).

[2] The urban informal sector is difficult to define, especially in Myanmar, for which no labour statistics are available. The term 'informal sector' is used here in a relatively vague manner to refer to those sectors that have low-productivity and a low-income, and are unregistered.

[3] If we choose some specific area (such as a slum) for the selection of labourers, it may avoid arbitrariness to a large extent, although a further problem arises that the labourers may be concentrated in a particular type of job.

[4] Myanmar's education system consists of: five years at primary school, four years at middle school, and two years at high school, before going to college/university.

[5] The high educational background of the urban informal sector labourers is

especially outstanding when compared with that of labourers in rural areas. If rural labourers are viewed as a pool of potential migrants to urban areas in the process of economic development, the current situation in Myanmar is highly problematic and serious, because it is difficult for agricultural labourers to move to urban areas and get jobs. About the educational background of the rural residents, see Chapter 7 of this book.

6   In terms of the rice wage rate, it was 5.8, 7.0, 7.6 and 8.9 kg per day, respectively.

7   The deposit is designed to discourage the drivers from making off with the trishaws and to compensate for any non-payment of rental fees. For a typical driver, the rental fee was 480 kyat, while the deposit was 13,156 kyat, making the deposited money equivalent to 27.4 days of the rental fee. In Yangon, when the drivers failed to pay their rental fees for a week, the owners took the trishaws from the drivers. Note that the price of new registered trishaws was about 500,000 kyat at the time of the survey. By contrast, the price in Bago was only 180,000 kyat. The excessive price in Yangon was due to controls over the total quantity of trishaws by the YCDC since April 2001 (Nang Mya Kay Khaing, 2004).

8   As our interview with a trishaw owner in Yangon revealed, the total cost of involved with renewing a trishaw license was 4,600 kyat (= 4.7 US$), including 1,000 kyat for the renewal fee, 100 kyat for the service charge, 2,500 kyat for the wheel tax, and 1,000 kyat for the contribution to the "welfare fund" (for the YCDC employees), and the total repair costs needed at the time of the license renewal was 5,000–10,000 kyat, according to the same owner.

9   The management section of the trishaw, the Slow Vehicle Regulation Department (SVRD) in YCDC, was transferred from the Tax Department to the Administration Department in April 2002, when the traffic regulations began to be strengthened and the penalties started to be collected more strictly; for instance, when the drivers stray beyond the designated business area, a verbal warning only was issued in the past, but a 2,000 kyat fine was imposed after the transfer. Thus, the revenue of the YCDC from the fines related to trishaw traffic violations increased rapidly year by year; see Nang Mya Kay Khaing (2004), who also reports the requisition of unregistered trishaws by the authorities.

10   The issue system of the trishaw driving license was simplified in April 2002; the driving test was abolished and examination is conducted solely by submitted documents. As a result, the number of persons with a trishaw driver's license in Yangon rapidly increased, from 16,777 in 2001/02 to 34,007 by September 8, 2003, so the labour market situation for trishaw drivers appears to be deteriorating.

11   Two drivers paid some commission to a broker who intermediated with the trishaw owners. The amount was 3,000 kyat (= 3.1 US$) in one case and 20,000 kyat (= 20.4 US$) in the other. Note that these commission fees are excluded in the estimated net income shown in Table 2.

12   In terms of the rice wage, it was 4.7–5.3 kg per day for male labourers and 3.5 kg per day for female labourers.

13   The vendors seek to raise the necessary working capital in various ways, other than the borrowing mentioned here. One is to buy on credit, only possible after gaining creditworthiness among the suppliers, while another is to join rotating savings and credit associations (*sume:*). According to our survey in Yangon and Bago, contributions by the members are collected daily, usually 500 kyat (= 0.5 US$) per unit share, and the leader of the association (*sume: gaun:*) gets the first round, then the others get it in turn by drawing lots.

14   Authorized pawnshops are private pawnshops which have obtained a license from the government. The license is issued either by the YCDC, MCDC (Mandalay City Development Corporation), or other City Development Committees (CDC) under the Ministry of Progress of Border Areas and National Races, and it must be extended every year. Authorized pawnshops need to follow the specific interest rate fixed by the government. According to our survey conducted in September 2003 at one of the authorized pawnshops in Bago, the operating system was as follows. Borrowers had to pledge gold (1 tical (231.5 grams) of gold is evaluated at 110,000 kyat, although its market price is more than 180,000 kyat) and an amount of money equivalent to the value of the gold can be borrowed for five months. Some other precious commodities can be accepted as well. The interest rate charged is 4 per cent per month. If borrowers fail to repay the principal and interest within five months, the item pawned will be forfeited. Besides the authorized pawnshops, there are unauthorized pawnshops, and public sector pawnshops (the Myanma Small Loans Enterprise run by the Ministry of Finance) in Myanmar.

15   See Table 13 in Fujita (2003), for evidence.

BIBLIOGRAPHY

Articles and Books

Adas, Michael. 1974. *The Burma Delta: Economic Development and Social Change on an Asian Rice Frontier, 1852–1941.* Madison: The University of Wisconsin Press.

Ahmed, R., S. Haggblade, and T. Chowdhury eds. 2000. *Out of the Shadow of Famine: Evolving Food Markets and Food Policy in Bangladesh.* Baltimore: Johns Hopkins University Press.

Asian Development Bank (ADB), Japan Bank for International Cooperation (JBIC) and World Bank. 2005. *Connecting East Asia: A New Framework for Infrastructure.* Manila.

Asian Population and Development Association. 2001. *Report on the Basic Surveys on Agricultural and Rural Development by Progress Stage in Asian Countries — The Union of Myanmar.* Tokyo.

Balino, Tomas J.T., Adam Bennett, and Eduardo Borensztein. 1999. "Monetary Policy in Dollarized Economies," *IMF Occasional Paper* 171, Washington D.C.: International Monetary Fund.

Bank of the Lao PDR. 2003. *Annual Report 2002,* Vientiane: Bank of the Lao PDR.

Barth, J., G. Caprio, and R. Levine. 2004. "Bank Regulation and Supervision: What Works Best?," *Journal of Financial Intermediation* 13, 2: 205–48.

Berglof, E., and P. Bolton. 2000. "The Great Divide and Beyond: Financial Architecture in Transition," *Journal of Economic Perspective* 16, 1: 77–100.

Choiyang Chuchart and Sopin Tongpan. 1965. *The Determination and Analysis of Policies to Support and Stabilize Agricultural Prices and Incomes of the Thai Farms (with special reference to rice premium).* Bangkok: Ministry of National development; Kasetsart University; SEATO.

Choeun, H., Y. Hayami, K. Kalirajam, D. Ma, and Y. Godo. 2004. *Welfare Effects of Rice Export Taxation in Thailand: Historical Simulation Analysis, 1950–1985,* mimeo.

Central Statistical Organization (CSO). 1997. *Report of 1997 Household Income and Expenditure Survey.*

Economic Intelligence Unit (EIU). 2004. *Country Profile 2004 Myanmar (Burma).* London.

——— 2006. *Country Report November 2006 Myanmar (Burma)*. London.

Enoch, C., Gulde, A.M., and D. Hardy. 2002. "Banking Crises and Bank Resolution: Experiences in Some Transition Economies," *IMF Working Paper* No. 02/56.

Fertilizer Advisory, Development and Information Network for Asia and the Pacific (FADINAP). 1987. *Supply, Marketing, Distribution and Use of Fertilizer in Burma.* Bangkok.

Freixas, Xavier and Jean-Charles Rochet. 1997. *Microeconomics of Banking.* Cambridge, MA., and London: MIT Press.

Fukui, Ryu. 2004. "Myanmar ni okeru Kinyu Sekutar no Hatten to Genjyo [Development of Financial Sector in Myanmar]," in *Shijo Keizai Ikou Ka no Myanmar: Sono Hatten Katei oyobi Genjyou [Myanmar Economy under the transition: Development Process and Current Situation]*, edited by Koichi Fujita. Chiba: Institute of Developing Economies.

Fujita, Koichi. 2003. "90 Nendai Myanmar no Ine-Nikisakuka to Nougyo-Seisaku Nouson-Kinyu: Irawaji-Kanku Ichi-Noson-Chousa-Jirei wo Chushin ni [Policy-Initiated Expansion of Summer Rice under Constraints of Rural Credit in Myanmar in the 1990s: Perspectives from a Village Study in Ayeyarwaddy Division]," *Keizai Kenkyu (The Economic Review)* 54, 2: 300–14.

——— 2005. *Bangladesh Nouson Kaihatsu no Noukano Kaiso Hendou: Hinkon Sakugen no tameno Kiso Kenkyu [Rural Development and Changing Class Structure in Bangladesh]*. Kyoto: Kyoto University Press.

——— 2007. "Myanmar no 'Hinkon Mondai': Syokuryou Seisaku to no Kanren wo Chushin ni ['Poverty Problems' in Myanmar: With Special Reference to the Relations with Food Policy]," in *Myanma Keizai no Jitsuzo: Naze Gunsei ha Ikinokoreta Noka [Real Image of Myanmar Economy: How did the Military Regime Survive?]*, edited by Toshihiro Kudo. Chiba: Institute of Developing Economies.

Fujita, Koichi and Ikuko Okamoto. 2000. "Myanmar Kanki-Kangai-Inasaku-Keizai no Jittai: Yangon Kinko-Noson Field Chosa yori [An Economic Study on Irrigated Summer Rice Production in Myanmar: The Case of a Village near Yangon]," *Tonan Ajia Kenkyu (Southeast Asian Studies)* 38, 1: 22–49.

Garcia, Y.T., Garcia, A.G., Malar Oo, Mahabub Hossain. 2000. "Income Distribution and Poverty in Irrigated and Rainfed Ecosystems: The Myanmar Case," *Economic and Political Weekly*, December 30, pp. 4670–76.

Giovannini, A. 1985. "Saving and the Real Interest Rate in LDCs," *Journal of Development Economics* 18, 2–3: 197–217.

Goto, Kenta. 2002. "Coordinating Risks and Creating Value: The Challenges for the Vietnam Textile and Garment Industry," *NEU-JICA Discussion Paper* No. 5.

Hattori, Ryozo. 1998. "Vietnam no Kinyuu Kaikaku to Ginkou Kiki [Financial Reforms and Banking Crises in Vietnam]," in *Kinyu kiki to Kinyu Kisei [Financial Crises and Regulation]*, edited by Shin'ichi Watanabe. Tokyo: Institute of Developing Economies, pp. 283–326.

Hill, Hal and Sisira Jayasuriya. 1986. *An Inward-looking Economy in Transition: Economic Development in Burma since the 1960s*. Singapore: Institute of Southeast Asian Studies.

Hla Myint. 1971. *Economic Theory and the Underdeveloped Countries*. London: Oxford University Press.

Hong, C., Y. Hayami, K. Lalirajan, D. Ma, and Y. Godo. 2004. *Welfare Effects of Rice Export Taxation in Thailand: Historical Simulation Analysis, 1950–1985*. Preliminary Draft, Tokyo, August 2004.

International Monetary Fund (IMF). 1999a. *Vietnam: Selected Issues*, IMF Staff Country Report No. 99/55.

———— 1999b. *Myanmar: Recent Economic Developments*, IMF Staff Country Report No. 99/134.

Khin Maung Kyi. Ronald Findlay, R.M. Sundrum, Mya Maung, Myo Nyunt, Zaw Oo eds. 2000. *Economic Development of Burma: A Vision and Strategy*. Stockholm: Olof Palme International Center.

Kudo, Toshihiro. 1998. "Political Basis of Economic Policies under Burmese Socialism," *Southeast Asian Studies*, Tokyo University of Foreign Studies, No. 4, Tokyo.

———— 2003. "Myanmar no Sato Sangyo [Sugar Industry in Myanmar]," *Ajiken Waludo Torendo (Ajiken World Trend)*, No. 89: 36–42.

———— 2005a. "Stunted and Distorted Industrialization in Myanmar," *IDE Discussion Paper Series* No. 38, Institute of Developing Economies.

———— 2005b. "The Impact of United States Sanctions on the Myanmar Garment Industry", IDE *Discussion Paper Series* No. 42, Institute of Developing Economies.

———— 2006. "Myanmar's Economic Relations with China: Can China Support the Myanmar Economy?," *IDE Discussion Paper Series* No. 66, Institute of Developing Economies.

———— 2008. "Kaiho Keizaika to Myanma Sangyo Hatten [Myanmar's Industrial Development in the Transition to an Open Economy]," in *Myanma Keizai no Jitsuzo: Naze Gunsei ha Ikinokoreta Noka [Real Image of Myanmar Economy: How did the Military Regime Survive?]*, edited by Toshihiro Kudo. Chiba: Institute of Developing Economies.

Kudo, Toshihiro ed. 2001. *Industrial Development in Myanmar: Prospects and Challenges*, ASEDP No. 60, Chiba: Institute of Developing Economies.

Kurita, K., I. Okamoto, T. Kurosaki, and K. Fujita. 2004. "Myanmar ni okeru Kome Zousan Shijyo Seisaku to Nouson Keizai- Hakkason Kakei Chosa Data ni yoru Syotoku Bunseki wo Chusin ni- [Rice Production Oriented Policies in Myanmar and Farm Economy: Centering on Income Analysis based on Household Survey in Eight Villages]," *Ajia Keizai (Asian Economy)* 45, 8: 2–37.

Kurosaki, Takashi. 2005. "Myanmar ni okeru Nougyo Seisaku to Sakutsuke Kettei, Nouka Shotoku [Agricultural Policies, Crop Choice and Farm Economy in Myanmar]," *Keizai Kenkyu (The Economic Review)* 56, 2: 97–110.

Kurosaki, Takashi, Ikuko Okamoto, Kyosuke Kurita and Koichi Fujita. 2004. "Rich Periphery, Poor Center: Myanmar's Rural Economy under Partial Transition to Market Economy," *COE Discussion Paper*, No. 23, Institute of Economic Research, Hitotsubashi University, Tokyo.

Lintner, Bertil. 1990. *The Rise and Fall of the Communist Party of Burma (CPB)*. Ithaca: Southeast Asian Program, Cornell University.

_____ 1994. *Burma in Revolt: Opium and Insurgency since 1948*. Boulder, San Francisco, Oxford and Bangkok: Westview Press and White Lotus.

_____ 1998. "Drugs and Economic Growth: Ethnicity and Exports," in *Burma: Prospects for a Democratic Future*, edited by Rotberg, Robert I. The World Peace Foundation and Harvard Institute for International Development, Washington D.C.: Brookings Institution Press.

Ministry of Agriculture and Irrigation (MOAI) 2000(a). *Agricultural Marketing in Myanmar*. Yangon: Ministry of Agriculture and Irrigation, Market Information Service Project (TCP/MYA/8821).

_____ 2000 (b). *The Long term Agricultural Plan – 2000/01 to 2030/31*. Yangon: Ministry of Agriculture and Irrigation (in Burmese).

Ministry of Information. 2000. *Myanmar: facts and figures*. Yangon: Ministry of Information.

_____ 2003. *Magnificent Myanmar (1988–2003)*. Yangon: Ministry of Information.

Mizuno, Atsuko. 2004. "Myanmar to Tyugoku no Keizai Kyouryoku Kankei [The economic relationship between China and Myanmar]," *Kikan Keizai Kenkyu* (*The Quarterly Economic Review*) 27, 1–2: 175–200.

Moe Kyaw. 2001. "Textile and Garment Industry: Emerging Export Industry," in *Industrial Development in Myanmar: Prospects and Challenges*, edited by Kudo Toshihiro. ASEDP No. 60, Chiba: Institute of Developing Economies.

Mizoguchi, Fusao. 1958. *Biruma no Nougyo Keizai [Agricultural Economy in Burma]*. Tokyo: Council for Productivity Improvement for Agriculture, Forestry, and Fisheries.

Mya Maung. 1970. "The Burmese Way to Socialism beyond the Welfare State," *Asian Survey* (June 1970) 10: 533–51.

_____ 1991. *The Burma Road to Poverty*. New York: Praeger.

Myanmar Agricultural Produce Trading (MAPT). 1991. *MAPT in Figures*. Yangon: MAPT (in Burmese).

_____ 2003. *History of Rice Marketing in Myanmar*. Yangon: MAPT. (in Burmese).

Mya Than. 1992. *Myanmar's External Trade*. Singapore: Institute of Southeast Asian Studies.

_____ 2005. "Myanmar's Cross-Border Economic Relations and Cooperation with the People's Republic of China and Thailand in the Greater Mekong Sub-region," *Journal of GMS Development Studies* 2, 1 (October 2005).

Myat Thein. 2003. "Banking Crisis in Myanmar: A Matter of Fundamentals," mimeo.
———— 2004. *Economic Development of Myanmar.* Singapore: Institute of Southeast Asian Studies.
Myat Thein and Mya Than. 1995. "Transitional Economy of Myanmar" in *Asian Transitional Economies: Challenges and Prospects,* edited by Naya Seiji and Loong-Hoe Tan. Singapore: Institute of Southeast Asian Studies.
———— 2000. *Financial Resources for Development in Myanmar: Lessons from Asia,* Singapore: Institute of Southeast Asian Studies.
Mya Than and Nobuyoshi Nishizawa. 1990. "Agricultural Policy Reforms and Agricultural Development in Myanmar," in *Myanmar Dilemmas and Options,* edited by Mya Than and Joseph L.H. Tan. Singapore: Institute of Southeast Asian Studies, pp. 89–116.
Nang Mya Kay Khaing. 2004. Myanmar ni okeru Toshi Infomaru Sekutar: Saika Untensyu oyobi Rotensyo no Jittai wo Tyuusin ni [*Urban Informal Sector in Myanmar: With Special Reference to Trishaw Drivers and Vendors*], in *Shijo Keizai Ikou Ka no Myanmar: Sono Hatten Katei oyobi Genjyou* [*Myanmar Economy under the transition: Development Process and Current Situation*], edited by Koichi Fujita. Chiba: Institute of Developing Economies.
Nicholas, M. and F. Goletti. 2000. *Rice Market Liberalization and Poverty in Viet Nam,* Research Report No. 114, Washington: International Food Policy Research Institute.
Nishizawa, Nobuyoshi. 2001. *Myannar no Keizai Kaikaku to Kaihou Seisaku* [*Economic Reform and Liberalization in Myanmar*]. Tokyo: Keiso Shobo.
Norås, Hildegunn Kyvik. 2004. "The Global Textile and Clothing Industry post the Agreement on Textiles and Clothing," *Discussion Paper* No. 5, World Trade Organization.
Okamoto, Ikuko. 1993. "Myanmar ni okeru Kome Ryuutus Jiyuka [Rice Marketing Liberalization in Myanmar]," *Ajia Trendo (Asian Trend)* IV: 98–114.
———— 2004. "Myanmar ni okeru Shin-Sakumotsu Fukyuu to Hi-Noka-Sou-Nousanbutsu Ryutsu Jiyuukago no Mame-Sanchi Sankason no Jirei kara- [Impact of Newly Introduced Crops on Non-Farm Households in Myanmar: The Case of Three Villages in a Pulse Producing Area]," *Ajia Keizai (Asian Economy),* 45, 2: 2–27.
———— 2008. *Economic Disparity in Rural Myanmar: Transformation under Market Liberalization.* Singapore: National University of Singapore Press.
Rao, K.S. Ramachandra. 1994. "*An Analysis of Production Trends in Pulses,*" Reserve Bank of India Occasional Papers 15, 2: 145–73.
Saito, Teruko. 1979. "Biruma no Momimai Kyousyutsu-seido to Nouka Keizai-Kyungale mura no Jirei [Paddy Procurement System in Burma and Farm Economy: Case of Kyungale Village]," *Ajia Keizai (Asian Economy)* 20, 6: 2–25.
———— 1980. "Shimo-biruma Beisakuson no Nogyo Rodosya-Kyungalay mura ni okeru Sono Jittai [Agricultural Labourers in a Rice Village in Lower Burma: Realities in Kyungale Village]", *Ajia Keizai (Asian Economy)* 21, 11: 76–91.

_____ 1981. "Farm Household Economy under Paddy Delivery System in Contemporary Burma," *Developing Economies* 19, 4: 367–97.

_____ 1982. "Biruma ni okeru Nogyo Rodosya Kaisou no Keisei [Formation of Agricultural Laborers Class in Burma]," in *Tonanajia Noson no Teisyotokusya Kaiso* [*Low Income Class in Southeast Asian Rural Areas*], edited by Tsutomu Takigawa. Tokyo: Institute of Developing Economies, pp. 235–64.

_____ 1987. "Biruma ni okeru Suitou Koushyuryo Hinsyu no Dounyu to Tenkai-Jittai to Mondai-[Introduction and Development of High Yielding Variety in Burma: Reality and Problems]," in *Tonan Ajia no Nougyou Gijyutu Kakushin to Nouson Syakai* [*Agricultural Technological Innovation and Rural Society in Southeast Asia*], edited by Tsutomu Takigawa. Tokyo: Institute of Developing Economies, pp. 167–91.

San Thein. 2006. *Agro-based Industries in Myanmar: The Long Road to Industrialization.* V.R.F. Series No. 414. Chiba: Institute of Developing Economies.

San Thein and Toshihiro Kudo. 2008. "Myanmar Sugar SMES: History, Technology, Location and Government Policy," *Discussion Paper Series* No. 147. Chiba: Institute of Developing Economies.

Steinberg, David. I. 1981. *Burma's Road toward Development: Growth and Ideology under Military Rule.* Boulder: Westview Press.

State Bank of Vietnam. 2003. *Annual Report 2002.* Hanoi: State Bank of Vietnam.

Takahashi, Akio. 1992. *Biruma Deruta no Beisaku-son: Shakaisyugi Taiseika no Noson-Keizai* [*A Rice Village in the Burma Delta: Rural Economy under the Socialist Regim*]. Tokyo: Institute of Developing Economies.

_____ 2000. *Gendai Myanmar no Noson-Keizai: Iko-Keizai-ka no Nomin to Hi-Nomin* [*Myanmar's Village Economy in Transition: Changing Rural Life in a Market-Oriented Economy*]. Tokyo: University of Tokyo Press.

_____ 2001. "Myanmar- Konnann na Shjyo Keizai he no Iko [Myanmar- Difficult Transition to a Market Economy," in *Ajia Keizai Ron: Shin Pan* [*Asian Economies New Edition*], edited by Hara, Yonosuke. Tokyo: NTT Press, pp. 295–323.

_____ 2002. "Myanmar no Kokuei Seitou-gyo to Kousau Nomin [State sugar industry and farmers in Myanmar]," *Toyo Bunka* [*Oriental Culture*], pp. 137–63.

Thawnghmung, Ardeth Maung. 2003. *Behind the Teak Curtain: Authoritarianism, Agricultural Policies and Political Legitimacy in Rural Burma.* London: Kegan Paul.

Theingyi Myint. 2007. *Myanmar Rice Market: Market Integration and Price Causality.* Unpublished Doctoral Thesis submitted to Yezin Agricultural University.

Tin Soe. 1994. "Policies and Institutions related to Grain Trade: Problems and Prospect both in the Short-run and the Medium Term," Paper presented at the Training Seminar of Developing an Efficient Marketing System for Food Grains. Yangon.

Tin Soe and Brian S. Fisher. 1990. "An Economic Analysis of Burmese Rice Policies" in *Myanmar Dilemmas and Options*, edited by Mya Than and Joseph L.H. Tan. Singapore: Institute of Southeast Asian Studies, pp. 117–66.

Tin Maung Maung Than. 2007. *State Dominance in Myanmar: The Political Economy of Industrialization.* Singapore: Institute of Southeast Asian Studies.

Turnell, Sean. 2003. "Myanmar's Banking Crisis," *ASEAN Economic Bulletin* 20, 3: 272–82.

―――― 2006. "Burma's Economy 2004: Crisis Masking Stagnation," in *Myanmar's Long Road to National Reconciliation*, edited by Trevor Wilson. Singapore: Institute of Southeast Asian Studies and Asia Pacific Press.

Tsujii, Hiroshi. 1975. "Tai koku Rice Premium Seisaku no Jissyoteki Keizai Bunseki [Economic Analysis of the Rice Premium Policy of Thailand]," *Tonan Ajia Kenkyu (Southeast Asian Studies)* 13, 3: 358–84.

Turnell, S. and A. Vicary. 2003. "Burma's Banking Crisis: A Commentary," *Burma Economic Watch*, 6 March.

United Nations [UN]. 1997. *Prospects for Pulses in South Asia: International and Domestic Trade Under UNDP Regional Trade Program* (RAS/92/035). New York: United Nations.

Unteroberdoerster, O. 2004. "Banking Reform in the Lower Mekong Countries," *IMF Policy Discussion Paper*, PDP/04/5.

Usui Susum and Tokuzo Mishima. 1994. *Kome Ryutsu/Kanri Seido no Hikaku Kenkyu Kankoku • Tai • Nippon [Comparative Study of Rice Marketing and Control Systems in Korea, Thailand and Japan].* Sapporo: Hokkaido Daigaku Tosyo Kankoukai.

U Tin Htut Oo and Toshihiro Kudo eds. 2003. *Agro-Based Industry in Myanmar: Prospects and Challenges.* ASEDP No. 67. Chiba: Institute of Developing Economies.

Wang, Sandra. 2004. "Private Banks in Myanmar (1990–2004)," mimeo.

Watanabe, Shin'ichi. 2004. "Ibdoshina Sankoku ni okeru doru-ka to Kinyu shisutemu no Hatten [Dollarization and the Development of the Financial Systems in Three Indochinese Countries]," in *Kinyu Globaru-ka to Tojyoukoku [Financial Globalization and Developing Economies]*, edited by Kozo Kunimune and Koji Kubo. Chiba: Institute of Developing Economies, pp. 21–44.

Watanabe, Shin'ichi. 1998. "Ikoukeizai ni okeru Ginko Kiki no Tokusei [Banking Crises in Transition Economies]," in *Kinyu kiki to Kinyu Kisei [Financial Crises and Regulation]*, edited by Shin'ichi, Watanabe. Chiba: Institute of Developing Economies. pp. 242–81.

World Bank 2002. *Banking Sector Review: Vietnam.* Washington D.C.

―――― 2005. *World Development Report 2005: A Better Investment Climate for Everyone.* Washington D.C.

Zaw Oo. 2003. "Throwing Good Money after Bad: The Banking Crisis in Burma," *Asian Tribune*, 10 March.

Statistics

Asian Development Bank (ADB). various issues. *Key Indicators.* Manila.

―――― 2001. *Country Economic Report: Myanmar 2: Statistical Appendixes.* Manila.

Bangladesh Bureau of Statistics (BBS). 2003. *Report of the Household Income & Expenditure Survey, 2000.*

Central Statistical Organization (CSO). various issues. *Selected Monthly Economic Indicators.* Yangon.

_____ various years. *Review of the Financial, Economic and Social Conditions (RFES).* Yangon.

_____ various years. *Statistical Yearbook.* Yangon.

_____ 1997. *Agricultural Statistics (1985–86 to 1995–96).* Yangon.

_____ 2001. *Myanmar Agricultural Statistics (1989–90 to 1990–2000).* Yangon.

Economic Research Department. 2001. *Economic and Financial Sector Statistics.* Vientiane.

FAO, *FAOSTAT.*

Government of India. 2003. *Agricultural Statistics at a Glance.*

International Monetary Fund (IMF). various years. *International Financial Statistics.* Washington, DC.

_____ 1999c. *Cambodia: Statistical Annex,* IMF Country Report No. 99/33.

_____ 2003. *Vietnam: Statistical Appendix,* IMF Country Report No. 03/382.

_____ 2004. *Cambodia: Statistical Appendix,* IMF Country Report No. 04/330.

_____ 2005. *Lao People's Democratic Republic: Selected Issues and Statistical Appendix,* IMF Country Report No. 05/9.

Ministry of Agriculture and Irrigation (MOAI). various issues. *Marketing Information System* (MIS).

Ministry of Home Affairs. 1993. *Estimated Population by States/Divisions & Townships 1993.* Yangon.

Ministry of Labor. 1993. *Report on Myanmar Labor Force Survey 1990.* Yangon.

Ministry of Immigration and Population. 1995. *Population Changes and Fertility Survey 1991.* Yangon.

Myanma Agricultural Service (MAS). 1994. *Crop Production Situation (Union),* Yangon.

Saito, Teruko and Lee Kin Kiong. 1999. *Statistics on the Burmese Economy: The 19th and 20th Centuries.* Singapore: Institute of Southeast Asian Studies.

CONTRIBUTORS

Fujita Koichi, Professor, Center for Southeast Asian Studies (CSEAS), Kyoto University.

Fukui Ryu, Manager, Tokyo Development Learning Center, The World Bank.

Kubo Koji, Associate Senior Research Fellow, Institute of Developing Economies, JETRO.

Kudo Toshihiro, Senior Research Fellow, Institute of Developing Economies, JETRO.

Mieno Fumiharu, Professor of Economics, Graduate School of International Cooperation Studies, Kobe University.

Nang Mya Kay Khaing, Lecturer (part-time), Faculty of Foreign Studies, Tokyo University of Foreign Studies.

Okamoto Ikuko, Associate Senior Research Fellow, Institute of Developing Economies, JETRO.

INDEX

190–1, 196, 206, 208–14, 216,
218–9, 221–3, 225, 231–2, 236–9,
243, 247, 254–8, 264–7, 276–80,
301
fertilizer, 50, 116, 170, 187–8, 190–1,
198, 213, 247, 253, 255–6
FDI, *see* foreign direct investment
FECs, *see* Foreign Exchange
Certificates
Financial Action Task Force on Money
Laundering (FATF), 153
Financial Institution Law, 26, 48, 128,
130–1, 133, 152, 162
financial sector, 13, 15–6, 24, 26,
28–9, 31, 55, 61–2, 129, 131,
149, 151–2, 154, 161–2, 165
First Myanmar Investment (FMI), 50,
64
fishery products, 174, 178–9, 204
Foreign Exchange Certificates (FECs),
5, 27, 36, 40, 76, 94, 122, 152
foreign direct investment (FDI), 4,
10–1, 13–4, 16, 26, 28, 42, 63,
103, 107, 117, 119–21, 124, 127
foreign exchange market, 4, 14–5
Foreign Investment Law of 1988
(FIL), 101, 103, 117, 121–2, 133
Foreign Investments Commission
(FIC), 117

garment industry, 13, 15, 25, 40, 63,
68, 76–7, 79–83, 85, 94, 97, 102,
124, 127, 282
GDE, *see* gross domestic expenditure
GDP, *see* gross domestic product
General Service Companies (GSCs),
61, 64, 149, 151–3, 162, 165
globalization, 103
Greater Mekong Sub-region Economic
Cooperation (GMS–EC), 111
gross domestic expenditure (GDE),
42, 63

gross domestic product (GDP), 3, 7,
10, 12, 29–34, 38–41, 44, 63, 67,
69, 88–90, 101, 105–6, 124, 142,
147, 157, 171–2, 276

hotel industry, 10, 28, 42, 121–2, 124
Hong Kong, 50, 79, 120, 125
Htantabin, 186, 188–9, 253

import substitution, 2, 72
industries, 67, 72–3, 75, 78, 83,
97, 106
policy, 1
sectors, 45, 62
income, 19, 32–3, 109, 140, 173,
189, 196, 199, 209, 214, 227,
239, 242, 247, 250, 252, 255,
263–6, 276–7, 279, 282–3,
286–301, 304, 306
independence, 1
India, 110–2, 115, 125, 192, 236,
262, 277, 304
Indonesia, 120, 125, 192, 197
Industrial Revolution, 66
industrial sector, 66–7, 86, 101
industrialization, 1–4, 10, 15, 19, 25,
42, 60, 62, 66, 68, 169, 209
export-oriented, 14
labour intensive, 14
infrastructure, 13, 15, 61, 67–8, 83,
85–6, 88–91, 94, 96–7, 101, 115,
131–2, 163, 204, 229, 241
informal sector, 17–9
International Monetary Fund (IMF),
100, 158
irrigation, 88, 182–3, 186, 188–9,
191, 196–7, 212–3

Japan, 80, 95, 104, 110, 112, 120,
125, 192, 223, 246
jute, 4, 178–9, 206